Integrity of Heart,
Skillfulness of Hands

Donald K. Campbell

Integrity of Heart, Skillfulness of Hands

Biblical and Leadership Studies
in Honor of Donald K. Campbell

Edited by
Charles H. Dyer
and Roy B. Zuck

Baker Books

A Division of Baker Book House Co
Grand Rapids, Michigan 49516

Dallas
Theological Seminary

Published by Baker Books
a division of Baker Book House Company
P.O. Box 6287, Grand Rapids, MI 49516-6287

Printed in the United States of America

Library of Congress Cataloging-in-Publication Data

Integrity of heart and skillfulness of hands : biblical and leadership studies in
   honor of Donald K. Campbell / edited by Charles H. Dyer and Roy B. Zuck.
      p.   cm.
  Includes bibliographical references
  ISBN (invalid) 0-8010-3027-5
    1. Christian life—Biblical teaching. 2. Christian leadership. I. Dyer, Charles
H., 1952– . II. Zuck, Roy B. III. Campbell, Donald K.
BS680.C47   1994
220.6—dc20   94-180

Contents

Part 2 Skillfulness of Hands—*Essays in Christian Leadership*

Contributors

All contributors are members of the faculty of Dallas Theological Seminary, unless designated otherwise.

J. Kerby Anderson, Adjunct Teacher in Pastoral Ministries, Dallas Theological Seminary; and Executive Vice-president, Probe Ministries, Dallas, Texas

Mark L. Bailey, Associate Professor of Bible Exposition

Darrell L. Bock, Professor of New Testament Studies

Robert B. Chisholm, Jr., Professor of Old Testament Studies

Peter V. Deison, Director of Leadership Development, Center for Christian Leadership, and Associate Professor of Discipleship

Charles H. Dyer, Professor of Bible Exposition

Kenneth O. Gangel, Vice-president for Academic Affairs, Academic Dean, and Senior Professor of Christian Education

John D. Hannah, Chairman and Professor of Historical Theology

Homer Heater, Jr., Academic Dean, Capital Bible Seminary, Lanham, Maryland; former Professor of Bible Exposition, Dallas Theological Seminary

Howard G. Hendricks, Chairman, Center for Christian Leadership, and Distinguished Professor

Harold W. Hoehner, Director of Ph.D. Studies, and Chairman and Senior Professor of New Testament Studies

Wendell G. Johnston, Vice-president for Planning and Advancement

William D. Lawrence, Executive Director, Center for Christian Leadership, and Professor of Pastoral Ministries

David E. Malick, Assistant Professor of Field Education

Aubrey M. Malphurs, Chairman and Professor of Field Education

Eugene H. Merrill, Professor of Old Testament Studies

J. Dwight Pentecost, Distinguished Professor of Bible Exposition, Emeritus

Michael Pocock, Chairman and Associate Professor of World Missions

Robert A. Pyne, Assistant Professor of Systematic Theology

James O. Rose, Pastor, Calvary Baptist Church, New York City, New York

James R. Slaughter, Professor of Christian Education

Stephen R. Spencer, Professor of Systematic and Historical Theology

Joseph M. Stowell III, President, Moody Bible Institute, Chicago, Illinois

Stanley D. Toussaint, Senior Professor of Bible Exposition, Emeritus

Jack A. Turpin, Retired Chairman of the Board, Hall-Mark Electronics Corporation, Dallas, Texas; and Chairman of the Board of Incorporate Members, Dallas Theological Seminary

John F. Walvoord, Chancellor, Minister-at-large, and Professor of Systematic Theology, Emeritus

Timothy S. Warren, Professor of Pastoral Ministries

Roy B. Zuck, Chairman and Senior Professor of Bible Exposition, and Editor of *Bibliotheca Sacra*

Acknowledgments

Putting together a festschrift volume takes a great deal of effort and coordination. We want to thank every author who agreed to contribute to this volume. Each article, in its own way, serves as a tribute to Dr. Donald K. Campbell. We also want to thank Baker Book House for agreeing to be part of this project from its inception. Their expertise and cooperation were instrumental in bringing the project to completion. Also, we extend a special word of thanks to Mrs. Roger Redhair who retyped many of the manuscripts—and did so "over and above" her other full-time responsibilities. Her work is *greatly* appreciated.

Dr. Charles H. Dyer
Dr. Roy B. Zuck

Biographical Introduction

Howard G. Hendricks

Donald K. Campbell has faithfully served the Lord and Dallas Theological Seminary as a faculty member and administrator for forty years. His leadership has touched thousands of lives. On resigning as seminary president effective June 1994, he will devote more time to preaching, teaching, and writing. This festschrift volume commemorates his distinguished, dedicated seminary service.

Dr. Campbell's colleagues and former students bestow this tribute. Unfortunately, space limitations prevent including countless other contributors.

Don Campbell, blessed with fine Christian parents, trusted in Christ as his Savior at an early age. Dwight and Evelyn Campbell reared five children. Don's father, Dwight Campbell, devotedly served as a church organist and pianist for forty-seven years.

As a student at Wheaton College, Don Campbell's life changed course in September 1945. Uneasy about his future direction, Don debated whether to accept a promising chemistry laboratory assistantship. Don's immediate thoughts quickly quenched a desire for Christian service, but his spirit continued to trouble him. Struggling within, Don sought out the college's dean of students, Dr. Charles Brooks. Dr. Brooks counseled the earnest youth wisely, assuring Donald that God would never mislead those honestly seeking his will. Don followed the elder's suggestion. Alone in his room Don quietly read the Bible and prayed. A verse vividly spoke to his heart: "Therefore do not be foolish, but understand what the Lord's will is" (Eph. 5:17). A deep conviction overcame him. He was sure God had called him to minister. That day Don offered the Lord his life and career.

Don graduated from Wheaton College with highest honors in 1947. Having graduated from Wheaton the year before, I had promptly enrolled at Dallas Seminary. An inquisitive Don asked me about the seminary. I wrote him enthusiastically about the fine program. At that time the school had 130 students and 10 faculty members. When Don and his wife Bea arrived, my wife Jeanne and I enjoyed a celebration dinner with them at the Adolphus

Hotel. As I vaguely recall, our modest budgets allowed only a fruit salad for each of us.

Don rapidly excelled as a student. He earned his Master of Theology degree in 1951 and by 1953 added a Doctor of Theology degree, majoring in his first love, Bible exposition. Don managed to pastor a local Dallas church, Pilgrim Chapel, from 1949 to 1953 despite his rigorous academic schedule. Don also taught at Dallas Bible Institute. After graduation, the Campbells journeyed to Bryan College, Dayton, Tennessee, where Don chaired the Bible and Philosophy Department for one year before beginning an illustrious Dallas Seminary career in 1954.

Dr. Campbell served Dallas Seminary in many important posts. He handled the demanding registrar's job from 1954 to 1967; continued to teach as an assistant professor of Bible exposition (1954–1961); served as acting chairman of the Bible Exposition Department (1960–1961); and functioned as academic dean from 1961 to 1984. He was appointed executive vice-president in 1985, and president in 1986. He has been a professor of Bible exposition since 1961. Liberty University honored him with a Doctor of Divinity Degree in 1989, and Dallas Baptist University added the Doctor of Humanities Degree to his many accolades in 1993.

Dr. Campbell became the school's third president. Seminary founder Dr. Lewis Sperry Chafer and the legendary Dr. John F. Walvoord mentored Don. His predecessors confidently handed Don Campbell God's glorious torch, which led to even greater achievements during his sterling tenure.

The Lord granted President Campbell far-sighted vision and the honor of fulfilling many wonderful dreams. The seminary constructed the luxurious 40,000-square-foot Turpin Library, which houses one of the finest theological libraries in the world, and acquired the Howard G. Hendricks Center for Christian Leadership in 1988. Campus facilities grew to encompass the Mitchell Ministries Center in 1990 and dedicated the impressive Margie Seay Leadership Resource Center in 1991.

Bricks and mortar, however, only supplemented exciting academic innovations. Dallas Theological Seminary's pioneer Th.M. program benefited from enhanced spiritual life and ministry skill additions. Small-group accountability and nurturing help build character, strengthening men and women as they train to reach the world for Christ. The Center for Christian Leadership develops servant leadership among students, alumni, Christian workers, and laypeople in their homes, churches, ministries, and communities. Extension courses now reach Houston, Philadelphia, San Antonio, and Dayton, Tennessee. The groundbreaking Master of Arts in Cross-Cultural Ministries degree program began in 1987, and the Certificate of Graduate Studies program started in 1991. Dr. Campbell also chartered the Dallas Seminary Foundation in 1987 and launched the CD Word Library.

Today more than 7,000 Dallas Seminary alumni around the world serve the Lord. The seminary campus has acquired an international flavor as 160 students from 40 countries contribute to the burgeoning student body. In addition, as many as 200 women lend grace to the seminary academic halls while Christians from varied cultural and ethnic backgrounds actively prepare for far-flung service. The future looks bright for this sixth largest seminary in the world.

Amidst rapid change, Dr. Campbell well represents the Dallas tradition of teaching the entire Bible as the inerrant, authoritative Word of God. He solidly reaffirms the seminary's initial charge: Preach the Word!

Yet Dr. Campbell's ministry has extended far beyond the Dallas Seminary academic halls. He has served as interim pastor for churches in both Dallas and Fort Worth. His reputation as a Bible conference speaker spans the country: Mount Hermon, Torrey Memorial, Heart of America, West Coast Prophetic, New England Prophetic, Pine Cove, Glen Eyrie (Navigators), America's Keswick, Camp-of-the-Woods, and Church of the Open Door Prophecy conferences. In addition, he has spoken at numerous churches and schools around the world.

Dr. Campbell serves on the corporate board of Covenant Life Insurance Company, and on the board of advisors of Dallas Christian Leadership, Dallas Association for Decency, Barnabas International, Fair Park Friendship Center, and Mount Hermon Association. He also serves on the board of reference for Christian Counseling Center, the Foundation for Thought and Ethics, Family Ministry, Outreach, Inc., Patkai Christian College, Uppsala Biblical Theological Seminary, Capturing Poland for Christ, and Nashville Bible College, and on the Steering Committee of Citizens of Dallas.

The leadership theme consistently surfaces in Dr. Campbell's writings. He authored four books: *Nehemiah: Man in Charge; Joshua: Leader under Fire; Daniel: God's Man in a Secular Society;* and *Judges: Leaders in Crisis Times*.

In his book on Nehemiah he lists twenty-one principles of leadership demonstrated in Nehemiah's character and behavior, characteristics exemplified by Dr. Campbell.

Nehemiah established a reasonable and attainable goal.
He had a sense of mission.
He was willing to get involved.
He rearranged his priorities in order to accomplish his goal.
He patiently waited for God's timing.
He showed respect to his superior.
He prayed at crucial times.
He made his request with tact and graciousness.
He was well prepared and thought of his needs in advance.
He went through the proper channels.

He took time (three days) to rest, pray, and plan.
He investigated the situation firsthand.
He informed others only after he knew the size of the problem.
He identified himself as one with the people.
He set before them a reasonable and attainable goal.
He assured them God was in the project.
He displayed self-confidence in facing obstacles.
He displayed God's confidence in facing obstacles.
He did not argue with opponents.
He was not discouraged by opposition.
He courageously used the authority of his position.[1]

Joshua is doubtless one biblical personality with whom Don Campbell particularly identifies. As he points out in his book on Joshua, "continued obedience to God's commands was essential to continued enjoyment of His blessing."[2] "A believer has only one *must,* and that is to be faithful to the Lord."[3]

Dr. Campbell has published numerous articles in *Moody Monthly, Kindred Spirit, Good News Broadcaster,* and *Bibliotheca Sacra.* He contributed commentaries on Joshua and Galatians in *The Bible Knowledge Commentary* (1983, 1985); he edited *Walvoord: A Tribute* (1982) and authored "The Church in God's Prophetic Program," in *Essays in Honor of J. Dwight Pentecost* (1986). Dr. Campbell also served as consulting editor for an abridged edition of Chafer's *Systematic Theology* (1988). He co-edited *A Case for Premillennialism: A New Consensus* (1992), and contributed to the *Baker Encyclopedia of the Bible* (1988).

Don Campbell never neglected his leadership role at home. He encouraged his children to read avidly. He advised them to pursue ministries in college. His four children retain fond memories of their family station-wagon vacations to visit relatives in California and Illinois. As a grandfather Don Campbell makes time to watch his grandchildren play soccer and takes each one on special luncheon dates.

Don Campbell demonstrates unexcelled leadership from his life on the campus to his duties as family man. His hands-on technique inspires others through service, ministry, and example.

Don carried a great burden during many years of his presidency as his beloved wife Bea suffered from cancer. Don never wavered in his duty even when his treasured lifelong companion departed to be with the Lord in 1991. He trusted all to God's faithfulness. On June 27, 1992, Dr. Campbell mar-

1. *Nehemiah: Man in Charge* (Wheaton, Ill.: Victor Books, 1979), p. 23.
2. *Joshua: Leader under Fire* (Wheaton, Ill.: Victor Books, 1981), p. 133.
3. Ibid., p. 134.

ried Bea's sister, La Vonne, whose husband had died of heart failure several years earlier. In announcing his wedding Don wrote the seminary family, "Weeping may remain for a night, but rejoicing comes in the morning" (Ps. 30:5).

His friends, the faculty and staff, and students past and present heartily wish Dr. Campbell the Lord's best as he passes the torch of leadership to his successor after forty wonderful years of service. All Don's associates join with him in reciting the title of his favorite hymn, "Great Is Thy Faithfulness." This volume to Donald K. Campbell stems from deep respect, gratitude, and love.

Part 1

Integrity of Heart
Essays in Biblical Studies

Deuteronomy,
New Testament Faith,
and the Christian Life

Eugene H. Merrill

The Christian who engages in the study of Old Testament theology, no matter what the reason for undertaking that pursuit, must at some point ask what relevance it has for the Christian faith and life. Anterior to this is the question as to the nature of Old Testament theology and its relationship to a total biblical theology of the Old and New Testaments. Only as that conundrum is addressed satisfactorily can the larger issues of authority and timeless relevance be encompassed.

A perusal of the history of the biblical theology movement reveals the uncertainties regarding the very possibility of doing Old Testament theology (or New Testament theology, for that matter).[1] The issue lies in the exclusiveness of the term "Old Testament" theology, a term that presupposes the end of the theological process to be the end of the Old Testament itself. That is, "Old Testament" theology suggests a self-contained unit in which the canon of the Old Testament provides the sole sum and substance of the theological data.

Jewish theologians can, of course, attempt such a theology, for the Old Testament *is* their canon. It follows that they need not and cannot turn to other sacred writings in their attempt to search out and organize the great theological themes that define their faith and provide a platform for their life in the world.[2] Christians who take both Testaments seriously as Scripture,

---

1. John H. Hayes and Frederick Prussner, *Old Testament Theology: Its History and Development* (Atlanta: John Knox, 1985), pp. 53–71.

2. Gerhard Hasel, *Old Testament Theology: Basic Issues in the Current Debate*, 4th ed. (Grand Rapids: Eerdmans, 1991), pp. 34–37. Jon D. Levenson, a Jewish scholar, laments that Old Testament theology is almost exclusively a Gentile affair. He himself is an exception, however, and has published several brief studies showing at least his perception of the discipline. See the chapter on Levenson in *The Flowering of Old Testament Theology*, ed. Ben C. Ollenburger, Elmer A. Martens, and Gerhard F. Hasel (Winona Lake, Ind.: Eisenbrauns, 1992), pp. 427–44.

however, cannot stop with the Old Testament for they must see it as open-ended toward the future, an unfinished revelation that finds its completion and fulfillment in the New.[3] It is impossible, then, for them to view the Old Testament "as though the New Testament did not exist," for it does exist for them as the capstone of revelation without which the Old Testament is a headless torso.

In light of this insistence on the wholeness of biblical revelation, the closest the Christian theologian can come to an Old Testament theology is either to approach it descriptively or to view it constantly through the lens of the New Testament and thus as a part of biblical theology. The former option reduces the Old Testament to a history of Israel's religion or, at best, understands Old Testament theology to be a record of what ancient Israel believed as opposed to what normative value, if any, it has for the church. The second option—that Old Testament theology is part of biblical theology—is the only one that allows the Old Testament to have continuing meaning and authority for the contemporary Christian.

Also important is the point that there can be no such thing as an exclusively New Testament theology, for if the Old Testament is open-ended to the New, the New Testament everywhere presupposes that open-endedness. Far from asserting its independence of what has gone before, that is, of the Hebrew Scriptures, the New Testament, whether the Gospels or the Epistles, reveals its Old Testament roots, declares its continuity with and development from them, and refuses to see itself as something qualitatively different from the earlier revelation. To pick up on a metaphor used already, the New Testament implicitly insists that without the Old it is a grotesque head without a body.[4]

There can be only one kind of theology, then, and that is biblical theology, an approach to God's Word that recognizes the unity of the Testaments; is sensitive to the open-endedness of the Old Testament to the New; and insists on a retrospective stance, one that understands the impossibility of developing a normative New Testament faith that rejects or even is ignorant of its Old Testament foundation. With these introductory remarks as a platform, attention will now be given to further implications of the unity of the Testaments; the New Testament use of the Old as illustrated specifically with Deuteronomy; two passages in Deuteronomy especially favored by the New Testament; and the application of these texts and truths to the Christian life.

3. Cf. Walther Zimmerli, "Biblical Theology," *Horizons in Biblical Theology* 4 (1982): 95–130.
4. For a full discussion of the "continuity-discontinuity" issue, see D. L. Baker, *Two Testaments: One Bible* (Downers Grove, Ill.: InterVarsity, 1976), pp. 19–93, 363–74.

The Unity of the Bible

The notion that the Old and New Testaments constitute a single revelation of Yahweh, the God of Israel and the church, is, of course, a Christian theological deduction. But it is more than that. The Old Testament continues to look forward with anticipation, even in the last stages of its canonical development. Most of the great promises to the fathers and prophecies of the seers of Israel remain unfulfilled, including those having to do with redemption and restoration. Though Second Temple Judaism appears not to have expected an ongoing canonical revelation and in fact eventually closed the door on such a possibility, such a closure bore no evidence of divine sanction.[5] The fact that the early church could refer to its apostolic writings as "Scripture" shows that whatever natural inclinations existed to accept the received Jewish tradition of a "closed canon" were not sufficient to preclude its "reopening" to these writings as a continuation, indeed, fulfillment, of God's ancient revelation to Israel.[6] Whatever attitude the Jews may have had toward the finality of the Old Testament witness, the church, under the Holy Spirit, proclaimed with boldness that God had finished his self-revelation only in his Son and in the (New Testament) Scriptures that spoke of him.

The idea of the unity of the Bible as a theological deduction is supported by the use of the Old Testament by the New Testament speakers and writers. Jesus (Matt. 4:6–10; 5:31, 33, 38–43; 9:13; 11:10; 12:3, 5; 13:14–15, 35; and Synoptic parallels) and the apostles (Rom. 1:17; 2:24; 3:4, 10–18; 4:3, 7–8, 17–18; 7:7; *passim* in Paul; *passim* in Heb.; 1 Pet. 1:16–17, 24–25; 2:6–8; 3:10–12) cited the Old Testament text scores of times, not just in support of new ideas or movements but as the basis for what they taught and advocated. There is no sense of the outmodedness or sharp discontinuity of the Old Testament on their part but, to the contrary, a recognition that their own message and ministry was a dynamic continuation of what preceded them in the Hebrew Scriptures.

At the same time, of course, Jesus and the apostles viewed their own inspired utterances as transcending or fulfilling those of the Old Testament in important respects. Thus, there are the well-known formulas in the Sermon on the Mount, "You have heard that it was said . . . but I tell you" (Matt. 5:27–28) and "It has been said . . . but I tell you" (5:31–32). Here

5. Roger Beckwith, *The Old Testament Canon of the New Testament Church* (Grand Rapids: Eerdmans, 1985), pp. 274–77.

6. F. F. Bruce, "New Light on the Origins of the New Testament Canon," in *New Dimensions in New Testament Study*, ed. Richard N. Longenecker and Merrill C. Tenney (Grand Rapids: Zondervan, 1974), pp. 6–8.

Jesus did not deny the authority or theological normativity of the quoted Old Testament texts (Exod. 20:14; Deut. 24:1) but elevated their significance to include not only act but attitude. His true estimate of the matter is clear from his statement in the same sermon that he had not "come to abolish the Law or the Prophets . . . but to fulfill them." In fact, he said, "until heaven and earth disappear, not the smallest letter, not the least stroke of a pen, will by any means disappear from the Law until everything is accomplished" (Matt. 5:17–18). He could hardly have made a stronger case for the unity and continuity of revelation.

What is discontinuous are the particular ceremonial or cultic practices demanded by the Mosaic covenant. Having been designed for Israel the servant people as a means of securing and maintaining their special covenant status, these ceremonial matters do not hold authority for the church, a body with a different meaning and mission. Moreover, they became obsolete in the perfect servanthood of Jesus, who fulfilled their requirements in every way. In fact, this is what it meant for Jesus to fulfill the Law and the Prophets.[7] His obedience imputes the same possibility to all who appropriate his perfection by faith.

In a more technical sense the relationship of the Testaments may be described in terms of various approaches to hermeneutics. In general these may be called fulfillment of prophecy if one defines prophecy as any suggestion in the New Testament that it somehow corresponds to something forward-looking in the Old.[8] Thus typology, analogy, correspondence, and the like may be seen as fulfillment of some kind or other. Indeed, it is not always possible to tell whether fulfillment of prophecy in the strict sense is in view when the New Testament speaker or writer makes an allusion to the Old. While the lines are frequently blurred between these avenues of usage, certain rhetorical or literary formulas provide some measure of guidance in the hermeneutical process.

It is impossible here to enter the discussion of hermeneutics as it bears on the matter of intertestamental continuity and discontinuity.[9] The sample texts to be examined presently afford us opportunity to see the great variety of possibilities that exist and to derive principles of interpretation useful to both an understanding of New Testament hermeneutics and a meaningful application to the contemporary church and its world.

7. Craig L. Blomberg, *Matthew*, New American Commentary (Nashville: Broadman, 1992), pp. 103–5.

8. John Goldingay, *Approaches to Old Testament Interpretation* (Downers Grove, Ill.: InterVarsity, 1981), pp. 97–122.

9. See the essays on this issue in *Continuity and Discontinuity: Perspectives on the Relationship Between the Old and New Testaments,* ed. John S. Feinberg (Westchester, Ill.: Crossway Books, 1988).

The New Testament Use of Deuteronomy

According to the *Index locorum* of Nestle's *Novum Testamentum Graece*[10] Deuteronomy is quoted or otherwise cited at least 95 times in the New Testament (compared to 103 for Genesis, 113 for Exodus, 35 for Leviticus, and 20 for Numbers), making it one of the favorite Old Testament books of Jesus and the apostles. When tempted by Satan in the desert, Jesus quoted Deuteronomy three times to offer biblical support for his refusal to acknowledge Satan's sovereignty (Matt. 4:1–11; Mark 1:12–13; Luke 4:1–13). In the Sermon on the Mount in his instruction concerning murder, adultery, divorce, the swearing of oaths, and the lex talionis, Jesus appealed to Deuteronomy five times, thereby reaffirming its continuing authority while elevating its precepts to even higher, more interiorized dimensions (Matt. 5:21, 27, 31–32, 33, 38–42).

While the New Testament use of Deuteronomy is pervasive (all but chapters 3, 12, 15, 16, 20, 26, 34 being cited at least once), it is striking that four passages stand out as being the clear centers of focus: 6:4–5; 18:15–19; 21:22–23; and 30:11–14. Though statistical data by themselves do not tell the whole story, it is quite obvious that the attention paid to these texts compared to the relative neglect of others is significant. The reason for the significance becomes apparent when their theological content is brought to bear on the New Testament message of hope in a redeeming Messiah who will (and has) brought a fallen and alienated world back into fellowship with the sovereign God of the universe. The remainder of this study will be devoted to two of these passages, addressing in turn the Old Testament exegesis, the theology, the New Testament citation, and the New Testament use of each of them.

Deuteronomy 6:4–5: The Shema

> Hear, O Israel: The LORD our God, the LORD is one. Love the LORD your God with all your heart and with all your soul and with all your strength.

The Decalogue of Deuteronomy 5:6–21 (= Exod. 20:2–17) embodies the great principles of covenant relationship that outline the nature and character of God and spell out Israel's responsibilities to him. It is thus an encapsulation or distillation of the entire corpus of covenant text. The passage at hand is a further refinement of that great relational truth, an adumbration of an adumbration, as it were.[11] It is the expression of the essence of all of God's

10. D. Eberhard Nestle, ed., *Novum Testamentum Graece*, 21st ed. (Stuttgart: Privileg. Wurtt. Bibelanstalt, 1952), pp. 658–61.

11. Eugene H. Merrill, "A Theology of the Pentateuch," in *A Biblical Theology of the Old Testament*, ed. Roy B. Zuck (Chicago: Moody, 1991), p. 78.

Person and purposes in sixteen words of Hebrew text. Known to Jewish tradition as the Shema (after the first word of v. 4, the imperative of the Hebrew verb *šāmaʿ*, "to hear"), this statement, like the Decalogue, is prefaced by its description as "commands, decrees, and laws" (or the like) and by injunctions to obey them (6:1–3; cf. 4:44–5:5).

Postbiblical rabbinic exegesis understood the role of the Shema in precisely this way, for when Jesus was asked about the greatest of the commandments he cited this (and its companion in Lev. 19:18) as the fundamental tenet of Jewish faith, an opinion with which his hearers obviously concurred (Matt. 22:34–39; Mark 12:28–31; Luke 10:25–28).[12] So much so did the centrality of this confession find root in the Jewish consciousness that to this very day observant Jews recite the Shema at least twice daily.[13]

It is possible to understand verse 4 in several ways, but the two most popular renderings of the final clause are: (1) "The LORD our God, the LORD is one" (so NIV) or (2) "The LORD our God is one LORD."[14] The former stresses the uniqueness or exclusivity of Yahweh as Israel's God and so may be paraphrased "Yahweh our God is the one and only Yahweh" or the like. This takes the noun *ʾeḥād* ("one") in the sense of "unique" or "solitary," a meaning that is certainly well attested.[15] The latter translation focuses on the unity or wholeness of the Lord. This is not in opposition to the later Christian doctrine of the Trinity but rather functions here as a witness to the self-consistency of Yahweh who is not ambivalent and who has a single purpose or objective for creation and history. The ideas clearly overlap to provide an unmistakable basis for monotheistic faith. Yahweh is indeed a unity, but beyond that he is the only God. For this reason the exhortation of verse 5 has practical significance.

The confession of Yahweh's unique oneness leads to the demand that Israel recognize him as such by obedience to all that that implies. In language appropriate to covenant terminology, that obedience is construed as love, that is, to obey is to love God with every aspect and element of one's being.[16] This equation has already been made clear in the Decalogue in which Yahweh said, in reference to the second commandment, that he displays covenant faithfulness *(ḥesed)* to the thousands who love him and keep his commandments (Deut. 5:10). In covenant terms, then, love is not so much emotive in its connotation (though this is not excluded) as it is of the nature of obligation, of legal demand. Thus because of who and what he is in refer-

---

12. Moshe Weinfeld, *Deuteronomy 1–11,* Anchor Bible (Garden City, N.Y.: Doubleday, 1991), pp. 349–54.

13. Isidore Epstein, *Judaism* (Baltimore: Penguin Books, 1959), pp. 162–63.

14. See Eugene H. Merrill, "Is the Doctrine of the Trinity Implied in the Genesis Creation Account?" in *The Genesis Debate,* ed. Ronald F. Youngblood (Grand Rapids: Baker, 1990), pp. 123–24.

15. *Theological Dictionary of the Old Testament,* s.v. "אֶחָד *ʾechādh,"* by Norbert Lohfink and Jan Bergman, 1:194.

16. W. L. Moran, "The Ancient Near Eastern Background of the Love of God in Deuteronomy," *Catholic Biblical Quarterly* 25 (1963): 77–87.

ence to his people whom he elected and redeemed, Yahweh rightly demands of them unqualified obedience.

The depth and breadth of that expectation are elaborated on by the fact that it encompasses the heart, soul, and strength of God's people, here viewed collectively as a covenant partner. The heart *(lēb)* is, in Old Testament anthropology, the seat of the intellect, equivalent to the mind or rational part of humankind.[17] The "soul" (better, "being" or "essential person" in line with the commonly accepted understanding of *nepeš*) refers to the invisible part of the individual, the person *qua* person including the will and sensibilities.[18] The strength *(mĕʾōd)* is, of course, the physical side with all its functions and capacities. The word occurs only here and in 2 Kings 23:25 as a noun with nonadverbial nuance and even here the notion is basically that of "muchness."[19] That is, Israel must love God with all her essence and expression.

Jesus said that this was "the first and greatest commandment" (Matt. 22:38), an observation that is profoundly correct in at least two respects. First, it qualifies as such since it constitutes the essence of the Deuteronomic covenant principle and requirement. As stated before, the Shema is to the Decalogue what the Decalogue is to the full corpus of covenant stipulations. But it also is first and greatest because it is a commentary on the very first of the Ten Commandments—"You shall have no other gods before me" (Deut. 5:7).[20] This affirmation of the uniqueness and exclusiveness of Yahweh as Israel's Sovereign and Savior finds full endorsement and explication in the Shema, for to recognize Yahweh's unity and solitariness and to respond to that confession with total obedience is the strongest possible way of demonstrating adherence to the first commandment.

Jesus' use of the Shema is attested in all three Synoptic Gospels (Matt. 22:37–38; Mark 12:29–30; Luke 10:27). Matthew and Mark placed it immediately after the Sadducees' denial of a resurrection, whereas Luke recorded it as a response to the lawyer's question, "What shall I do to inherit eternal life?" In fact, in Luke's account it is the lawyer who quoted the second half of the Shema (Deut. 6:5) in answer to Jesus' follow-up question to him, "What is written in the Law?"

What seems clear here is that the Shema was cited on two occasions: once by Jesus in his reply to the Pharisee lawyer concerning the greatest commandment and once by the seeker who desired to know the way of life.[21] Doubtless

17. Hans Walter Wolff, *Anthropology of the Old Testament* (Philadelphia: Fortress, 1974), pp. 40–44.

18. Ibid., pp. 17, 53.

19. *Theological Wordbook of the Old Testament*, ed. R. Laird Harris, Gleason L. Archer, Jr., and Bruce K. Waltke (Chicago: Moody, 1980), s.v. "מאד," 1:487.

20. J. A. Thompson, *Deuteronomy*, Tyndale Old Testament Commentaries (Downers Grove, Ill.: InterVarsity, 1974), p. 121.

21. For evidence pro and con, see I. Howard Marshall, *The Gospel of Luke* (Grand Rapids: Eerdmans, 1978), pp. 440–41.

these instances are not exhaustive of all the citations of the Shema in Jesus' public ministry and, indeed, they may reflect a widespread recognition of its centrality in Jewish religious thought. It is striking, to say the least, that the "great commandment" (so Matthew) or the "first of all" (so Mark) is the very one which, if followed, leads to life (Luke 10:28). All this must be understood against the background of the Shema in Deuteronomy, where, as already noted, it serves as the essence of the Decalogue and, indeed, of all the Law. It is first and most important precisely because it encapsulates all God's saving intentions and provisions. To love God is to place oneself within the orbit of his saving grace, for the Shema, the heart and core of the Old Testament Law, was designed, as Paul wrote, to be "put in charge to lead us to Christ that we might be justified by faith" (Gal. 3:24).

It is not possible here to engage in a full discussion of the textual variants among the Synoptic renditions of the Shema,[22] but it is worth noting that only Mark cited Deuteronomy 6:4 ("Hear, Israel, the Lord our God is one Lord") and only Mark used the preposition *ek* ("with"), as does the Septuagint, in rendering "with all your heart." Matthew and Luke employ *en*, clearly reflecting the Hebrew preposition *b (bêt)*. On the other hand, Matthew alone limits the list of psychophysical terms to "heart," "soul," and "mind" (*dianoia*, almost always the translation of Heb. *lēb*, "heart," in LXX). Matthew seems to distinguish between "heart" and "mind" by viewing "heart" *(kardia)* as synonymous with love or affection.[23] This is likely the way Mark and Luke take "heart" as well. They both, however, add to the list "strength" *(ischys)*, a translation of the Hebrew *mĕʾōd*. The Septuagint also translates the Hebrew noun as "strength" but by a different Greek noun *(dynamis)*. A comparison of the order—heart, soul, mind (Matthew); heart, soul, mind, strength (Mark); heart, soul, strength, mind (Luke); heart, soul, strength (the Masoretic Text); and mind, soul, strength (the Septuagint)— among the various lists suggests that Mark and Luke added "mind" to the Hebrew/Septuagintal formula whereas Matthew substituted "mind" for "strength."

Again, it is impossible here to enter the debate about Synoptic traditions,[24] but several observations may be made about the New Testament use of this Old Testament text and its implications for theology.[25] First, it is clear that citation is not necessarily synonymous with quotation. Second, the variety of

22. For detailed discussion, see Wilhelm Dittmar, *Votus Testamentum in Novo: Die alttestamentlichen Parallelen des Neuen Testaments* (Göttingen: Vandenhoeck & Ruprecht, 1903), pp. 50–51.

23. Walter Bauer, William F. Arndt, and F. Wilbur Gingrich, *A Greek-English Lexicon of the New Testament and Other Early Christian Literature*, 2d ed., rev. F. Wilbur Gingrich and Frederick W. Danker (Chicago: University of Chicago Press, 1979), p. 404.

24. Cf. Marshall, *Gospel of Luke*, p. 443.

25. For the principles of interpretation involved in the New Testament use of the Old Testament in general, see O. Palmer Robertson, "Hermeneutics of Continuity," and Paul D. Feinberg, "Hermeneutics of Discontinuity," in *Continuity and Discontinuity*, pp. 89–108, 109–28.

ways in which New Testament authors cited the same Old Testament texts reveals that their concern was not with the letter of the cited passage but with its intent, its fundamental message. Third, in this case, at least, nothing was subtracted from the meaning of the Old Testament passage by the Gospel writers. In fact, Mark and Luke fleshed out the original text by dividing the Hebrew term *lēb* into its proper semantic categories of emotion (or feeling) and mind (the intellect). As for Matthew's use of "mind" for original "strength" or "might," it is possible, with many scholars, to understand mind as both the formulator and expediter of action, that is, thought at work.[26] In any event, all three citations of the Shema agree in demanding that we love God with all our being if we are to claim to be obedient to the first and great commandment.

Deuteronomy 18:15–19: The Prophet Par Excellence

The LORD your God will raise up for you a prophet like me from among your own brothers. You must listen to him. For this is what you asked of the LORD your God at Horeb on the day of the assembly when you said, "Let us not hear the voice of the LORD our God nor see this great fire anymore, or we will die." The LORD said to me: "What they say is good. I will raise up for them a prophet like you from among their brothers. I will put my words in his mouth, and he will tell them everything I command him. If anyone does not listen to my words that the prophet speaks in my name, I myself will call him to account."

This passage is nowhere cited *in toto* in the New Testament but verses or parts of verses appear with great frequency, especially in the Gospels and most especially, of course, with reference to Jesus. John's use of the Deuteronomy passage is especially striking (approximately twenty-four out of forty-two occurrences).

Deuteronomy 18:15–19, which describes the Moses-like prophet to come, is a part of a larger pericope dealing with the prophets of Yahweh and how their authenticity can be determined (vv. 14–22). This unit in turn is set in juxtaposition and opposition to a preceding one in which the abominable heathen practices of witchcraft and divination are set forth in detail (vv. 9–13). In this context of such perversion of prophetism Moses spoke of the emergence of an order of true prophets in Israel, a line that would find ulti-mate expression in a single Prophet par excellence.

Regardless of the precision with which the satanic practices of the Canaanite seers can or cannot be identified, the most important point to be made in the text is that any means employed by the heathen to gain informa-

---

26. Cf. Robert Horton Gundry, *The Use of the Old Testament in St. Matthew's Gospel* (Leiden: E. J. Brill, 1967), pp. 22–23.

tion from their gods or even to manipulate them to a certain course of action must be strictly avoided by God's elect people.[27] Such practices are detestable *(tōʿēbâ)* as are those who engage in them. Indeed, it is because the nations of Canaan are involved in such nefarious behavior that they will be expelled from the land (v. 12). In contrast to such wicked ways, the servants of Yahweh must be blameless *(tāmîm,* "upright") in all their relationships and associations with him (v. 13).

However, this does not mean that Israel would have no means of access to God, with no way to determine his purposes for them. They were not to emulate the divination of the peoples whom they would dispossess (v. 14); instead of these purveyors of lies an order of God's own prophets would speak true revelation (v. 15). This order is first spoken of in the singular—"a prophet like me" and "listen to him"—but the continuing context makes it clear that the term is being used in a collective sense to refer to prophetism as an institution (cf. "a prophet" and "that prophet" in vv. 20, 22).[28] There is nonetheless a lingering importance to the singular "prophet," for in late Jewish and New Testament exegesis there was the expectation of an incomparable eschatological prophet who would be either a messianic figure or the announcer of the Messiah (cf. John 1:21, 25; Acts 3:22; 7:37).[29] The ambiguity of the individual and collective being expressed in the grammatical singular is a common Old Testament device employed to afford multiple meanings or applications to prophetic texts.[30]

The promised prophet in Israel would differ from the charlatans described in verses 9–14 (cf. chap. 13) in that he would be like Moses and would come from among his own people. Moreover, he would speak with authority and so must be heeded by the people (v. 15). There had already been persons designated as prophets *(nābî)* in Israel's past; some, like Abraham, were named (Gen. 20:7), and others were anonymous (Num. 11:29; 12:6–8). However, Moses introduced something new, a channel of revelation to whom Yahweh spoke "face to face" and "not in riddles" (Num. 12:8). The composer of Moses' epitaph went on to say that no one up to his own time had equaled Moses as a prophet, one whom Yahweh knew "face to face" and whom he used to accomplish signs and wonders (Deut. 34:10–11).

The reason for a prophetic voice like that of Moses was (as Moses himself wrote) that the awesomeness of Yahweh in his epiphanic glory at Horeb ter-

27. Cf. A. Malamat, "Prophetic Revelations in New Documents from Mari and the Bible," *Vetus Testamentum Supplements* 15 (Leiden: E. J. Brill, 1966), pp. 207–27.

28. Willem A. Van Gemeren, *Interpreting the Prophetic Word* (Grand Rapids: Zondervan, 1990), pp. 28–34.

29. For the literature on this subject, see Peter C. Craigie, *The Book of Deuteronomy*, New International Commentary on the Old Testament (Grand Rapids: Eerdmans, 1976), pp. 262–64.

30. This is most clearly seen in the singularity and plurality of the Servant in the "Servant Songs" of Isaiah (42:1–4; 49:1–6; 50:4–9; 52:13–53:12). See H. Wheeler Robinson, *Corporate Personality in Ancient Israel* (Philadelphia: Fortress, 1964), pp. 15–17.

rified the people (18:16). They could not bear to look on his radiant presence nor could they listen to his words because of their transcendent quality. This point was already made most forcefully in Deuteronomy 5:23–27 (cf. Exod. 20:18–19). What was needed was a mediator who could approach God for them and who could then transmit the divine revelation to them. Future, post-Mosaic generations would also need such spokespersons to bear the message of heaven. This would particularly be the case when the peculiar role of Moses (and of Joshua after him) as covenant mediator came to an end. The new situation would require some individual or institution to carry on the ministry of revelation and of covenant enforcement. This would fall to the order of the prophets from then on.

The prophetic function is most clearly spelled out. The Moses-like spokespersons, called by God from among the people of Israel, will receive and speak only those things committed to them by Yahweh (v. 18). So great will be their authority that anyone who disobeys their word will be disobeying the word of Yahweh and accordingly be made accountable (v. 19). Moreover, any persons who profess to speak for Yahweh but in fact do not, or who speak on behalf of other gods, must be executed (v. 20). This latter contingency is also addressed in Deuteronomy 13:1–11. There are thus at least two kinds of false prophets: prophets of Yahweh who proclaim a false message, and prophets of false gods.

The history of the biblical use of this passage, especially that part that speaks of the prophet par excellence, begins not with the New Testament but within the Old Testament itself. Here it is not possible to speak of citation per se, certainly not in the sense of quotation, but of inner-biblical or progressive development of a theme. With this in mind, it is helpful to turn to the least doubtful Old Testament use of the ideal, eschatological prophet to come, namely, Malachi 4:5–6 (Heb. 3:23–24). Here that prophet is identified with Elijah, who, indeed, did appear with Moses and Jesus in the theophanic splendor of the Transfiguration (Matt. 17:3, 11; Mark 9:4; Luke 9:30).[31]

But in what sense can one identify Elijah with that prophet to come? Answers to this question are varied. The Old Testament record reveals that Elijah did not die but was translated bodily into heaven (2 Kings 2:11). His coming thus could be more easily explained and made possible without the impediment of death. His very ascension perhaps was for the purpose of his later eschatological appearance as forerunner of the Messiah. Jewish tradition from earliest times has viewed it in this way, as even the New Testament

31. Linkage between Moses and Elijah is found in the fact that both encountered Yahweh at Sinai (or Horeb; 1 Kings 19:8–18) as well as on the Mount of Transfiguration. For further connections, see Joyce G. Baldwin, *Haggai, Zechariah, Malachi*, Tyndale Old Testament Commentaries (Downers Grove, Ill.: InterVarsity, 1972), pp. 251–52.

suggests.[32] When the Jewish masses learned of the ministry of John the Baptist in the wilderness, they went out to him and inquired as to his identity (John 1:19–28). Was he the Messiah, they wondered, or Elijah, or the prophet, that is, the prophet of Deuteronomy 18? To each of these his answer was no. But the very question reflects anticipation of a coming Elijah and/or of a coming prophet.

Jesus, in an apparent contradiction of John's own testimony, identified John as Elijah albeit in a highly nuanced way (Matt. 11:14). John's inquisitors had wondered if he was not actually Elijah in the flesh returned to earth. This he was not, as he made clear in his reply. But he was, however, an Elijah figure, one who came in the spirit and power of Elijah. This is why Jesus qualified his assessment of the Elijah–John identification by saying, "If you are willing to receive him, this is Elijah who is to come." That is, John the Baptist stands in fulfillment of the promise of Malachi concerning the coming of Elijah, but only in the sense that he announced the coming of Christ.

Jesus touched on this point again in the Transfiguration narrative (Matt. 17:1–13; cf. Mark 9:2–13; Luke 9:28–36). When he appeared on the mountain in glory, he was accompanied by Moses and Elijah, the same two figures mentioned by Malachi (4:4–5). In later discussion with his disciples about his resurrection, they reminded him that before the messianic manifestation could come to pass Elijah must first appear (Matt. 17:10). Jesus agreed that Elijah must restore all things, but then he announced that Elijah had already come, only to be rejected. They then understood that Jesus once more was connecting Elijah with John the Baptist.

Why Elijah and not someone else is predicted in Malachi may have to do with his role as a prophet without parallel. Moses is mentioned in Malachi 4:4 in connection with the Law; Elijah is mentioned in the next verse, perhaps in connection with the Prophets. Thus, the whole canon of Malachi's day is represented, attesting univocally to the certainty of Yahweh's coming salvation. This sublime act of final redemption is confirmed by the word of two witnesses (Deut. 19:15), just as the anticipatory revelation in the Transfiguration of our Lord was accompanied by the same two witnesses, Moses and Elijah (Matt. 17:3).

The establishment of a linkage between the prophet of Deuteronomy 18 and Elijah in Malachi may appear to be somewhat tenuous in that the New Testament suggests a sharp demarcation among the Messiah, Elijah, and "the prophet" in first-century Jewish thought (cf. John 1:20–21, 25). John the Baptist denied that he was any one of these. Jesus, however, not only asserted that John was Elijah in some sense (Matt. 11:14) but that he was a prophet, indeed, "more than a prophet" (11:9).[33] He then identified John with the messenger of Malachi 3:1, a spokesman whom most interpreters

32. Joseph Klausner, *The Messianic Idea in Israel* (New York: Macmillan, 1955), pp. 451–57.

connect in turn with the Elijah of Malachi 4.[34] In this manner Jesus linked the prophet par excellence with Elijah (and with John), no matter the prevailing Jewish dissociation of the two.[35]

John himself pointed to another who would succeed him—One mightier than he (Matt. 3:11). In context the superiority of John's Successor would be in his baptizing ministry. Whereas John baptized with water, the One to come would baptize with the Holy Spirit. Subsequent events would reveal that John had much more than this in view, for after the demise of John the Baptist it became increasingly clear that his prophetic identity and role as the great eschatological prophet were not exhausted in him but transmitted to Jesus Christ, of whom the Baptist had spoken as the mightier One.

This is already hinted at in Luke's account of John's imprisonment and execution, for in the passage just before that account Jesus had raised to life the son of the widow of Nain whereupon the witnesses to the miracle glorified God and asserted that "a great prophet has appeared among us" (Luke 7:16). The transition of fulfillment of the promise of the great prophet of Deuteronomy from John the Baptist to Jesus is addressed even more specifically in the Gospel of John. There John denied that he was the long-awaited prophet just as he also denied that he was Elijah (John 1:21, 25). As noted already, however, he was indeed Elijah in a provisional and anticipatory sense until the true Elijah should appear. Likewise, he should in the same sense be seen as the prophet of Deuteronomy, the one Jesus called "more than a prophet," until that prophet should be revealed in his fullest manifestation in Christ.

The Samaritan woman perceived that Jesus was a prophet in a general sense (John 4:19; cf. Matt. 21:11; Luke 7:39), but the multitude whom Jesus fed with the five loaves and two fish acclaimed him as "the Prophet who is to come into the world" (John 6:14). The definite article before the word "prophet" *(ho prophētēs)* puts beyond any doubt that this crowd saw in Jesus the Prophet par excellence of Deuteronomy 18, an identification that Jesus left unchallenged.[36] The identical assertion was made at the temple on

---

33. The Greek *perissoteron prophēton,* if masculine, suggests "one who is more than a prophet" (Bauer, Arndt, and Gingrich, *Greek-English Lexicon of the New Testament and Other Early Christian Literature,* p. 651), that is, as Stein says, "the one who fulfilled the prophecy of Mal 3:1," namely, Elijah (Robert H. Stein, *Luke,* New American Commentary [Nashville: Broadman, 1992], p. 230). This is another way of speaking of a prophet par excellence, the only ones described in such ultimate terms in the Old Testament being Moses (Num. 12:7–8; Deut. 18:15, 18; 34:10–12) and to a lesser extent Elijah (1 Kings 18:36–38; 19:11–13; 2 Kings 2:10–12). Close attention to the parallels between Moses and Elijah supports the view that "the prophet" is Moses, then Elijah, then John, and then Jesus.

34. Craig L. Blomberg, "Elijah, Election, and the Use of Malachi in the New Testament," *Criswell Theological Review* 2 (1987): 102–8.

35. Marshall cites Oscar Cullmann to the effect that Jesus here was identifying John with the great eschatological prophet, a view Marshall rejects (*Gospel of Luke,* p. 295).

36. Raymond E. Brown, *The Gospel According to John (i–xii),* Anchor Bible (Garden City, N.Y.: Doubleday, 1966), pp. 234–35.

the occasion of the Feast of Tabernacles, when Jesus issued his invitation to the people assembled there to "come to me and drink" for "whosoever believes in me . . . streams of living water will flow from within him" (John 7:37–38). The spontaneous response was, "Surely this man is the Prophet" (v. 40), an attribution that our Lord did nothing to dispel.

The most indisputable linkage between the Deuteronomy prophet and Jesus was established by Peter in his sermon following the healing of the man at the temple gate (Acts 3:12–26). After arguing that God had revealed his saving purposes through a whole line of Old Testament prophets, he presented Jesus as both the fulfillment of the unanimous prophetic witness and the very greatest of the prophets. To put the matter beyond doubt he quoted Deuteronomy 18:15, 19, one of only two places in the New Testament where this crucial text is actually cited at length (cf. also Acts 7:37).

In summary, the New Testament use of Deuteronomy 18:15–19, though somewhat complicated by its apparent prior appropriation by Malachi, is well established. Inasmuch as the Lord Jesus appears as both ideal King and ideal Priest, thus fulfilling these respective offices in the Old Testament (Gen. 49:10; 2 Sam. 7:12–13; Pss. 2:6; 110:1–3, 4; Zech. 6:13, respectively), it is only reasonable to expect that he would likewise fulfill the third Old Testament institutional role, that of prophet. And this is precisely what Deuteronomy 18 has in view when it described the Prophet par excellence. True to the progressively unfolding nature of biblical revelation, this ultimate prophet is successively the whole order of prophets (Acts 3:18, 21; Deut. 18:20–22), Elijah (Mal. 4:4–5; cf. 3:1), John the Baptist (Matt. 11:9–14), and the Lord Jesus Christ (Acts 3:22). All the others may prefigure him, but only Christ fully satisfies the requirements of the prophet without parallel of Deuteronomy 18. Perhaps this is in part what the great prophet of the Judean wilderness meant when he said, "He must become greater; I must become less" (John 3:30).

Application to Life

This essay has focused on two of the more profound and important texts of Deuteronomy that find extensive citation in the New Testament, the so-called Shema of 6:4–5 and the prophecy of the Prophet par excellence of 18:15–19. Even brief reflection on the matter makes plain how theologically significant and interlinked these passages are and how crucial they are to Christian faith and life. The confession that Yahweh is the one and only God and that he must be loved and served with all one's being is at the core of ancient Israel's confession. The Ten Commandments and in fact the entire Old Testament Law find their center and meaning in this brief passage and the prophets and sages of Israel address their own communities in terms of its requirements. There is little wonder that Jesus understood the Shema to be the adumbration of all that we must believe and do if we are to know God and to obey him.

Another theme pervades Old Testament revelation as well and that is the sinfulness of Israel and of all humankind and the resulting consequence of alienation between the Creator and those he made as his image on the earth. Yahweh is one, indeed, and he must be obeyed and served unreservedly. But that cannot be understood and applied without the divine interposition of grace that atones for, forgives, and restores. Thus the salvific purpose is introduced and while running its course throughout Old Testament times from Genesis 3:15 onward, it always is open-ended and forward-looking, never achieving its historical reality until the Prophet comes who announced the kingdom and made salvation available by his sacrificial death and triumphant resurrection. The Shema describes the ideal, and the coming Prophet par excellence makes it a living and dynamic reality in the lives of those who believe. This is surely the intent of the message of the author of Hebrews who wrote, "In the past time God spoke to our forefathers through the prophets at many times and in various ways, but in these last days he has spoken to us by his Son, whom he appointed heir of all things, and through whom he made the universe. The Son is the radiance of God's glory and the exact representation of his being, sustaining all things by his powerful word. After he had provided purification for sins, he sat down at the right hand of the Majesty in heaven" (Heb. 1:1–3).

Tribute

It is a pleasure, on the occasion of his retirement from long and faithful service to Dallas Theological Seminary, to honor Donald Campbell with this contribution dealing with Deuteronomy. One of the themes of that book is transition of leadership from Moses to Joshua (Deut. 3:28; 31:14, 23; 34:9) so it is appropriate that one who is about to pass on the mantle to his successor be recognized for his many significant achievements. It is hoped that this study will to some extent reflect the esteem and appreciation due its recipient.

The Role of Women in the Rhetorical Strategy of the Book of Judges

Robert B. Chisholm, Jr.

The Book of Judges demonstrates, albeit in a negative manner, the importance of competent leadership to the people of God. After a notice of the great leader Joshua's death (1:1; cf. 2:8), the book tells how God raised up "judges" to deliver certain Israelite tribal groups from their enemies. Though these leaders often accomplished great military victories through God's power, many failed miserably in other respects. Despite their military successes, the spiritual climate in Israel grew bitterly cold as violence and anarchy swept through society. The book's final chapters include a sordid account of idolatry, gang rape, civil war, and kidnapping. The book concludes with the somber words, "In those days Israel had no king; everyone did as he saw fit" (21:25; cf. 17:6; 18:1; 19:1), setting the stage for the rise of Samuel and David, through whom God restored some semblance of covenantal loyalty and societal order.

We cannot read through the Book of Judges without noticing that women appear at several strategic points in the narrative. They assume a variety of roles, including heroine, seductress, and innocent victim, among others.[1] Their changing roles vis-à-vis the male characters contribute powerfully to the book's portrayal of the disintegration of Israelite society.[2] This portrait culminates in 1 Samuel 1 with the oppressed figure of Hannah, through whom the Lord reverses the downward spiral detailed in Judges and brings to realization the leadership ideal presented at the beginning of the book. This essay examines the interrelationship between the male and female characters in Judges to explain how the changing function of the women charac-

---

1. For a helpful general survey of the role of women in Judges, see M. O'Connor, "The Women in the Book of Judges," *Hebrew Annual Review* 10 (1986): 277–93.
2. Jay G. Williams comments on the changing roles of certain key women characters and asks if "this juxtaposition of roles is purely a matter of happenstance." However, he fails to develop this observation. See "The Structure of Judges 2.6–16.31," *Journal for the Study of the Old Testament* 49 (1991): 82.

ters provides a key to understanding the book's overall evaluation of Israel's male leadership during this time period. It also attempts to show how two of the women set the stage for the appearance of Hannah in a particularly pointed manner.

Declining Male Leadership and Changing Female Roles

A Warrior Wins a Wife and a Father Blesses His Daughter (Judg. 1–3)

Following the book's two introductory panels (1:1–2:5; 2:6–3:6), which record Joshua's death, Israel's partial success in taking the promised land, and the gradual spiritual decline of the Israelites, the author relates the exploits of Othniel, Ehud, and Shamgar, three judges who bravely delivered Israel from foreign oppressors (3:7–31). Though the accounts are relatively brief, the author paints a picture of militarily effective men who displayed daring and courage. He presents Othniel as a divinely empowered warrior who demonstrated military efficiency in an almost matter-of-fact way.[3] Ehud, who seems to have "ice in his veins," exhibited unhesitating courage and remarkable cunning in assassinating Eglon and subduing the Moabites. Shamgar, though mentioned in only one verse, displayed extraordinary military prowess.[4]

---

3. Judges 1:13 declares simply that Othniel, in response to Caleb's offer, "took it" (i.e., Debir). In a similar straightforward fashion, 3:10 reports that Othniel "went to war" and "overpowered" the enemy.

4. Block challenges the traditional idealistic view of the judges as "saviors of the nation." Instead, he suggests that the book's redactor intended to present them as "part of the problem that plagued Israel" during this period. He then attempts to show how the book negatively portrays the judges, including Ehud and Shamgar (Daniel I. Block, "The Period of the Judges: Religious Disintegration under Tribal Rule," in *Israel's Apostasy and Restoration: Essays in Honor of Roland K. Harrison,* ed. Avraham Gileadi [Grand Rapids: Baker, 1988], pp. 48–51). I agree generally with Block's thesis that the judges are portrayed in a tragic rather than heroic light, but would question whether this is the case with the three judges mentioned in chapter 3.

In the case of Othniel, little if any information is given about his personality or spiritual condition. Nevertheless, as Block observes (ibid., p. 48), what information is provided, both in 1:12–13 and in 3:7–11, can be viewed in a positive light. (Note the threefold reference in 3:9–10 to Othniel's role as the Lord's instrument.) The brevity and positive focus of the account are what we would expect when a character occupies a purely paradigmatic role. Cf. David M. Gunn, "Joshua and Judges," in *The Literary Guide to the Bible,* ed. Robert Alter and Frank Kermode (Cambridge, Mass.: Harvard University Press, 1987), p. 113.

As for Ehud, his use of deception and violence may be repugnant to modern sensibilities and ideas of propriety, but it is doubtful this would be the case for an ancient Israelite audience (note the glorification of Jael's bloody and cunning deed in 5:24–27), or if the pattern of Ehud's behavior is distinctly Canaanite (as Block suggests ["Period of the Judges," p. 49]). As Webb observes, this account is satiric, even comic (Barry G. Webb, *The Book of Judges: An Integrated Reading* [Sheffield: JSOT, 1987], pp. 129–31). The story is crafted to appeal to the audience's sense of humor and disdain for the Moabites. The utter humiliation of obese, stupid Eglon and his oppressive countrymen would make the reversal accomplished through Ehud that much sweeter for an ancient Israelite audience hearing of his exploits.

Acsah, the daughter of Caleb, is the first woman to appear in Judges (1:12–15). Caleb promised the conqueror of Debir his daughter's hand in marriage (v. 12), thereby guaranteeing that she would have a worthy husband and that Caleb would have a capable son-in-law who shared his faith and bravery. Othniel, Caleb's nephew (or younger brother),[5] responded to the challenge, took the city, and won the promised bride (v. 13). To complement her land holdings in the Negev, Acsah asked her father for "springs of water," a request with which he readily complied (vv. 14–15).[6]

Though there is little information pertaining to Ehud's personal faith, his battle cry (3:28), because it echoes the Lord's commission recorded at the beginning of the book (1:2), should be viewed as a significant expression of faith, not a mere "rallying slogan" (as Block suggests ["Period of the Judges," p. 49]).

In his speech to the foreign king Eglon (3:20), Ehud's use of Elohim instead of Yahweh, rather than suggesting a deficient faith (as Block implies [ibid.]), seems natural (cf. George F. Moore, *A Critical and Exegetical Commentary on Judges*, International Critical Commentary [Edinburgh: T. & T. Clark, 1895], p. 98) and is perhaps employed to avoid any hint of hostile intentions. After all, using the special covenantal name in such a context might suggest an overly patriotic attitude (cf. Jephthah's use of the covenantal name when negotiating with foreigners, 11:27) and/or conjure up images of past exploits by Israel's mighty warrior God (2:7).

Finally, the references to Ehud's "turning from" and "passing through" the images at Gilgal (3:19, 26) may carry a positive symbolic significance and, in the words of Polzin, "provide . . . an important ideological frame to Ehud's deliverance of Israel" (Robert Polzin, *Moses and the Deuteronomist: A Literary Study of the Deuteronomic History, Part One* [New York: Seabury, 1980], p. 160).

In the case of Shamgar, Block is correct in observing that "the brevity of the account precludes a clear interpretation of his role" ("Period of the Judges," p. 49). In this case one's interpretation of the preceding accounts will of necessity influence his or her understanding of Shamgar's role. Since I have argued that Othniel and Ehud are presented in a positive, even paradigmatic way, I tend to see the brief notice of Shamgar's extraordinary exploits in the same light. However, I would also admit that this account has its peculiar, perhaps even negative, elements. The omission of any direct reference to the Lord's enablement is curious (contrast 3:9–10, 15, 28), though it is possible that the Lord's involvement is implied in the wording of the text (Webb, *Book of Judges*, pp. 132–33). Shamgar's name (which seems to be foreign in its etymology) and identity (lit. son of Anath) are also puzzling. Though Block probably overstates the significance of these (he observes that Shamgar's "identification as 'son of Anath' hardly commends him for his Yahwistic piety" ["Period of the Judges," p. 49]), the appearance of the name "Anath," with its obvious Canaanite connotations (Peter C. Craigie, "A Reconsideration of Shamgar Ben Anath [Judges 3:31 and 5:6]," *Journal of Biblical Literature* 91 [1972]: 239–40), does seem to cast a cloud over the narrative. Nevertheless, the reference to Shamgar's apparent foreignness, rather than having a negative intent, may emphasize that Yahweh's "chosen means" of providing deliverance "may not be so easy to predict or explain" (Webb, *Book of Judges*, p. 133), a theme that has already been hinted at in the Ehud narrative and will emerge clearly in the story of Jael in chapters 4–5 (ibid., pp. 132, 137). Also if the author, with polemical design, likens the exploits of Deborah and Jael to those of the Canaanite deities Anath and Athtart (Peter C. Craigie, "Deborah and Anat: A Study of Poetic Imagery [Judges 5]," *Zeitschrift für die alttestamentliche Wissenschaft* 90 [1978]: 374–81; and J. Glen Taylor, "The Song of Deborah and Two Canaanite Goddesses," *Journal for the Study of the Old Testament* 23 [1982]: 99–108), then the reference to Shamgar as "son of Anath" might be a somewhat tongue-in-cheek foreshadowing of what is to come.

5. For discussion of the two options, see Moore, *Critical and Exegetical Commentary on Judges*, p. 27. Boling understands "brother" in its political sense of "ally" here (Robert G. Boling, *Judges*, The Anchor Bible [Garden City, N.Y.: Doubleday, 1975], p. 56).

6. Verses 14–15 have sometimes been misunderstood to suggest that Othniel is here presented in a negative light as one who was controlled by his wife or (if we follow the Septuagint) unduly greedy. However, if we understand the suffix on the form *wattᵉsîṭēhû* "she urged (or better, 'beguiled') him," as referring to Caleb (not Othniel) and take the infinitive *lišʾôl* as a gerund ("by asking"), it becomes

In many ways this brief account sets the stage for the rest of the book. Othniel is a model of the ideal warrior, for he followed Joshua's directive, bravely defeated the enemy, and aggressively took the land God had given to his people. Later we read again of his exploits, as the Spirit of God enabled him to rid the land of the foreign oppressor Cushan-Rishathaim (3:7–11). Unfortunately, no Israelite warrior would fully measure up to the ideal established by Othniel until David emerged on the scene hundreds of years later.[7]

Acsah's role as the maiden won by bravery in battle contrasts sharply with that of the women described later in the book. Rather than inspiring great military acts, subsequent female characters are forced to assume the typically male role of warrior because of character flaws in male leaders; and, by the end of the book, Israelite women are brutally abused by their own countrymen.

Caleb's gift to his daughter provides more than a pleasant, heart-warming touch to the story. Like his acquisition of a worthy husband for his daughter, Caleb's gift illustrates the protective concern that Israelite men should display toward their wives and daughters.[8] However, as the story unfolds, women become the victims of male oppression rather than the beneficiaries of male protection. The life-giving springs, which symbolize fertility and are actually called a "blessing," stand in sharp contrast to the death and infertility that another Israelite daughter would experience as a result of her father's misguided zeal and lack of foresight (11:34–40; see discussion on p. 42).

To summarize, the book's first three chapters, while not entirely positive in their assessment of Israel's early history, paint a somewhat ideal picture of heroic warriors and of an Israelite woman who inspires great deeds and receives a blessing from her father.

A Courageous Woman Lures a Foreign Warrior to His Death (Judg. 4–5)

Unfortunately, this ideal becomes somewhat tarnished in chapter 4, the opening verses of which state that Jabin of the Canaanites had been oppressing the Israelites for twenty years (vv. 2–3). A woman, Deborah, was exercising leadership in Israel at the time. Her duties included prophesying and

---

apparent that Othniel, rather than being placed in a bad light, is simply absent from this scene. See Paul G. Mosca, "Who Seduced Whom? A Note on Joshua 15:18//Judges 1:14," *Catholic Biblical Quarterly* 46 (1984): 18–22.

7. On the paradigmatic function of Othniel, see, among others, Gunn, "Joshua and Judges," p. 113; Lilian R. Klein, *The Triumph of Irony in the Book of Judges* (Sheffield: Almond, 1988), pp. 33–34; and Marc Brettler, "The Book of Judges: Literature as Politics," *Journal of Biblical Literature* 108 (1989): 405–6.

8. The Book of Ruth, which is specifically set against the background of the Judges period, also presents this ideal in the person of noble Boaz.

judging the people's legal disputes (vv. 4–5). She summoned Barak, of the tribe of Naphtali, and delivered a message from the Lord: "The LORD, the God of Israel, commands you: 'Go, take with you ten thousand men of Naphtali and Zebulun and lead the way to Mount Tabor. I will lure Sisera, the commander of Jabin's army, with his chariots and his troops to the Kishon River and give him into your hands'" (vv. 6b–7). Barak's reaction was less than enthusiastic. He said to Deborah, "If you go with me, I will go; but if you don't go with me, I won't go" (v. 8). Deborah's response suggests that Barak's attitude was inappropriate: "Very well, I will go with you. But because of the way you are going about this, the honor will not be yours, for the LORD will hand Sisera over to a woman" (v. 9).[9]

With a little more prodding from Deborah (v. 14), Barak hesitantly led the Israelite forces to a rousing victory (vv. 15–16). However, the Canaanite general Sisera escaped Barak's clutches and fled from the battle. Exhausted and thirsty, he came to the tent of a woman named Jael, the wife of Heber, a Kenite ally of Sisera. Despite her husband's allegiance to Sisera, Jael's loyalties were to Israel. She invited Sisera into her tent, gave him some milk, tucked him into bed, and then, while he lay sleeping, drove a tent peg through his head. Barak arrived on the scene a little too late and discovered, in fulfillment of Deborah's words, that the honor of slaying the Canaanite general belonged to a woman (vv. 17–22).

Judges 5 records Deborah and Barak's song of celebration. While Barak receives honorable mention (vv. 12, 15), Deborah and especially Jael are the focus of attention. Verses 7 and 12 speak of Deborah's role in the victory, while verses 24–27 rehearse at length Jael's courageous, though devious, exploits.

Judges 5:28–30 introduces another woman, Sisera's mother, who peered out her window in anticipation of her son's return. At first she was concerned about the delay, but then she realized that the warriors were probably plundering the enemy. She assumed that each warrior was grabbing "a girl (lit. womb, vagina) or two" to satisfy his lust (v. 30). The text is dripping with sarcasm at this point. Rather than brutally raping "a girl or two," the unfortunate Sisera met his violent demise at the feet of a courageous woman.[10] Furthermore, the language of sexual submission that permeates the descrip-

---

9. On Barak's spiritual insensitivity and hesitancy, see, among others, John H. Stek, "The Bee and the Mountain Goat: A Literary Reading of Judges 4," in *A Tribute to Gleason Archer,* ed. Walter C. Kaiser, Jr. and Ronald F. Youngblood (Chicago: Moody, 1986), pp. 64–65; and Meir Sternberg, *The Poetics of Biblical Narrative* (Bloomington, Ind.: Indiana University Press, 1987), p. 274.

10. See Mieke Bal, *Murder and Difference: Gender, Genre, and Scholarship on Sisera's Death,* trans. Matthew Gumpert (Bloomington, Ind.: Indiana University Press, 1988), p. 134; Athalya Brenner, "A Triangle and a Rhombus in Narrative Structure: A Proposed Integrative Reading of Judges IV and V," *Vetus Testamentum* 40 (1990): 133; and Andrea Cohen-Kiener, "Three Women," *Jewish Bible Quarterly* 19 (1991): 208.

tion of Sisera's death adds to the irony of his mother's words.[11] However, not only do these verses lend dramatic irony to the present context, but they also set up a tragic contrast with the book's final chapters (see page 45 for further discussion).

What are we to make of this account of Barak's victory over the Canaanites? Though Barak enjoyed success, he failed to display the courage of his predecessors. On the contrary, when God challenged, indeed commanded, him to lead Israel's armies into battle, he hesitated. Unlike Othniel, who charged into battle to win Acsah's hand in marriage, Barak demanded the military support of a woman, Deborah, before agreeing to go into battle. He thereby forfeited to Jael, another woman, the blessing that could have been his.

Ironically the warrior ideal established in Judges 3 was carried on by a woman rather than by Barak. As Brenner notes, Jael "goes about her task in a true 'male' manner."[12] Webb observes that Jael's actions mirrored the exploits of Ehud, another "lone assassin" who used deception to slay a foreign oppressor behind closed doors (cf. 3:12–30). Webb also notes parallels between Jael and Shamgar: "Like Shamgar she is a makeshift fighter who uses an improvised weapon. And if Shamgar was *probably* not an Israelite, Jael is *certainly* not; she is a member of a Kenite splinter group which is at peace with Jabin, Israel's arch enemy."[13]

By the end of the story we sense that Israel had taken a step backward, at least in male leadership. Fortunately, two courageous women rose to the occasion and compensated for Barak's weakness. However, the necessity of women playing a militaristic role, rather than inspiring the hero, was symptomatic of a decline in the quality of male leadership.

A Woman Delivers Israel from a Power-Hungry Oppressor (Judg. 6–9)

Gideon, despite being famous for his great victory over the Midianites with a force of only three hundred men, was less than an ideal ruler.[14] Like Barak, he was initially hesitant when called to action by the Lord (6:12–22, 36–40) and responded to the divine challenge with the word "if." When Barak heard the Lord's promise of victory, he told Deborah, "*If* you go with me, I will go; but *if* you don't go with me, I won't go" (4:8). Similarly Gideon, in response to the Lord's promises of his presence and military success, said,

---

11. See Robert Alter, *The Art of Biblical Poetry* (New York: Basic Books, 1985), pp. 43–49; and Susan Niditch, "Eroticism and Death in the Tale of Sisera," in *Gender and Difference in Ancient Israel*, ed. Peggy L. Day (Minneapolis: Fortress, 1989), pp. 47–51.

12. Brenner, "Triangle and a Rhombus in Narrative Structure," p. 132.

13. Webb, *Book of Judges,* p. 137.

14. For a list of his numerous faults, see J. Paul Tanner, "The Gideon Narrative as the Focal Point of Judges," *Bibliotheca Sacra* 149 (1992): 154. Also see D. W. Gooding, "The Composition of the Book of Judges," *Eretz Israel* 16 (1982): 74*–75*.

"*If* now I have found favor in your eyes, give me a sign that it is really you talking with me" (6:17). Later he proposed, "*If* you will save Israel by my hand as you have promised—look I will place a wool fleece on the threshing floor. *If* there is dew only on the fleece and all the ground is dry, then I will know that you will save Israel by my hand, as you said" (vv. 36–37). No wonder the Lord later declared, "*If* you are afraid to attack, go down to the camp with your servant Purah and listen to what they are saying. Afterward, you will be encouraged to attack the camp" (7:10–11).

Though ridding the land of a foreign oppressor, Gideon also contributed to the religious decline and political disintegration of Israel by failing to exercise the spiritual sensitivity and wisdom needed by a truly competent leader. He made a golden ephod that became a stumbling block for the nation and for his family (8:23–27). He took many wives (who gave him seventy sons), and kept a concubine at Shechem, who gave him a son named Abimelech (vv. 30–31). The power struggle inherent in this less than ideal family situation eventually became reality. Power-hungry Abimelech convinced the people of Shechem to hand over his seventy half-brothers whom he murdered, with the exception of Jotham. Conflict broke out between Abimelech and the Shechemites, which ended with Shechem being burned, in fulfillment of Jotham's curse. Abimelech met his demise at Thebez when an unidentified woman, perched in a tower, dropped an upper millstone on his head (9:53). The text emphasizes her singularity and states that she "threw" the stone on him, a touch of hyperbole that suggests a heroic act of strength and tends to cast the woman in the role of a warrior.[15]

A comparison of this account with the narrative of Sisera's death is instructive. In the earlier account a woman (Jael) delivered Israel from a *foreign* oppressor. In the account of Abimelech's death a woman delivered Israel again (once more, ironically, by a fatal blow to the head with an unconventional weapon; cf. 5:26 with 9:53), only this time from an oppressive *Israelite*.[16] The quality of Israelite leadership had steadily regressed as the brave warrior Othniel was replaced by hesitant Barak and unwise and timid Gideon, who in turn gave way to the "antijudge" Abimelech, a power-hungry and bloodthirsty initiator of civil discord. The changing roles of the women are symptomatic of this decline. Unlike Acsah, who inspired worthy and brave deeds, women were forced to assume the role of warrior, first to

15. See J. Gerald Janzen, "A Certain Woman in the Rhetoric of Judges 9," *Journal for the Study of the Old Testament* 38 (1987): 35, 37 n. 6.
16. Gooding also notes this parallel and comments on its implications: "Things have seriously deteriorated when the bondage from which Israel has to be delivered in this fashion is no longer a bondage to some foreign power but a bondage to one of Israel's own number who, instead of being a deliverer of Israel, has installed himself as a tyrant, and is maintaining his tyranny by ruthless destruction" ("Composition of the Book of Judges," p. 74*). O'Connor also notes the similarity between Jael and Abimelech's slayer, calling the latter "a sister to Jael" who "acts in a woman's sphere, i.e., from the inside, in killing an oppressing male" ("Women in the Book of Judges," p. 286).

deliver the nation from a foreign oppressor (Sisera) and then from a power-hungry countryman (Abimelech).

An Israelite Warrior Wins a Battle but Brings a Curse on His Daughter (Judg. 10–12)

Jephthah, identified as a "mighty warrior" and the son of a prostitute (11:1), was cut from the same mold as Barak and Gideon. Though he won military victories, he also demonstrated uncertainty before charging into battle. Despite being divinely empowered for battle (11:29), he bargained with God by making a vow (v. 30). Like Barak and Gideon (4:8; 6:17, 36–37), his use of "if," before the battle testifies to his uncertainty about its outcome.[17] The precise wording of his vow also attests to his sense of desperation and his lack of confidence. The description of the promised offering (11:31) suggests that Jephthah intended to offer a human being, not an animal, perhaps thinking that such a radical (but, alas, pagan!) proposal would guarantee divine support.[18]

Of course, the vow proved to be a rash and foolish one, for as Jephthah returned victorious from battle he was shocked to see that his daughter, his only child, was the first to come out of the house to meet him. True to his word and at the insistence of his daughter (v. 36), he sacrificed her as a burnt offering to the Lord (v. 39). But in accord with her request he first allowed her two months to mourn the fact that she would never have the opportunity to be a wife and mother.[19] Ironically Jephthah, who should have been a great

---

17. In Judges when *ʾim* is followed by the imperfect, the particle is usually conditional and the imperfect hypothetical (cf. 4:8, 20; 6:37; 13:16 [here *ʾim* seems to have the force of "even if"]; 14:12–13; 16:7, 11, 13). The only clear exception to this is in 15:7, where the context indicates that *ʾim* has the force of "since" and that the imperfect is customary or present progressive. We could possibly translate, "If you continue to act like this . . . ," but since Samson immediately carried out his vow without apparently giving the Philistines opportunity to change (v. 8), the NIV rendering ("Since you've acted like this") is preferable. The NIV translates 21:21, "When the girls of Shiloh come out," but the hypothetical nuance of the imperfect may be retained (cf. NASB). On the basis of past custom, the elders were anticipating that the girls would come out to dance, but their words leave open the possibility that they might not.

The closest parallels to Jephthah's vow are found in 14:12 and 16:11. In both passages, as in 11:30–31, the protasis has the conditional *ʾim* followed by the infinitive absolute and imperfect, while the apodosis, introduced by a perfect consecutive, states a promise or guaranteed outcome if the action proposed in the protasis is realized. Phyllis Trible suggests that the presence of the infinitive absolute in Jephthah's vow also signals his uncertainty and insecurity. By using this emphatic form, he appears to be "pushing the bargaining mode of discourse to its limit" (*Texts of Terror: Literary-Feminist Readings of Biblical Narratives* [Philadelphia: Fortress, 1984], p. 96).

Outside of Judges, close parallels to Jephthah's vow are found in Genesis 28:20–22; Numbers 21:2; 1 Samuel 1:11; and 2 Samuel 15:7–8, all of which have an introductory reference to a vow (as in Judg. 11:30). See David Marcus, *Jephthah and His Vow* (Lubbock, Tex.: Texas Tech, 1986), pp. 18–21. In each case *ʾim* is conditional and the imperfect hypothetical.

18. Cf. ibid., pp. 13–18; and Moore, *Critical and Exegetical Commentary on Judges*, pp. 299–300.

19. On the interpretive debate over the precise fate of Jephthah's daughter, see Marcus, *Jephthah and His Vow*.

hero because of his military success, ended up being one of the most tragic figures in the pages of Scripture because of his lack of faith and foresight. His "allegiance" to God (if we dare call it that) took the grotesque form of human sacrifice and brought a curse, rather than a blessing, on his daughter.

Once again the crisis in Israelite leadership at this period is evident. The radically changing role of the story's major female character draws attention to this. In the earlier stories, women heroically delivered the nation from oppressors; now an Israelite woman became an innocent victim of her own father's lack of wisdom. In contrast to Acsah, who received a blessing and a source of agricultural fertility from her father, Jephthah's daughter was doomed to a brief life of infertility culminating in a cruel and unnecessary death. To make matters worse, Jephthah's slaughter of his own flesh and blood foreshadowed the battle between the Gileadites and Ephraimites (12:1–7) and the bloody civil war described in the final chapters of the book, in which many Israelite women, like Jephthah's daughter, became victims of a misplaced oath and male brutality.[20]

A Foreign Woman Lures an Israelite Warrior to His Death (Judg. 13–16)

On the surface, Israel's most famous judge, Samson, seems to have the qualities necessary for a great leader. His supernatural conception seemingly placed him in line with the great patriarchs Isaac, Jacob, and Joseph. Like Othniel, he was divinely empowered and did not hesitate to attack the Lord's enemies. His apparent delight in riddles suggests a capacity for cunning, much like Ehud possessed. Like Shamgar, he was able to slaughter hundreds, even with an unconventional weapon.

However, we do not have to read far before noticing chinks in Samson's armor. His rash behavior and lack of foresight, as in the case of Jephthah, led to the violent death of an innocent young woman (14:1–15:6; both Jephthah's daughter and Samson's Timnite bride died by fire; 11:31, 39 and 15:6). Regardless of how we evaluate Samson's marriage to the Timnite woman,[21] his later involvement with a Philistine prostitute (16:1–3) is proof

---

20. Cf. J. Cheryl Exum, "The Centre Cannot Hold: Thematic and Textual Instabilities in Judges," *Catholic Biblical Quarterly* 52 (1990): 423, 430. By interpreting Judges 12:1–7 as exalting Jephthah, Trible misses the foreshadowing function of the story's conclusion (*Texts of Terror*, p. 107). Gooding, who sees this event in a negative light, explains that Jephthah's actions contrast with those of Ehud's: "Ehud with the Ephraimites takes the fords of Jordan against the Gentile enemy and slaughters them. Jephthah adopts precisely the same tactics with equal success. Alas, he uses them not against the Gentile enemy but against his fellow nationals, the Ephraimites" ("Composition of the Book of Judges," p. 74*).

21. Initially one is inclined to agree with Samson's parents (14:3) and question the propriety of his desire for a Philistine wife. However, the issue is not this simple, for verse 4 suggests that God was responsible for Samson's desire. Was this a divinely authorized exception to the general Old Testament prohibition against foreign wives, justified by the end in view (cf. v. 4b, which states that the Lord "was seeking an occasion to confront the Philistines")? Or does verse 4 mean that the Lord intended

of his moral weakness, and his disastrous affair with Delilah (16:4–22) reveals an embarrassing naiveté and lack of wisdom on a par with Eglon's.

Samson, following the pattern established by Barak, Gideon, and Jephthah, made several statements beginning with the word "if," the last of which led to his downfall. In their case "if" drew attention to their weak faith; in Samson's use "if" highlighted his lack of wisdom. At his wedding feast, he challenged the Philistines with a riddle (14:14) and proposed the following wager: "*If* you can give me the answer within the seven days of the feast, I will give you thirty linen garments and thirty sets of clothes. *If* you can't tell me the answer, you must give me thirty linen garments and thirty sets of clothes" (14:12–13a). The Philistines forced Samson's wife to persuade him to reveal the answer to the riddle. When Samson realized what they had done, he killed thirty men of Ashkelon, took their clothes to pay the debt, abandoned his Timnite wife, and went home to his parents.

Samson's inability to anticipate the Philistines' ingenuity (if their threat of 14:15 may be labeled in this way!) and his willingness to capitulate to his wife's pleas foreshadow his fateful encounter with Delilah, recorded in chapter 16. Once again the cunning Philistines used a woman to coax important information from Samson. Delilah asked about the secret of Samson's success. Three times he toyed with her before yielding (in each case he prefaced his lie with the word "if"—16:7, 11, 13). Exasperated by Delilah's constant nagging, he finally revealed the true secret of his strength: "*If* my head were shaved, my strength would leave me, and I would become as weak as any other man" (16:17).[22] Samson's lack of foresight brought about his personal downfall. Once his hair was cut, the Lord departed from him, enabling the Philistines to subdue him. The Philistines then blinded him,[23] forced him to grind grain, and publicly taunted him.

At this point the story has come full circle from the account of Jael and Sisera. On that earlier occasion Israel's ally Jael lured a *foreign* general to his death; now the Philistine Delilah had lured the greatest of *Israel's* warriors to his demise. Samson was now in the role of Sisera, and Delilah in the role of Jael.[24] Ironically, the great warrior Samson had been reduced to the posi-

---

to utilize Samson's lust for the Philistine woman, without approving of it, similar to the way he brought something good out of Joseph's brothers' immoral actions (Gen. 50:19–20)? For discussions of this difficult problem, see James L. Crenshaw, *Samson: A Secret Betrayed, A Vow Ignored* (Atlanta: John Knox, 1978), pp. 78–83; and Klein, *Triumph of Irony in the Book of Judges,* pp. 116–17.

22. The very wording of the statement signals that it is different in nature from the three lies. This time Samson prefaced his remarks with a theological explanation for his strength and he used a passive *qatal* verbal form after *ʾim* instead of an active *yiqtol* form as in verses 7, 11, and 13.

23. Ironically the blinding of Samson prevented him from looking with lust on any more Philistine women (cf. 14:1 and 16:1, where the verb *rāʾāh* appears).

24. Both Webb (*Book of Judges,* p. 164) and Klein (*Triumph of Irony in the Book of Judges,* p. 137) note thematic and verbal links between the Jael–Sisera and Delilah–Samson accounts. Also see O'Connor, "Women in the Book of Judges," p. 289. In addition to the more obvious parallels, the Philistine assembly that gathers to celebrate the captivity of Samson may correspond to Deborah and

tion of a woman. He was forced to perform the typically female task of grinding grain,[25] and, as in the case of Sisera, the suggestive language of sexual submission is used to describe his humiliation.[26]

Samson's story does not end on an entirely sour note, however. God's sovereign power, revealed in response to Samson's desperate suicidal plea for revenge, brought destruction to the taunting Philistines. Their confidence in their god Dagon, coupled with their failure to notice Samson's growing hair, contributed to their defeat.[27]

Despite this divine victory, Samson's death in the rubble of the Philistine temple makes the decline in Israel's leadership complete. Deficient faith has given way to lack of wisdom. No more individual leaders will appear in the book, the final chapters of which describe a period of anarchy that surpasses the turmoil produced earlier by the antijudge Abimelech.

Israelite Women Oppressed by Their Countrymen (Judg. 17–21)

Devoid of effective spiritual leadership, it is little wonder that the people of Israel, with their propensity to rebel, fell away from the Lord. Chapters 17–21 of Judges illustrate the depths of Israel's moral decline, describing the rise of an idolatrous cult and the outbreak of civil war.

In Judges 19–21 Israelite women play a prominent role, tragically, like Jephthah's daughter, as innocent victims. In chapter 19 we read of a Levite who was traveling with his concubine. He decided it would be safer to spend the night in Israelite territory than in the land of the foreign Jebusites. One of the men of Gibeah invited them in for a meal and lodging. However, a group of local thugs surrounded the house and demanded that the Levite be sent out so they could have homosexual relations with him. (The parallel to the Sodom–Gomorrah account is obvious.) The Levite and his host sent the concubine out instead and the thugs raped her all night and left her to die.

Once news of this crime reached the rest of the tribes, they demanded that the Benjamites hand over the perpetrators. When the Benjamites refused, a civil war erupted; its women, children, and soldiers were killed. Only six

---

Barak in the earlier account. Just as Deborah and Barak celebrated Israel's victory over Sisera in song so the Philistine lords and ladies praised Dagon for giving Samson into their hands (16:23–24).

25. See Susan Niditch, "Samson as Culture Hero, Trickster, and Bandit: The Empowerment of the Weak," *Catholic Biblical Quarterly* 52 (1990): 616–17.

26. Ibid., p. 617. See also Mieke Bal, *Death and Dissymmetry: The Politics of Coherence in the Book of Judges* (Chicago: University of Chicago Press, 1988), p. 26.

27. Samson's experience is representative of Israel's. Despite his tremendous God-given potential, he foolishly succumbed to the allurements of a foreigner and endured harsh ridicule and intense oppression. Nevertheless, God in the end mercifully responded to the sufferer's cry and vindicated him. For further discussion of this point, see Webb, *Book of Judges*, p. 179; and George W. Savran, *Telling and Retelling: Quotation in Biblical Narrative* (Bloomington, Ind.: Indiana University Press, 1988), p. 85.

hundred men escaped to the hills. The other tribes took an oath that they would not allow any of their daughters to marry the Benjamite survivors. Unfortunately, this oath, like Jephthah's, brought suffering in its wake.[28] Not wanting the tribe of Benjamin to disappear entirely, the Israelites devised a two-part plan to supply the remaining Benjamites with wives. Because the town of Jabesh Gilead failed to send a contingent to the war, it was wiped out, with the exception of four hundred virgins who were given to the Benjamite men. But two hundred more women were needed, so the remaining wifeless Benjamites were told to go to Shiloh, hide in the trees, and kidnap some of the girls who came out to dance in the vineyard in celebration of the harvest. As Exum observes, the Israelites, though initially appalled by the treatment of the Levite's concubine, "repeat on a mass scale the crimes they found so abhorrent in the men of Gibeah."[29]

By the end of the book Israel's moral decline is complete. Women, who at the beginning of the book inspired Israelite men to great deeds and then played the role of national deliverers, were raped, slaughtered (21:16), and kidnapped by their countrymen.[30] Ironically the brutalization of Israelite women anticipated by Sisera's mother (5:28–30) is realized, not through a ruthless foreign conqueror, but through Israelite men.

Summary

The early chapters of Judges present an ideal of male leadership, especially through the portrait of Othniel. Unfortunately, later judges, who were plagued by a weak faith (Barak, Gideon, Jephthah)[31] and/or lack of wisdom (Gideon, Jephthah, Samson), failed to live up to this ideal. By the end of Samson's story, Israel's greatest warrior was reduced to a helpless and vulnerable female role, much like the Canaanite general Sisera earlier in the book. By the end of the book, there are no leaders. Instead, Israelite men war with each other and cause untold suffering for Israelite women.

The changing roles of the women vis-à-vis the male leaders contribute to this account of Israel's societal decline. In contrast to Acsah, who inspired mighty deeds, women were soon forced into other roles. Due to Barak's weak

---

28. Exum, "Centre Cannot Hold," p. 430.

29. Ibid., pp. 430–31. See also Stuart Lasine, "Guest and Host in Judges 19: Lot's Hospitality in an Inverted World," *Journal for the Study of the Old Testament* 29 (1984): 49; and Trible, *Texts of Terror*, pp. 83–84. Contrast the fate of Benjamin's women (cf. 20:48; 21:16) and the actions of its men (cf. 21:14, 23) with the idyllic portrait painted in 12:9, where Ibzan, a fertile, divinely blessed Bethlehemite judge, peacefully arranges marriages for his thirty sons and thirty daughters.

30. Cf. Klein, *Triumph of Irony in the Book of Judges,* pp. 172–73; and Exum, "Centre Cannot Hold," p. 416.

31. It is beyond the scope of this study to harmonize this observation, which is validated by a close reading of the Hebrew text, with the generalized statement of Hebrews 11:32, which commends Gideon, Barak, and Jephthah for their faith. Suffice it to say that even weak faith can find commendation from God (as in Heb. 11:32), but such faith hardly guarantees effective spiritual *leadership* (as illustrated by Judges).

faith and Gideon's lack of wisdom, Deborah, Jael, and the unnamed woman in Thebez assume the role of warriors, demonstrating the same courage, cunning, and prowess as the earlier heroes Othniel, Ehud, and Shamgar. As the male leaders continued to lose effectiveness and then disappeared altogether, the highly valued and heroic women of the early chapters were replaced by the brutalized victims of the later chapters. In contrast to Acsah, who received her father's rich blessing, Jephthah's daughter was forced to swallow the bitter pill of infertility and death by her father. Her painful experience foreshadowed the widespread oppression and bloodshed that stain the pages of the book's final chapters.

Paving the Way for Hannah

The downward spiral outlined in Judges reaches its lowest point in 1 Samuel 1. Here we encounter Hannah, who was oppressed not by a man, but by another woman. Though greatly loved by her husband, barren Hannah experienced the constant taunts of a rival wife, a type of oppression in some respects worse than the physical oppression described in Judges. Hannah is a pivotal figure whose experience foreshadows that of Israel. God supernaturally delivered her from oppression, allowing her to give birth to a son whom she consecrated to the Lord in fulfillment of her earlier vow. Through this son, Samuel, the Lord revived Israel's prophetic movement and paved the way for the arrival of the great king David.

In addition to tracing a pattern of oppression that culminated in Hannah, the Book of Judges sets the stage for her appearance in another way. The reader has probably observed that two significant women characters, the unnamed mothers of Samson and Micah, were omitted from the earlier survey of Judges. While not fitting into the scenario outlined earlier, these women play a vital role in the unfolding plot for they and their sons serve as foils for Hannah and her son.

The accounts in which these three women play an important role begin in the same way:[32]

> Judges 13:2   "Now there was a certain man from Zorah"
> Judges 17:1   "Now there was a man from the hill country of Ephraim"
> 1 Samuel 1:1 "Now there was a certain man from Ramathaim"

At first glance the formula "now there was a (certain) man from (place name)" seems to be merely a stylized way of introducing a new pericope.

---

32. The similarity between Judges 13:2 and 17:1 is noted by Exum, "Centre Cannot Hold," p. 425. Cf. also Lyle M. Eslinger, *Kingship of God in Crisis: A Close Reading of 1 Samuel 1–12,* Bible and Literature Series 10 (Sheffield: Almond, 1985), p. 285.

However, in Judges and 1 Samuel this formula appears only in these three passages and in 1 Samuel 9:1, where Saul's family background is introduced.[33] A comparison of the accounts reveals significant thematic connections, suggesting that the introductory formula is a linking device at the macrostructural level.

Samson's Mother (Judg. 13:1–14:3)

Samson's life began with great promise. An angel appeared to the barren wife of Manoah and announced that she would give birth to a son, whom she was to dedicate to the Lord's service. When she told her husband Manoah of her extraordinary experience, he requested another visitation from the Lord so that he might receive instructions about the promised child's training. The angel reappeared, essentially repeated his earlier instructions to Manoah's wife, and then left. Shortly thereafter Samson was born.

The angelic announcement of Samson's birth and his mother's supernatural conception offered tremendous hope for Israel, for they recalled the birth accounts of the patriarchs Isaac (cf. Gen. 17–18, 21), Jacob (Gen. 25:21), and Joseph (Gen. 30:22–23). However, despite Samson's being consecrated to the Lord from birth, his potential and promise were only partially realized. Only God's sovereignty was able to salvage a victory out of the blinded warrior's tragic death in a Philistine temple.

The experience of Samson's mother is parallel in many respects to that of Hannah. Though both were barren, the Lord supernaturally enabled them to conceive sons destined to become leaders in Israel. Samson's mother was instructed by the angel to dedicate her son to the Lord's service from birth; Hannah, though not receiving an angelic visitation, devoted Samuel to the Lord from infancy in fulfillment of her earlier vow. Both of these long-haired servants of the Lord won victories over the Philistines.

However, the resemblance ends there. Samson's career came to a tragic end as his moral weakness and lack of wisdom led to his humiliation and death. Samuel, on the other hand, was the catalyst for Israel's political and religious revival. Samson's career was at best a mere first step in the subduing of the Philistines (as recorded in Judg. 13:5, God stated, "he will *begin* the deliverance of Israel from the hands of the Philistines"), while Samuel and David, whom Samuel anointed king, accomplished a more complete and lasting victory (cf. 1 Sam. 7:14; 17:1–58; 2 Sam. 5:17–25; 8:1).[34]

---

33. The introductory formulas in Judges 17:7 ("Now there was a young man from Bethlehem") and 19:1 ("Now there was a Levite staying in the remote parts of the hill country of Ephraim") are similar, but they differ in important ways. In 17:7 *na^{c}ar* is used instead of *ʾîš*; in 19:1 a participle and the preposition *b^e* follow *ʾîš* rather than *min*.

34. Like Samson, Saul contrasts with Samuel (and with David). In fact, there are numerous parallels between the foils of Samson and Saul. The same formula introduces the narratives in which they are commissioned for service (cf. Judg. 13:2 with 1 Sam. 9:1). In both cases a traditional type scene is

Micah's Mother (Jug. 17:1–5)

The author portrays Micah's mother, who is also a foil for Hannah, as a misguided devotee of Yahweh (17:1–5). When her son (the meaning of whose name ["Who is like Yahweh"] seems to attest to his mother's devotion) confessed that he was the one who had stolen 1,100 shekels of silver from her, she blessed rather than rebuked him. When he returned the money, she consecrated it to the Lord and commissioned her son to have a carved image and a cast idol made from a portion of the silver. Like earlier vows (11:30–31) and later vows (21:1, 7, 18) in the Lord's name, her oath led to nothing but trouble. This image and idol, once stolen from Micah, were used by the Danites to establish an unauthorized religious cult in competition with the tabernacle at Shiloh (18:30–31).[35]

Like Micah's mother, Hannah also made a solemn vow to the Lord. However, the resemblance ends there. The misguided vow of Micah's mother led to an idolatrous form of Yahwism opposed to the authorized cult located at Shiloh. Hannah's appropriate vow led to the revival, though shortlived, of the declining Shiloh cult (cf. 1 Sam. 3:21) and to the continuance of genuine Yahwistic religion in Israel. Unlike Micah, who provided (unwillingly) the personnel and equipment for an unsanctioned, idolatrous Danite cult, Samuel became a channel of renewed divine revelation and a powerful spokesman for the Lord.

Summary

In contrast to Samson's mother, whose miraculously conceived son failed to realize his potential, Hannah supernaturally gave birth to a son through whom the Lord restored effective leadership to Israel. In contrast to Micah and his mother, whose misguided zeal led to a polluted, unauthorized cult,

---

used (or altered) for rhetorical effect. Samson's miraculous conception seemingly places him in line with the patriarchs of old, but the utilization of the barren-mother type scene in his birth account only makes his subsequent failure that much more disappointing. The betrothal type scene is utilized in the story of Saul. Isaac (through his proxy, Abraham's servant, Gen. 24), Jacob (Gen. 29), and Moses (Exod. 2) all met their future brides at wells. In the case of Jacob and Moses, certain actions performed on this occasion foreshadowed their careers (cf. Gen. 29:10; Exod. 2:17). However, as Alter observes, in 1 Samuel 9:11–12, where Saul met the girls on their way to the well, this type scene is "aborted," foreshadowing Saul's unrealized potential. Unlike the patriarchs and Moses, he and his descendants would not play a significant, ongoing role in the future of the covenant community (Robert Alter, *The Art of Biblical Narrative* [New York: Basic Books, 1981], pp. 60–61). Like Samson, Saul only accomplished a partial victory over his enemies, expired with a death wish on his lips (1 Sam. 31:1–6) and became the object of public ridicule among the Philistines (vv. 8–10).

35. On the author's overall negative assessment of the incidents recorded in chapters 17–18, see Yairah Amit, "Hidden Polemic in the Conquest of Dan: Judges XVII–XVIII," *Vetus Testamentum* 40 (1990): 7–8; and Dale Ralph Davis, "Comic Literature—Tragic Theology: A Study of Judges 17–18," *Westminster Theological Journal* 46 (1984): 161. Davis calls the narrator a "hostile critic" of what he relates.

Hannah's devotion to the Lord led to the revival of genuine Yahwism in Israel through the spiritual direction provided by Samuel.

Epilogue: Another Othniel Arrives

The birth of Samuel marked a significant turning point in Israel's history. Though the tragic death of Phinehas's wife (1 Sam. 4:19–20) carries on the theme of female suffering and oppression so characteristic of Judges, the supernatural reversal of Hannah's situation signaled the dawning of a new era. Quality male leadership was about to be restored. After the notice of Phinehas's wife's death, the next women characters to appear in the story (omitting the girls who give Saul directions; 9:11–13) are the singers and dancers who celebrated the victories of Saul and David (18:6–7).[36] Shortly thereafter Saul's daughters Merab and Michal, like Acsah of old, were offered (in their respective turns; 18:17–21) to a conquering hero as a reward for bravery in battle (17:25). In David, the conqueror of Goliath, another Othniel had arrived—at least for a time.

Tribute

I consider it a privilege to contribute to this volume dedicated to Dr. Donald K. Campbell, whose strong faith, godly wisdom, and spiritual leadership are exemplary.

---

36. There may be an intentional contrast with Jephthah's daughter (Judg. 11:34) and the girls of Shiloh (21:21, 23), whose dancing was quickly transformed into brutality. Trible discusses parallels and contrasts between Judges 11:34 and Exodus 15:19–21/1 Samuel 18:6–7 (*Texts of Terror*, pp. 100–101). She notes that Jephthah's daughter, unlike Miriam and the women of 1 Samuel 18:6–7, "comes alone and no words of a song appear on her lips." She adds, "The difference accents the terrible irony of an otherwise typical and joyful occasion." In addition to Trible's observations, we should also note that, in contrast to Miriam and the women of 1 Samuel 18:5–6, other women only join Jephthah's daughter in her lamentation (Judg. 11:38–40).

Young David and
the Practice of Wisdom

Homer Heater, Jr.

"In everything he did he had great success *(maśkîl),* because the LORD was with him" (1 Sam. 18:14). "The Philistine commanders continued to go out to battle, and as often as they did, David met with more success *(śākal)* than the rest of Saul's officers, and his name became well known" (1 Sam. 18:30). "My lord [David] has wisdom *(ḥākam)* like that of an angel of God—he knows everything that happens in the land" (2 Sam. 14:20). "One of the servants answered, 'I have seen a son of Jesse of Bethlehem who knows how to play the harp. He is a brave man and a warrior. He speaks well and is a fine-looking man. And the LORD is with him'" (1 Sam. 16:18). "Now David the son of Jesse was wise, and enlightened like the light of the sun, literate, and discerning, perfect in all his ways before God and men. Yahweh gave to him a spirit of discernment and enlightenment" (Qumran 11QPsa).[1]

A number of attempts have been made to demonstrate that portions of the Bible outside the areas traditionally assigned to "wisdom" (Job, Proverbs, Ecclesiastes, and some psalms) were sourced in wisdom circles.[2] In 1969 Crenshaw set out five observations or criteria by which one might evaluate whether a piece of literature came from "wisdom circles."[3] His criticism of the three works mentioned in note 2 have effectively squelched optimism in trying to find "wisdom" material outside the places where it is usually found.[4]

---

1. J. A. Sanders, ed., *The Psalms Scroll of Qumran Cave 11 (11QPsa)* (Oxford: Clarendon, 1965), p. 48 (translation mine).
2. Three important examples are R. N. Whybray, *The Succession Narrative* (Naperville, Ill.: A. R. Alleson, 1968); S. Talmon, "'Wisdom' in the Book of Esther," *Vetus Testamentum* 13 (1963): 419–55; and Gerhard von Rad, "The Joseph Narrative and Ancient Wisdom," *The Problem of the Hexateuch and Other Essays,* ed. W. Trueman Dicken (London: Oliver & Boyd, 1966), pp. 292–300.
3. James L. Crenshaw, "Method in Determining Wisdom Influence upon 'Historical' Literature," *Journal of Biblical Literature* 88 (1969): 129–42.
4. This is the assessment of Leo G. Perdue ("The Testament of David and Egyptian Royal Instructions," in *Scripture in Context II: More Essays on the Comparative Method,* ed. W. W. Hallo, J. C. Moyer, and Leo G. Perdue [Winona Lake, Ind.: Eisenbrauns, 1983], pp. 79–96). But the effort has not been abandoned. See, for example, Walter Brueggemann, "On Coping with Curse: A Study of 2 Sam.

Crenshaw criticizes a failure to take into account the history of wisdom. He questions attributing great wisdom influence to the time of Solomon (and Hezekiah).[5] However, he seems to be too conservative in light of the extensive emphasis placed on wisdom in the biblical narratives. On the other hand, four of his criteria are valid as he demonstrates by applying them to Genesis, Samuel, and Esther with convincing results.

With Crenshaw's caveats in mind, this essay looks at young David in the light of wisdom teaching. Crenshaw was right in saying that the story of David is not the direct product of wisdom circles, but surely the people who went to such pains to show Solomonic wisdom would have been derelict if they had not also pointed out David's wisdom.[6] Of the David and Goliath story Rofé wrote, "It is remarkably paradigmatic. This paradigmatic quality can be seen, first and foremost, in the portrayal of David as a paragon of virtue."[7] This statement can be extended to other parts of David's life. Perhaps we can avoid the pitfall Crenshaw points out by speaking of David's life as more of an unconscious paradigm of wisdom practices than a formal setting forth of such an idea. Brueggemann says, "Although wisdom literature in the Bible is often dated much later than David, and in the tradition intrudes with Solomon, it seems legitimate to suggest that David made this intrusion possible."[8]

Certainly the absence of the basic word for "wisdom" (*ḥokmāh*)[9] should caution us against too much enthusiasm for a connection between "wisdom" and David. At the same time 1 Samuel 18:14 contains the word *maśkîl,* a word used frequently in Proverbs. It is applied to Abigail (1 Sam. 25:3, nominal form), Solomon (2 Chron. 2:12, nominal form), and the Levites in Hezekiah's day (2 Chron. 30:22, verbal form). The critical wisdom word "ways" also occurs in 1 Samuel 18:14. Surely there is some sense in which David is being shown as a wise person.[10]

16:5–14," *Catholic Biblical Quarterly* 36 (1974): 175–92; and C. Fontaine, "The Bearing of Wisdom on the Shape of 2 Samuel 11–12 and 1 Kings 3," *Journal for the Study of the Old Testament* 34 (1986): 61–77.

5. Crenshaw, "Method in Determining Wisdom Influence upon 'Historical' Literature," p. 135.

6. Rose says, "It is our thesis that the chapter [1 Samuel 16] is uniquely formulated in categories of thought, and with literary features, similar to those found in the traditionally defined wisdom literature (Job, Proverbs, Qoheleth, Aḥiqar, Ben Sira', Pirqe Aboth)" (Ashley S. Rose, "The 'Principles' of Divine Election: Wisdom in 1 Samuel 16," in *Rhetorical Criticism: Essays in Honor of James Muilenberg,* ed. J. J. Jackson and M. Kessler [Pittsburgh: Pickwick, 1974], p. 44). He says further that Yahweh's response to Samuel's attempt to evaluate Jesse's sons follows teacher-student patterns (ibid., p. 47). He calls these "torah units."

7. Alexander Rofé, "The Battle of David and Goliath," in *Judaic Perspectives on Ancient Israel,* ed. J. Neusner, B. A. Levine, and E. S. Prerichs (Philadelphia: Fortress, 1987), p. 126.

8. Walter Brueggemann, *In Man We Trust* (Richmond, Va.: John Knox, 1972), p. 32.

9. Except in the description of and in the mouth of the wise woman of Tekoa (2 Sam. 14:2, 20).

10. The perception of David as a wise man was held by some at Qumran as well. The sentence cited above is found in a fragment sandwiched between parts of 2 Samuel 24 and Psalm 140.

David and Yahweh: The Fear of the Lord[11]

What in David's life can be categorized as wisdom? Wisdom in the Old Testament is multifaceted. It has to do with proper conduct in the king's court as well as everyday deportment. But above all there is a spiritual dimension unique to the wisdom of the Old Testament.[12] David brought to Israel a robust confidence in Yahweh that profoundly changed the way people thought about God and life. He was able to integrate "faith and life" as few before or since him have been able to do.

The spiritual dimension of wisdom is referred to throughout Proverbs. The fear of the Lord is the foundation and linchpin of human existence. Wisdom (Prov. 9:10; 15:33) and knowledge (1:7, 29; 2:5) are identified with the fear of the Lord. In the Old Testament wisdom includes the idea of knowledge (1 Kings 4:29–34), but knowledge of data separated from piety is meaningless in Old Testament wisdom.

The fear of the Lord is also attached to the practice of avoiding evil (Job 1:1, 8; 2:3; Prov. 3:7; 8:13; 14:16; 16:6). Evil is made more specific in Proverbs 8:13: it is pride, arrogance, evil behavior (lit. the evil way), and perverse speech. A psalm attributed to David reads, "Men of perverse heart shall be far from me; I will have nothing to do with evil" (Ps. 101:4). According to Psalm 10:4, "In his pride the wicked does not seek him; in all his thoughts there is no room for God." "In his arrogance the wicked man hunts down the weak, who are caught in the schemes he devises" (Ps. 10:2). In another Davidic psalm these evil practices are castigated: "Let their lying lips be silenced, for with pride and contempt they speak arrogantly against the righteous" (Ps. 31:18).

As a young shepherd, David learned that "the fear of the LORD is the beginning of wisdom" (Prov. 9:10), and so he fearlessly faced a lion and a bear, but it was Yahweh who delivered him from their paws (1 Sam. 17:34–37).[13] From his youthful victory over Goliath through his constant mistreatment by Saul, David feared God and turned from evil. His response to Nathan's indictment reflects this humility before God as he accepted the charge and submitted to whatever consequence God would lay on him. This

11. On wisdom and the fear of the Lord, see Henri Blocher, "The Fear of the Lord as the 'Principle' of Wisdom," *Tyndale Bulletin* 28 (1977): 3–28; and Roy B. Zuck, "A Theology of the Wisdom Books and the Song of Songs," in *A Biblical Theology of the Old Testament*, ed. Roy B. Zuck (Chicago: Moody, 1991), pp. 214–17.

12. Brueggemann, *In Man We Trust*, pp. 40–41. Also see R. B. Y. Scott, *The Way of Wisdom in the Old Testament* (New York: Macmillan, 1971), pp. 4–5; Roland E. Murphy, *The Tree of Life* (Garden City, N.Y.: Doubleday, 1990), pp. 3–5; James L. Crenshaw, *Old Testament Wisdom* (Atlanta: John Knox , 1981), pp. 11–25.

13. "At this point we merely note the two factors which made the heroic possible, viz. David's zeal for the reputation of Israel's God—'that all the earth may know' (v. 46) and his utter trust in God's ability to preserve him against all odds (vv. 37, 45–47)" (R. Gordon, *I & II Samuel* [Grand Rapids: Zondervan, 1986], p. 153).

demeanor contrasts sharply with that of many of his descendants (Rehoboam, Joash, and Jehoiakim, to name a few).

The opposite of the fear of the Lord is the fear of man. No greater contrast of these opposing fears could be presented than when David confronted Goliath. Saul and his men feared Goliath the man, but David by virtue of his fear of Yahweh did not. "Fear of man will prove to be a snare, but whoever trusts in the LORD is kept safe" (Prov. 29:25).

David and His Father: Honoring Parents

"Even a child is known by his actions, by whether his conduct is pure and right." (Prov 20:11)

David is also an example of wisdom in his response to his parents. The biblical narrative gives no interchanges between David and his father. We read only of his father sending for him (1 Sam. 16:12) or sending him to Saul (16:20) or to his brothers (17:17–18). Later David left his parents in the Transjordan with the king of Moab (22:3). Since David's father was elderly when the account begins, we have no way of knowing whether he was able to enjoy the fruits of David's success. But he and others would surely have been able to say, "A wise son brings joy to his father" (Prov. 10:1; 15:20), "A wise son heeds his father's instruction" (13:1), and "The father of a righteous man has great joy" (23:24).

David's obedience to his father was first evident when he was called from the field where he was watching sheep. The fact that he was not included with his other brothers when Samuel first came, and his older brother was later sarcastic in referring to David's work (1 Sam. 17:28), may indicate that David's role as a shepherd was deemed insignificant. Even so, David cheerfully assumed the responsibility placed on him by his father, and his onerous task became a stepping stone to success.[14] He is consistently linked metaphorically and literally with the flock (1 Sam. 16:19; 17:15, 20, 34; 2 Sam. 5:2; 7:8; 1 Chron. 11:2; 17:6–7; Ps. 78:70–71; Ezek. 34:23; 37:24). He came from the flock to be anointed (1 Sam. 16:12); he was tending the flock when Saul sent for him (16:19); he went back and forth between Gibeah and Bethlehem to care for the flock (17:15); and his brother upbraided him for leaving his puny flock to watch the battle (17:28).

It is not surprising then that later the leaders of Israel said, "In the past, while Saul was king over us, you were the one who led Israel on their military campaigns. And the LORD said to you, 'You will shepherd my people Israel,

---

14. David and Joseph are often compared (Graham S. Ogden, "Historical Allusion in Qoheleth IV 13–16?" *Vetus Testamentum* 30 [1980]: 309–15). In this case both came from "dead-end" positions to exaltation.

and you will become their ruler'" (2 Sam. 5:2). David's cheerful obedience to his father prepared him to do battle against Goliath and to lead the people of God over whom he was placed as a shepherd. When Jeremiah issued a diatribe against the shepherds of Israel, he also promised that God would raise up good shepherds, specifically an offshoot of David who will "reign wisely" and bring about deliverance and security for God's people (Jer. 23:4–6). During the exile, Ezekiel said, "I will place over them one shepherd, my servant David, and he will tend them; he will tend them and be their shepherd" (Ezek. 34:23). The scion of David will assume the role of shepherd in the eschaton (Mic. 5:4–5).

David and Saul: Respect for Authority

"Fear the LORD and the king, my son, and do not join with the rebellious." (Prov. 24:21)

Perhaps no greater example of wisdom practice is found than in David's response to Saul. His attitude appears first when Saul recruited him to play music to soothe him when he was troubled (1 Sam. 16:17–23). The servant's description of David shows what a wonderful young man he was.[15] He presented David as the ideal man, a paragon of virtue. He was talented, brave, and a warrior. Furthermore he spoke well, and was a fine-looking man. Above all, "Yahweh was with him," a theme the historian began developing in 1 Samuel 16.[16] How much better could the "wise son" of Proverbs be described? Something about David caused Saul to love him and to make him his armor bearer. "David is evidently a man with particularly attractive features, as we are shown here and often elsewhere; he takes hearts by storm, and everyone falls for him. He is indeed someone 'with whom' the Lord is (16.18; 17.37)."[17] There must have been an open and gracious spirit about this young man that endeared him to the king. In this sense he was wisdom personified.

David assumed a humble role when Saul offered his older daughter to him. He should have received Merab as one of the terms of his victory over Goliath (1 Sam. 17:25), but apparently Saul went back on that part of the bargain. Not only did David not complain; he even affirmed that he was not

15. "The ideal Israelite hero was clever with words, as the stories of Jacob, Joseph, Esther, Daniel, and the rest (except Moses) show" (P. Kyle McCarter, *1 Samuel*, Anchor Bible [Garden City, N.Y.: Doubleday, 1980], p. 281).

16. "This part of the description explains all the previous parts: the young man's success, strength, manners, and looks are the result of divine favor. The expression 'Yahweh is with him/David' now becomes a kind of leitmotif running through the stories of David and Saul. 'David was successful in all his undertakings, for Yahweh was with him' (18:14)" (ibid.).

17. H. W. Hertzberg, *I & II Samuel*, Old Testament Library (Philadelphia: Westminster, 1964), p. 154.

worthy of Saul's house.[18] When Saul treacherously gave his older daughter to another man, David did not demur. He accepted a second offer of marriage to Michal, Saul's other daughter, and killed two hundred Philistines to provide the dowry. David's conduct sounds like Job's: "in all this, Job did not sin in what he said" (Job 2:10). Job was a "blameless" *(tām)* man. Small wonder that the nameless writer of Qumran uses the same word *(tāmîm)* to describe David (11QPsa).

In the instances in which he had opportunity to kill Saul, David exemplified the proverb, "Fear the LORD and the king, my son, and do not join with the rebellious" (Prov. 24:21). David and his men were hiding in a cave at Engedi when Saul entered. David's men were convinced that Yahweh had delivered David's enemies into his hand so that he could wreak vengeance. David conceded only to cutting off part of Saul's robe for later proof.[19] Even this act, however, David interpreted as a form of rebellion against the king, and he said to his men, "The LORD forbid that I should do such a thing to my master, the LORD's anointed, or lift my hand against him; for he is the anointed of the LORD" (1 Sam. 24:6). The phrase "the anointed of the LORD" carries a sense of awe in the Book of Samuel. Hannah said in her psalm, "those who oppose the LORD will be shattered. He will thunder against them from heaven; the LORD will judge the ends of the earth. 'He will give strength to his king and exalt the horn of his anointed'" (1 Sam. 2:10). As a wise man David respected the leaders the Lord raised up. Consequently he could not bring himself to lift his hand against Saul.

He expressed the same sentiment when a second opportunity presented itself (1 Sam. 26:9, 11, 23). David carried out this philosophy against the Amalekite who killed Saul, asking, "Why were you not afraid to lift your hand to destroy the LORD's anointed?" (2 Sam. 1:14). Years later when David was fleeing from his son Absalom, General Abishai no doubt remembered David's response to Saul. Shimei was calling down curses on David's head as he trudged ignominiously up the slope of the Mount of Olives. Abishai said, "Why should this dead dog curse my lord the king? Let me go over and cut off his head" (2 Sam. 16:9). But David refused to allow Shimei to be killed, arguing that Yahweh was probably using Shimei to punish him.[20] After his victory over Absalom, David encountered Shimei again.

---

18. An Egyptian proverb says, "Preserve thy tongue from answering thy superior, and guard thyself against reviling him" ("The Instructions of Amen-em-opet," in *The Ancient Near Eastern Texts*, ed. J. B. Pritchard [Princeton, N.J.: Princeton University Press, 1969], p. 423).

19. Hertzberg wonders whether David, at the urging of his men, intended to kill Saul, but changed his mind and cut off the robe (*I & II Samuel*, p. 196). Further, he does not see David's act as that of a humble, generous person, but of one who knew he was in line for the kingship and who had been spared by God from misinterpreting the situation. Gordon sees much more significance in David's cutting off the robe (*I & II Samuel*, p. 179).

20. "The alternative is to respond, i.e. answer at the level of the self, in a way chosen by free men after considering alternatives. David realizes that it is beneath his dignity to argue with Shimei and that

Again Abishai said, "Shouldn't Shimei be put to death for this? He cursed the LORD's anointed" (2 Sam. 19:21). David's respect for the anointed office had not diminished, but as the Lord's anointed he chose to exercise mercy (vv. 22–23).

David and Abigail: The Counterpoise of Wisdom

The story of the stupid sheepherder with a beautiful and intelligent wife is one of the most delightful in Samuel. Its purpose is to lay one more brick in the edifice of David's legitimacy, however, and not to entertain.[21] Yet the narrative is presented in a unique way in that Abigail's wise actions, not David's, prevented his rash act.

David as a youngster was "ruddy, with a fine appearance and handsome features" (1 Sam. 16:12), and Abigail was "an intelligent and beautiful woman" (25:3).[22] In contrast her husband was stupid (in Hebrew his name means "stupid") and besides belonging to the Dog clan (Calebites), he acted like a dog![23]

The situation developed when David and his men provided security for Nabal's shepherds and their flocks, and, even though this service was no doubt forced on Nabal's men, it was appreciated (25:14–16). David sent messengers to collect his "protection money," but Nabal rebuffed them with insults. The reaction of David, unlike his later response to Shimei, was visceral and violent. He was about to attack fellow Judeans and wipe out a whole family. This act would surely have brought reprobation on David and would have undone all his carefully crafted relationships with his fellow Israelites.

Abigail, like the wise woman of Proverbs 31, was sufficiently intelligent to take matters into her own hands, bypass her husband, and appeal directly to David. She spoke to her superior wisely; she was humble and deferential to David;[24] and she even affirmed David's right to the throne (1 Sam. 25:30).

---

it is a trap for himself to step into Shimei's system" (J. P. Fokkelman, *Narrative Art and Poetry in the Books of Samuel* [Assen: Van Gorcum, 1981], pp. 198–99).

21. Gordon interprets Nabal as a sort of surrogate of Saul who, like Saul, insulted and calumniated David (*I & II Samuel*, p. 181).

22. "To the listener familiar with Israel's traditions, the contrast is more poignant, for Abigail's qualities, intelligence and beauty, are precisely those of the man who the audience may thus already suspect will become her new husband, and very appropriately so. . . . Abigail is as well matched with David as she is mismatched with Nabal" (J. D. Levenson, "1 Samuel 25 as Literature and History," *Catholic Biblical Quarterly* 40 [1978]: 17–18).

23. Hertzberg translates "a real Calebbite dog" (*I & II Samuel*, p. 199). Levenson shows at length the way the "fool" in Proverbs fits Nabal ("1 Samuel 25 as Literature and History," pp. 13–17).

24. Abigail sounds much like the noble wife of Proverbs 31 who is probably a prototype of wisdom in contrast to the "strange woman." "David is like the young man to whom so much of the Book of Proverbs is addressed, who finds himself in contact with the proverbial 'fool' . . . and the proverbial 'stalwart' woman . . . 'who opens her mouth with wisdom'" (Prov. 31:26) (McCarter, *1 Samuel*, p. 401).

In fact, she appealed to his inevitable position to deter him from his contemplated violent act.

David gladly acceded to her request, and he also praised "the LORD, the God of Israel, who has sent you today to meet me" (v. 32). He further praised her for her intelligence *(tāʿam)*. Wisdom had prevailed, but it was Abigail's, not David's. He, however, had learned an important lesson. Yahweh must go before him. When Nabal died of a stroke, the historian stated that it was Yahweh, not David, who struck him (v. 38).[25]

This valuable lesson is positioned between David's two opportunities to kill Saul (1 Sam. 24 and 26). The circumstances in chapter 26 seemed to be directing David to eliminate his adversary. Abishai wanted to kill Saul, and he even said that Yahweh had delivered Saul into David's hand (v. 8). David forbade Abishai's action, saying, "As surely as the LORD lives the LORD himself will strike him; either his time will come and he will die, or he will go into battle and perish" (v. 10).

Later in David's life, in the midst of internecine squabbles with Absalom, a wise woman of Tekoa challenged him to do the right thing by his son (2 Sam. 14:1–20). She was like Lady Wisdom who calls out; "on the heights along the way, where the paths meet, she takes her stand; beside the gates leading into the city, at the entrances, she cries aloud: 'To you, O men, I call out; I raise my voice to all mankind. You who are simple, gain prudence; you who are foolish, gain understanding'" (Prov. 8:2–5).

David and Jonathan: Enduring Friendship

"A friend loves at all times, and a brother is born for adversity." (Prov. 17:17)

Something about David drew people to him. After his defeat of Goliath, "Jonathan became one in spirit with David, and he loved him as himself" (1 Sam. 18:1). Jonathan was already a tested warrior, so his reaction was not from youthful sentimentalism.[26] Even Saul, who later became David's archenemy, at one time loved David (16:21).[27] "He who loves a pure heart and

---

25. Hertzberg, *I & II Samuel*, p. 204.

26. Jonathan had already played a key role in the battles against the Philistines (1 Sam. 13–14). "Here Jonathan goes beyond the personal feelings of a friendly disposition and makes a solemn 'covenant' which was certainly concluded under Yahweh's eyes and in a fixed (cultic) form" (ibid., pp. 154–55). Jobling argues that Jonathan is a transition figure in turning the kingdom over to David (D. Jobling, *The Sense of Biblical Narrative I* [Sheffield: JSOT, 1978], p. 12). "But that from a relatively early moment Jonathan regarded David as the natural and proper successor to Saul in the kingship over Israel is indicated by his likening David to Saul (I Sam 20:13ff.) and also quite probably by his stripping off his outer robe and other articles of apparel and clothing David in them (I Sam. 18:4)" (J. Morgenstern, "David and Jonathan," *Journal of Biblical Literature* 78 [1959]: 322–25).

27. The NIV rendering, "liked him," is too mild. The word is *ʾāhab* as in the Jonathan passages.

whose speech is gracious will have the king for his friend" (Prov. 22:11). Saul's daughter, Michal, loved David (1 Sam. 18:20), as did all Israel (18:16).[28] Jonathan's devotion never wavered. He made a covenant with David (18:3).[29] He warned David of his father's malevolent plot to kill him, and he mediated reconciliation (19:1–7).[30] He conspired with David to learn of Saul's true attitude and to help David escape (20:1–42). Jonathan made another covenant with David because of his love for him (v. 16). He even defended David publicly and was almost killed by his father as a result (vv. 32–33). This bitter episode was concluded when Jonathan stood with David in the field and said, "Go in peace, for we have sworn friendship with each other in the name of the LORD" (v. 42).

Even when David became a fugitive and it was dangerous for Jonathan to be his friend, Jonathan made the trip into southern Judah to encourage him (23:15–18). He affirmed David's right to the throne[31] and for the third time he made a covenant with David. Wisdom teaches, "Perfume and incense bring joy to the heart, and the pleasantness of one's friend springs from his earnest counsel" (Prov. 27:9).

Two facts show that David reciprocated Jonathan's love. First, when Jonathan and his father were killed in the Philistine battle, David wrote and sang a lament that became a permanent part of Israel's literature. "I grieve for you, Jonathan my brother; you were very dear to me. Your love for me was wonderful, more wonderful than that of women" (2 Sam. 1:26). Second, after David's ascent to the throne, he asked whether there was anyone left from Saul's family "to whom I can show kindness for Jonathan's sake" (9:1). He then made full and generous provision for Mephibosheth, the disabled son of his old and dear friend.

28. "It is therefore important that one after another, Saul's daughter Michal, the prophetic leader Samuel, and now, too, the crown prince and heir to the throne, should all have helped David's flight" (Hertzberg, *I & II Samuel*, p. 171).

29. Some have read more than affection into Jonathan's action. The Hebrew word "love" has at times the idea of "choice," but even though it bears the burden of a wide semantic range, it is speculative to argue that it means "loyalty" here, and that Jonathan was pledging his fealty to the young David. See McCarter, *1 Samuel*, p. 305; and J. A. Thompson, "The Significance of the Verb *Love* in the David–Jonathan Narratives in I Samuel," *Vetus Testamentum* 24 (1974): 34–38. Gordon is skeptical of this line of reasoning, but he does believe that by Jonathan's handing over his robe and armor, he was virtually abdicating to David (*I & II Samuel*, p. 159). Wozniak compares this covenant with those of the Hittites, Syrians, and Assyrians and argues for dependency on them (J. Wozniak, "Drei Verschiedene literarische Beschreibungen des Bundes zwischen Jonathan und David," *Biblische Zeitschrift* 27 [1983]: 213–18).

30. As Hertzberg observes, this was a real test of Jonathan's friendship (*I & II Samuel*, p. 163).

31. "David (and the reader!) are to be assured that David is to be the future 'king over Israel.' So Jonathan strengthens David 'in God.' He himself fades into the background, like the 'friend of the bridegroom' when the hour comes. We shall learn later, in still more detail, that as Jonathan says, Saul is indeed clear about this divinely ordained course of events. The covenant, renewed afresh, seals the friendship and shows how seriously Jonathan means what he has said" (Hertzberg, *I & II Samuel*, pp. 193–94).

Such affection is rarely seen, particularly between men. One is reminded of wisdom's statement, "A man of many companions may come to ruin, but there is a friend who sticks closer than a brother" (Prov. 18:24). The Hebrew of the first hemistich is difficult, but the proverb seems to mean that though it is impossible to be friends with everyone, a close and vital friendship is better than that of a relationship with a sibling. David was such a friend, and he inspired such confidence that men were willing to die for him and women danced in the streets, praising his name.

David at Hebron: Awaiting the Throne

"No one from the east or the west or from the desert can exalt a man. But it is God who judges: He brings one down, he exalts another." (Ps. 75:6–7)

David showed wisdom beyond his years when he refused to kill Saul, and to take his destiny into his own hands. He knew that he had been anointed to be king over all Israel. He also knew that Saul was the king and therefore in some sense was under divine protection. David chose not to intrude until the Lord opened the door. At Hebron, his patient wait continued. He spent seven years waiting to inherit the northern tribes. David learned the wisdom of Proverbs 4:8: "Esteem her [wisdom], and she will exalt you; embrace her, and she will honor you." Likewise Lady Wisdom is the source of good rule: "By me kings reign and rulers make laws that are just; by me princes govern, and all nobles who rule on earth" (Prov. 8:15–16). A series of actions on his part as he waited the denouement shows how wise he was.[32]

After Saul's death, when it would have been natural for David to exult over his enemy, David put an end to the young Amalekite's expectation of reward for news about Saul's death by having him killed (2 Sam. 1:1–16). While Saul was alive, David was unwilling to lift his hand against him. How dare this foreigner lift his hand against the Lord's anointed as he was dying. David thereby served notice that even in death Saul, as the Lord's anointed, was to receive respect.

The first recorded act of David as king of Judah was to reward the Jabesh Gileadites for removing Saul's and Jonathan's bodies from the wall at Beth Shan and giving them decent burials. Saul's first act as king (1 Sam. 11) had been to deliver the Jabesh Gileadites from Nahash the Ammonite, and they were forever grateful to him.[33] David's actions were political as well as compassionate, but even that is wisdom. "When a man's ways are pleasing to the

32. See Homer Heater, "A Theology of Samuel and Kings," in *A Biblical Theology of the Old Testament*, ed. Roy B. Zuck (Chicago: Moody, 1991), p. 142.

33. Merrill suggests that Saul's ancestors were the Jabesh Gileadites who were brought in to marry the few men left in Benjamin (Judg. 21) (Eugene H. Merrill, *Kingdom of Priests* [Grand Rapids: Baker, 1987], p. 181). This would explain Saul's interest in this city.

LORD, he makes even his enemies live at peace with him" (Prov. 16:7). Since the Jabesh Gileadites were strategically located in the Transjordan, it was appropriate for David to cultivate their friendship. Furthermore, it was in that very area (Mahanaim) that Abner, Saul's old general, had set up a rump government with Ish-Bosheth, Saul's son.

The life-long tension between David and his nephews (the sons of Zeruiah) began to manifest itself in the Abner incident. Abner, in a tiff with Ish-Bosheth, decided to throw in with David. This was a strategic move on the part of all concerned. Abner had long been a popular and effective general in Saul's army, and David had served under him. So to bring in this military representative was to bring in the northern tribes. David made a pact with him. Joab, when he learned of the pact, was furious. After all, his own position of authority was threatened. There would not be two generals. Consequently Joab treacherously assassinated Abner. It is difficult to believe that any advantage could accrue to David through this death.[34] When he avowed his innocence, the people believed him. He followed Abner's bier to the tomb, weeping and reciting a lament for this veteran of the Lord's campaigns. Then he fasted for the remainder of the day. The people—and, more important, *all Israel*—"knew that the king had no part in the murder of Abner son of Ner" (2 Sam. 3:37).

Two entrepreneurs later killed Ish-Bosheth and brought his head to David. Surely David would be happy to learn that the heir of Saul who was blocking David's way to rule over all Israel was now dead. However, as wisdom states, "Do not gloat when your enemy falls; when he stumbles, do not let your heart rejoice" (Prov. 24:17). David was moving inexorably to the throne, but it had to be in God's time, not his. Yahweh, who anointed David to be king, also brought him to rule in the place of Saul and his descendants.

Conclusion

Young David had now become king. Second Samuel 5–8 records David's triumph through Yahweh. The key elements in David's rule are summarized in these few chapters. The wisdom of the pink-cheeked shepherd boy, his faith in Yahweh, his unassuming attitude, his faithfulness and loyalty to those in authority and to his friends, had brought him to this place. Though some of his later actions departed from clear wisdom teaching (especially in the matter of Bathsheba),[35] his rise to power is almost without blemish. These narratives are not merely court flatteries; there is a ring of simplicity and verity about them with which "every man" may identify. David became

---

34. Hertzberg argues to the contrary (*I & II Samuel*, p. 261), but if David's goal is the uniting of the two kingdoms, how could Abner's death help him?

35. Most works that relate wisdom to the David narratives work with the latter part of 2 Samuel. See, for example, Fontaine, "Bearing of Wisdom on the Shape of 2 Samuel 11–12 and 1 Kings 3."

the most famous king in Israel's history and the prototype of the coming ideal Ruler, Jesus Christ, who will rule with the "Spirit of wisdom and of understanding, the Spirit of counsel and of power, the Spirit of knowledge and of the fear of the LORD" (Isa. 11:2).

Tribute

The past eight years I have spent on the faculty of Dallas Theological Seminary have overlapped much of the tenure of Dr. Donald Campbell as president of the seminary (1988–94). It is not easy being the president of a school these days, and I appreciate the gargantuan effort Dr. Campbell has exerted as a good administrator, a wise leader, and a friend. I wish him the best in his new endeavors, and am grateful for the opportunity of working with him in the vital task of training men and women for the ministry.

Waistbands, Water, and the Word of God: Where Did Jeremiah Bury His Girdle?

Charles H. Dyer

In Jeremiah 13:1–7 the Lord commanded Jeremiah to buy a linen waistband, wear it for a time, take it to a location called Perath, and bury it.[1] Later God told the prophet to go back to Perath, dig up the waistband, observe its ruined condition, and explain the point of the message to the people. Jeremiah was to perform this symbolic act to drive home God's message of judgment to the disobedient people of Judah and Jerusalem.

The "sign of the soaked waistband" has received several different interpretations.[2] Jeremiah's symbolic act has been said to refer to the *results* of God's impending judgment on Judah, the *cause* for God's impending judgment on Judah, or the *nature* of God's impending judgment on Judah. Part of the difficulty in interpreting this symbolic act is determining the location of Perath. This location has been identified with the Euphrates River, with the village of Parah in the Wadi Farah, and with a place called Perath not attested to in any other Old Testament passage. The rationale behind these identifications will be examined and their contribution to the interpretation of the passage will be explored.[3]

---

1. One of the problems in Jeremiah 13:1–7 is the exact spelling of the word in question. I have adopted the English spelling as it appears in the New International Version translation. There is some question as to whether the Hebrew word in Jeremiah 13 should be spelled *pĕrāt* or *pārāh*. This will be examined later in this essay.

2. These specific interpretations will be discussed later in the section, "The Evidence in Jeremiah."

3. Other identifications have been proposed, but they have not found wide acceptance. Some have proposed that Perath should be identified with Ephrathah or Bethlehem (cf. Mic. 5:2). However, von Orelli dealt a deathblow to this position with his insightful comment that "apart from the absence of א, there is no sign of water [near Bethlehem], and the significance of the locality would be quite inexplicable" (C. von Orelli, *The Prophecies of Jeremiah,* trans. J. S. Banks [reprint, Minneapolis: Klock & Klock, 1977], p. 114). Others have proposed that the entire event was nothing more than a vision and that Jeremiah did not physically travel anywhere. Calvin wrote that "the Prophet . . . did not indeed mean that he actually went [to the Euphrates]6, but his object was to give the Jews a vivid representation" (John Calvin, *Commentaries on the Book of the Prophet Jeremiah and the Lamentations,* trans. John Owen [Grand Rapids: Eerdmans, n.d.], 2:163). Others who hold to this position include A. Weiser (*Das Buch des Propheten Jeremia,* p. 112) and M. Cunliffe-Jones (*Jeremiah* [London: SCM, 1960], p. 111). However, nothing in the story suggests that it should be taken in a symbolic fashion.

The Euphrates Identification

Perhaps the most common interpretation of Perath is "to the Euphrates," with the understanding that *pĕrāt* in Jeremiah 13:4–7 refers to the Euphrates River in Mesopotamia.[4] At least three arguments have been presented to support the identification with the Euphrates River.

The Arguments for Identifying Perath as the Euphrates River

The normal interpretation of Perath. The identification of Perath with the Euphrates River can be made on three lines of evidence. First, Perath normally refers to the Euphrates River. Outside the Book of Jeremiah the Hebrew word *pĕrāt* occurs ten times, and it always refers to the Euphrates River.[5] In eight of the ten occurrences it is specifically called *nĕhar-pĕrāt*, "the River Euphrates" (Gen. 15:18; Deut. 1:7; 11:24; Josh. 1:4; 2 Kings 23:29; 24:7; 1 Chron. 5:9; 18:3). Even in the remaining two references the identification is obvious. In Genesis 2:14 *pĕrāt* was one of the four rivers that flowed from the garden of Eden (mentioned just after the Tigris). In 2 Chronicles 35:20 *pĕrāt* is identified as the place where Carchemish was located. Thus, *pĕrāt* clearly refers to the Euphrates River in each of its occurrences outside the Book of Jeremiah.

Within the Book of Jeremiah there is also evidence for interpreting *pĕrāt* as Euphrates. The word is used four times near the end of the book to describe the Euphrates River. In chapter 46 the prophet delivered an oracle of judgment against Egypt. In verse 2 the background to the prophecy is stated. The prophecy concerned "the army of Pharaoh Neco king of Egypt, which was by the Euphrates River *[nĕhar-pĕrāt]* at Carchemish, which Nebuchadnezzar king of Babylon defeated in the fourth year of Jehoiakim the son of Josiah, king of Judah." This prophecy came in 605 B.C., after the defeat of the Egyptians at Carchemish by Babylon. In verses 6 and 10 Jeremiah refers to this defeat "in the north beside the river Euphrates" (again, *nĕhar-pĕrāt*). In context he must be referring to the Euphrates River where it flows by the city of Carchemish. In 51:63 Jeremiah commanded Seraiah to tie a stone to a scroll and throw it "into the middle of the Euphrates" *(pĕrāt)*. The identification of *pĕrāt* is clear in the context. In Jeremiah 51:59–61 the prophet wrote that Seraiah was traveling with Zedekiah to the city of Babylon. When Seraiah arrived in the city he was to read the words of Jeremiah's scroll and then cast the scroll "into the Euphrates." Thus, *pĕrāt* must refer

---

4. This is the translation of Perath in the Authorized Version, the American Revised Version, the Revised Standard Version, and the New American Standard Bible. The only modern versions that do not follow this translation are the New International Version and the New English Bible, both of which read "Perath."

5. Francis Brown, S. R. Driver, and Charles A. Briggs, *A Hebrew and English Lexicon* (Oxford: Clarendon, 1906), s.v. *"pĕrāt,"* p. 832.

to the Euphrates River, which flowed through the midst of the city of Babylon. These four occurrences of *pĕrāt* in Jeremiah 46–51 clearly refer to the Euphrates River.

The Hebrew word *pĕrāt* occurs fourteen times in the Old Testament apart from the passage under discussion. In each of these occurrences the word refers to the Euphrates River. Thus, there is strong and compelling evidence to interpret *pĕrāt* in the same way in Jeremiah 13.

The one difference between Jeremiah 13 and the other Old Testament texts is that Jeremiah 13 refers to *pĕrātāh* while the other texts refer to *pĕrāt*. However, the presence of the *h* at the end of the word can be explained as a directional *h*.[6] The addition of the directional *h* would be expected since the Lord was commanding Jeremiah to go *to* the Euphrates.

The later understanding of Perath. A second argument for translating Perath as "Euphrates" is that this is the historical understanding of the word. Most ancient translations assume that Perath should be translated as Euphrates.[7] Perhaps the major translation is the Septuagint, which renders Perath as *epi ton Euphratēs* ("to the Euphrates"). The point here is that the "normal" understanding of *pĕrātāh* (i.e., the Hebrew word *pĕrāt* plus the directional *h*) as "to the Euphrates" was recognized by later generations as the best interpretation.

The significance of Perath in the interpretation of the story. The third argument for interpreting Perath as Euphrates focuses on the interpretation of the symbolic act being performed by Jeremiah. The Euphrates River would have more geographical significance to Jeremiah's audience since that was the origin of the nation being sent to punish Judah for her sin. "Moreover, the hiding of the girdle in the region of the Euphrates may have carried with it some implication about the Chaldean invasion. It would be the Chaldeans who would 'spoil' Judah."[8]

The point of this argument is that the purpose behind Jeremiah's symbolic act was the prediction of Judah's coming defeat by the Babylonians as well as her exile in Babylon. Bright writes that "the soaking [at *pĕrāt*] is symbolic of the Exile through which Yahweh will punish the great pride of his disobedient people."[9] Thus, according to this argument the name "Perath" is a vital part of the interpretation of the symbolic act designed to show Judah the place of her exile.

---

6. Gesenius, Kautzsch, and Cowley note that the directional *h* was appended to the substantive "most commonly to express *direction towards* an object, or *motion to a place*" (*Gesenius' Hebrew Grammar*, 2d English ed., ed. E. Kautzsch and A. E. Cowley [Oxford: Clarendon, 1910], p. 249).

7. Von Orelli saw this as a strong argument. "By *prt* nothing else is to be understood than the Euphrates (so all ancient versions) = *nhr prt*" (von Orelli, *Prophecies of Jeremiah*, p. 114).

8. J. A. Thompson, *The Book of Jeremiah*, New International Commentary on the Old Testament (Grand Rapids: Eerdmans, 1980), p. 364.

9. John Bright, *Jeremiah: A New Translation with Introduction and Commentary*, Anchor Bible (Garden City, N.J.: Doubleday, 1965), p. 96.

An Evaluation of the Euphrates Identification

The normal interpretation of Perath. It is true that Perath always refers to the Euphrates River in the biblical passages cited earlier. This is perhaps the strongest argument for identifying Perath with the Euphrates River. However, this argument rests on two assumptions. First, it assumes that the Hebrew word used by Jeremiah in chapter 13 is *pĕrāt*. Second, it assumes that *pĕrāt* can mean only "Euphrates." Both of these assumptions have been challenged in recent years.

The first assumption is based on the belief that the Hebrew word *pĕrātāh* in Jeremiah is formed from the word *pĕrāt* ("Euphrates") with the addition of the directional *h*. However, this is not the only Hebrew word which, with the addition of a directional *h*, would form the word *pĕrātāh*. For example, the same word would be formed if a directional *h* had been added to *pārāh*.[10] This possibility will be examined in a later section, but it should be noted here that a village called Parah *(pārāh)* was included in the land allotted to the tribe of Benjamin (Josh. 18:23).

Another important item in evaluating the association of *pĕrātāh* with the Euphrates River is the fact that the directional *h* was never used to describe movement to the Euphrates River elsewhere in the Old Testament. In all the other occurrences of the word *pĕrāt* where direction toward the Euphrates was intended, the writer employed the prepositions *'ad* (Gen. 15:18; Deut. 1:7; Josh. 1:4), *'al* (2 Kings 23:29; 24:7; 2 Chron. 35:20; Jer. 46:2, 6), *'al* (Jer. 46:10; 51:63), or *bĕ* (1 Chron. 18:3). Admittedly this is an argument from silence, but it is still significant because the use of the directional *h* combined with the absence of *nāhār* does set Jeremiah 13 off from the other passages that refer to the Euphrates River.

The later understanding of Perath. The second reason for interpreting Perath as Euphrates is the argument from history. As already noted, the word was translated as *epi ton Euphratēs* ("to the Euphrates") in the Septuagint. However, Aquila transliterated *pĕrātāh* as *eis pharan*, reflecting a different interpretation of Perath than Euphrates.[11] Thus, while we can say that "Euphrates" was the normal interpretation based on the Septuagint, there was at least some variation from that position.

The significance of Perath in the interpretation of the account. If the purpose of Jeremiah's symbolic action was to show Judah's captivity in Babylon because of her sin, then burying the garment at the Euphrates River would

---

10. Ibid. Bright writes, "Indeed 'to Parah' . . . and 'to the Euphrates' would be spelled identically *(prth)*, thus causing later readers to suppose that Jeremiah went twice to the Euphrates."

11. See Jeremiah 13:4–7 in *Septuaginta, Vetus Testamentum Graecum Auctoritate Academiae Scientiarum Gottingensis,* ed. Josephus Ziegler, vol. 15, *Ieremias, Baruch, Threni, Epistula Ieremiae.* Also see Joseph Reider, *An Index to Aquila,* rev. Nigel Turner, Supplements to Vetus Testamentum (Leiden: E. J. Brill), p. 249. Aquila transliterated the Hebrew words *pĕrātāh* (Jer. 13:4, 6) and *pā'rān* (Hab. 3:3) as *Pharan.*

be significant to the story. The purpose of the story will be examined in more detail below, but it may be that the purpose was not to show Judah's captivity in Babylon.[12] If this can be proven, then the identification of Perath with the Euphrates River may not be central to the interpretation of Jeremiah's symbolic act.

A second problem in identifying Perath in Jeremiah 13 as the Euphrates River is the great distance Jeremiah would have had to travel if he did bury the garment at the Euphrates River. The distance from Jerusalem to the closest point on the Euphrates River has been estimated as between 250 and 350 miles,[13] with 350 miles being the better estimate.[14] Thus, if Jeremiah did make two trips to the Euphrates River, he would have traversed some 1,400 miles. None of the people to whom Jeremiah was prophesying would have followed him for that distance. Such lengthy journeys are possible, but they do pose difficulties.[15]

The Wadi Farah Identification

A second identification given for Perath is the village of Parah in the Wadi Farah,[16] located about four miles northeast of Anathoth within the land

12. So Southwood writes: "The interpretation of the symbolic act as a reference to the exile is a well-established one . . . but it is one which lays undue stress perhaps on a single element of the narrative—that Jeremiah makes a journey to bury the girdle—at the expense of other elements" (Charles H. Southwood, "The Spoiling of Jeremiah's Girdle (Jer. xiii 1–11)," *Vetus Testamentum* 29 [1979]: 232).

13. Harrison believes that the trip to and from the Euphrates would be "a journey of at least 500 miles" (R. K. Harrison, *Jeremiah & Lamentations: An Introduction and Commentary,* Tyndale Old Testament Commentaries [Downers Grove, Ill.: InterVarsity, 1973], p. 99). Nicholson states that "to have gone to the Euphrates would have involved two round trips of some 700 miles (about 1,126 km) each for Jeremiah" (Ernest W. Nicholson, *The Book of the Prophet Jeremiah, Chapters 1–25,* Cambridge Bible Commentary [Cambridge: University Press, 1973], p. 121).

14. Assuming that Jeremiah traveled to the Euphrates along the normal trade routes using the shortest route possible, he would have traveled east from Jerusalem past Jericho to Rabbath-ammon, north along the King's Highway to Damascus, and then northeast to the nearest point on the Euphrates River about 50 miles south of Carchemish and about 50 miles east of Aleppo. This route would involve a round trip journey of almost 700 miles. For an accurate map of the area, see "Operational Navigational Chart (ONC) series G-4 (Cyprus, Iran, Iraq, Israel, Jordan, Lebanon, Saudi Arabia, Syria, Turkey, USSR), 1:1,000,000."

15. Thompson notes, "In Ezra 7:9 the journey from Persia to Jerusalem, about 800 miles, took about 100 days." Thus, he believes that if Jeremiah had actually taken two physical trips to the Euphrates, it would have involved "a three months' disappearance by the prophet" (Thompson, *Book of Jeremiah,* p. 364).

16. The English spelling of this wadi varies. Older writers identified it as "Farah" (Conder and Kitchener, *The Survey of Western Palestine,* vol. 3, *Judea* [London: Committee of the Palestinian Exploration Fund, 1883], pp. 174–80; J. Simons, *The Geographical and Topographical Texts of the Old Testament,* [Leiden: E. J. Brill, 1959], p. 33) or "Fara" (George Aaron Barton, *A Year's Wandering in Bible Lands* [Philadelphia: Ferris & Leach, 1904], p. 138). This preserves the Arabic pronunciation, which has no hard "p" sound. However, modern Israeli maps identify the wadi as both Nahal Perat and Wadi Farah ("Survey of Israel Maps, Sheet 11-12 [Yerushalayim], 1:100,000"). The name "Farah" preserves toponymically the Hebrew name "Parah," which is mentioned in Joshua 18:23. In

apportioned to the tribe of Benjamin. The identification of Perath with the Wadi Farah is also based on three lines of evidence.

The Arguments for Identifying Perath as the Wadi Farah

The similarity of name. The first argument given to support the identification of Perath with the Wadi Farah is the similarity in spelling between Parah and Euphrates. Bright writes, "Indeed 'to Parah' . . . and 'to the Euphrates' would be spelled identically *(prth)*, thus causing later readers to suppose that Jeremiah went twice to the Euphrates."[17] Both *pārāh* and *pĕrāt*, with the addition of the directional *h*, are spelled *pĕrātāh*.[18] Since the spelling for "to Parah" and "to the Euphrates" is identical, Jeremiah 13 could refer to either location.

The argument that "to Parah" and "to the Euphrates" would both be spelled *pĕrātāh* is important because it answers one of the main assumptions underlying the Euphrates identification, namely, that *pĕrātāh* comes from the root *pĕrāt*. The root of *pĕrātāh* can also be *pārāh,* and this would eliminate the need to have the Euphrates River in the passage. Even Simons, who believes that "Euphrates" is the correct interpretation, grudgingly allows for the possibility of this interpretation:

> The answer to the well-known question whether in Jer. xiii 4–7 *pĕrāt* does not refer to the E[uphrates] but to wadi farah which is close to the prophet's birthplace 'ANATHOTH (§337, nº 12), largely depends upon the general interpretation of the so-called "prophetic actions." The passage of Jer. xiii is often quoted as a proof against the view that the respective texts are to be understood in a literal sense, on the ground that the E[uphrates] is too far from Jeremiah's home for a twice repeated journey to that river being regarded a sensible idea. On this view the passage implies that wadi farah anciently bore the same name as the great river in the far north. Although this supposition is as improbable as it is arbitrary, one has to allow for the possibility of a word-play based on the ancient name of wadi farah and that of the E[uphrates] bearing some sort of resemblance (perath-parah? cp. the city-name PARAH in Josh. xviii 23).[19]

The difficulty with the Euphrates identification. The second argument in

---

this essay the spelling "Farah" is used to refer to the wadi, but the spelling "Parah" or "Perath" is used for specific locations associated with the wadi.

17. Bright, *Jeremiah,* p. 96.

18. According to Brown, Driver, and Briggs *pārāh* is from the root *prr* and is closely related to the feminine noun *pārāh* ("heifer, cow") (Brown, Driver, Briggs, *A Hebrew and English Lexicon,* s.v. *"pārāh,"* pp. 830–31). The addition of the directional *h* to feminine nouns ending in *h* is very precise. "In the case of feminines ending in *âh* the *âh local* is added to the original feminine ending *at* (§ 80 *b*), the *ă* of which (since it then stands in an open tone-syllable) is lengthened to *ā*" (Kautzsch, *Gesenius' Hebrew Grammar,* p. 251, § 90 *i*).

19. Simons, *The Geographical and Topographical Texts of the Old Testament,* p. 33, n. 13.

favor of interpreting Perath as the Wadi Farah is the physical difficulty involved in the Euphrates identification. Two major geographical difficulties inherent in the Euphrates identification are resolved with the Wadi Farah identification.

The first geographical difficulty with identifying Perath as the Euphrates River in Jeremiah 13 is the fact that the distance from Jerusalem to the Euphrates would have prohibited the people of Judah from observing Jeremiah's symbolic actions. Taking two journeys of 700 miles (350 miles each way) to the Euphrates River would have separated Jeremiah and his symbolic act from the people of Judah to whom it was given. The purpose of Jeremiah's symbolic act was to provide a visual object lesson to the disobedient people of Judah and Jerusalem. Both the hiding of the linen waistband among the rocks and its later uncovering were important elements of this symbolic act. Walking several hundred miles to the Euphrates River would have removed some of the immediate impact of the lesson if Jeremiah 13 describes a literal action rather than a vision.[20]

The second geographical difficulty with identifying Perath as the Euphrates River in Jeremiah 13 is the fact that the area of the Euphrates to which Jeremiah most likely would have traveled would not have met the physical requirements mentioned in the account. Jeremiah was commanded by the Lord to "hide" (*ṭāman*, "to bury, hide"[21]) the linen garment in "a crevice of the rock." The word for "crevice" *(nāqîq)* is used only three times in the Old Testament, and in the two other occurrences it describes the rocky crevices that pocket the landscape of Judah.[22] The word for "rock" *(selaʻ)* refers to jagged cliffs or crags.[23] Jeremiah was commanded to bury the linen garment in a crevice of jagged rocks or cliffs near the body of water in question.

The problem in identifying Perath with the Euphrates River is that the physical characteristics of the Euphrates River from Carchemish south do not fit this identification. The middle and lower courses of the Euphrates River are a relatively level plain void of cliffs and rocky crags.[24] Bewer

20. Abel noted that a trip to the Euphrates River would have placed the action outside the framework of Jeremiah's prophetic activities to the people of Judah (F.-M. Abel, *Géographie de la Palestine*, Tome II, *Géographie Politique. Les Villes*, 3d ed. [Paris: Librairie Lecoffre, 1967], p. 404).

21. The word *māman* has the idea of "to hide, conceal esp[ecially] in earth" (Brown, Driver, Briggs, *A Hebrew and English Lexicon*, s.v. "*māman*," p. 380).

22. Ibid., s.v. "*nāqîq*," p. 669. The other two occurrences of *nāqîq* are found in Isaiah 7:19 and Jeremiah 16:16.

23. Ibid., s.v. "*selaʻ*," pp. 700–701. The word comes from a root meaning "jagged cliff, crag, isolated (split off) rock" (ibid.). Jeremiah used the word to refer to the rocky heights of Judah (Jer. 16:16) and Edom (Jer. 49:16).

24. "Operational Navigational Chart (ONC) series G-4 (Cyprus, Iran, Iraq, Israel, Jordan, Lebanon, Saudi Arabia, Syria, Turkey, USSR), 1:1,000,000." The ONC map identifies the entire Euphrates basin south of what was once Carchemish as "flat or relatively level terrain." One must travel farther toward the headwaters of the Euphrates in what is now southern Turkey to find any rocky crags. The general terrain south of Carchemish is pictured in the article on Tell Hadidi by Dornemann

believes that this is a strong reason for interpreting Perath as Parah instead of Euphrates.[25]

Thus, the problems of distance and topographical inconsistency mitigate against the identification of Perath as the Euphrates River. If two interpretations of Perath are possible, one should choose the interpretation that better fits all the topographical statements in the passage. That would seem to be the Wadi Farah.

The proximity of the Wadi Farah to Anathoth. The third argument in favor of the Wadi Farah is its proximity to Anathoth in the territory of Benjamin. This argument is supported by historical, toponymic, and topographical evidence. The first part of this argument is the historical evidence. The Hebrew word *pĕrātāh* can be interpreted "to Parah" rather than "to the Euphrates," but for such an argument to be valid one must also show that a place called Parah actually existed and that it would have had some geographical significance to the account in Jeremiah 13. Joshua 18:23 provides the key to this identification.

In Joshua 18:11–28 the tribal inheritance of Benjamin is described. Verses 11–20 trace the borders of Benjamin, which extended like a rough parallelogram from the Central Benjamin Plateau just north of Jerusalem eastward toward the Jordan Valley. The allotment was relatively small, but it was extremely significant because it controlled the very productive Central Benjamin Plateau, the major intersections between the north/south and east/west trade routes, and the three major routes into the hill country from the Jordan Valley near Jericho.[26]

Verses 21–28 describe the cities located within the territory allotted to the tribe of Benjamin. This list is divided into two groups of twelve and fourteen cities respectively.[27] Included among the first twelve cities is Parah *(pārāh)*. The city of Anathoth is not listed in the tribal allotment of Benjamin in

---

(Rudolph H. Dornemann, "Salvage Excavations at Tell Hadidi in the Euphrates River Valley," *Biblical Archaeologist* 48 [March 1985]: 49–59).

25. Bewer admits that Perath normally refers to the Euphrates River, but rejects this interpretation because of the distance and the lack of rocks along the branch of the Euphrates River nearest to Judah. "This means a journey of many days, undertaken twice, cf. vv. 5–7, which seems unlikely. Therefore some read *Parah*, a town (Josh. 18:23) in the Wady Farah, c. 3 m. NE of Anathoth, Jeremiah's home. Here would be *rocks,* which are not on the banks of the middle and lower Euphrates" (Julius A. Bewer, *The Prophets* [New York: Harper & Brothers, 1955], p. 211).

26. For a description of the territory allotted to Benjamin, see James M. Monson, *The Land Between: A Regional Study Guide to the Land of the Bible* (Jerusalem: By the author, 1983), pp. 178–82; James M. Monson, *Student Map Manual* (Jerusalem: Pictorial Archive [Near Eastern History], 1979), sections 6-2, 6-3; Herbert G. May, ed., *Oxford Bible Atlas,* 3d ed. (New York: Oxford University Press, 1984), pp. 62–63.

27. Yohanan Aharoni, *The Land of the Bible: A Historical Geography,* rev. ed., trans. Anson F. Rainey (Philadelphia: Westminster, 1979), p. 315. He sees the twofold division between the twelve northern cities in the territory (Josh. 21:21–24) and the fourteen southern cities in the territory (vv. 25–28).

Joshua 18, but it is included in the cities allotted to the Levites in Joshua 21:17–18: "And from the tribe of Benjamin . . . Anathoth with its pasture lands."

In addition to the city list in Joshua 18, Aquila's transliteration of *perātāh* in Jeremiah 13 as *eis pharan* could also support the identification of Perath with the Wadi Farah. His interpretation would imply that he knew a place called Parah and accepted it as the location to which Jeremiah went.

Parah and Anathoth are linked historically, but it is also possible to link them toponymically. The name of Anathoth, Jeremiah's hometown, has been associated with the modern village of 'Anata, which is located approximately three miles northeast of Jerusalem.[28] Just over three miles to the northeast of 'Anata is a spring that bears the name "Spring of Parah" *('ên pārān)*, and it is located in the Wadi Farah.[29] The identification of the Spring of Parah *('ên pārān)* with the Parah of Joshua 18:23 has been accepted by many scholars.[30] In summary, there is strong toponymic evidence linking Anathoth and Parah in the same general location in the territory allotted to Benjamin. This adds some support for interpreting *pĕrātāh* as "to Parah" rather than "to the Euphrates" because the Spring of Parah in the Wadi Farah preserves the name *pārāh*, and it is close enough to Anathoth so that Jeremiah could easily make two journeys there.[31]

A third line of evidence linking Parah with Anathoth is topographical. Two items are important topographically. First, the geographical proximity of the Wadi Farah to Anathoth argues in favor of interpreting *pĕrātāh* as "to Parah." The people of Judah would have been able to follow Jeremiah on his journey from Anathoth to the Wadi Farah to bury the linen waistband, and

28. Armerding writes, "The present-day village of 'Anata, 5 km. (c. 3 mi.) NE of Jerusalem, preserves the name of Jeremiah's native town" (*The New International Dictionary of Biblical Archaeology*, s.v. "Anathoth," by Carl E. Armerding, p. 28). Aharoni places ancient Anathoth at Ras el-Kharrubeh about one-half mile to the southwest of the modern village of 'Anata (Aharoni, *Land of the Bible*, p. 410). For additional information on 'Anata and Anathoth, see E. P. Blair, "Soundings at 'Anata," *Bulletin of the American Schools of Oriental Research* 62 (1936): 18–21; A. Bergman, "Soundings at the Supposed Site of OT Anathoth," *Bulletin of the American Schools of Oriental Research* 62 (1936): 22–25; and A. Bergman, "Anathoth?" *Bulletin of the American Schools of Oriental Research* 63 (1936): 22.

29. "Survey of Israel Maps, Sheet 11-12 [Yerushalayim], 1:100,000." The map indicates that ruins have been discovered at the Spring of Parah and that the Wadi Farah continues southwest from the Spring of Parah and passes within one-half mile of 'Anata.

30. Parah "may with some confidence be identified with Farah on Wady Farah, which runs into Wady Suweinit, about 3 miles N.E. of 'Anata" (*International Standard Bible Encyclopedia*, 1939 ed., s.v. "Parah," 4:2247). Abel suggested reading Parah in place of Euphrates in Jeremiah 13 because: (a) the Euphrates River was too far away from Jeremiah's prophetic activities; (b) the Wadi Farah preserves the name of Parah in Judges 18:23; and (c) the Wadi Farah is close enough to Anathoth to fit the context of Jeremiah's symbolic act (Abel, *Géographie de la Palestine*, 2:404).

31. Conder and Kitchener tentatively identified Parah with "Khurbet Farah" in the Wadi Farah (*Survey of Western Palestine*, 3:174, 180), and that identification has been accepted by later scholars (cf. Marten Woudstra, *The Book of Joshua*, New International Commentary on the Old Testament [Grand Rapids: Eerdmans, 1981], p. 278).

they could also have returned there with him later when he dug it up. The symbolism of the action is more significant because the people could *see* the object lesson God had asked Jeremiah to perform.

The second topographical item is the physical description of the Wadi Farah, which fits well with the details given in the biblical account. The Wadi Farah cuts deeply through the Cenomanian hard limestone and Senonian chalk as it drops from approximately 700 meters (ca. 2,300 feet) above sea level near 'Anata to 140 meters (ca. 460 feet) above sea level where it joins the Wadi Qilt. From there it continues its journey down to Jericho some 240 meters (ca. 787 feet) below sea level. Near the Spring of Parah the wadi reaches a depth of several hundred feet.[32]

In 1984 Dr. Don Campbell and I hiked down the Wadi Suweinit (also called the Nahal Mikhmas)[33] from near Jaba and Mukhmas (sites of ancient Geba and Michmash)[34] to its confluence with the Wadi Farah at the spring called *Ein El Fawwar* where the two wadis join to form the Wadi Qilt. From there we turned to the southwest and followed the Wadi Farah from *Ein El Fawwar* to the Spring of Parah where we ascended from the gorge. Visual sightings within the wadi confirm the contour lines of the survey map. The Wadi Farah was characterized by steep, rocky cliffs on either side that extended to a great height. The use of *sela'* ("jagged cliffs or crags") would be appropriate to describe the Wadi Farah.[35]

In conclusion, the historical, toponymic, and topographical information offers strong evidence for interpreting *perātāh* as "to Parah" rather than "to the Euphrates." The village of Parah was situated in the tribe of Benjamin, and the available toponymic evidence points to its location near Jeremiah's hometown of Anathoth. Its geographical proximity is matched by its topographical uniformity. The Wadi Farah (in contrast to the Euphrates) is a place of steep, jagged cliffs in which a linen waistband could be hidden.

An Evaluation of the Wadi Parah Identification

Much of the material that would appear in an evaluation of this position has already been examined. The topographical and toponymic evidence for

---

32. "Survey of Israel Maps, Sheet 11-12." According to the survey map the floor of the Wadi Farah near the Spring of Parah is 375 meters (1,230 feet) while the rim of the canyon is 500 meters (1,640 feet). This would give the wadi a depth of approximately 410 feet. The contour lines are accurate to within 25 meters (82 feet). A visual observation of the wadi confirms its depth, though its vertical drop appeared to be more like 200 feet instead of 400 feet.

33. "Survey of Israel Maps, Sheet 11-12"; "Survey of Israel Maps, Sheet 7-8 [Tel Aviv-Yafo], 1:100,000"; and Monson, *Student Map Manual*, section 5-4.

34. On the identification of Geba and Michmash (Jaba and Mukhmas), see Aharoni, *Land of the Bible*, pp. 118–20; and Monson, *Student Map Manual*, section 15-2.

35. For a visualization of the crags and rocky cliffs in this area, see the picture of the Wadi Farah in T. H. Robinson, *The Decline and Fall of the Hebrew Kingdoms: Israel in the Eighth and Seventh Centuries B.C.*, The Clarendon Bible (Oxford: Clarendon, 1926), p. 193.

locating Parah near Anathoth seems to be strong. The one assumption that must be evaluated closely is the argument that *pĕrātāh* could be translated "to Parah" just as easily as it could be translated "to the Euphrates."[36]

The word in question occurs four times in Jeremiah 13. In verses 4, 6, and 7 the directional *h* is included as part of the word *pĕrātāh*. As noted earlier, in each of these instances the root word could be *pĕrāt* ("Euphrates") or *pā-rāh* ("Parah"). However, verse 5 has *biprāt*, without the directional *h* appended. Instead it has the prefix *b* ("in, at") with the root. This is the one instance in the passage in which the root is not ambiguous, and the root is *pĕrāt* rather than *pārāh*. This must be considered as a major obstacle to the position that *pĕrātāh* should be translated as "to Parah" rather than "to the Euphrates."

The Perath Identification

A third proposal is to identify Perath as "Perath,"[37] a location in Benjamin near Anathoth not mentioned in any other Old Testament texts.

The Arguments for Identifying pĕrātāh as "to Perath"

The textual argument. The basic textual argument is that an examination of all four references to *pĕrātāh* in Jeremiah 13 indicates that the root is *pĕrāt* rather than *pārāh*. However, there are some problems, examined above, with making this *pĕrāt* refer to the Euphrates River. Thus, *pĕrāt* must refer to some other Perath. One should look for Perath in the general location of Anathoth or Jerusalem.

The toponymic argument. Apart from Jeremiah 13 no Old Testament sites in Israel are called "Perath." However, one piece of toponymic evidence may help in the identification. In the Wadi Farah, approximately one-half mile to the west of the Spring of Parah *('ên pārāh)* is another spring called the Spring of Perath *('ên pĕrāt).*[38] The history behind the name of this spring cannot be determined, so it is uncertain how long the spring has had that name. However, it is still significant to note that a spring in the Wadi Farah, which is located near the ancient sites of both Anathoth and Parah, bears the name "Perath."

The historical argument. Locating Perath in Judah near Anathoth and Jerusalem has some good historical support. First Maccabees 9:50 records a number of cities in Judah that were fortified by Bacchides in his war with Jonathan. These included Jericho, Emmaus, Beth-horon, Bethel, Thamnatha, Pharathoni, and Taphon. The city in question in 1 Maccabees 9:50 that has

36. Bright, *Jeremiah*, p. 96.
37. The most recent examples of this solution are the translation of *perātāh* as "to Perath" in the New English Bible and the New International Version.
38. "Survey of Israel Maps, Sheet 11-12 [Yerushalayim], 1:100,000."

some bearing on the location of Perath is Pharathoni *(pharathōni)*. Is this a reference from the intertestamental period to the Perath of Jeremiah 13?

Before establishing the possibility of a relationship between Pharathoni and Perath, one must first try to locate Pharathoni historically. The locations for Jericho, Emmaus, Beth-horon, and Bethel are well established;[39] they formed a ring of fortifications along the northern perimeter of Jerusalem and Judah.[40] However, the locations of Thamnatha, Pharathoni, and Taphon are not as clear. Abel proposed identifying Thamnatha with Timnath-serah (Josh. 19:50; 24:30), Pharathoni with Pirathon (Judg. 12:13, 15), and Taphon with Tappuah (Josh. 16:8; 17:8).[41] Goldstein agrees with Abel and suggests that the common thread among all these sites is the writer's theological purpose in trying to parallel the events of Jonathan and Bacchides to those of Joshua.[42] Even though the site identifications proposed by Abel are outside the territory of Judah,[43] the writer of Maccabees describes them as being "strong cities in Judæa" because he "uses 'Judæa' of all Palestinian territory inhabited by Jews."[44]

If the identification of Pharathon with Pirathon is correct, then 1 Maccabees 9:50 has no bearing on the location of Perath. However, some have challenged Abel's identification of the three cities in dispute. The first challenge focuses on the purpose for identifying these specific cities by the writer of 1 Maccabees. Were the cities selected by the writer of 1 Maccabees for theological reasons, or were they selected by Bacchides for military reasons? The second option is clearly indicated by the text. Unfortunately, apart from the possible exception of Timnath-serah the fortification of the sites proposed by Abel would have provided no military advantage to Bacchides. Pirathon and Tappuah were remote locations off the main routes in the inaccessible hill country of Ephraim,[45] while Timnath-serah merely duplicated the function of Bethel since it was located on the road from Aphek to Bethel.

The second challenge to Abel's identification focuses on the underlying assumption that the description of these cities in 1 Maccabees 9:50 as "strong cities in Judæa" is broad enough to encompass Abel's proposed iden-

39. Jonathan A. Goldstein, *I Maccabees*, Anchor Bible (Garden City, N.Y.: Doubleday, 1976), p. 386. (Also see his comments on pp. 247, 259–60.)

40. "The new bases were established at Emmaus and Beth-Horon to the north-west; at Bethel, due north; at Jericho, north-east of the capital" (Moshe Pearlman, *The Maccabees* [New York: Macmillan, 1973], p. 208).

41. F.-M. Abel, "Topographie des campagnes machabéenes (Suite)," *Revue Biblique* 33 (1924): 202–8.

42. Goldstein, *I Maccabees*, p. 386.

43. For the location of Timnath-serah, Pirathon, and Tappuah, see Monson, *Student Map Manual*, section 7-3. All three locations were located on the western side of the watershed ridge between Shechem in the north, Bethel in the south, Shiloh in the east, and Aphek in the west.

44. Goldstein, *I Maccabees*, p. 386.

45. Monson, *The Land Between: A Regional Study Guide to the Land of the Bible*, p. 120; Aharoni, *Land of the Bible*, pp. 28–29.

tifications. The Bible never associates the cities proposed by Abel with the
territory of Judah. Timnath-serah was described as a city "in the hill country
of Ephraim" (Josh. 19:50); Pirathon was located "in the land of Ephraim, in
the hill country of the Amalekites" (Judg. 12:15); and Tappuah was a border
city between the tribes of Ephraim and Manasseh (Josh. 17:8). As Avi-Yonah
notes, "All these are outside the boundaries of Judæa, and the two later [i.e.,
Pirathon and Tappuah] were never included in Judæa, not even in the days
of its greatest extent."[46]

The difficulties with Abel's proposed indentifications have caused Avi-
Yonah to suggest alternative indentifications for the cities within the territory of Judah. He proposes identifying Thamnatha with Timnah of Judah,
Pharathon with the Wadi Farah/Brook of Perath, and Taphon with Tekoa.[47]
This proposed identification places all the cities mentioned in 1 Maccabees
9:50 within the borders of Judah that existed at the time when 1 Maccabees
was written. It also connects all the cities in verse 50 with those listed in verse
52. These cities formed a defensive ring around Jerusalem and covered key
roads and approaches within Judah.[48]

One difficulty with Avi-Yonah's indentification is his association of
Taphon with Tekoa. This association has no toponymic support in
1 Maccabees. However, Avi-Yonah is basing the identification on a textual
variant preserved in Josephus. Josephus quotes 1 Maccabees 9:50 in his discussion of the conflict between Jonathan and Bacchides. His spellings vary
slightly, but side-by-side comparison of the two accounts shows their essential agreement apart from the last entry.

1 Maccabees 9:50	Josephus (*Ant.* 13.15)
Ierichō (Jericho)	*Ierichounta* (Jericho)
Emmaoun (Emmaus)	*Ammaoun* (Emmaus)
Baithōrōn (Beth-horon)	*Baithōrōn* (Beth-horon)
Baithēl (Bethel)	*Baithēlē* (Bethel)
Thamnatha (Thamnatha)	*Thamnatha* (Thamnatha)
Pharathōni (Pharathoni)	*Pharathō* (Pharatho)
Tephōn (Taphon)	*Tochoan* (Tekoa)

Josephus's reading of *Tochoan* (Tekoa) in place of *Tephōn* (Taphon) makes
more sense topographically because Tekoa was included within the bound-

46. Michael Avi-Yonah, *The Holy Land from the Persian to the Arab Conquests (536 B.C. to A.D.
640): A Historical Geography* (Grand Rapids: Baker, 1966), p. 53.
47. Ibid., pp. 53–54. For the locations of these cities see Monson, *Student Map Manual*, sections
9-4, 11-4; and Yohanan Aharoni and Michael Avi-Yonah, *Macmillan Bible Atlas* (New York: Macmillan, 1968), map 197.
48. Pearlman notes that these fortifications "effectively ringed the province" (Pearlman, *Maccabees*, p. 208).

aries of Judah and did guard an important route into the hill country of Judah and Jerusalem from En Gedi.[49]

Both 1 Maccabees 9:50 and Josephus locate a city called Pharathoni or Pharatho within the territory occupied by Judæa. Avi-Yonah identifies this site with the Perath of Jeremiah 13 for three reasons: (1) the toponymic association between Perath and Pharathoni;[50] (2) the archaeological discovery of a stronghold or fort in the Wadi Farah;[51] and (3) the geographical location of Pharathoni in the account of 1 Maccabees and Josephus.[52] Perath would be the only Old Testament city with the same name in the same general vicinity.

A second historical reference that identifies a place in Judah with a name that is similar to Perath is found in Josephus's *The Jewish War*. In 4.511–12 Josephus describes the activity of Simon ben-Giora. Simon's attacks against the Zealots of Judah extended from Acrabeta in the north to Idumea in the south.[53] He established his headquarters "in the valley of Pheretae" *(Pheretai)*, which had "many convenient caves" and enough water to meet the needs of his expanding army. The place was close enough to Jerusalem to be used as a staging ground for Simon's planned attack against the city.[54] Some have identified *Pheretai* with the Perath of Jeremiah 13 and have located it in the Wadi Parah.[55]

Both 1 Maccabees and Josephus identify a location in Judah that preserves the name "Perath." In both accounts a location to the northeast of Jerusalem fits best. Josephus identified the site as a valley that contained many caves. Thus, there is strong historical support for identifying a site in Judah in the general location of Anathoth as Perath.

49. The importance of Tekoa and the route it guarded can be seen historically. Tekoa was fortified by Rehoboam in an effort to protect his kingdom from attack (2 Chron. 11:6); and the route past Tekoa was the planned invasion route of the Moabites and Ammonites during the reign of Jehoshaphat (2 Chron. 20:1–30).

50. Avi-Yonah, *The Holy Land*, pp. 53–54. He associated Pharathoni with "the biblical Brook of Perath" and with "the Valley of Pheretae of Josephus." This second location will be examined in a later section.

51. For a brief discussion of this stronghold, see Abel, *Géographie de la Palestine*, 2:404.

52. Avi-Yonah notes the strategic importance of these cities: "If we accept these corrections, we obtain a logical line of fortifications intended to protect the approaches to Jerusalem on all sides: Thamna on the south-west, Emmaus and Beth-Horon in the west, Bethel in the north, Pharathon in the north-east, Jericho in the east, Tekoah in the south-east and Beth-Zur (which is mentioned in a separate list in the same passage) on the south" (Avi-Yonah, *Holy Land*, p. 54).

53. Acrabeta was located to the southeast of Shechem while Idumea was the dry-lands south of Hebron. Simon's activities thus stretched from central Samaria into the Negeb. See Monson, *Student Map Manual*, section 12-2; and Aharoni and Avi-Yonah, *Macmillan Bible Atlas*, map 254.

54. So Josephus noted, "His object was obvious: he was training his army in readiness for an attack on Jerusalem" (Josephus, *Jewish War* 4.513).

55. So Cornfeld writes that the "*Valley of Pheretae* is the present gorge of *Wadi Fara* and *Fawar* 10 and 12 kms northeast of Jerusalem. Simon moved out of the wilderness into these well-watered canyons and established his headquarters there" (Gaalya Cornfeld, *Josephus: The Jewish War* [Grand Rapids: Zondervan, 1982], p. 302). See also Karl Heinrich Rengstorf, ed., *A Complete Concordance to Flavius Josephus*, Supplement I, *Namenwörterbuch zu Flavius Josephus*, s.v. "*Pheretai*," p. 123.

An Evaluation of the Perath Identification

The identification of *pĕrāt* with a place called Perath in Israel has much to make it attractive. It helps preserve the name *pĕrāt*, which seems to be the actual name given to the site in the text. It also does justice to the topographical details of the text that call for a place with high, jagged cliffs to which Jeremiah could walk. The chief weakness of the position is the lack of a specific place in Israel identified in the Old Testament as Perath. However, 1 Maccabees 9:50 and Josephus provide extrabiblical evidence for the location of a city in Judah called Perath. The location of *'ên pĕrāt* in the Wadi Farah does provide some toponymic support for identifying the Perath in Jeremiah 13 with this specific location in Israel.

The Evidence in Jeremiah

The possible identifications of Perath have been examined, but every proposed location has some difficulty. The next step is to examine the text of Jeremiah 13:1–7 to see if the account itself provides any help in the identification of Perath.

The Purpose of the Symbolic Act

To predict the results of God's judgment. The first point that must be examined is the purpose behind Jeremiah's symbolic act. What message did God intend to convey through this action? Some interpreters believe that the point of the action was to predict the results of God's judgment on Israel. Bright feels the purpose was to predict Israel's exile in Babylon.[56] To come to this conclusion he interprets Perath as an ultimate reference to the Euphrates River (though he feels Jeremiah could have accomplished the symbolic act at Parah); and he believes that verse 9 points to the fact that "the nation's pride will be destroyed in Exile."[57]

This interpretation has two serious flaws.[58] First, if the burial at the Euphrates was to indicate Judah's exile, then Judah was not "marred" before her

56. Bright, *Jeremiah*, p. 96. He writes, "But what is the meaning of the parable? Jeremiah clearly acts the part of Yahweh while, clearly, the waistcloth represents Israel. But what is the significance of the soaking in Euphrates water that ruins the waistcloth? Some argue that this refers to political entanglements with the Mesopotamian powers, which have corrupted the character of the nation. This, however, does violence to the sense of vs. 9, where it is clearly indicated that the soaking is symbolic of the Exile through which Yahweh will punish the great pride of his disobedient people."

57. Ibid. Others who hold this position include Nicholson (*The Book of the Prophet Jeremiah, Chapters 1–25*, p. 122), Calvin (*Commentaries on the Prophet Jeremiah and the Lamentations*, pp. 160–65); and Harrison (*Jeremiah & Lamentations*, p. 99).

58. Southwood writes, "The interpretation of the symbolic act as a reference to the exile is a well-established one . . . but it is one which lays undue stress on a single element of the narrative—that Jeremiah makes a journey to bury the girdle—at the expense of other elements" (Southwood, "The Spoiling of Jeremiah's Girdle," p. 232).

exile into Babylon. This interpretation of the symbolic act would imply that the Babylonian captivity was the event that marred Judah because Jeremiah's symbolic marring took place *after* the waistband was buried. However, the text indicates that Judah had become spiritually separated from Yahweh *before* her impending captivity.[59] The removal of the waistband was symbolic of Israel's and Judah's departure from Yahweh. "For as the waistband clings to the waist of a man, so I made the whole house of Israel and the whole house of Judah cling to Me . . . but they did not listen" (Jer. 13:11). Second, the burial was connected with the sins of both Israel and Judah. However, Israel was not taken into captivity to the Euphrates River but to the Tigris. Thus, if the symbolic act was designed to illustrate the *results* of God's judgment (i.e., exile in Babylon), the reference to Israel is awkward. But if the symbolic act was designed to show the cause or the nature of God's judgment, Israel's parallel to Judah is clearer.

To predict the cause for God's judgment. Other interpreters have felt that the symbolic action was intended to show the cause for God's judgment on Judah. God would judge Judah because of the corruption that resulted from her contact with Babylon. "There may have been an alternative inference that it was influences from the Euphrates direction, that is, from Assyria and Babylon, that had spoiled Judah, in particular the worship of Astral deities (Amos 5:26–27). Certainly under Ahaz and Manasseh these influences were considerable (2 K. 16:10–16; 21:3–8). Perhaps Jeremiah was declaring that there would be no salvation because there was nothing left to save."[60]

In this second interpretation the Euphrates River becomes not the location for punishment but the *source* of corruption. Israel and Judah were marred through their contact with the paganism and idolatry of the civilizations along the Euphrates.[61] This interpretation does have some basis in the text because verse 10 attributes the marring of the waistband to the corrupting influences of idolatry that had overtaken both Israel and Judah. However, the problem comes in trying to narrow the idolatry that caused Judah's downfall to that which came from the area of the Euphrates. Some of the false gods specifically singled out for condemnation by Jeremiah in his prophecies against Judah include Baal (cf. 7:9; 11:13, 17; 12:16; 19:5; 23:13,

---

59. Ibid., p. 235. He writes, "To sum up: the symbolic action of Jeremiah reported in Jer xiii 1–11 threatens Judah with an invasion from Babylon as a consequence of her apostasy from Yahweh to whom she had formerly clung closely and safely."

60. Thompson, *Jeremiah*, p. 364. Feinberg agrees with this interpretation when he writes, "Why the Euphrates? The purpose of the trip may have been to underscore the influence of Mesopotamia in corrupting the nation religiously, beginning with ungodly Manasseh (2 Kings 21)" (Charles L. Feinberg, *Jeremiah: A Commentary* [Grand Rapids: Zondervan, 1982], p. 106).

61. T. Miles Bennett, "Jeremiah: Outline and Exposition," *Southwestern Journal of Theology* 24 (Fall 1981): 50. He writes, "Just so the chief glory and purpose of Judah was to cleave to the Lord. But they refused, choosing rather to cleave to other gods. Therefore, like the loincloth, they are spoiled and have become *good for nothing.*"

27; 32:29, 35) and Molech (32:35)—two non-Babylonian deities that had led the people astray.[62] Jeremiah did mention the two distinctly Babylonian deities—Bel and Marduk—but he included them only in his judgment against Babylon. The point here is that to argue that Perath indicates the corrupting influence of the gods of the Euphrates is very arbitrary. The gods most often condemned by Jeremiah were Canaanite, not Babylonian or Assyrian. Thus, this interpretation falls short when it tries to identify the burial at Perath as an indication of the source of Israel's and Judah's corruption.

To predict the nature of God's judgment. A third interpretation of the symbolic action is that it is intended to predict the nature of God's judgment. Southwood represents this position when he writes, "The hiding of the girdle in the crevice of the rock signals both the apostasy of Judah, which is in hiding from Yahweh for 'many days' (v. 6); as well as the inevitable outcome of this apostasy: Judah in hiding from the invading flood."[63] This interpretation sees Jeremiah's actions symbolizing Judah's vain attempt to hide from Yahweh's judgment that was about to break out on the nation because of her sin.

Two elements are crucial in this interpretation. The first is the emphasis on water. The waistband, when uncorrupted, was not to be placed in water (13:1). The waistband became corrupted when it was buried beside the water.[64] The water was the instrument of corruption. The waistband had been removed from Jeremiah's body before being marred, but it was the contact with the water that destroyed it.

Jeremiah used imagery of water and a flood to describe the advance of the Babylonians. In 1:13 the Babylonian invasion was pictured as a boiling pot spilling its contents on the land of Judah. In 47:2 Jeremiah described the rising power of Babylon that swept Egypt from her place of influence in Palestine as an overflowing flood sweeping through the land: "Thus says the LORD: 'Behold, waters are going to rise from the north and become an overflowing torrent, and overflow the land and all its fulness, the city and those who live in it.'"

A second element important in this interpretation is the focus on God's specific identification of the hiding place. Most have labored over the identification of Perath, but God specifically told Jeremiah to "hide" the garment "in a crevice of the rock *(binqîq hassāla').*" This phrase is used one other time in the Book of Jeremiah to describe the care with which the Babylonians

---

62. Baal was the "supreme fertility-god of the Canaanites" (*International Standard Bible Encyclopedia,* s.v. "Baal," by K. G. Jung, 1 [1979]:377) while Molech was the supreme god of the Ammonites (*Zondervan Pictorial Encyclopedia of the Bible,* s.v. "Molech," by B. K. Waltke, 4:269). For additional information on these gods, see William Foxwell Albright, *Yahweh and the Gods of Canaan: A Historical Analysis of Two Contrasting Faiths* (reprint, Winona Lake, Ind.: Eisenbrauns, 1968), pp. 124–29 (Baal), 236–42 (Molech/Moloch).

63. Southwood, "The Spoiling of Jeremiah's Girdle," p. 236.

64. At this point the exact location of Perath is not the point of the story. Whether it was the Euphrates, Parah, or Perath, the garment was still to be placed in a damp place where it would rot.

would hunt out the Judeans who were trying to hide from them. "'Behold, I am going to send for many fishermen,' declares the LORD, 'and they will fish for them; and afterwards I shall send for many hunters, and they will hunt them from every mountain and every hill, and from the clefts of the rocks' (*ûminneqîqê hasselā'îm)*" (16:16). In this passage the "clefts of the rocks" were the remote hiding places in which the people of Judah tried to conceal themselves from the invading Babylonians. Jeremiah used similar imagery in 4:29 to picture the people trying to hide from the invading Babylonians: "They go into the thickets and climb among the rocks."

The point here is that elsewhere Jeremiah used the imagery of water to describe the army of the Chaldeans that would invade Judah, and the imagery of hiding among the rocks to picture the vain attempts of the Judeans to hide from these invaders. "The spoiling of the girdle at *pĕrāt* links the humbling of the pride of Judah with Babylon, seen not as the place of Judah's exile, nor as the source of corrupting religious influence, but as an armed invading power."[65] This interpretation seems to make the most sense in the context. It accounts for the reference to both Israel and Judah in verse 11 (Israel was judged by an invading army in the past just as Judah would be judged in Jeremiah's day); and it allows verse 9 (God's statement that he would destroy the pride of Judah) to remain as the main point of Jeremiah's symbolic action. The points could be summarized as follows:

1. Jeremiah represented Yahweh and the waistband represented Judah.
2. The unwashed waistband around Jeremiah's waist represented the relationship of Judah to Yahweh as his covenant people and the protection afforded them because of that relationship.
3. The removal of the waistband represented Judah's departure from the Lord to serve other gods.
4. The hiding of the waistband among the crevice of the rocks represented Judah's vain attempt to hide or protect herself from the threatened Babylonian invasion, which was punishment for her sin.
5. The location of Perath was not the main point of the action though the similarity of names ("Perath" and "Euphrates") pointed toward Babylon as the destructive nature of the Babylonians.
6. The marring of the waistband pictured Judah's destruction by the Babylonians.

The Physical Description of the Burial Place

God told Jeremiah to bury the waistband "in a crevice of the rock" (Jer. 13:4). As noted earlier the phrase used is *binqîq hassāla'*. These two words in construct are found together only in Isaiah 7:19; Jeremiah 13:4; and Jere-

---

65. Southwood, "The Spoiling of Jeremiah's Girdle," pp. 235–36.

miah 16:16.[66] In Isaiah 7:19 the phrase was used in connection with the invasion of Israel by Gentile nations, most notably Egypt and Assyria. Isaiah's point was that even the remote place in Judah (the crevices in the cliffs, the steep ravines, etc.) would feel the presence of these Gentile invaders. In Jeremiah 16:16 the point is similar to that of Isaiah 7:19. Those Judeans who tried to hide in "the clefts of the rocks" would be hunted down and captured by the Babylonians.

Two observations can be made concerning the phrase *binqîq hassāla'* in its two other occurrences. First, the phrase is used to refer to the remote places in the land of Judah. The "crevices" referred to those rocky crags that dominate the hill country of Judah, especially on the eastern side of the watershed ridge. Second, the "crevices of the rocks" were pictured as natural hiding places used by Judeans to try to escape from invading armies. The use of this phrase in Isaiah 7:19 and Jeremiah 16:16 does not demand a parallel meaning in Jeremiah 13:4, but it does lend support to such an interpretation. Certainly the hill country near Anathoth and Parah are better suited to this description than the relatively flat Euphrates River basin south of Carchemish.

Conclusion

The exact location of Perath cannot be determined with certainty. However, a number of geographical, topographical, historical, and textual markers do seem to point away from the Euphrates River toward a location in the land of Israel. The specific location is not the dominant factor in the interpretation of Jeremiah's symbolic act because his action was designed to show primarily the *nature* of the coming judgment (the overflowing waters of judgment) rather than the cause or results of the coming judgment (i.e., the Euphrates River as the location of the coming army or as the place of the impending exile). However, Jeremiah might have used "Perath" because of the wordplay with "Euphrates" to show that the waters of judgment would come from Babylon.

The toponymic evidence is mixed. Perath could mean "to the Euphrates," but the phrase can also be translated "to Parah" or "to Perath." The location of a Benjamite city named Parah near Anathoth as well as the location of a spring called Parah about three miles northeast of Anathoth provide some support for this interpretation. However, Jeremiah 13:5 militates against Parah as the root of Perath because there the word appears without the directional *h* (*pĕrāt* rather than *pārāh*). The possibility of a location near Parah

---

66. *The Mandelkern Biblical Concordance*, s.v. *"nāq îq,"* p. 767. In Isaiah 7:19 and Jeremiah 16:16 both *nāq îq* and *sela'* are plural, indicating numerous crevices among the many cliffs. In Jeremiah 13:4 both words are singular, indicating one crevice located at a rocky place. One would expect the singular form in Jeremiah 13:4 because Jeremiah was being instructed to bury a single item at a specific location.

with the name "Perath" receives some toponymic support with the location of a spring called the Spring of Perath in the Wadi Farah.

The topographical data are often overlooked, but they point toward a location in Judah for Perath. Jeremiah was to bury the waistband in the "crevice of a rock," and the phrase indicates a crevice in a rocky crag or cliff. One would have to travel to the upper reaches of the Euphrates River north of Carchemish to find a location to fit this description. However, the rocky crags in the Wadi Farah near Anathoth fit perfectly. Also supporting this view is the fact that the other two occurrences of the phrase are used to describe remote places in the land of Judah.

The tentative identification for Perath is the Spring of Perath in the Wadi Farah. This view has historical support in 1 Maccabees and Josephus, and it fits the available toponymic and textual evidence. It also fits the details of the account, and it is located close enough to Jerusalem and Anathoth so that the people of Judah could have followed Jeremiah and observed his actions.

Tribute

In 1984 I journeyed to Israel for the first time to study with a group from Dallas Seminary at the Institute of Holy Land Studies. That trip opened up new vistas in my approach to the Bible, especially the Old Testament. I developed a love for historical geography that resulted in my writing my doctoral dissertation on selected geographical problems in the Book of Jeremiah.

One of the leaders on that study tour was Dr. Donald K. Campbell, then academic dean at Dallas Seminary. Dr. Campbell's love of Israel was infectious. We participated in several "extracurricular" hikes through the land of Israel. One hike was an all-day excursion following the Wadi Suweinit from a spot near biblical Geba and Michmash to the beginning of the Wadi Qilt. We then turned and traveled up the Wadi Farah and ended our journey near Jeremiah's ancient hometown of Anathoth.

That journey with Dr. Campbell eventually became the subject of a chapter in my dissertation. The images from that trip still remain sharp in my memory. Because of that trip to Israel—and especially because of the day-long journey down the wadis walked by Jeremiah—Dr. Donald K. Campbell became more than just a faculty member and administrator under whom I had studied. He became a friend. This chapter is affectionately dedicated to him in fond remembrance of those days in Israel.

The Progression of Events in Ezekiel 38–39

Harold W. Hoehner

The contents of Ezekiel 38–39 have engendered much discussion over the years. Although scholars must admit that the text of these chapters is well preserved, these chapters are among the most difficult parts of the book.[1] Some question Ezekiel's authorship of these chapters, thinking they may have been penned by one of Ezekiel's disciples or an editor who compiled Ezekiel's work and thought that these chapters fit best here. More recently some commentators are willing to see that parts of these chapters, if not all, are from the hand of Ezekiel.[2]

The Placement of the Chapters in the Book

One problem that concerns many commentators is the location of these chapters. In chapters 33–37 Ezekiel discussed the restoration of Israel. This is particularly emphasized in chapters 36–37, which end with the promise that God's sanctuary will be set in the midst of Israel (37:26–28). The same theme is continued in chapters 40–48, where the details of the sanctuary are given. However, chapters 38–39 describe the battle of Gog and Magog, which interrupts the restoration theme. These chapters talk about the enemies of Israel. This is a theme that Ezekiel had already discussed in the oracles against the nations (chaps. 25–32). Why do chapters 38–39 appear where they do? Should they instead be part of the oracles against the nations?

---

1. Cf. Walter Eichrodt, *Ezekiel: A Commentary,* Old Testament Library, trans. Cosslett Quinn (Philadelphia: Westminster, 1970), pp. 519–21; G. A. Cooke, *A Critical and Exegetical Commentary on the Book of Ezekiel,* International Critical Commentary (Edinburgh: T. & T. Clark, 1936), pp. 406–8; Peter C. Craigie, *Ezekiel,* Daily Study Bible (Philadelphia: Westminster, 1983), pp. 265–67.
2. Walther Zimmerli, *Ezekiel,* trans. James D. Martin, ed. Paul D. Hanson and Leonard P. Jay Greenspoon (Philadelphia: Fortress, 1983), 2:302–4; Leslie C. Allen, *Ezekiel 20–48,* Word Biblical Commentary (Dallas: Word, 1990), pp. 202–4.

Taylor suggests that chapters 38–39 are a separate composition added as a postscript to chapters 1–37 and that chapters 40–48 were a later appendix based on the original work of chapters 1–37. This would explain the links between 37:24–28 and chapters 40–48 and the lack of links between 37:24–28 and chapters 38–39.[3]

Although Ezekiel is primarily dealing with Israel's restoration in chapters 33–37, he intertwines elements of judgment. Two observations must be considered. First is the setting of this section. In 33:21 Ezekiel states, "In the twelfth year of our exile, in the tenth month, on the fifth day of the month . . ." (i.e., January 8, 585 B.C.). It was at this time that a messenger from Jerusalem announced the news of Jerusalem's destruction to the Jewish captives in Babylon. The night before the messenger's arrival Ezekiel gave the oracles of chapters 33–39 (33:22). The next chronological note is given in 40:1: "In the twenty-fifth year of our exile, at the beginning of the year, on the tenth day of the month, in the fourteenth year after the city was conquered . . ." (i.e., April 28, 573 B.C.). Ezekiel then discussed the future temple and land for Israel.

A second observation pertains to the themes of restoration and judgment in chapters 33–37. Immediately after the time note Ezekiel declared the destruction of Jerusalem and discloses Israel's hypocrisy (33:21–33). In chapter 34 he describes the false shepherds of Israel who will be replaced by the true shepherd, the Messiah. Chapter 35 depicts the desolation of Israel's enemy, Edom, and chapters 36–37 describe Israel's restoration. At that time Israel will be judged and restored (chap. 36) and regathered as a nation to the promised land (chap. 37). All the land promises of the Abrahamic covenant will be fulfilled, and Israel as a redeemed nation will fulfill the new covenant. In addition, the rule of Messiah over this nation in her land will fulfill the Davidic covenant. Chapters 38–39 portray the attempt of people and nations to possess the land that belongs to Israel. Yet they will be defeated by God so that Israel will be able to occupy the land God promised her in his covenants with her. This will show Israel and the nations that he is truly God (38:16, 23; 39:7, 21–22, 28–29). After God's victory over the nations and Israel's filling by the Spirit, the temple will be built for worship by Israel during the reign of Messiah. Thus, chapters 38–39 fit well into the flow of the argument of this portion of Ezekiel. Although the primary theme is the restoration of Israel, the theme of judgment is woven throughout this entire section of the book.

The time frame referred to in these chapters is important. Although some think Ezekiel was foretelling the overthrow of Babylon, much like Jeremiah (chaps. 50–51), most think it is apocalyptic in nature and thus refers to some

---

3. John B. Taylor, *Ezekiel: An Introduction and Commentary,* Tyndale Old Testament Commentaries (Downers Grove, Ill.: InterVarsity, 1969), p. 242.

future date.[4] The familiar expressions "after many days," "in the latter days" (38:8), and "in the last days" (38:16) refer to the time of the tribulation (Deut. 4:27–30; Dan. 2:28; 8:19, 23; 10:14) and/or the millennial restoration (Isa. 2:2–4; Mic. 4:1–7). The context must determine the setting. Here in Ezekiel 38–39 it must refer to the time of great tribulation for Israel. This is demonstrated in 38:8 by the expressions "after many days" and "the latter days," which are followed by a description of war and the taking of spoils by the various nations. Also the expression "in the last days" in 38:16 is followed by "in those days" and "on that day" (vv. 17, 19), which depict a time of trouble that will be followed by a day of restoration and peace (39:22–29).

Ezekiel 38–39 speaks of nations making an attack on Israel in her land but being defeated by God and his armies. The identification of these nations has been much discussed—sometimes with questionable speculations due to the paucity of evidence. In 38:2 mention is made of Gog and Magog, Rosh, Meshech, and Tubal. Although it is difficult to be certain, it is probable that Gog refers to a personage, whether by title or name.[5] Magog is the land over which Gog rules. Rosh,[6] Meshech, and Tubal have been identified with Russia, Moscow, and Tobolsk. However, this is "based on similar sounds to the hearing between the two terms, but such etymological footwork is not linguistically sound at all."[7] It is more likely that Rosh, Meshech, and Tubal are constituent parts of Magog. This territory could be the mountainous area between and south of the Black and Caspian seas, which includes Turkey and south-central Russia.[8] The countries mentioned in 38:5 are easier to identify. Persia is modern Iran, Cush is Ethiopia (29:10), and Put is Libya (30:5; Jer. 46:9). Ezekiel 38:6 mentions Gomer and Togarmah or Beth-togarmah. Gomer refers to the descendants of Japheth. They were among the Indo-Europeans and were known to the Greeks as Cimmerians who settled in the

---

4. Cooke mentions those who hold to the foretelling of Babylon's future overthrow although he maintains that it is an apocalypse composed after Ezekiel's day (Cooke, *Critical and Exegetical Commentary on the Book of Ezekiel*, p. 408). For a different view, see Michael C. Astour, "Ezekiel's Prophecy of Gog and the Cuthean Legend of Naram-Sin," *Journal of Biblical Literature* 95 (December 1976): 567–79.

5. Ralph H. Alexander, "A Fresh Look at Ezekiel 38 and 39," *Journal of the Evangelical Theological Society* 17 (Summer 1974): 161; W. F. Albright, "Contributions to Biblical Archaeology and Philology," *Journal of Biblical Literature* 43 (1924): 378–85.

6. Rosh (רֹאשׁ) is translated as an adjective ("*chief* prince of Meshech and Tubal") in AV, RSV, TEV, NIV, NJB, NRSV, whereas it is translated as a proper noun ("prince of *Rosh*, Meshech, and Tubal") in RV, ASV, NASB, NEB, JB. The proper noun is preferred contextually as well as from extrabiblical evidence (James D. G. Price, "Rosh: An Ancient Land Known to Ezekiel," *Grace Theological Journal* 6 [Spring 1985]: 67–89).

7. Alexander, "Fresh Look at Ezekiel 38 and 39," p. 161. Cf. Carl Armerding, "Russia and the King of the North," *Bibliotheca Sacra* 120 (January–March 1963): 50–55; John Ruthven, "Ezekiel's Rosh and Russia: A Connection?" *Bibliotheca Sacra* 125 (October–December 1968): 324–33.

8. Alexander, "Fresh Look at Ezekiel 38–39," pp. 161–62. For a brief discussion of the identity of these places, see Edwin M. Yamauchi, *Foes from the Northern Frontier: Invading Hordes from the Russian Steppes* (Grand Rapids: Baker, 1982), pp. 19–27.

northeastern part of modern-day Turkey.[9] Togarmah or Beth-togarmah is probably in the northwestern part of Turkey or possibly in Azerbaijan. Hence, those who will attack Israel will be from the north and south.

Suggested Interpretations of Ezekiel 38–39

The timing of these events has been the subject of much discussion as well. First, some believe that the events will occur before the tribulation.[10] It is suggested that since Israel will dwell safely or securely (38:8, 11, 14), this must precede and not follow the tribulation. However, the context of chapters 38–39 is the latter days of Israel and not the latter days of the church.[11]

Second, a popular proposal is that the events occur in the middle of the tribulation.[12] It is argued that the invasion is to be equated with the invasion of the king of the north in Daniel 11:40–41. Before this invasion Israel will make a covenant with the "prince who shall come," the Antichrist, for seven years (Dan. 9:27). This covenant would give Israel the security mentioned in Ezekiel 38:8, 11, 14. However, this covenant is broken in the middle of the seven years because Gog, the king of the north, will invade Israel and will be destroyed. Furthermore, according to this view, it makes good sense to see his destruction in the middle of the tribulation because there is no mention of him at the end of the tribulation, the time when the beast and the false prophet are cast into the lake of fire.

There are several problems with this view. First, why would weapons be burned (39:9–10) in the middle of the tribulation? Military personnel preserve all the weapons they can in the midst of battle. Second, to cleanse the land by burying the dead (39:11–16) at the height of the occurrence of the abomination of desolation is highly improbable. Third, the occurrence of birds eating carcasses (39:17–20) is portrayed elsewhere in Scripture (Zech. 14:12; Matt. 24:28; Rev. 19:17–21) as taking place at the end of the tribulation at the time of Christ's return. Fourth, the fact that the Lord's name would not be profaned again among the nations (39:7, 22, 25) contradicts other references that refer to profanity during the last half of the tribulation (Matt. 24:9–26; Mark 13:5–23; Luke 21:8–24; Rev. 6–19). Therefore, the midtribulation view of these events is incongruous with several important passages of Scripture.

---

9. Yamauchi, *Foes from the Northern Frontier,* pp. 49–61.

10. David L. Cooper, *When Gog's Armies Meet the Almighty: An Exposition of Ezekiel Thirty-eight and Thirty-nine* (Los Angeles: Biblical Research Society, 1940), pp. 80–81.

11. J. Dwight Pentecost, "Where Do the Events of Ezekiel 38–39 Fit into the Prophetic Picture?" *Bibliotheca Sacra* 114 (October–December 1957): 337; Charles H. Dyer, "Ezekiel," in *The Bible Knowledge Commentary, Old Testament,* ed. John F. Walvoord and Roy B. Zuck (Wheaton, Ill.: Victor, 1985), 1300.

12. Pentecost, "Where Do the Events of Ezekiel 38–39 Fit into the Prophetic Picture?" pp. 334–46; J. Dwight Pentecost, *Things to Come* (Findlay, Ohio: Dunham, 1958), pp. 350–52.

A third explanation is that these events culminate at the end of the tribulation.[13] In this view Gog's invasion is a part of the final rebellion of all those assembled against Messiah as seen in Zechariah 12 and 14:1–4. Such a scheme appears to make good sense of some of the objections raised in the midtribulation view. Furthermore, the concept of the latter or last days of Israel (Ezek. 38:8, 16) would support this view. However, the latter days could include more than the end of the tribulation and in fact it can refer to the entire tribulation and the millennium (Isa. 2:2–4; Jer. 30:24; Dan. 10:14). Another difficulty with this view is the idea that Israel lives safely or securely (38:8, 11, 14) in the last half of the tribulation. Feinberg describes it as imagined security,[14] but how can one imagine such security in the midst of the greatest turmoil in history? Revelation 12:14–17 shows that "Israel is not going to dwell in the land in peace and safety during the latter half of the seventieth week, but will be the special target of Satan's attack."[15] Consequently, this view does not satisfy all the demands of Ezekiel 38–39, especially chapter 38.

A fourth suggestion is that the events in Ezekiel 38–39 will take place at the beginning of the millennium.[16] Gaebelein anticipates some of the problems and tries to answer them. Since Israel will be safely in her land with Christ, and since Satan will be bound, how could these nations invade Messiah's land? Gaebelein thinks that the prince of Rosh will have been so inspired and blinded by Satan that he will make a last attempt to destroy Israel.[17] However, it is inconceivable that anyone would attack Israel after Messiah is already ruling there and Satan is bound. It is commendable that Gaebelein wants to preserve the idea of safety and security, which is a hallmark of the millennium. But it will hardly be a millennium if there is a horrendous war! Further, Gaebelein also seeks to answer the problem of this unlikely attack by suggesting that the judgment of the nations (Matt. 25:31–46) will cover a long period of time and that this nation (or nations) will be the last one to be judged.[18] However, Scripture leaves the impression that the judgment will be swift. There is no idea that Jesus will be "putting out brush fires" when he judges the nations. Gaebelein wants to have peace and

13. W. K[elly], *Notes on Ezekiel* (London: G. Morrish, n.d.), pp. 200–201; Louis S. Bauman, *Russian Events in the Light of Bible Prophecy* (New York: Fleming H. Revell, 1942), pp. 174–77; Charles Lee Feinberg, *The Prophecy of Ezekiel: The Glory of the Lord* (Chicago: Moody, 1969), pp. 218–19. Cf. also *The Scofield Reference Bible*, ed. C. I. Scofield (Oxford: Oxford University Press, 1909), p. 883; and *The New Scofield Reference Bible*, ed. C. I. Scofield, E. Schuyler English, et al. (Oxford: Oxford University Press, 1967), pp. 881–82.

14. Feinberg, *Prophecy of Ezekiel*, pp. 222–24.

15. Pentecost, "Where Do the Events of Ezekiel 38–39 Fit into the Prophetic Picture?" p. 339.

16. Arno C. Gaebelein, *The Prophet Ezekiel: An Analytical Exposition* (New York: Publication Office "Our Hope," 1918), p. 251.

17. Ibid., pp. 255–56.

18. Ibid., p. 256.

war simultaneously. But we cannot have our cake and eat it too.

A fifth proposal places these events at the end of the millennium.[19] A strong argument for this position is the explicit mention of Gog and Magog in Revelation 20:7–10. However, this view has some definite problems. First, in Ezekiel 38:2 only the northern (local) power is identified as Gog and Magog, whereas in Revelation 20:8 all nations are identified as Gog and Magog. Second, in Ezekiel 38:2 Gog is prince and Magog is the land that includes Rosh, Meshech, and Tubal; in Revelation 20:8 Gog and Magog represent all the nations. Third, in Ezekiel 38:15–16 Gog goes against Israel, but in Revelation 20:8–9 Gog and Magog go against the saints and Jerusalem. Fourth, in Ezekiel 39:4, 17 the invaders fall on Israel's mountains, whereas in Revelation 20:8–9 fire from heaven will devour the invaders. Fifth, in Ezekiel 39:11–16 after the war people are burying war victims for seven months, whereas in Revelation 20:1–15 Satan is cast into the lake of fire, the earth and heavens flee, and the Great White Throne judgment for all unbelievers takes place. Sixth, in Ezekiel 39:9–10 the weapons are burned for heat, whereas in Revelation 20 there is no mention of burning of weapons and there probably is no need for heat in the new heavens and the new earth described in Revelation 21–22. Seventh, in Ezekiel 39:11 Gog and his multitude are buried in Israel in the Valley of Hamon Gog, whereas in Revelation 20:10 Satan will be cast into the lake of fire with the beast and the false prophet. Eighth, in Ezekiel 39:17–20 after the battle, there is a great feast of corpses (which fits well with Revelation 19:17–21 at the end of the tribulation before the millennium), whereas in Revelation 20:1–6 after the battle, Satan is cast into the lake of fire at the end of the millennium. Ninth, in Ezekiel 38–39 the events fit chronologically before the restored millennial temple, whereas in Revelation 20 the events fit chronologically after the millennium. Therefore, though "Gog and Magog" are mentioned in both Ezekiel 38 and Revelation 20:8, there are too many contradictory details for them to be referring to the same event.

A Fresh Look at the Chapters

It is interesting to note that all the above views see the events of Ezekiel 38–39 as occurring at one time. None of the views separates the two chapters. However, these two chapters should be viewed as describing events that are spread over a period of time. Such a solution has some clear advantages textually. Chapter 38 refers to events in the *middle* of the tribulation, and

19. H. L. Ellison, *Ezekiel: The Man and His Message* (London: Paternoster, 1956), pp. 133–34; Alexander, "Fresh Look at Ezekiel 38 and 39," pp. 164–69; Ralph H. Alexander, "Ezekiel," in *The Expositor's Bible Commentary* (Grand Rapids: Zondervan, 1986), 6:940. In this last reference, Alexander is a little optimistic when he says that the majority of expositors hold to his view and he cites only two.

chapter 39 refers to events at the *end* of the tribulation. Rather than one battle, there will be a campaign or a series of battles lasting three and one-half years. Ezekiel 38:2–6 mentions the nations that are both north (Rosh, Meshech, Tubal, Gomer, and Togarmah) and south (Persia, Cush, and Put) of Israel. On the other hand 39:1–2, 6, 11 refer only to the north. Furthermore, the description in chapter 39 regarding the defeat of Gog (vv. 1–8), the burning of weapons (vv. 9–10), the seven-month burial of the dead (vv. 11–16), the carnage eaten by birds and animals (vv. 17–20), and the restoration of Israel under God's protection (vv. 21–29), fits much better at the end of the tribulation than at the middle.

This scenario of the events of Ezekiel 38–48 fits well with the flow of the context. The broader context of Ezekiel 33–39 is the restoration of the nation, Israel. In chapter 33 Ezekiel is designated as the true watchman for Israel who predicted judgment on Israel's faithlessness and eventually her restoration. Chapter 34 contrasts Israel's false shepherds (vv. 1–10) and the future true shepherd, God, who will care for his sheep (vv. 11–31). Chapter 35 describes the destruction of the oppressor, Edom, Israel's long-time enemy. Chapter 36 records God's dealing with Israel in punishing and scattering them among the nations and then in promising a new covenant with her. She will be gathered from among the nations, cleansed from sin, and indwelt with the Spirit for empowerment to live in the restored promised land (vv. 22–38). This is a reiteration of the new covenant in Jeremiah 31. It is fitting, for Jeremiah revealed the new covenant to those who had not gone into captivity and Ezekiel informed those who had gone into captivity. In chapter 37 Ezekiel prophesied Israel's restoration to her land. This is a restoration, not a physical resurrection, because the portrayal is not death but dispersion among the nations as the bones figuratively commiserate with one another regarding their dispersion (v. 11). The bones are gathered with no breath in them until after they are in the land (vv. 7, 12, 14), which implies they are gathered to their land in unbelief. This makes good sense, for Israel in her unbelief will confirm a covenant with the godless prince of the west at the beginning of the tribulation (Dan. 9:27). Such a covenant would be unlikely if they were believers who were trusting God. Chapters 38–39 speak of the campaigns that begin in the middle of the tribulation and finish at the end of the tribulation. Chapters 40–48 speak about the restoration of the temple and its worship and then describe the land in which Israel will dwell.

More particularly, chapters 38–39 support the idea of a progression of events from the middle to the end of the tribulation. In 38:2–6 Israel is faced with the nations of the north and south and yet Israel rests securely (38:8, 11, 14) in her land. The term "'security' (בֶּטַח) does not have the idea of 'peace' but instead means 'to feel secure, be unconcerned,' or, . . . the reason for the security, 'to rely on something or someone.' However, quite often this general meaning has a negative ring: the thing on which one relies turns out to be deceptive, so that the words derived from the root *bṭḥ* are actually used to indicate a false security, a *securatas.*"[20]

This makes good sense with other prophetic Scripture. Daniel 9:27 points out that the western confederacy or prince of the west will confirm (not make) a covenant with Israel for one week or seven years. Thus, this covenant will be made at the beginning of the seven-year period of tribulation. The content of the covenant is not given by Daniel. However, it may be the confirmation of a treaty (much like the 1948 United Nations treaty) that probably will guarantee her autonomy and make her feel secure even though she will be surrounded by enemies. Nevertheless, in the middle of the week, that is, after three and one-half years, the covenant will be broken by the prince of the west. As a result, Israel will lose her political independence and her religious freedom and must worship the abomination of desolation (Dan. 9:27). Why will the prince of the west break this covenant in the middle of the seven-year period? It is logical that the northern and southern nations mentioned in Ezekiel 38:2–6 will make the invasion. This would make it necessary for the prince of the west to come to Israel to protect his interests.

Moreover, such a scenario fits well with Daniel 11:40–43. In the endtime the king of the south and the king of the north will make war against the prince of the west (called a "king" in Dan. 11:36), who will magnify himself above every god (vv. 36–39). The prince of the west will then enter the promised land, head south, and defeat Egypt, Libya (= Put; Ezek. 38:5), and Ethiopia (= Cush; Ezek. 38:5) as well as Edom, Moab, and Ammon (Dan. 11:41–43). Although nothing is mentioned specifically about the defeat of the northern nations, Daniel stated that the prince of the west will stretch out his hands against other countries, which could include at least part of the north. Also, Ezekiel 38:17–23 indicates that Gog will be judged and will thus withdraw. Although Gog is not specifically mentioned in Daniel 11:40–43 nor is the king of the north specifically mentioned in Ezekiel 38–39, it is most likely that Gog and the king of the north refer to the same person. God will judge him, and it may be that the prince of the west is the instrument of that judgment. This marks the commencement of the Battle of Armageddon.

This fits well with other Scripture passages that indicate that in the middle of the tribulation Satan will be cast out of heaven and Israel will be the center of his attention (Rev. 12). During this time the prince of the west will set himself up as god, as the Abomination of Desolation in the temple (Dan. 9:27; Matt. 24:15; 2 Thess. 2:4; Rev. 13:5). As a result of this persecution, Israel will flee the promised land (Matt. 24:16–20; Rev. 12:15–17). Consequently, unbelieving Israelites will be deceived by the false prophet (Matt. 24:11–18)

---

20. *Theological Dictionary of the Old Testament,* s.v. בָּטַח, by Alfred Jepsen, 2 (1979): 88. Also see Francis Brown, S. R. Driver, and Charles A. Briggs, *A Hebrew and English Lexicon of the Old Testament* (Oxford: Clarendon, 1906), p. 105.

and will go into apostasy (Matt. 24:12; 2 Thess. 2:11) while believing Israelites will proclaim the gospel of the kingdom to the whole world (Matt. 24:14; Rev. 7:1–8; 14:1–5). Hence, the events portrayed in Ezekiel 38 harmonize well with other prophetic Scriptures describing the middle of the tribulation.

Several factors indicate that Ezekiel 39 is referring to the end of the tribulation. First, in verses 1–8 there is another prophecy against Gog, prince of Rosh, Meshech, and Tubal.[21] There is no mention of the nations of the south because they will have already been destroyed. This battle in Ezekiel 39 looks like a consummating battle and thus will occur at the end of the tribulation. God declared that the nations will know his holy name in the midst of his people Israel and that his name will no longer be profaned (vv. 7–8). This cannot be true in the middle of the tribulation because Israel will have fled the land. Moreover, certainly God's name will be profaned from the middle to the end of the tribulation when the Abomination of Desolation will be set up in the temple in Jerusalem. Therefore, it must refer to the end of the tribulation. This fits well with Daniel 11:44, when the prince of the west will defeat the king of the south. At that time he will hear of rumors from the east and the north. Although he will try to destroy those enemies, he will be defeated.

Second, there is also the destruction of the weapons for firewood (38:9–10). Such an action is more likely to take place at the end of a war rather than in the middle of a war. This agrees with the picture of the future kingdom in which nations will beat their swords into plowshares and their spears into pruning hooks (Isa. 2:4; Mic. 4:3).

Third, there will be a massive burial of people to cleanse the land. This will take seven months (39:11–16). How could Israel be burying its dead in the middle of the tribulation when the people are told to flee (Matt. 24:16)? Hence, the burying of the dead will be a mopping-up operation after the war.

Fourth, a description of the birds and animals feeding on the carnage of the enemy (Ezek. 39:17–20) is also portrayed in Zechariah 14:12, Matthew 24:28, and Revelation 19:17–21 as occurring at the end and not the middle of the tribulation.

Fifth, Ezekiel 39 depicts Israel as a restored nation that has been cleansed and indwelt with the Holy Spirit and is living securely with God's protection in the land that was promised to them (vv. 21–29).[22] Chapters 40–48 continue this theme of a restored and cleansed nation in their land. The pouring out of the Spirit at the end of the tribulation is also mentioned in Zechariah

---

21. Possibly the break should be at Ezekiel 38:17 rather than 39:1. However, the break at 39:1 seems preferable because 38:17–23 could refer to the prince of the west pushing the king of the north out of Israel in the middle of the tribulation.

22. Cf. Daniel I. Block, "Gog and the Pouring Out of the Spirit: Reflections on Ezekiel XXXIX.21–29," *Vetus Testamentum* 37 (July 1987): 257–70.

12:10 and Joel 2:28. Thus, the events described in Ezekiel 39 fit well at the end of the tribulation.

Summary

Ezekiel 38–39 is best considered as covering the last half of the tribulation: chapter 38 refers to events in the middle of the tribulation, chapter 39 refers to events at the end of the tribulation. This suits the context well. In brief, chapter 36 gives the revelation of the new covenant and chapter 37 describes the restoration of Israel in unbelief. Next, chapter 38 speaks about the first half of the tribulation, when Israel will rest in security but then will be attacked in the middle of the tribulation. This is followed by chapter 39, which depicts the end of the tribulation when Gog will be destroyed and God will cleanse the land, restore his people to the land, and pour out his Spirit on them. Then chapters 40–48 portray the worship of the people in their new land.

We can outline the chronology of events in Ezekiel 38–39 and related prophetic Scriptures regarding the tribulation in the following way:

1. Israel will be regathered to her land (Ezek. 37).
2. At the beginning of the tribulation:
   a. Israel will sign a covenant with a western confederacy headed by the prince of the west (Dan. 9:27).
   b. As a result, Israel will be secure in the land (Ezek. 38:8, 11, 14).
3. In the middle of the tribulation:
   a. The north and the south will invade the promised land (Dan. 11:40; Ezek. 38:2, 5, 13).
   b. The prince of the west will break his covenant (Dan. 9:27), enter the promised land (Dan. 11:40, 41), and defeat Egypt, Libya (= Put; Ezek. 38:5), and Ethiopia (= Cush; Ezek. 38:5; Dan. 11:42, 43). Apparently, the king of the north will withdraw voluntarily (or God or the west will force him back) as the prince of the west enters the land. However, Daniel 11:40 states that the prince of the west will enter many countries, which may include the north. Also Ezekiel 38:17–23 indicates that the north will be judged and thus will withdraw.
   c. The Battle of Armageddon will commence.
   d. Satan will be cast out of heaven (Rev. 12:9–10).
   e. The prince of the west will set himself up as god, as the Abomination of Desolation in the temple is set up (Dan. 9:27; Matt. 24:15; 2 Thess. 2:4; Rev. 13:5).[23]

---

23. The harlot in Revelation 17 is seen as a spiritual leader (vv. 2, 5), a power broker over the political leaders (v. 3), rich and profane (v. 4), the persecutor of the saints (v. 6), and influential over the world (v. 15). She will be destroyed by the beast, the Antichrist (vv. 16–17).

   f. Israel will be persecuted and will flee the promised land (Matt.
      24:16–20; Rev. 12:15–17). Unbelieving Israelites will be deceived
      by the false prophet (Matt. 24:11–18) and will go into apostasy
      (Matt. 24:12; 2 Thess. 2:11); believing Israelites will proclaim the
      message (Matt. 24:14; Rev. 7:1–8; 14:1–5).
4. At the end of the tribulation:
   a. The kings of the north and of the east will attack Israel (or the
      western confederacy) (Ezek. 39; Dan. 11:44; Rev. 16:12). They
      will attempt to get rid of Israel and secure world domination.
   b. The Messiah will appear and as a result the nations will oppose
      him (Zech. 14:4; Matt. 24:30; Rev. 19:19).
   c. He will destroy them in order to show that he is God (Ezek. 39:6–
      7, 13, 21–22, 28; Dan. 11:45).
5. After the tribulation:
   a. Weapons will be destroyed (Ezek. 39:9–10).
   b. Carcasses will be buried and other carcasses will be eaten by birds
      and beasts (Ezek. 39:11–20; Zech. 14:12; Matt. 24:28; Rev.
      19:17–21).
6. The millennium (Ezek. 39:21–29; 40–48; Rev. 20).

Tribute

"Never be lacking in zeal, but keep your spiritual fervor, serving the
Lord" (Rom. 12:11). It has been apparent over the years that Dr. Don Campbell has taken Paul's admonition seriously. His commitment to the ministry
of Dallas Theological Seminary has been exemplary. May God bless him as
he continues to serve him in the years ahead.

A Literary Approach to the Birth Narratives in Luke 1–2

David E. Malick

Though many writers claim to approach Luke 1–2 from a literary standpoint, they tend to place thematic or linear categories of the text before working with its structure.[1] The literary approach in this study is synoptic/synthetic, emphasizing the narrative logic of the units in Luke 1–2. Instead of a look at the trees, this is a look at the forest; instead of a look at the buildings, it is a glance at the skyline; instead of a step into the depth of grammatical, historical, and lexical analysis, it is a climb up the scaffold of literary structure.

In narrative literature, message-units are often defined and communicated through the logic of literary connections. This essay supports the contention that a literary approach to Luke 1:5–2:52 will substantiate the grouping of the many units into a major division of thought and will also aid in communicating the message of that division.

The Structure of Luke 1:5–2:52

An Overview of the Unit

Rather than approaching the text in a linear or thematic fashion it seems better, in view of Luke's choice of the literary technique of interchange, to examine the text from the perspective of balance. The following chart expresses the architecture of Luke 1:5–2:52:

---

1. René Laurentin, *Structure et Theologie de Luc I–II* (Paris: Gabalda, 1964); Charles H. Talbert, *Patterns, Theological Themes, and the Genre of Luke–Acts* (Missoula, Mont.: Scholars, 1974); David Gooding, *According to Luke: A New Exposition of the Third Gospel* (Grand Rapids: Eerdmans, 1978); Raymond Brown, *The Birth of the Messiah: A Commentary on the Infancy Narratives in Matthew and Luke* (Garden City, N.Y.: Image, 1979); Charles Thomas Davis, "The Literary Structure of Luke 1–2," in *Art and Meaning*, ed. David J. A. Clines, David M. Gunn, and Alan J. Hauser (Sheffield: JSOT, 1982), pp. 215–29; James P. Martin, "Luke 1:39–47," *Interpretation* 36 (October 1982): 394–99; E. Earle Ellis, *The Gospel of Luke* (Grand Rapids: Eerdmans, 1983); Robert C. Tannehill, *The Narrative Unity of Luke–Acts: A Literary Interpretation*, vol. 1: *The Gospel According to Luke* (Philadelphia: Fortress, 1986).

	Zechariah and Elizabeth	Mary	Mary and Elizabeth	Zechariah and Elizabeth	Joseph and Mary
Historical Setting	Herod (1:5)	Nazareth (1:26)			Caesar and Quirinius (2:1–3)
Life Setting	Righteous, No children, Old (1:6–7)	A virgin engaged (1:27)			Of the house of David, engaged (2:4–5)
Announcement	1:8–20	1:26–37			
Response to the Announcement	Zechariah (1:21–23) Elizabeth (1:24–25)	1:38	Mary (1:39–40) Elizabeth (1:41–45) Mary (1:46–56)		
Birth				1:57	2:6–7
Response to the Birth				1:58	Angels and shepherds (2:8–20)
Circumcision				People (1:59–66) Zechariah (1:67–79)	Fact (2:21–24) Simeon (2:25–35) Anna (2:36–38)
Child's Growth				1:80	2:39–52

As the chart reveals, the structure of this major unit is one of interchange or balance. The movement of the chapters progresses in a comparison between "Zechariah and Elizabeth" and "Mary," and then between "Zechariah and Elizabeth" and "Joseph and Mary." In between these two poles, as a pivot, is a unit that is balanced between "Mary and Elizabeth" (1:39–56).

By following the verse notations vertically in each column from left to right the reader can see that this is not a contrived structure. There is a sequential flow from the upper left-hand corner of the chart to the lower right-hand corner. When Luke's structure is observed, balance becomes the technique by which to group the smaller units and thus interact with them. The pattern defines the boundaries of the larger message unit at 1:5 and 2:52 and suggests how best to interact with the inner units. Examining each individual pericope in an analytical manner would be to miss a portion of the message Luke intended his readers to capture through a careful comparison of the couplets.

As seen in the chart, specific textual clues reinforce this grouping. Each of the major "actors" in this large division is introduced by a historical setting: Zechariah (the priest) and his wife Elizabeth through Herod (the "king of the Jews"), Mary (a young woman in Nazareth of racially mixed Galilee),[2] and Joseph through the secular, international setting of Rome (Caesar Augustus and Quirinius, the governor of Syria).

It is true that Luke 3 includes another historical setting with the introduction of John the Baptist, but this is probably not to be connected with the birth interchange for several reasons: (1) John was already introduced in the record of his birth through Zechariah. (2) The parallel is not carried on with a historical introduction to Jesus in 3:21. (3) The initial parallels are completed with the reports about the children's growth. (4) A unit about the life of Jesus is introduced before the discussion of John without a historical introduction, thus breaking the order of interchange. (5) The historical introduction is a recapitulation of the one presented in 1:5, emphasizing a Jewish legal setting. Therefore it is more probable that 3:1–2 provides the setting for the next major unit. Perhaps the interchange in Luke 1–2 is a cameo of the rest of the book in which John's ministry is introduced and completed in 3:1–20

2. Before the exile of the northern kingdom of Israel, Galilee was considered a land inhabited by Gentiles (*gᵉlîl haggôyim*, Isa. 9:1 [Heb., 8:23]). It was primarily a Gentile area during the Maccabean period in the second century B.C. (1 Macc. 5:14–17, 20–23; Josephus, *The Antiquities of the Jews* 12.333–34; Emil Schürer, *The History of the Jewish People in the Age of Jesus Christ (175 B.C.–A.D. 135)*, rev. and ed. Geza Vermes, Fergus Millar, and Matthew Block, 2 vols. [Edinburgh: T. & T. Clark, 1973], 1:142; 2:8). By the conclusion of the Maccabean period Judaism extended no farther north than the province of Samaria, which became known as northern Judea (1 Macc. 9:50–52; Schürer, *History of the Jewish People in the Age of Jesus Christ (175 B.C.–A.D. 135)*, 1:117–18; 2:7–9). However, the Jewish community was never restored in Galilee as it was in Judea proper (Schürer, *History of the Jewish People in the Age of Jesus Christ (175 B.C.–A.D. 135)*, 2:7).

Concerning the Galilee of Mary's day, Smith writes, "The province, it is true, had been under the Law for only a little more than a century. Her customs and laws, even on such important matters as marriage and intercourse with the heathen, her coins and weights, her dialect, were all sufficiently different from those of Judæa to excite popular sentiment in the latter, and provide the scribes with some quotable reasons for their hostility" (George Adam Smith, *The Historical Geography of the Holy Land: Especially in Relation to the History of Israel and the Early Church* [New York: A. C. Armstrong and Son, 1904], p. 423; cf. Schürer, *History of the Jewish People in the Age of Jesus Christ (175 B.C.–A.D. 135)*, 2:13–14; *Mishnah*, Kethuboth 4:12; 13:10; Terumoth 10:8; Kethuboth 5:9; Pesachim 4:5). For more popular discussions of this subject, see J. Dwight Pentecost, *The Words and Works of Jesus Christ: A Study of the Life of Christ* (Grand Rapids: Zondervan, 1981), pp. 43–44, 516–24; and Alfred Edersheim, *The Life and Times of Jesus the Messiah*, 3d ed. (McLean, Va.: MacDonald, 1886), pp. 144–49.

and then Jesus' ministry is introduced in 3:21 and continued through the Gospel of Luke and the Book of Acts.

These historical settings define the message-units, but when grouped they also help communicate the message of the overall division. Luke was intimating through this historical progression that God is working in space and time through those within the core of Judaism, through those outside the core of Judaism who were committed to God, and through the world rule of Rome. The placement of the characters is conspicuous: the one who cannot receive the message in Jerusalem, the one who can receive the message outside Jerusalem, and the one to be the Savior of the world born under Roman rule.

Another observation from the chart is that all the "players" are related. Clearly there is an emphasis on the family of God. But in view of the difficulty experienced by each couple as they become the bearers of God's revelation, emphasis is placed on the support provided within the family of God to enable his children to perform his will. As God works among his people and on their behalf to bring about deliverance from evil for them, he provides the support they need to accomplish what he has called them to do. Mary would find support in Elizabeth, and both sets of parents would find confidence to face the brutality exerted against their children through their common experiences with the angel. Perhaps this theme would be important to Theophilus as he followed God against the Greco-Roman culture of his day.

The Annunciations

Many have noted in some detail the parallels between the announcements given to Zechariah and Mary, but there is more to see once we accept the fact that Luke intended for his readers to compare these units. Besides providing a subunit within the major division of 1:5–2:52, they are also a unit in balance. The parallels are as follows:

Zechariah	*Mary*
The angel appeared (vv. 11–14)	The angel appeared (vv. 26–28)
–to him	–to her
–in the holy place	–in Nazareth
The angel announced (vv. 13–17)	The angel announced (vv. 28–33)
–do not fear	–do not fear
–your prayers are heard	–you found favor
–you have a son	–you will have a son
–great	–great
–no wine, and the Holy Spirit	–Son of the Most High
–prepare for the King	–King over Jacob

The angel affirmed (vv. 19–20)	The angel affirmed (vv. 35–37)
–mute	–Holy Spirit
	–Elizabeth
	–God's Word

Davis notes many of the parallels with the annunciation to Zechariah,[3] but he does not develop their significance. The parallels clearly extend the boundaries of these units beyond the individual accounts to include both of them. What did Luke want his readers to see in the twin announcements? How does this structure contribute to his message?

The place and persons of appearance are radically different. One place is the holy place, the center of Jewish faith and holiness; the other is Nazareth, a place polluted by Gentiles and sin. One person is a priest fulfilling the holy work of a lifetime;[4] the other person is a woman in the common place of her home. Their character descriptions (compare 1:6–7 with 1:27) suggest both are morally upright. The reader would expect the priest to be the one who responds the most appropriately to the angel, but the opposite occurs. This surprise is a key to the theme of Israel responding inappropriately to the message of God while those outside Israel (Gentiles), yet sensitive to God, respond appropriately.[5]

The announcements themselves clearly emphasize God's work of grace. To both Zechariah and Mary the angel announced that God saw them and

3. (1) Minimum background, (2) angelic greeting, (3) a question, and (4) the angelic answer (Davis, "Literary Structure of Luke 1–2," p. 220). Like many others, he notes that they are present, but he does not unfold their importance.

4. Temple duties were conferred by lots on each of the twenty-four divisions of priests (1 Chron. 24:1–31; Josephus, *Antiquities of the Jews* 7.366–67; *Life of Josephus* 2), and then on individuals in each tribe for various tasks in the temple (*Mishnah*, Yoma 2:2–4; Schürer, *History of the Jewish People in the Age of Jesus Christ (175 B.C.–A.D. 135)*, 2:287). Because of the large number of priests (1 Chron. 9:13; Ezra 2:36–39, 64; Neh. 11:10–14) Zechariah may have had only one opportunity in his lifetime to perform this service. M. Stern suggests that the number of priests did in fact decrease after the second temple period ("Aspects of Jewish Society: The Priesthood and Other Classes," in *The Jewish People in the First Century: Historical Geography, Political History, Social, Cultural and Religious Life and Institutions*, ed. S. Safrai et al. [Assen: Van Gorcum, 1976], 2:595–96), but they would still have been numerous. In addition, the *Mishnah* limits the duty of "offering incense" to one who has never before performed it: "The third lot—Fresh priests, come and draw lots for the incense!" (*Mishnah*, Yoma 2:4). Blackman defines the term for "fresh" as follows: "Such of the *bêt 'aḇ* on duty that day as had never before officiated at the offering of the incense" (Philip Blackman, *Mishnayoth* [New York: Judaica, 1984], vol. 2: *Order Yoma* 2:4 n. 2, p. 280). Therefore, this was a prestigious opportunity for Zechariah.

5. Perhaps the question being asked by Theophilus (a Gentile Christian?) and those with him was, How is it that Christianity is primarily Gentile in nature if it came from Judaism? Therefore, Luke wrote Luke–Acts to argue that the Christian gospel is not anti-Semitic, but rooted in the Hebrew Scriptures' promise of salvation to both Jews and Gentiles. Believing Gentiles share in the initiation of the spiritual promises to Israel. They are stewards of the promises to Israel. The reason Christianity is primarily Gentile in nature is that the Jews rejected the message of Jesus as Messiah. Nevertheless the Jews as a people are not rejected by God. The promises will yet be consummated for the nation through the resurrected Jesus, the Hope of Israel.

chose to be gracious to them. God was being gracious to Zechariah by answering his and Elizabeth's personal prayers for a son and his national prayers (on that day) for his people. God was being gracious to Mary by choosing her, a woman in Nazareth, to be the earthly mother of the Messiah. Mary later developed this theme in her Magnificat.

Comparison between the sons shows their unique place in these announcements of grace: (1) both would be great (vv. 15, 32); (2) their character was presented—John would be unique for God and the Holy Spirit would work through him (v. 15); and Jesus is God himself—very God (v. 32); and (3) their tasks were delineated—John would prepare for the King (vv. 16–17), and Jesus would be the King (vv. 32–33).

The responses of both Zechariah and Mary elicit a message of affirmation from Gabriel. It is common to view Zechariah's being speechless as an act of divine judgment. However, when the sign is placed in parallel with Gabriel's words to Mary, the reader understands that this is affirmation, not condemnation.[6]

In light of Mary's response to Gabriel's message, it is apparent that the angel's words were an affirmation to her. Mary was able to respond to the "word" and was therefore given three affirmations of the truth of this oracle: (1) the child would be supernaturally conceived by God (v. 35); (2) God had done a similar miracle of enabling her cousin Elizabeth to conceive (v. 36); and (3) whatever God says is possible (v. 37).[7]

Likewise Gabriel's response to Zechariah is an affirmation. He was a "servant" of God performing one of the highest duties of a lifetime in the temple, and yet he was hardened so that he would not receive the word of God. Wren suggests that less than the full sense of Malachi 4:6 is quoted in Luke 1:17[8] for the sake of emphasis in this opening unit: "The emphasis is on the need of the old to beware of the impact of the arrival of the new."[9] This lends support to the idea of Zechariah's hardness and his inability to receive the word

6. Gooding identifies Zechariah's doubtful questioning as subversive to the entire gospel in that God's inability to provide for their physical needs meant that he was unable to provide for the needs of creation and humankind itself. This seems to come close to but misses the point of the narrative interchange. He reasons in a linear fashion rather than in a literary one. Likewise he explains the dumbness of Zechariah in terms of his inability to proclaim the gospel in faith, rather than as a confirming sign provided by Gabriel just as he later did for Mary (Gooding, *According to Luke*, pp. 33–36).

7. Wren notes well the play on words with ῥῆμα as Gabriel spoke to Mary (Malcolm Wren, "Sonship in Luke: The Advantage of a Literary Approach," *Scottish Journal of Theology* 37 [1984]: 301–11). Unlike Zechariah, Mary was able to receive the word of God.

8. Malachi 4:6 reads, "And he will restore the hearts of the fathers to their children, and the hearts of the children to their fathers"; and Luke 1:17 reads, "to turn the hearts of the fathers back to the children, and the disobedient to the attitude of the righteous."

9. Wren, "Sonship in Luke," p. 304. Brown makes a similar observation: "Luke . . . identifies the fathers with the disobedient whereas the children seem to be the just whose wisdom is noted" (Raymond Brown, "Luke's Method in the Annunciation Narratives of Chapter One," in *No Famine in the Land*, ed. J. W. Flanagan and Anita Weisbrod Robinson [Claremont, Calif.: Scholars, 1975], p. 190).

of God.[10] He was a religious leader who had been serving God all his life, and in his righteousness (1:6) he had not experienced the blessing of God through the birth of a child (1:7). Therefore, upon hearing another promise (a word from God), he doubted. So God's word would have to speak to him through the experience of life, before he could believe it. This then accounts for Zechariah's being speechless.

Zechariah was also placed in a representative role for the nation as priest (the people outside the temple were awaiting his return, 1:21–22). This allowed him to represent the nation that day in his response to the word. Davis draws a parallel between Zechariah and Israel, but purely on a theological basis without observing the narrative structure of the book.[11] Parsons, who argues for techniques of closure in Luke's Gospel, notes the typological role of Zechariah in this first appearance:

> The opening scene in the gospel (Luke 1:5–23) establishes the conflict between the people of God and his agents. . . . Zechariah, whom the narrator tells us was "righteous before God, walking in all the commandments of the Lord, blameless" (1:5–6), is one of God's people. While in God's sanctuary (the temple, v. 9), God's agent, an angel of the Lord (vv. 11, 19), appears to him. The conflict begins in 1:18 when Zechariah doubts the angel's prophecy that he and Elizabeth will have a son. The angel rebukes Zechariah, revealing to him that he is none other than Gabriel who "was sent to speak to you" (1:19). The conflict is resolved when Gabriel strikes Zechariah speechless. Zechariah then returns home. This initial episode provides the type-scene of the other synagogue/temple encounters. The tension seems to intensify with each subsequent conflict. The other conflict incidents between God's agents with God's people in God's house may be diagrammed in the following way.[12]

Text	God's Sanctuary	God's People	God's Agent	Conflict
1:5–23	Temple	Zechariah	Gabriel	1:18–20
2:41–51	Temple	Jesus' parents	Jesus	2:48–50
4:6–30	Synagogue	All	Jesus	4:23–30
6:6–11	Synagogue	Scribes and Pharisees	Jesus	6:8–11

10. Wren continues, "In the case of the child that is born Luke goes on to labour the fact that he does not take a patronym, but will be called John. He will not be a conventional elder son who walks in his father's footsteps; sonship in his case is a matter of *dis*continuity" ("Sonship in Luke," p. 304).

11. Davis notes the following correlation: "The fulfillment of the angel's word to Zechariah will simultaneously be the fulfillment of God's word to Israel, who like Zechariah has dared at times to question God's promises" ("Literary Structure of Luke 1–2," p. 220).

12. Mikeal C. Parsons, "Narrative Closure and Openness in the Plot of the Third Gospel: The Sense of an Ending in Luke 24:50–53," *Society of Biblical Literature Seminar Papers* (Atlanta: Scholars, 1986), pp. 209–10.

13:10–17	Synagogue	Synagogue ruler	Jesus	13:14–17
19:45–48	Temple	Chief priest and scribes	Jesus	19:47

This study emphasizes that the narrative structure of the units not only defines the grouping of subunits, but also aids in communicating the message of the book.

The Response to the Announcements

In this first interchange Luke's message is clarified even more as the responses to the angel's messages are charted:

Zechariah	*Elizabeth*	*Mary*
Troubled, fearful (v. 12)		Confused, wondered what this would mean (v. 29)
"Prove it" (perhaps a spirit of suspicion or doubt due to old age and being hardened (v. 18)		Questioned how this could occur since she had not known a man; yet she agreed (v. 38)
Is made mute (v. 22)		Received God's word
Went to the people (v. 22) and to his home to Elizabeth (v. 23) ⟶	⟵ Responded in a quiet way; kept herself in seclusion for five months ⟵ [until one month before Mary received the message] (v. 24)	Went to Elizabeth and rejoiced (vv. 39, 46–55)
	Responded in a joyful way (vv. 41–45) ⟶	

It does not seem appropriate to subsume Elizabeth's response under Zechariah's or Mary's, as many do.[13] On the contrary, she is highlighted as both

---

13. While Wren does note Elizabeth's seclusion following her pregnancy, he does not relate the unit to her response to Mary. Consequently he draws a less than full observation of the material: "This unexpected response serves as a literary device to maintain the reader's interest and anticipation of the outcome (for we are now to leave the sub-plot for a while), but primarily reinforces the sense of secrecy" ("Sonship in Luke," p. 305).

Wren's theological approach to Luke's Gospel overrides his literary approach when he speaks of Elizabeth's response to Mary: "John's recognition, in the form of a kick, is communicated to Elizabeth . . . who cries, 'Blessed are you among women, and blessed is the fruit of your womb!'—an exclama-

Zechariah and Mary travel to her. This helps explain Elizabeth's place as a pivot between the two broad groupings of parallelisms before and after the announcements.

Unlike Zechariah and Mary, Elizabeth only heard of the angel's visits; she had not seen the visions. Thus she stands in the place of the reader, who also is "hearing" a report of what happened. In each case she was able to respond appropriately; she chose to be quiet with her husband (vv. 24–25) and to rejoice with Mary (vv. 41–45). Both are expressions of faith. Just as Elizabeth was able to identify with their experience by properly receiving the word from those who heard it, so the reader is to enter into the benefits of God's Word through proper response to it (cf. v. 4).

Another theme that is highlighted from this comparison is that of being a servant of God. The story opens by noting that Zechariah was God's servant, having devoted his life to serving God in the temple. Though representing the people in the temple, he could not receive the word of God when it was spoken to him. On the contrary and to the surprise of the readers, the parallels reveal that Mary was the true servant of God. Her very words confirm this exalted position: "I am the Lord's servant. . . . may it be to me as you have said" (1:38). How ironic. The servant of God is not determined by gender, age, position, function, or location, but by the one who can receive the Word of God. So it is throughout Luke–Acts. Those who consider themselves servants of God (Israel) will not respond to the message of God as it is proclaimed, while those who are considered unlikely candidates (the Gentiles) will be seen as true servants of God as they believe his Word.

The Speeches

Progression of thought is evident in the speeches by Elizabeth, Mary, and

---

tion which Luke consciously recapitulates in 11.27, where it is made clear that such claims of understanding only reveal misunderstanding. For one of the major theological motifs in Luke's presentation of an 'unfolding epiphany' is his emphasis that those who think they recognize the significance of Jesus are in fact mistaken" (ibid., p. 306). The difficulty with this discussion is that Wren has read Luke 11:27 back into the response of Elizabeth in 1:42. Actually a comparison of Elizabeth's responses with those of Zechariah and Mary shows a positive affirmation rather than a negative one.

Davis explains Mary's visit to Elizabeth as a subscene emphasizing Mary's upcoming message that those of low degree are being lifted up. This misses the positive emphasis on Elizabeth. After all, it was she who spoke, not Mary. He also writes, "It is simply the question of how Jesus, the King, relates to John, the one who prepares the way. Normally servants visit the king. Why this surprising departure from convention? The *Magnificat* forms Mary's answer. God's King, like God himself reverses the expected pattern of power. Those of low degree are raised up" (Davis, "Literary Structure of Luke 1–2," p. 221).

In a similar way Brown places the response of Elizabeth with that of Mary. "Episode 3 [the visitation], which brings the mothers of J[ohn the] Bap[tist] and Jesus together, does not fit either side of a diptych arrangement. However, since it exalts Jesus, there is a tendency to put it on Jesus' side of the diptych pattern" (Brown, *Birth of the Messiah,* pp. 250–51).

Zechariah. Once again the message is communicated through an awareness
of the narrative techniques employed by Luke:

Elizabeth	Mary	Zechariah
Initial response: She said God had taken away her reproach (v. 25)	*Initial response:* She believed and asked for God's wonder-working word to be fulfilled in her (v. 38)	*Initial response:* He was disturbed and made silent about the introduction of John (vv. 18–20)
Later response: The child leaped (v. 41)	*Later response:* Her life showed how great God is; she magnified him (v. 46)	*Later response:* He praised God (v. 64)
She was filled with the Holy Spirit (v. 41)	She was filled with the Holy Spirit (v. 35)	He was filled with the Holy Spirit (v. 67)
She proclaimed loudly (v. 42)	In her spirit she rejoiced in the God of her salvation (v. 47)	He professed
Her message: Mary was exalted (vv. 43–45) She called Mary "the mother of my Lord" (v. 43) Her greeting caused Elizabeth's child to leap with joy (v. 44) She would be enriched for believing (v. 45)	*Her message:* God was exalted (vv. 48–55) God had done a wonderful thing with a girl from Nazareth (vv. 48–49) God had been merciful throughout history to those who fear him (vv. 50–51) –by humiliating the self-assured (vv. 50–51) –by exalting those with need who look to him (the humble, v. 52; the hungry, v. 53; the nation, vv. 54–55)	*His message:* The role of his son with Messiah was proclaimed (vv. 68–79): God visited his people (v. 68), redeemed them (v. 68), raised up the horn of salvation (v. 69) as he promised (vv. 70–75), for their child would proclaim the Messiah (v. 76), and prepare the people for the Messiah who would guide them (vv. 77–79)

The responses of the three are parallel, but in the content of the initial
responses and the messages, the development of thought becomes evident.
Because there are parallels with respect to the initial response, the later
response, praise, the filling of the Spirit, and the proclamation of a message,
there is validity in emphasizing the development of thought in the speeches.
Apparently Luke wanted his readers to compare this material, noting the
similarities, so that they would discover the progression of thought.

In the initial response both Elizabeth and Mary were positive, while Zechariah was negative. In the initial responses the order is Zechariah, Elizabeth, and Mary, and in the later responses the order is Elizabeth, Mary, and Zechariah. This exchange highlights Zechariah's speech as the climax of the three. Mary, who was with child, had already been filled by the Holy Spirit (1:35), and Elizabeth is said to have been filled with the Spirit before she spoke. This theme thus becomes the literary thread to correlate the words of Zechariah with those of Elizabeth and Mary when Luke wrote before Zechariah's speech that "Zechariah was filled with the Holy Spirit" (1:67). This is a surprise, for one would expect this to be the case with the women, but not with Zechariah after his rebellion in the temple.

The subject matter in the speeches then moves toward a logical climax. While Elizabeth hinted at exalting God but primarily supported Mary, Mary's emphasis was on the exaltation of God. Then when Mary hinted at the work of God for the nation Israel, Zechariah gave the specific application to the speeches of Elizabeth and Mary.[14] Besides exalting God, Zechariah also functioned as a prophet in explaining these life events.[15] He identified the roles of the children, focusing on Mary's son who would bring about sal-

14. Wren astutely observes the change in verb tenses as Mary alluded to the words of Hannah. In 1 Samuel 2 the verbs are in the present tense, but in Luke 1 they are in the past tense. "By the very acts of Jesus' conception God has acted to save his people" (Wren, "Sonship in Luke," p. 306).

Brown notes Mary's progression of thought: "Noblesse oblige would almost require that Mary in turn bless Elizabeth. But in Luke's version of the scene this is the appropriate moment to insert the Magnificat with the clear effect that if Elizabeth blesses Mary, 'the mother of the Lord' (1:43), Mary now blesses the Lord Himself" (Raymond Brown, "The Annunciation to Mary, the Visitation, and the Magnificat [Luke 1:26–56]," *Worship* 62 [May 1988]: 256).

Though approached from the vantage point of the "appropriate response of Mary to her blessing," Gooding likewise observes that "she does not add 'because I am to be the mother of the Son of God' but 'because the Mighty One has done great things for me' (1:49). In other words, what God has done, rather than what she is, is the aspect of the matter that is filling her mind" (Gooding, *According to Luke*, p. 43).

15. Gooding notes Zechariah's emphasis when he named his son: "In their society it was considered a disaster if a man died without a son to carry on the family name. The relatives therefore would have been tremendously relieved that Zechariah's branch of the family now had a son to keep the family name going, and they were already calling him Zechariah after his father when Elizabeth said, 'No: he had to be called John.' The relatives were shocked and tried to get her to see that this would break the family tradition completely (see 1:61). But Elizabeth insisted. They appealed over her head to Zechariah; and to their astonishment and dismay he agreed with his wife" (ibid., p. 47).

While this is an accurate observation, Gooding misses some of the significance of the event. He notes that John the Baptist "was destined to be the illustrious forerunner of Messiah," yet he says, "John eventually grew up, claimed to be the forerunner and announced Jesus as the Messiah. John was murdered, Jesus was crucified. We today still have to ask the question, Was John really the forerunner? And that means asking, among other things, what motives Zechariah had in naming his son John" (ibid., p. 48).

Gooding, however, does not note how John's name, when placed along with the names of his parents, literally communicates the message of this unit!

Haik argues for the literary contribution of the names when he writes, "That the meaning of the names have a connection with the narrative is not without significance. Zacharias is a frequent name in the Old Testament (*Zĕcaryâh*), and means *whom Jehovah remembers*. Elizabeth is the Greek name for *'ĕlîšebaʿ* and means *to whom God is the oath*, or *one who swears by God*. The name John (*Iōánvῃς*) is composed of *Yhwh* and *ḥāna*, and means *Jehovah shows grace*. The name of the forerunner

vation for the nation and the Gentiles. Zechariah, who at one point spurned the word of God and suffered for it, learned from the sign of his being unable to speak that the message was true, and then in faith he became the most articulate and complete spokesperson for what the Lord was doing.[16] As already noted, he serves as a type of the nation. The cameo foretells the future far beyond the specifics of the one man. He pictures what would be true of the nation someday.

The Circumcision

Davis does not comment on the parallel between the circumcision of the two children. Instead he views Luke 2:21 as "a tag added to an already completed drama."[17]

Brown likewise notes the difficulty authors have in correlating the presentation of Jesus in the temple with the finding of Jesus in the temple.[18] The summary statements about the growth or progress of each child as well as the circumcision parallels are helpful here because they place the units in their proper parallels.

The examination of the two passages in chart form sets forth the parallels:

Zechariah and Elizabeth	*Mary and Joseph*
Setting (1:59):	Setting (2:21):
–eight days	–eight days
–circumcision	–circumcision
Naming: John (1:59–63)	Naming: Jesus (2:21)

---

suggests the gracious character of the message and the age which he came to introduce. It refers to the grace of God which was to descend upon the people" (Paul S. Haik, "The Argument of the Gospel of Luke" [Th.D. diss., Dallas Theological Seminary, 1965], p. 85).

While one may wonder whether the significance of these Hebrew names would be lost on Luke's Gentile readers, there is evidence that Luke 1–2 is related to Hebrew concepts (as part of Luke's larger argument in Luke–Acts concerning the movement of the gospel from the Jews to the Gentiles) and possibly even to Hebrew sources (see Paul Winter, "Cultural Background of the Narrative in Luke 1 and 2," *Jewish Quarterly Review* 45 [January 1955]: 159–67, 230–42; idem, "Some Observations of the Language in the Birth and Infancy Stories of the Third Gospel," *New Testament Studies* 1 [November 1954]: 111–21; idem, "Two Notes on Luke 1–2 with Regard to the Theology of 'Imitation Hebraisms,'" *Studia Theologica* 7 [1953]: 158–65). Therefore, the meaning of the Hebrew names would be intricately related to the message of Luke 1–2.

16. Zechariah may foreshadow another hardhearted Hebrew who was initially hostile toward God's Word, but became its greatest spokesman—Saul of Tarsus (Acts 7; 9).

17. Davis, "Literary Structure of Luke 1–2," p. 223. He adds, "It belatedly corrects the narration of this scene and serves also to introduce the next scene: the presentation of the child in the Temple." This disregards Luke's structure.

18. He writes, "There are no narrative parallels in the J[ohn the] Bap[tist] story for episodes 6 [presentation of Jesus in temple] and 7 [finding in temple], and so these episodes cause difficulty for those who analyze into two divisions" (Brown, *Birth of the Messiah*, p. 251).

Speeches:
  –praise (1:64)
  –response (1:64–66)
  –salvation (1:67–75)
  –difficult ministry (1:76–79)

Growth: desert (1:80)

Speeches:
  –salvation (2:24–32)
  –response (2:33)
  –difficult ministry (2:38)
  –praise (2:38)

Growth: Nazareth (2:39–52)

Once again the parallels draw the reader to relate the two units with regard to their setting, the naming,[19] the speeches,[20] and the report about growth. However, topics in the speeches, though similar, are not given in the same order. The order is probably switched to emphasize the roles of the boys, with salvation being the first in Simeon's emphasis regarding Jesus (2:24–32) but third in Zechariah's speech regarding John the Baptist (1:67–75). Likewise the order of praise is inverted because Zechariah had already passed through difficulty and seen God work; therefore, it was normal for him to respond by initially extolling the good character of his Lord. However, in the case of Joseph and Mary the perspective of praise follows mention of a difficult ministry that would even pierce Mary's life. But through this ministry God would work to bring about redemption; therefore the praise comes last (2:38).

These parallels contribute to the meaning of the message when the audience of the speeches is noted. This observation would not gain its strength as a message from God if it were not for the strong textual/literary correlations of parallelism.

Zechariah and Elizabeth	*Mary and Joseph*
Parents spoke (1:42–45, 67–79)	Prophets Simeon and Anna spoke (2:28–32, 34–35, 38)
People responded (1:58)	Parents responded (2:33)
Speeches were for the benefit of the people	Speeches were for the benefit of the parents

In these speeches a polarization occurs. When Zechariah spoke, Luke was presenting the parents as the "actors." But in the parallel with Joseph and Mary the parents were not the "actors"; instead, the prophets were. The speeches of Zechariah and Elizabeth were for the benefit of the multitudes,

19. Again it is significant that the meanings of these Hebrew names contribute to the message. John means "Yahweh is gracious," and Jesus means "Yahweh saves." The gracious God who remembers his covenant (Zechariah, Elizabeth) was now moving to save his people.

20. Though the speeches occurred at different times—Zechariah's at Jesus' circumcision (1:59) and that of Simeon and Anna forty days later at Jesus' dedication in the temple—the content and placement within Luke's narrative suggest that they should be placed together in thought.

whereas the speeches to Mary and Joseph were for the benefit of the parents. Zechariah spoke of God as the One who cares for the people, the nation, and the multitudes (1:68–79), but the prophets spoke of God as the One who cares for individuals, namely, his servants, the parents. As God's servants, they had a difficult path to walk (2:34–36), and they could not possibly speak for God unless they also had some sense of what God was doing in their own lives. Therefore, God tailored these words for the sake of Mary and Joseph to help them in their task as they reared the Messiah. Perhaps this would also help serve Luke's intent for Theophilus (1:4).

Conclusion

Message-units in Luke's Gospel are often defined and clarified through the logic of literary connectives. A literary analysis defines the message-units in the birth announcements in the following ways. Luke 1:5–2:52 forms a major unit in the Gospel; the technique of balance places individual paragraphs alongside each other to extend their boundaries into larger units of comparison; and the role of problematic units (e.g., Elizabeth's response and the circumcision of John) is clarified.

A literary analysis also clarifies the message-units in the birth announcements in the following ways. Through comparing the historical settings that introduce each actor, God is seen working in space and time for all people; by comparing the responses of Zechariah and Mary to Gabriel's announcement, the sign on Zechariah may be understood as a sign of affirmation rather than condemnation; in the responses to Gabriel, Elizabeth can be seen as representing all who do not experience supernatural encounters but nevertheless respond appropriately; by observing the responses of Zechariah and Mary to the angel's message, Luke's meaning crystallizes—the servant of God is not necessarily one who functions in that role, but one who receives the Word of God; by comparing the speeches of Elizabeth, Mary, and Zechariah it becomes evident that the one who once spurned the Word of God grew in his understanding and graciously became the most articulate and complete spokesperson for what the Lord was doing in the events; and through comparing the speeches given at the circumcision and dedication of the two children, God is seen as the One who not only cares for his people corporately, but is also concerned for his people individually.

A literary approach is not the only exegetical technique necessary for the interpreter to understand Luke's presentation of the birth narratives. However, it is evident that a literary approach that follows the contour of Luke's narrative logic is a necessary step for the exegete in identifying and understanding the message-units in Luke's Gospel. When this approach is limited to a theological or thematic purpose, the message of Luke may be *mis*understood. However, when the narrative logic is allowed to speak, subtle but crucial elements spring forth as a genuine portion of the message.

Tribute

Dr. Donald K. Campbell has distinguished himself in my eyes not only as a biblical scholar but also as a gifted servant of God who has a rare ability to weave the narratives of Scripture deep into a person's soul. It is my privilege to dedicate this literary evaluation of the birth stories in Luke to a godly man through whom God continues to weave his story as he did through Zechariah, Elizabeth, Mary, and Joseph.

How Jesus Responded
to Questions

Roy B. Zuck

Questions provide one of the most important means by which teachers can involve students of all ages in the teaching-learning process. Questions can arouse student interest and curiosity, lead students to think more clearly about a subject, stimulate discussion, help teachers ascertain what students know, obtain student opinions, guide learners to new facts or ideas, encourage students to express themselves, correct students' misconceptions, clarify issues, present proofs or arguments, and exhort students to action.

More than eighty years ago DeGarmo wrote, "In the skillful use of the question more than anything else lies the fine art of teaching; for in such use we have the guide to clear and vivid ideas, the quick spur to imagination, the stimulus to thought, the incentive to action."[1] Skillful teachers work at using questions effectively.

However, research reveals that questions teachers ask do not always require thoughtful answers. H. C. Haynes found in 1935 that only 17 percent of teachers' questions in sixth-grade history classes required students to think. In 1940 S. M. Corey discovered that only 21 percent of the questions asked by high school teachers called for thoughtful answers. Only 20 percent of questions asked by elementary school teachers in 1960 required thoughtful responses, as reported by W. D. Floyd. J. J. Gallagher in 1965, O. L. Davis and D. C. Tinsley in 1967, and R. T. Pate and N. H. Bremer in 1967 found similar results.[2] Gall states that the findings in these studies on teachers' questions show that "about 60% of teachers' questions require students to recall facts; about 20% require students to think; and the remaining 20% are procedural."[3]

1. Charles DeGarmo, *Interest and Education* (New York: Macmillan, 1911), p. 179.
2. These findings are reported in Owen D. W. Hargie, "The Importance of Teacher Questions in the Classroom," *Educational Research* 20 (1978): 99–102; and Meredith D. Gall, "The Use of Questions in Teaching," *Review of Educational Research* 40 (December 1970): 712.
3. Gall, "Use of Questions in Teaching," p. 713. Also see James Weilgand, ed., *Developing Teacher Competencies* (Englewood Cliffs, N.J.: Prentice-Hall, 1971), p. 85.

Jesus' Use of Questions

Jesus asked numerous questions of his disciples and his opponents.[4] But in contrast to the findings in the above-mentioned research studies, only a handful of Jesus' questions were simply for purposes of recall.[5] His questions made people think, encouraged their response, and pierced their consciences, thus demonstrating his skill as the Master Teacher.[6] Christian teachers today can gain insight on ways to improve their own use of questions by studying the ways Jesus used the questioning method. Reeser presents twenty-eight ways Jesus used questions.[7] Fortosis suggests the following eight purposes of Jesus' questions: (1) to stimulate interest or form a point of contact, (2) to initiate thinking, (3) to verbalize the thinking process, (4) to test spiritual understanding or commitment, (5) to help learners apply truth, (6) to employ

4. Writers differ on the number of questions Jesus asked. Gibbons says the number is 110 (Joan Lyon Gibbons, "A Psychological Exploration of Jesus' Use of Questions as an Interpersonal Mode of Communication" [Ph.D. diss., Graduate Theological Union, Berkeley, Calif., 1979], pp. 1133–41a. Benson stated that Jesus asked more than 100 questions (Clarence Benson, *The Christian Teacher* [Chicago: Moody, 1940]), and Reeser claims Jesus used more than 200 questions (LaVerne Roy Reeser, "Jesus' Use of the Question in His Teaching Ministry" [M.R.E. thesis, Talbot Theological Seminary, 1968], p. 1). Another writer said the Gospels record 310 questions asked by Jesus, with 227 of them occurring only once (Norman Detlav Sorensen, "How Christ Used Questions" [Th.M. thesis, Dallas Theological Seminary, 1953], p. 45). I have found 225 *separate* questions (in the NIV). Because some of the same questions are cited by more than one Gospel writer, the total number of *recorded* questions is 304.

5. "Have you never read . . . ?" "What did Moses command you . . . ?" "Is it not written . . . ?" are questions in which Jesus asked his hearers to recall facts (Lilas D. Dixon, *How Jesus Taught* [Croydon, NSW: Sydney Missionary and Bible College, 1977], pp. 32–33).

6. That Jesus was a teacher is evident from the content he communicated, the variety of ways he communicated that content and involved students, and the fact that he was called "teacher" *(didaskalos)* by his disciples (Mark 4:38; Luke 7:40; 21:7; John 13:13–14), teachers of the law (Matt. 8:19; Luke 20:39), the Pharisees (Matt. 9:11; 12:38; 22:36; Mark 12:32; Luke 19:39; John 8:4), a Pharisee named Simon (Luke 7:40), an unnamed person from Jairus' house (Luke 8:49), tax collectors (Matt. 17:24), a father of a demon-possessed boy (Mark 9:17), John (Mark 9:38), a rich young man (Mark 10:17, 20), James and John (Mark 10:35), the Pharisees and Herodians (Matt. 22:16), the Sadducees (Matt. 22:23), a Pharisee (Luke 11:45), one of the disciples (Mark 13:1), someone in a crowd (Luke 12:13), and Martha (John 11:28). Several called Jesus "Rabbi," including Andrew and another disciple (John 1:38), Nathaniel (John 1:49), Nicodemus (John 3:2), Peter (Mark 9:5), the crowd (John 6:25), his disciples (John 11:8), Judas (Matt. 26:25, 49), and Mary (John 20:16). Four times Jesus referred to himself as the teacher (Matt. 23:10, in which he used a word, *kathēgētēs*, that occurs only here in the New Testament; Matt. 26:18; Mark 14:14; John 13:13–14). Because of his skill as a teacher people were amazed (Matt. 7:28; 22:23; Mark 1:22; Luke 4:32), and enjoyed listening to him (Mark 12:37), and his opponents said his teaching stirred up the people (Luke 23:5).

For works on Jesus as a teacher, see Dixon, *How Jesus Taught;* Matt Friedeman, *The Master Plan of Teaching* (Wheaton, Ill.: Victor, 1990); Herman Harrell Horne, *Jesus—The Master Teacher* (1920; reprint, Grand Rapids: Kregel, 1982); Claude C. Jones, *The Teaching Methods of the Master* (St. Louis: Bethany, 1957); Edward Kuhlman, *Master Teacher* (Old Tappan, N.J.: Revell, 1987); J. M. Price, *Jesus the Teacher* (Nashville: Sunday School Board, 1946); Robert H. Stein, *The Method and Message of Jesus' Teachings* (Philadelphia: Westminster, 1978); Clifford A. Wilson, *Jesus the Master Teacher* (Grand Rapids: Baker, 1974); and Roy B. Zuck, *Teaching as Jesus Taught* (Grand Rapids: Baker, forthcoming).

7. Reeser, "Jesus' Use of the Question in His Teaching Ministry," pp. 43–54.

disputation, argumentation, or logic, (7) to rebuke or point up spiritual inadequacy, and (8) to introduce a teaching.[8] Gibbons groups Jesus' questions in eight categories: (1) questions that locate an opposite, (2) questions that introduce a comparison, (3) questions that introduce the first half of a comparison, (4) questions that introduce the second half of a comparison, (5) questions that call on the hearer's experience in evoking a known side of a comparison, (6) questions that call on the religious tradition side of a comparison, (7) questions that challenge what is done or evoke the opposite, and (8) questions that present a choice or decision.[9] Warren discusses Jesus' many questions and concludes that "with both groups and individuals Christ used questions to achieve the following purposes: to reprove, to teach, to involve, and to determine the quality of their faith. With groups Jesus used questions to achieve these purposes: to awaken morally, to expose publicly, to silence, and to guide thought."[10]

Many of the Lord's questions engendered a verbal response, whereas other questions, which were rhetorical, anticipated an inner response of mind and heart. He asked questions not to test his hearers' memory of facts but to impress on them the importance and implications of truths and to impact their lives with those truths. Each question was aimed "to produce an effect."[11] It is interesting to compare Jesus' use of questions with the levels of questions suggested by Sanders, who discusses eight levels of classroom questions. Beginning with the lowest level, these categories are memory (factual recall), translation (restating information), interpretation (discerning relationships), application (applying learned facts to a new situation), analysis (identifying parts of a problem to see how they are similar or different), synthesis (putting together several elements to create a new communication), and evaluation (making value judgments).[12] These are adapted from Bloom's taxonomy of seven levels of thought,[13] except that Bloom's first level is "knowledge" and his second level is "comprehension" (basic understanding), which Sanders divided into "translation" and "interpretation."

Questions Addressed to Jesus

Teaching effectiveness can be measured not only by evaluating the kinds of questions teachers ask, but also by noting the questions students ask.

8. Stephen G. Fortosis, "Can Questioning Make Religious Educators More Effective in the Classroom?" *Christian Education Journal* 12 (Spring 1992): 92–97.

9. Gibbons, "Psychological Exploration of Jesus' Use of Questions as an Interpersonal Mode of Communication," pp. 1133–41a.

10. David Glenn Warren, "Christ's Use of Questions and Attention Getters" (M.A.B.S. thesis, Dallas Theological Seminary, 1978), p. 80.

11. Stein, "Method and Message of Jesus' Teachings," p. 24.

12. Norris M. Sanders, *Classroom Questions: What Kinds?* (New York: Harper and Row, 1966).

13. Benjamin S. Bloom, *Taxonomy of Educational Objectives* (New York: Longman and Green, 1956).

What kinds of questions do students ask? What kinds of questions should they be encouraged to ask? How can teachers encourage students to ask questions? How should teachers respond to student questions?

These questions call for more extensive research in education.[14] In addition, less study seems to have been made of Jesus' responses to questions addressed to him than to the questions he asked. A study of questions addressed to him and how he responded to them can help teachers today improve their own responses to students' verbal inquiries in class.

How many questions were addressed by individuals and groups to Jesus? Gibbons lists forty-one.[15] However, I have noted 103 questions addressed to Jesus. (See the chart at the end of this chapter.)

The fact that twenty individuals and twelve groups asked Jesus questions reveals how his teaching and his presence stimulated thought and interaction. Each of the following individuals asked one question each: his mother Mary, Nathaniel, Andrew, Martha, a healed blind man, an unnamed person, Judas Iscariot, Thomas, Judas (not Judas Iscariot), a thief on the cross, and Cleopas. Those who asked more than one question include John the Baptist (two questions), Nicodemus (two), the Samaritan woman (two), the high priest (two), an expert in the law (three), a rich young man (three), demons (two questions on each of two occasions), Pilate (nine), and Peter (nine). The fact that Peter asked nine questions of Jesus points to his inquisitive, loquacious nature, and Pilate's nine questions point to his frustration in whether to condemn Jesus or free him.

Of the groups who queried Jesus, his disciples posed seventeen questions. This is not surprising since he spent an extensive amount of time with them. Other follower groups, each of whom asked one question, included Andrew and another disciple; John's disciples; Peter, James, and John; and James and John. Enemies who interrogated him were the Jews (nine questions), the Pharisees (six questions), Pharisees and the teachers of the law (two), chief priests and elders (two), Pharisees and Herodians (two). In addition, the "crowd" asked him five questions. The chief priests and teachers of the law, and the Sadducees each asked him one question.

A variety of kinds of questions were addressed to the Lord. I have noted twelve kinds, with a few questions taking on more than one characteristic.[16]

14. Gall, "Use of Questions in Teaching," pp. 715–16.

15. Gibbons, "Psychological Exploration of Jesus' Use of Questions as Interpersonal Mode of Communication," 1158–63. Actually her list includes forty-seven, but six of them are questions *about* Jesus addressed to others.

16. In the chart at the end of this chapter, questions numbered 4 and 6 seem to be examples of questions containing two elements. Nathaniel's query to Jesus, "How do you know me?" (John 1:48) seems to reflect a desire for knowledge on how Jesus could have known Nathaniel before having met him and also reflects the emotion of surprise. In asking Jesus how he could restore Herod's temple in three days when it had already been under construction for forty-six years, the Jews seemed to be expressing confusion as to how he could do it and also denial that it was possible.

The largest group of questions were requests for information. These total thirty-nine. The next group, a total of twenty-one, include expressions of confusion (or implied requests for clarification). Others were expressions of denial (nine), challenge (eight), trickery (seven), expressions of anxiety (seven), requests for confirmation (three), surprise (three), requests for directives (three), expressions of rebuke (two), and one each of mockery and sarcasm.

Many of the requests for information came in response to Jesus' teaching, thus demonstrating that his teaching stimulated his hearers' interest and prodded them to think about what he said and to inquire further about what he meant. Twice the Jews who heard him were led to ask, "Who are you?" (John 8:25, 53). Hearing Jesus' comments about salvation after the rich young man refused to follow Jesus, Peter asked what benefit would come to those who did follow him (Matt. 19:27). After Jesus spoke of the stones of the temple being thrown down, the disciples wanted to know when it would happen (Matt. 24:3). They asked Jesus a similar question as he was teaching them just before he ascended (Acts 1:6). Jesus' comments about his betrayal led Peter to ask who would commit this act (John 13:25). When Jesus said he was going where the disciples could not go, Peter was prompted to ask where Jesus was going (John 13:36).

Because of their spiritual ignorance or insensitivity, those who heard Jesus did not always understand. However, though confused, they did not hesitate to express their confusion or to request an explanation or clarification. This was true of the Jews, who asked about Jesus' remarks about destroying the temple (John 2:20), of Nicodemus, who was confused about Jesus' comments about a second birth (3:4, 9), of the Samaritan woman in her confusion about physical and "living" water (4:9, 11), of the disciples who were confused about how to secure enough bread for five thousand men (Mark 6:37) and four thousand men (Matt. 15:33), and of Peter, who wondered about the application of a parable (Luke 12:41). Jesus' disciples wondered who could be saved (Matt. 19:25); they wondered about the quick withering of the fig tree (21:20); and in the Upper Room Discourse, Peter, Thomas, and Judas (not Iscariot) each asked Jesus a question for clarification (John 13:37; 14:5, 22).

Questions expressing anxiety were voiced by Jesus' mother when he was twelve (Luke 2:48), by demons when Jesus approached demoniacs (Matt. 8:29; Mark 1:24), and by the disciples who feared they would drown (Mark 4:38). Some questions addressed to Jesus were actually denials, as in the Samaritan woman's question, "Are you greater than . . . Jacob?" (John 4:12), in which she was presumably affirming that Jesus was *not* greater than Jacob. The Jews' similar question, "Are you greater than our father Abraham?" (John 8:53), also was a way of their denying that he surpassed Abraham in greatness. Similarly when they asked, "Have you seen Abraham?" (John 8:57), they were denying this possibility.

Some interrogations directed to the Lord were efforts to trick him by forcing him to take one or two views, either of which would pose a problem for him. By the question, "Is it lawful to heal on the Sabbath?" (Matt. 12:10), the Pharisees hoped to place Jesus in a dilemma. If he responded that it was lawful to heal on the Sabbath, they could then accuse him of violating the Mosaic law by working on the Sabbath. On the other hand, if he said it was unlawful, then he would be unable to restore to wholeness the man's withered hand.

Two questions about the law and divorce were voiced by Pharisees in Matthew 19:3, 7. With both questions they hoped to force Jesus to take one of two positions, either of which would mean some people would agree with him and others would disagree. The two questions about paying taxes to Caesar (Matt. 22:17), which were asked by the Pharisees and the Herodians together, were again designed to trick Jesus. If he denied the need to pay taxes, he would be stating disloyalty to Caesar, and would be offending the Herodians. Of if he affirmed the need to pay taxes, he would seemingly be siding with the Romans against Israel, which would offend the Pharisees and would deny his own right to kingship. Their intent was "evil," as Matthew noted (v. 18).

Another group, the Sadducees, also tried to trick Jesus with a question, by asking which of several brothers in the resurrection would be the husband of a woman who had married each of them (Matt. 22:28). The Sadducees, who denied the resurrection, hoped to present a situation Jesus could not answer successfully. The Pharisees then tried to trap him with a question by one of their experts: "Which is the greatest commandment in the Law?" (22:36). They hoped that his answer would demean whichever commandments were not cited, so that they could accuse him of denigrating much of the law.

Questions of challenge were voiced by those who were not followers of Jesus. The Pharisees challenged Jesus by a question on why his disciples were violating the Sabbath (Mark 2:24), and why they broke tradition by neglecting ceremonial washings (Matt. 15:2). On another occasion, when Jesus stated that two witnesses, himself and his Father, supported his testimony, the Pharisees challenged him to show them who his Father was. They asked, "Where is your father?" (John 8:19). They hoped to discredit his second witness by his inability to show them the One who they thought was his earthly father.

The question, "By what authority are you doing these things?" (Matt. 21:23), which the chief priests and elders asked of Jesus, was a challenge for him to declare the basis of the authority by which he taught and acted.

When Jesus was on trial before Caiaphas the high priest, he refused to answer two anonymous accusers. Disturbed, the priest stood up and asked, "Are you not going to answer?" (Matt. 26:62). This was a challenge for Jesus to respond. Later when standing before Pilate, Jesus refused to answer some of his questions also. His silence frustrated Pilate, so that he challenged Jesus:

"Do you refuse to speak to me? Don't you realize I have power either to free you or to crucify you?" (John 19:10). One of the two criminals crucified with Jesus challenged him by asking, "Aren't you the Christ? Save yourself and us!" (Luke 23:39).

Four times the Jews, enemies of Jesus, asked him to confirm what he was doing. On two occasions, with three questions, they requested a confirming miraculous sign (John 2:18; 6:30 [two questions]) so they could believe, and once they harshly accused him of being a demon-possessed Samaritan and asked him to confirm the truth of their accusation (John 8:48).

Surprise was expressed in the questions presented by Nathaniel (John 1:48), by Peter in the Upper Room (John 13:6), and by Cleopas on the Emmaus Road (Luke 24:18).

When Jesus approached Peter to wash his feet, Peter responded in surprise. "Lord, are you going to wash my feet?" (John 13:6). Apparently Peter felt this was inappropriate for Jesus. In Greek, Peter's sentence stresses the words "you" and "my"—"Lord, *you* are going to wash *my* feet?"—thereby expressing surprise.

Three times Jesus' disciples asked him for a directive on what to do. James and John wanted to know if he desired them to call down fire from heaven to destroy the Samaritan village where people had rejected him (Luke 9:52). One wonders how they thought they had the power to perform such a miracle. A similar inquiry in the face of opposition was made by his disciples when Jesus was being arrested: "Lord, should we strike with our swords?" (Luke 22:49). The other request for a directive from the Lord was their question about where they should prepare to share the Passover (Matt. 26:17).

Martha expressed a question of rebuke when she asked Jesus if he was concerned that Mary had left Martha to do all the housework herself (Luke 10:40). Another question of rebuke was stated by the chief priests and teachers of the law when children were praising Jesus in the temple area: "Do you hear what these children are saying?" (Matt. 21:16). They seemed to have been accusing them of their disturbing words and rebuking him for not chiding the children.

Mockery is seen in the Jews' question, "Who hit you?" when people slapped Jesus on the face at his trial (Matt. 26:68). Sarcasm may have been present in Pilate's response to Jesus, "Do you think I am a Jew?" (John 18:35).

When teachers today are presenting challenging content, they can expect students to respond with requests for further information. Other responses may reflect confusion or the desire for clarification. Still, other responses may occasionally be those of surprise, requests for a directive, requests for confirmation, or even expressions of anxiety. Occasionally what a teacher is presenting may be met with student questions that present a challenge to what he or she is teaching. Sometimes a student may even deny what is being taught. Some kinds of questions, however, may be considered unique to Jesus and his ministry. These would include questions expressing trickery, mockery, and sarcasm.

As teachers become aware of the kinds of questions they may expect from their students, they can be better prepared for their teaching tasks. In addition, they should seek to teach in such a way that students will be encouraged to ask for further information and for points of clarification.

Jesus' Answers to Questions Asked of Him

The Lord Jesus responded to questions in a great variety of ways. He was always eager to respond, and never refused to interact with his inquirers except when addressed by Caiaphas (Matt. 26:62), the Jews on one occasion (Matt. 26:68), Pilate (Matt. 27:13; John 18:38; 19:9—Jesus answered some of Pilate's questions but not others), and the thief on the cross (Luke 23:39). Also Herod plied Jesus "with many questions," but "Jesus gave him no answer" (Luke 23:9). As Barnard wrote:

> Very striking are those instances where the silence of Jesus was more eloquent than words could have been. It was useless to attempt any answer to the charges of witnesses brought against Him before judges who had procured their false evidence (Mk 14^{61} = Mt 26^{63}), or to similar charges before Pilate (Mk 15^5 = Mt 27^{14}) and Herod (Lk 23^9); it was useless to discuss with such a man as Pilate the nature of truth (Jn 18^{38}), or His heavenly mission (Jn 19^9). Only when such questions are asked in a right spirit is it worth answering them. When Pilate asked Him (Mk 15^2 = Mt 27^{11} = Lk 23^3, cf. Jn 18^{57}) whether He was "the King of the Jews," He gave an ambiguous answer—"Thou sayest": it was a title He himself had not claimed, and which belonged to Him only in a sense that Pilate could not understand. But Christ did not hesitate, in spite of the obvious danger, to give direct answers to questions concerning His own claims (Mk 14^{62} = Mt 26^{64}, cf. Lk 22^{70}).[17]

Jesus gave explanations in response to questions by John the Baptist; Nicodemus; John's disciples; his disciples; Peter, James, and John; the crowd; the Jews; Martha; the Pharisees; a rich young man; Peter; the Pharisees and the Herodians; the Sadducees; and an expert in the law.

Many times Jesus responded to a question with a question of his own. This is true of his reply to the first recorded question addressed to him. When his mother asked why he had stayed behind in the temple, twelve-year-old Jesus answered her with two questions: "Why were you searching for me? . . . Didn't you know I had to be in my Father's house?" (Luke 2:49). His parents, though, did not understand what he meant. He also voiced questions to

---

17. *Dictionary of Christ and the Gospels*, 1909 ed., s.v. "Questions and Answers," by P. M. Barnard, p. 462.

Nicodemus (John 3:10, 12), John's disciples (Matt. 9:15), the Pharisees (Matt. 12:11; 19:4), the disciples in the storm (Mark 4:40), the disciples with the five thousand (Mark 6:38) and the four thousand to be fed (Matt. 15:34), Peter (Luke 12:42; John 6:70; 21:22), an expert in the law who asked what he must do to inherit eternal life (Luke 10:26), the rich young man (Matt. 19:17), the chief priests and teachers of the law (Matt. 21:16), the chief priest and elders (Matt. 21:25), Pilate (John 18:34), and Cleopas (Luke 24:19). These counterquestions prompted his interrogators to think through the answers to their own questions or even to ask further questions.

When individuals requested information, Jesus always gave the facts they needed. This is seen in his responses to Andrew's question about where Jesus was staying (John 1:38), Nathaniel's question about how Jesus knew him (John 1:48), Peter's question about how many times to forgive (Matt. 18:21), the healed blind man's question about who Jesus was (John 9:36), the rich young man's question about which commandment to obey and what he still lacked (Matt. 19:18, 20), his disciples' questions about the sign of his coming (Matt. 24:3), their question about where to make preparations for the Passover (Matt. 26:17), and their questions about who would betray him (Matt. 26:22, 25; John 13:25).

Some questions, however, Jesus evaded or answered indirectly. Instead of answering them directly he answered in other ways. When the Pharisees asked, "Where is your father?" (John 8:19), he answered by stating, "You do not know me or my Father." After Jesus spoke of his return, when some would be taken with him and others would be left, his disciples asked, "Where, Lord?" (Luke 17:37), that is, "Where will they be taken?" Jesus replied somewhat enigmatically, "Where there is a dead body, there the vultures will gather." The idea in that response seems to be that much as a dead body inevitably results in vultures gathering around it, so dead people will certainly be confined to judgment if they are not ready for the Lord's return.

When the crowd asked Jesus about his statements that the Son of Man would be lifted up (John 12:34), he did not answer their question. Instead, he encouraged them to "trust in the light" (v. 36). He pressed on to their real need. Without telling specifically how he could wither a fig tree so quickly (Matt. 21:20), Jesus told the disciples that by exercising faith great things can be accomplished (v. 22).

Jesus cleverly avoided answering the question the chief priest and elders asked about his source of authority (Matt. 21:23) by asking them about the source of John the Baptist's authority (vv. 24–27). When Peter expressed surprise that Jesus was about to wash his feet (John 13:6), Jesus explained that later Peter would realize the significance of what he was about to do (v. 7). Nor did Jesus answer Peter's question about where he was going (v. 36). When Pilate queried, "Are you the king of the Jews?" (18:33), again Jesus did not answer the question but instead asked if that was Pilate's own idea

(v. 34). And when Pilate responded, "Do you think I am a Jew?" (v. 35), Jesus did not answer that question either. He replied, "My kingdom is not of this world" (v. 36).

To Thomas's direct question, "How can we know the way?" (John 14:5), that is, where Jesus was going, the Lord answered him indirectly but with an affirmation: "I am the way, the truth, and the life" (v. 6). And when Judas (not Judas Iscariot) asked for a reason why Jesus said he would show himself to them and not to the world (v. 22), Jesus responded indirectly. Instead of giving a reason, he emphasized that individuals who love him will be obedient to him (vv. 23–24), implying that the world does not love or obey him.

Sometimes Jesus' response to questions was in the form of a rebuke. This is true of his response to demons (Matt. 8:32; Mark 1:25), to the disciples in the storm (Mark 4:40), to James and John who asked about calling down fire from heaven (Luke 9:55), to the crowd who accused him of being demon-possessed (John 7:20) when he asked them why they were angry for his healing on the Sabbath (v. 23), to the chief priests and teachers of the law who asked him if he heard what the children were saying when they were praising him (Matt. 21:16), and when he asked if they had never read Psalm 8:2. He also rebuked the Pharisees and the Herodians by calling them hypocrites when they asked about taxes to Caesar (Matt. 22:18). The Lord also rebuked Peter (John 21:22) when the apostle asked about John.

A few times Jesus corrected the false teaching of his questioners. He pointed out to the Pharisees that Moses permitted divorce but did not command it as they had said (Matt. 19:7–8). The Sadducees' denial of the resurrection was corrected by Jesus' response to their query about marriage in the resurrected life (22:29–32). When on trial before Pilate, Jesus corrected Pilate's false assumption that he had power to release or crucify Jesus (John 19:10–11).

Occasionally Jesus found it necessary to give negative answers to his inquirers' questions. When the Jews asked him if he was a demon-possessed Samaritan, he simply replied, "I am not demon-possessed" (John 8:48–49). Then he used that occasion to point out the difference between those who do not honor him and those who do keep his word (vv. 49–50). When Peter asked, "Why can't I follow you now?" and affirmed, "I will lay down my life for you" (13:37), Jesus negated Peter's supposed readiness to die for him by asking, "Will you really lay down your life for me?" (v. 38). At his ascension when the disciples wanted to know if he would restore the kingdom to Israel then (Acts 1:6), Jesus simply told them he could not inform them of the time (v. 7). He then proceeded to disclose a truth of greater importance to them at that time, namely, the fact that they would receive spiritual power from the Holy Spirit on the day of Pentecost (v. 8).

Questions from his audiences also gave Jesus opportunity to teach in parables. He did this on at least four occasions. When John's disciples wondered why Jesus' disciples did not fast (Matt. 9:14), he spoke in parabolic statements about old garments and new cloth and old wineskins and new wine (vv. 16–17). Jesus' parable of the unforgiving servant (Matt. 18:23–35) followed Peter's question about the number of times one should forgive others (v. 22). The well-known parable of the good Samaritan (Luke 10:30–36) was given in response to the question of the expert in the law, "Who is my neighbor?" (v. 29).

Jesus' replies to questions included affirmations of truth. "How much more valuable is a man than a sheep!" (Matt. 12:12), was his reply to the Pharisees' question about healing on the Sabbath. In response to Pilate's question to Jesus, "Do you think I am a Jew?" Jesus affirmed, "My kingdom is not of this world" (John 18:35). And in response to Peter's query, "What then will there be for us?" (Matt. 19:27), the Lord said, "Many who are first will be last, and many who are last will be first" (v. 30).

Queries addressed to Jesus gave him opportunity to challenge his interrogators to action. When the crowd asked when Jesus had arrived at Capernaum (John 6:25), he ignored the question and used the occasion to challenge them to "work . . . for food that endures to eternal life" (v. 27), rather than follow him for the sake of material food. When the disciples asked, "Who is the greatest in the kingdom of heaven?" (Matt. 18:1), he challenged them to be humble, to become like little children (v. 3). A rich young man who asked, "What do I still lack?" (Matt. 19:20), was challenged to sell his possessions and to follow Jesus (v. 21). When the crowed asked about Jesus being lifted up as the Son of Man (John 12:34), he challenged the people to trust in him, the Light (v. 36).

On fifteen occasions the responses of the questioners to Jesus' answers included additional questions. These were asked by Nicodemus (John 3:9), the Samaritan woman (John 4:11), Jesus' disciples (Mark 4:41), the crowd at Capernaum (John 6:28, 30), the Jews (John 8:53), the Pharisees (Matt. 19:7), the rich young man (Matt. 19:18, 20), Peter (John 13:25, 36–37), Judas (Matt. 26:25), Caiaphas (Mark 14:61), and Pilate (John 18:35; 19:10).

Implications

A number of implications for teachers today can be drawn from this study of the scores of questions addressed to Jesus and how he responded to them:

1. Teachers should be open to students' questions and should give them thoughtful, appropriate answers. Jesus never called any questions foolish or unnecessary.
2. Teachers should teach in such a way that students are stimulated to think about the content and to ask questions about the material communicated.

3. Teachers should recognize the variety of kinds of questions students may ask. Students may want additional information; they may desire clarification; they may even express anxiety or surprise.

4. Teachers should respond to students' questions with attentiveness and give appropriate answers with explanations and clarifications. Some questions, however, may call for indirect answers or for correction of false concepts, for additional questions, for additional teaching (by way of truths or illustrations of truths), or for challenges to action.

As Fortosis wrote, "When students are posing questions freely in the classroom, it is usually a very positive sign. It suggests that there is a relaxed atmosphere and an accepting attitude on the part of the instructor. It also suggests that students are motivated to learn more about the subject matter."[18]

Students' questions and teachers' responses to them comprise a highly significant element in the teaching-learning classroom. Teachers do well to learn from Jesus how to stimulate and respond to questions.

Tribute

I have been privileged to work closely with Dr. Campbell for almost two decades, as his assistant academic dean and associate academic dean. Then when he was appointed president of Dallas Seminary and I was academic dean, we continued to work closely together.

I know him as a man of wisdom, integrity, administrative skill, love for the Lord and his Word, and genuine concern for others. The Lord has used him greatly in these forty years of administrative leadership and faculty service at the seminary.

With deep personal appreciation I dedicate this chapter—and this book— to one who, like Jesus Christ, knows how to ask and answer questions with honesty, gentleness, and godliness.

18. Fortosis, "Can Questioning Make Religious Educators More Effective in the Classroom?" p. 100.

Questions Addressed to Jesus and His Responses

Passage*	Person(s) Who Asked	Question	Kind of Question or Problem	Place	Jesus' Answer	Kind of Answer by Jesus	Immediate Response of the Questioner(s)
1. Luke 2:48	Mary, Jesus' mother	"Son, why have you treated us like this?"	Anxiety	Temple in Jerusalem among the teachers	"Why were you searching for me? Didn't you know I had to be in my Father's house?"	Explanation	Mary and Joseph did not understand his response
2. Matthew 3:14	John the Baptist	"I need to be baptized by you, and do you come to me?"	Expression of confusion	Jordan River	"It is proper for us to do this to fulfill all righteousness."	Explanation	John consented to baptize Jesus.
3. John 1:38	Andrew and another disciple	"Rabbi, where are you staying?"	Request for information	Bethany beyond the Jordan River	"Come, and you will see."	Information	They went with him.
4. John 1:48	Nathanael	"How do you know me?"	Request for information; surprise	Galilee	"I saw you while you were still under the fig tree before Philip saw you."	Information	Nathanael said Jesus was the Son of God and the King of Israel.
5. John 2:18	Jews	"What miraculous sign can you show us to prove your authority to do all this?"	Request for confirmation	Temple in Jerusalem	"Destroy this temple and I will raise it again in three days."	Enigmatic statement	They misunderstood what he was referring to.
6. John 2:20	Jews	"It took forty-six years to build this temple, and you will raise it up in three days?"	Expression of confusion; denial	Temple in Jerusalem	None (apparently he left them confused).	None	None recorded

* The passages are listed in chronological order. The references in parentheses are parallel passages, though the wording often differs from one Gospel to another.

Reference	Person	Question/Statement	Type	Location	Jesus' Response	Response Type	Result
7. John 3:4	Nicodemus	"How can a man be born when he is old?"	Expression of confusion	With Jesus at night	Jesus explained that he was speaking of spiritual rebirth.	Explanation	Nicodemus asked a second question, again reflecting confusion.
8. John 3:9	Nicodemus	"How can this be?"	Expression of confusion	With Jesus at night	Jesus expanded on the way of salvation.	Two questions (vv. 10, 12) and further explanation	None recorded
9. John 4:9	Samaritan woman	"How can you ask me for a drink?"	Expression of confusion	Samaria	Jesus explained that if she knew who he was, she would have received "living water."	Explanation	She asked a second question, again reflecting confusion.
10–11. John 4:11–12	Samaritan woman	"Where can you get this living water? Are you greater than . . . Jacob?"	Expression of confusion; denial	Samaria	Jesus explained the meaning of living water.	Explanation	She requested water.
12–13. Mark 1:24 (Luke 4:34)	Demon	"What do you want with us, Jesus of Nazareth? Have you come to destroy us?"	Anxiety	Capernaum	"Be quiet!"	Rebuke	The demon departed.
14. Matthew 9:14 (Mark 2:18)	John's disciples	"Why do we and the Pharisees fast, but your disciples do not fast?"	Request for information	Capernaum	Jesus said that the bridegroom's attendants "cannot mourn as long as the bridegroom is with them, can they?" Then he said they will fast later, and he spoke of old garments and parabolically wineskins.	A question, an explanation, and parables	None recorded

Passage	Person(s) Who Asked	Question	Kind of Question or Problem	Place	Jesus' Answer	Kind of Answer by Jesus	Immediate Response of the Questioner(s)
15. Mark 2:24	Pharisees	"Look, why are they doing what is unlawful on the Sabbath?"	Challenge	Galilee	Jesus answered with a question and a quotation, and said, "The Sabbath was made for man, not man for the Sabbath."	A question, a quotation, and an explanation	None recorded
16. Matthew 12:10	Pharisees	"Is it lawful to heal on the Sabbath?"	Trickery	Galilean synagogue	Jesus asked if on the Sabbath they would lift a sheep out of a pit, and then said man is more valuable than sheep.	A question (by an illustration) and a statement of a truth	Pharisees discussed how to kill him.
17. Matthew 11:3 (Luke 7:20)	John the Baptist	"Are you the One who was to come, or should we expect someone else?"	Expression of confusion	Galilee	Jesus referred to his miracles.	Presentation of evidence by which they could draw a conclusion	None recorded
18. Matthew 13:10	Jesus' disciples	"Why do you speak to them in parables?"	Expression of confusion	In a boat by the shore of the Sea of Galilee	Jesus explained that parables enabled believers to comprehend further and parables further blinded unbelievers.	Explanation	None recorded
19. Mark 4:38	Jesus' disciples	"Teacher, don't you care if we drown?"	Anxiety	In a boat in the Sea of Galilee	Jesus calmed the storm and then rebuked them by asking, "Why are you so timid? How is it that you have no faith?"	Two questions of rebuke	Fear and confusion expressed by the question, "Who then is this?"

Reference	Who	Question	Type	Location	Jesus' Response	Response Type	Result
20–21. Matthew 8:29 (Mark 5:7; Luke 8:28)	Demons	"What do you want with us, Son of God? Have you come here to torment us before the appointed time?"	Anxiety	Gerasa	Jesus exorcised the demons.	None	The demons went out of the man and into pigs.
22. Mark 6:37	Jesus' disciples	"Are we to go and spend that much on bread and give it to them to eat?"	Expression of confusion	Bethsaida	"How many loaves do you have? Go and see."	A question and a directive	The disciples found five loaves and two fish.
23. John 6:9	Andrew	"Here is a boy with five small barley loaves and two small fish, but how far will they go among so many?"	Expression of confusion	Bethsaida	Jesus ignored the question, and told the disciples to have the people sit down.	Evasion of the question, and a directive	The disciples obeyed.
24. John 6:25	Crowd	"Rabbi, when did you get here?"	Request for information	Capernaum	Jesus ignored the question, and then encouraged them to do work of eternal significance.	Evasion of the question, and a challenge	They asked him another question.
25. John 6:28	Crowd	"What must we do to do the works God requires?"	Request for information	Capernaum	"The work of God is to do this: to believe in the One he has sent."	Explanation	They asked him a third question.
26–27. John 6:30	Crowd	"What miraculous sign then will you give that we may see it and believe you? What will you do?"	Request for confirmation	Capernaum	Jesus poke of himself as the "true bread form heaven," a sign already given by God the Father.	Explanation	They requested the true bread.
28. John 6:68	Peter	"Lord, to whom shall we go? You have the words of eternal life."	Request for information	Capernaum	Jesus asked, "Have I not chosen you, the Twelve? Yet one of you is a devil."	A question that evaded Peter's question	None recorded

Passage	Person(s) Who Asked	Question	Kind of Question or Problem	Place	Jesus' Answer	Kind of Answer by Jesus	Immediate Response of the Questioner(s)
29. Matthew 15:2 (Mark 7:5)	Pharisees and teachers of the law	"Why do your disciples break the tradition of the elders?"	Challenge	Gennesaret	Jesus asked, "And why do you break the command of God for the sake of your tradition?"	A question, a quotation, and denunciation	None recorded
30. Matthew 15:12	Jesus' disciples	"Do you know that the Pharisees were offended when they heard this?"	Request for information	Gennesaret	Jesus said that plants not planted by God will be pulled up and that the Pharisees should be left alone because they were blind guides.	Explanation by an illustration	Peter asked Jesus to explain the "parable."
31. Matthew 15:33 (Mark 8:4)	Jesus' disciples	"Where would we get enough bread in this remote place to feed such a crowd?"	Expression of confusion	By the Sea of Galilee	Jesus asked, "How many loaves do you have?"	A question	They commented that they had seven loaves of bread and a few small fish.
32. Matthew 17:10 (Mark 9:11)	Peter, James, and John	"Why then do the teachers of the law say that Elijah must come first?"	Expression of confusion	Mount of Transfiguration	Jesus explained that Elijah had already come.	Explanation	They understood that he was referring to John the Baptist.
33. Matthew 17:19 (Mark 9:28)	Jesus' disciples	"Why couldn't we drive it [a demon] out?"	Expression of confusion	Near the Mount of Transfiguration	"Because you have so little faith."	Explanation	None recorded
34. Matthew 18:1	Jesus' disciples	"Who is the greatest in the kingdom of heaven?"	Request for information	Capernaum	Placing a child among them, Jesus talked about humility and not causing children to sin.	Explanation and challenge by an illustration	None recorded

Reference	Speaker	Question	Type	Location	Jesus' Response	Response Type	Result
35–36. Matthew 18:21	Peter	"Lord, how many times shall I forgive my brother when he sins against me? Up to seven times?"	Request for information	Capernaum	Jesus said 490 times and then told the parable of the unforgiving servant.	Information and a parable	None recorded
37. Luke 9:54	James and John	"Lord, do you want us to call fire down from heaven to destroy them?"	Request for a directive	A Samaritan village	"Jesus turned and rebuked them."	Rebuke	None recorded
38. John 7:20	Crowd	"You are demon-possessed. Who is trying to kill you?"	Denial	Temple courts in Jerusalem	"Why are you angry with me for healing . . . on the Sabbath?"	Explanation and a rebuke by a question	Some doubted that he was Christ.
39. John 8:5	Teachers of the law and Pharisees	"In the law Moses commanded us to stone such women. Now what do you say?"	Trickery	Temple courts in Jerusalem	Jesus did not answer the question, but wrote on the ground.	Evasion of the question and a rebuke	They left, trapped by their own trap.
40. John 8:19	Pharisees	"Where is your father?"	Challenge	Temple courts in Jerusalem	"You do not know me or my Father."	Evasion of the question	None recorded
41. John 8:25	Jews	"Who are you?"	Request for information	Temple courts in Jerusalem	"Just what I have been claiming all along."	Evasion of the question	They did not understand.
42. John 8:33	Jews	"How can you say that we shall be set free?"	Denial	Temple courts in Jerusalem	"Everyone who sins is a slave to sin."	Explanation	They protested, "Abraham is our father."
43. John 8:48	Jews	"Aren't we right in saying that you are a Samaritan and are demon-possessed?"	Request for confirmation	Temple courts in Jerusalem	"I am not demon-possessed."	Denial	They affirmed, "Now we know you are demon-possessed," and they asked two other questions.

Passage	Person(s) Who Asked	Question	Kind of Question or Problem	Place	Jesus' Answer	Kind of Answer by Jesus	Immediate Response of the Questioner(s)
44–45. John 8:53	Jews	"Are you greater than our father Abraham? . . . Who do you think you are?"	Denial; request for information	Temple courts in Jerusalem	"My Father . . . . Abraham saw [my day] and was glad."	Explanation	They could not believe he was older than Abraham.
46. Luke 10:25	An expert in the law	"Teacher, what must I do to inherit eternal life?"	Request for information	Judea	"What is written in the Law? How do you read it?"	Two questions	The man quoted Leviticus 19:18.
47. Luke 10:29	An expert in the law	"And who is my neighbor?"	Request for information	Judea	Jesus gave the parable of the good Samaritan	A parable to illustrate who is one's neighbor.	None recorded
48. Luke 10:40	Martha	"Lord, don't you care that my sister has left me to do the work by myself?"	Rebuke	Bethany	Jesus said Mary had chosen what was better.	Explanation	None recorded
49. Luke 12:41	Peter	"Lord, are you telling this parable to us, or to everyone?"	Expression of confusion	Judea	"Who then is the faithful and wise manager?"	A question and information about a wise manager and his servants	None recorded
50. John 9:2	Jesus' disciples	"Rabbi, who sinned, this man or his parents, that he was born blind?"	Request for information	Jerusalem	Jesus said, "Neither," and then gave the reason for the man's blindness.	Explanation	None recorded
51. John 9:36	Healed blind man	"Who is he, sir?"	Request for information	Jerusalem	"You have now seen him."	Information	The man believed and worshiped Jesus.

Reference	Questioner	Question	Attitude	Location	Jesus' Response	Type of Response	Result
52–53. John 9:40	Pharisees	"What? Are we blind too?"	Surprise; denial	Judea	"If you were blind, you would not be guilty of sin; but now that you claim you can see, your guilt remains."	Enigmatic statement and rebuke	None recorded
54. John 10:24	Jews	"How long will you keep us in suspense? If you are the Christ, tell us plainly."	Request for information	Jerusalem	"I did tell you, but you do not believe. . . . I and the Father are one."	Explanation	The Jews started to stone him.
55. Luke 13:23	Someone	"Lord, are only a few people going to be saved?"	Request for information	Perea	Jesus gave an affirmative answer by speaking of few entering a narrow door.	Explanation by an illustration	None recorded
56. John 11:8	Jesus' disciples	"Rabbi, a short while ago the Jews tried to stone you, and yet you are going back there?"	Anxiety	Perea	Jesus asked, "Are there not twelve hours of daylight?" and then he said Lazarus was sleeping.	A question and an explanation	They were confused.
57. Luke 17:37	Jesus' disciples	"Where, Lord?"	Request for information	Between Samaria and Galilee	"Where there is a dead body, there the vultures will gather."	Indirect answer by an enigmatic statement	None recorded
58. Matthew 19:3 (Mark 10:2)	Pharisees	"Is it lawful for a man to divorce his wife for any and every reason?"	Trickery	Perea	Jesus asked, "Haven't you read . . . ?" and quoted Genesis 1:27 and 2:24 and affirmed the permanency of marriage.	A question and an explanation	They asked him another question.

Passage	Person(s) Who Asked	Question	Kind of Question or Problem	Place	Jesus' Answer	Kind of Answer by Jesus	Immediate Response of the Questioner(s)
59. Matthew 19:7	Pharisees	"Why then did Moses command that a man give his wife a certificate of divorce and send her away?"	Trickery	Perea	Jesus corrected them about Moses and again affirmed the permanence of marriage.	Correction and explanation	The disciples responded with a statement expressing confusion.
60. Matthew 19:16 (Mark 10:17; Luke 18:18)	A rich young man	"Teacher, what good thing must I do to get eternal life?"	Request for information	Perea	"Why do you ask me what is good? . . . Obey the commandments."	Information	The man asked which commandments he should obey.
61. Matthew 19:18	A rich young man	"Which ones?"	Request for information	Perea	Jesus stated six commandments.	Information	The man asked what he still lacked.
62. Matthew 19:20	A rich young man	"What do I still lack?"	Request for information	Perea	"Sell your possessions [and] follow me."	Information and challenge	The man went away sad.
63. Matthew 19:25 (Mark 10:26; Luke 18:26)	Jesus' disciples	"Who then can be saved?"	Expression of confusion	Perea	"With God all things are possible."	Explanation	Peter asked a question.
64. Matthew 19:27	Peter	"We have left everything to follow you. What then will there be for us?"	Request for information	Perea	"You who have followed me will also sit on twelve thrones. . . . Many who are last will be first."	Explanation and the parable of the vineyard workers	None recorded
65. Matthew 21:16	Chief priests and teachers of the law	"Do you hear what these children are saying?"	Rebuke	Temple in Jerusalem	Jesus said "Yes" and then asked if they had ever read Psalm 8:2.	Affirmation and a question in the form of a rebuke	Jesus left them.

Reference	Audience	Question	Type	Location	Jesus' Response	Response Type	Outcome
66–67. John 12:34	Crowd	"How can you say, 'The Son of Man must be lifted up'? Who is this 'Son of Man'?"	Denial; request for information	Jerusalem	Jesus encouraged them to "trust in the light."	Evasion of the question in the form of a challenge	Jesus left them.
68. Matthew 21:20	Jesus' disciples	"How did the fig tree wither so quickly?"	Expression of confusion	Between Bethany and Jerusalem	Jesus said that by faith great things can be done.	Evasion of the question by an explanation	None recorded
69–70. Matthew 21:23 (Mark 11:28; Luke 20:2)	Chief priests and elders	"By what authority are you doing these things? And who gave you this authority?"	Challenge; denial	Temple courts in Jerusalem	Jesus asked them about the origin of John's baptism.	Evasion of the question by asking a question that put them on the horns of a dilemma.	They admitted they could not answer his questions.
71–72. Matthew 22:17 (Mark 12:14–15; Luke 20:22)	Pharisees and Herodians	"Tell us then, what is your opinion? Is it right to pay taxes to Caesar or not?"	Request for information; trickery	Jerusalem	Jesus rebuked them ("You hypocrites"), asked why they were trying to trap him, and then answered their question by referring to a coin.	Rebuke, a question, and an explanation by using an object	They were angered and left.
73. Matthew 22:28 (Mark 2:23; Luke 20:33)	Sadducees	"Now then at the resurrection, whose wife will she be of the seven, since all of them were married to her?"	Trickery	Jerusalem	Jesus explained that in the resurrection people will not marry and then he corrected their denial of the resurrection.	Explanation and correction	None recorded

Passage	Person(s) Who Asked	Question	Kind of Question or Problem	Place	Jesus' Answer	Kind of Answer by Jesus	Immediate Response of the Questioner(s)
74. Matthew 22:36 (Mark 12:28)	An expert in the law	"Teacher, which is the greatest commandment in the Law?"	Trickery	Jerusalem	Jesus quoted Deuteronomy 6:5 and Leviticus 19:18.	Explanation	None recorded
75–76. Matthew 24:3 (Mark 13:4; Luke 21:7)	Jesus' disciples	"When will this happen, and what will be the sign of your coming and the end of the age?"	Request for information	Mount of Olives	Jesus gave his lengthy Olivet discourse.	Information	None recorded
77. Matthew 26:17 (Mark 14:12; Luke 22:9)	Jesus' disciples	"Where do you want us to make preparations for you to eat the Passover?"	Request for a directive	Jerusalem	Jesus told them to go to the city and find a large upper room.	Information	They did as he said.
78. John 13:6	Peter	"Lord, are you going to wash my feet?"	Expression of surprise	Jerusalem	"You do not realize now what I am doing, but later you will understand."	Evasion of the question by an explanation	Peter said Jesus would never wash his feet.
79. Matthew 26:22	Jesus' disciples	"Surely not I, Lord?"	Expression of confusion	Jerusalem	"He who has dipped his hand into the bowl with me will betray me."	Information	Peter asked a question.
80. John 13:25	Peter	"Lord, who is it?"	Request for information	Jerusalem	"It is the one to whom I will give this piece of bread."	Information	Judas asked a question.
81. Matthew 26:25	Judas	"Surely not I, Rabbi?"	Denial	Jerusalem	"Yes, it is you."	Information	Judas left the upper room
82. John 13:36	Peter	"Lord, where are you going?"	Request for information	Jerusalem	"Where I am going you cannot follow now, but you will follow later."	Evasion of the question by an explanation	Peter asked another question.

Reference	Speaker	Statement	Type	Location	Jesus' Response	Response Type	Result
83. John 13:37	Peter	"Lord, why can't I follow you now? I will lay down my life for you."	Expression of confusion	Jerusalem	"Will you really lay down your life for me? . . . Before the rooster crows you will disown me three times."	Denial by asking a question	None recorded
84. John 14:5	Thomas	"Lord, we don't know where you are going, so how can we know the way?"	Expression of confusion	Jerusalem	"I am the way, the truth, and the life."	Indirect answer by an affirmation	None recorded
85. John 14:22	Judas (not Judas Iscariot)	"But, Lord, why do you intend to show yourself to us and not to the world?"	Expression of confusion	Jerusalem	Jesus explained that those who love him obey him.	Indirect answer by an affirmation	None recorded
86. Luke 22:49	Jesus' disciples	"Lord, should we strike with our swords?"	Request for a directive	Mount of Olives	Before Jesus answered, Peter cut off the ear of the high priest's slave, Malchus. Then Jesus healed the man's ear, and told Peter to stop.	Directive	None recorded
87–88. Matthew 26:62 (Mark 14:60)	Caiaphas, the high priest	"Are you not going to answer? What is this testimony these men are bringing against you?"	Challenge; request for information	High priest's courtyard in Jerusalem	Jesus remained silent.	Silence	The high priest asked another question.
89. Mark 14:61 (Luke 22:70)	High priest	"Are you the Messiah, the Son of the Blessed One?"	Request for information	High priest's courtyard in Jerusalem	"I am."	Affirmation	The high priest accused Jesus of blasphemy.
90. Matthew 26:68 (Luke 22:64)	Jews	"Who hit you?"	Mockery	High priest's courtyard in Jerusalem	None recorded	Silence	Pilate was greatly amazed.

Passage	Person(s) Who Asked	Question	Kind of Question or Problem	Place	Jesus' Answer	Kind of Answer by Jesus	Immediate Response of the Questioner(s)
91. John 18:33	Pilate	"Are you the King of the Jews?"	Request for information	Pilate's hall	"Is that your own idea or did others talk to you about me?"	Evasion of the question by asking another question	Pilate asked another question.
92–93. John 18:35	Pilate	"Do you think I am a Jew? . . . What is it you have done?"	Sarcasm; request for information	Pilate's hall	"My kingdom is not of this world."	Evasion of the question by stating a truth	Pilate answered his own questions by stating, "You are a king, then."
94. Matthew 27:11 (Luke 23:3)	Pilate	"Are you the king of the Jews?"	Request for information	Pilate's hall	"Yes, it is as you say."	Affirmation	None recorded
95. John 18:38	Pilate	"What is truth?"	Request for information	Pilate's hall	None recorded	None recorded	Pilate told the people he found no fault in Jesus.
96. Matthew 27:13 (Mark 15:3)	Pilate	"Don't you hear how many things they are accusing you of?"	Request for information	Pilate's hall	Jesus did not answer.	Silence	Pilate was greatly amazed.
97. John 19:9	Pilate	"Where do you come from?"	Request for information	Pilate's hall	Jesus did not answer.	Silence	Pilate asked another question.
98–99. John 19:10	Pilate	"Do you refuse to speak to me? Don't you realize I have power either to free you or to crucify you?"	Challenge	Pilate's hall	"You would have no power over me if it were not given to you from above."	Correction	Pilate tried to set Jesus free.
100. Luke 23:39	Thief on the cross	"Aren't you the Christ? Save yourself and us?"	Challenge	Golgotha	None	Silence	The other thief answered the first thief.

Reference	Speaker	Statement	Type	Location	Response	Response Type	Result
101. Luke 24:18	Cleopas	"Are you the only one living in Jerusalem who doesn't know the things that have happened there in these days?"	Expression of surprise	Emmaus road	"What things?"	Question	They answered that they were referring to Jesus.
102. John 21:21	Peter	"Lord, what about him?"	Request for information	Near the Sea of Tiberias	"What is that to you?"	Rebuke in the form of a question	None recorded
103. Acts 1:6	Jesus' disciples	"Lord, are you at this time going to restore the kingdom to Israel?"	Request for information	Jerusalem	Jesus answered that they were not to know the times or dates.	Denial	None recorded

The Apostles' Use of Jesus' Predictions of Judgment on Jerusalem in A.D. 70

J. Dwight Pentecost

The prophets of the Old Testament proclaimed a message of hope, even in times of judgment. Their predictions caused the nation of Israel to anticipate the fulfillment of the covenants and promises God had made with them. David's "Son," the Messiah, would come to bring peace, righteousness, and prosperity to Israel. He would come as the Savior to redeem and as the Sovereign to reign. Nations that had persecuted Israel would be subjugated to him and she would experience peace that he, the Prince of Peace, would bring. Israel's accumulated sins would be put away and she would have forgiveness and a new life of righteousness. Such was the hope of Israel.

How glorious then was the message the angel of the Lord proclaimed to the shepherds: "Today in the town of David a Savior has been born to you; he is Christ the Lord" (Luke 2:11). The coming of the Messiah heralded the fulfillment of all the promised and covenanted blessings so often repeated in the Old Testament. His coming would bring "glory to God in the highest" and "on earth peace" (Luke 2:14). Simeon announced that God's salvation had been revealed in the One he held in his arms, this One who was "a light for revelation to the Gentiles, and for a glory to your people Israel" (v. 32).

Jesus' Claims

Years after these announcements of the realization of Israel's hopes John the Baptist officially proclaimed to Israel, "Repent, for the kingdom of heaven is near" (Matt. 3:2). The reference to the kingdom needed no explanation; it was the covenanted kingdom under David's descendant, the Messiah, of which the prophets had so clearly spoken and for which the nation was waiting. To those assembled in the Nazareth synagogue, Jesus read the messianic portrait in Isaiah 61:1–2 and then proclaimed, "Today this scripture is fulfilled in your hearing" (Luke 4:21). Clearly God was being faithful to his covenanted promises to Israel. All they had been waiting for was on the horizon.

The fact that Jesus was the son of David was indisputable. The fact that he was the Son of God was not so evident. So he performed numerous miracles to authenticate that fact. What Jesus did as well as what he said were designed to demonstrate that he was both the son of David and the Son of God, thus qualifying him to fulfill all that had been written in the prophets about him. The nation was called on to believe the facts he presented to them about himself. They were not asked to believe the truth concerning his person blindly but to believe because of the evidence he presented.

What was this Jesus of Nazareth who claimed to be the son of David and the Son of God? Was he what he claimed to be? If so, he truly is the promised and covenanted Messiah. If not, he is a blasphemous imposter worthy of death. These questions plunged the nation into a debate. Jesus made his claims clear, validated them convincingly, and then challenged the people to accept his claims and to place their faith in him. By doing so they would receive a righteousness from him that would enable them to enter his coming kingdom. His invitation to the nation is best summarized in these words: "Come to me, all you who are weary and burdened, and I will give you rest. Take my yoke upon you and learn from me, for I am gentle and humble in heart, and you will find rest for your souls. For my yoke is easy and my burden is light" (Matt. 11:28–30).

Israel's Responses to Jesus' Claims

From the beginning of Jesus' ministry two responses to his presentation were evident, as summarized in John 1:12: "He came to that which was his own [things], but his own [people] did not receive him. Yet to all who received him, to those who believed in his name, he gave the right to become children of God." Many, like those in Nazareth, rejected his claim to be the One to fulfill the prophecy of Isaiah 61:1–2. As seen in the climactic incident recorded in Matthew 12:22–24, some expressed willingness to accept him as the messiah, whereas others rejected the evidence in support of his claims. Only two supernatural powers can perform miracles: Satan's and God's. If the leaders had acknowledged that Jesus performed his miracles by God's power, they would be without excuse for their unbelief. But if he performed miracles by Satan's power, they felt they were justified in rejecting his claim to deity. So they sought to dissuade those who believed by saying, "It is only by Beelzebub, the prince of demons, that this fellow drives out demons" (v. 24).

This question about the person of Jesus was so crucial that he did on this occasion what he had done only once before. Just as in the debate over his person in reference to Sabbath observation (12:10–12), Jesus defended himself. He offered three conclusive proofs that he could not have been performing miracles by Satan's power (vv. 25–30).

Jesus viewed this explanation by the religious leaders as indicative of the course that generation would follow. He viewed their rejection of him as though it were final, even though it was not finalized until his trial and crucifixion. The message he then began to proclaim was no longer, "Come to me, all you who are weary and burdened, and I will give you rest" (11:28). Now the message was one of impending judgment: "And so I tell you, every sin and blasphemy will be forgiven men, but the blasphemy against the Spirit will not be forgiven. Anyone who speaks a word against the Son of Man will be forgiven, but anyone who speaks against the Holy Spirit will not be forgiven, either in this age or in the age to come" (12:31–32). Jesus spoke here of a physical, temporal judgment that would fall on that generation if they persisted in their rejection of the Messiah.

There were three witnesses to the validity of Christ's claim to be the Messiah. The first was the witness of God the Father (3:17; 17:5). If the nation rejected that witness, they had a second witness, that of the Son himself (John 8:13–18). If that was rejected, they had a third witness, the witness of the Holy Spirit borne through the miracles Jesus performed by the Spirit. If this third witness was also rejected, no further witness would be given to persuade them that Jesus is the promised Messiah. The announced judgment then would be inevitable. Viewing the nation as confirmed in her rejection and unbelief, Jesus from that time on spoke of coming judgment.

Jesus' Pronouncements of Judgment

In the parable of the wicked vinedressers (Matt. 21:33–44) Israel is portrayed as the vineyard, God as the owner of the vineyard, and the leaders as the vinedressers. The leaders, bent on killing Jesus, fail to present fruit to the owner (God). So, after they kill the heir (Jesus), the owner "will bring those wretches to a wretched end" (v. 41). Then Jesus added, "Therefore I tell you that the kingdom of God will be taken away from you [that generation in Israel] and given to a people [or generation] who will produce its fruit. He who falls on this stone will be broken to pieces, but he on whom it falls will be crushed" (vv. 43–44; cf. Luke 20:18). Like grain cast into a mill to be ground into flour, Israel would be judged.

Jesus depicted this same judgment in Matthew 22:1–7. The guests (Israel) who had been invited to a wedding banquet (Messiah's kingdom) but refused to come suffered serious consequences. The king "sent his army and destroyed those murderers and burned their city" (v. 7). This parable reveals the form the judgment would take: Roman armies, under Titus, would destroy the city of Jerusalem and kill or disperse its inhabitants. This parabolic announcement views the destructive judgment as inescapable because of that generation's rejection of the Messiah.

Another specific prediction of the coming judgment is given in Matthew 23:37–24:2. Using the figure of a hen gathering her chicks under her wings to protect them from danger, Jesus declared he had sought to provide peace and security for Israel. However, the Israelites "were not willing" (23:37). This implies that Jesus' generation understood what he was offering them but that they knowingly rejected him and his proffered blessings. Therefore, he announced, "Look, your house is left to you desolate" (23:38). The house could refer to the temple, Jerusalem (where the temple stood), or the Davidic line whose throne would be empty. The severity of the judgment is seen in his declaration that "not one stone here will be left on another; every one will be thrown down" (24:2).

In the parable of the minas (pounds) the nobleman said of some unfaithful stewards, "Those enemies of mine who did not want me to be king over them—bring them here and kill them in front of me" (Luke 19:27). Judgment fell on those who refused to submit themselves to the one who had the right to reign. This was the sin of that generation in Israel. They refused to accept Christ as their rightful ruler, and so they would be judged.

Again Jesus predicted coming judgment in forceful terms:

> When you see Jerusalem surrounded by armies, you will know that its desolation is near. Then let those who are in Judea flee to the mountains, let those in the city get out, and let those in the country not enter the city. For this is the time of punishment in fulfillment of all that has been written. How dreadful it will be in those days for pregnant women and nursing mothers! There will be great distress in the land and wrath against this people. They will fall by the sword and will be taken as prisoners to all the nations. Jerusalem will be trampled on by the Gentiles until the times of the Gentiles are fulfilled. (Luke 21:20–24)

Jesus said the Father had given him the right to judge: "For as the Father has life in himself, so he has granted the Son to have life in himself. And he has given him authority to judge, because he is the Son of Man" (John 5:26–27). This Judge (the Lord Jesus) declared, "For judgment I have come into this world" (9:39). "As for the person who hears my words but does not keep them, I do not judge him. For I did not come to judge the world, but to save it. There is a judge for the one who rejects me and does not accept my words; that very word which I spoke will condemn him at the last day" (12:47–48). These words make it clear that those who willfully reject the Messiah will be judged.

Initially Jesus' message offered hope, blessing, and salvation. However, after the leaders announced that Jesus received his power from Satan and that he was a blasphemous imposter, Jesus' message to that generation in Israel was a message of judgment. This was not the message of eternal condemnation because individuals are sinners. Instead, it was a special message about physical, temporal judgment that would fall on *that* generation in Israel because they rejected Jesus as the promised Messiah. This announcement did not cancel the covenants and promises given to Israel concerning the earthly kingdom of David's greater Son; it only postponed the realization of those hopes. Yet it did consign that generation to an inescapable physical and temporal judgment (Luke 19:27).

The Apostles' Preaching on Physical Judgment on Israel

Referring to the temple, Jesus told his disciples, "Not one stone here will be left on another; every one will be thrown down" (Matt. 24:2). They asked, "When will this happen, and what will be the sign of your coming and of the end of the age?" (v. 3). Clearly they understood him to have said that the temple would be totally destroyed. Without the temple there could be no national life for Israel, and by implication, Israel's promises and hopes would terminate. However, in answering their questions, Jesus outlined God's prophetic events for Israel, thus assuring them of the eventual fulfillment of all that God had promised the nation (Matt. 24:4–25:51). Their questions revealed that Jesus' prediction of judgment on that generation had made a profound impression on those men who, after his resurrection, would be sent into the world to proclaim the gospel.

Jesus had anticipated that the Twelve would not understand all he had been teaching them about the postponement of the Davidic kingdom, the introduction of a new form of the theocracy, the establishment of the church, and the inclusion of Gentiles in the program of God. He stated, "I have much to say to you, more than you can now bear" (John 16:12). But he added a promise: "When he, the Spirit of truth, comes, he will guide you into all truth" (16:13); "All this I have spoken while still with you. But the Counselor, the Holy Spirit, whom the Father will send in my name, will teach you all things and will remind you of everything I have said to you" (14:25–26). The things they were unable to comprehend would be made clear to them when the promised Holy Spirit was given to indwell them (16:7).

Peter's Preaching on Physical Judgment on Israel

Just before his ascension the Eleven asked Jesus, "Lord, are you at this time going to restore the kingdom to Israel?" (Acts 1:6). This shows they had not understood all he had revealed to them. However, when the Holy Spirit came on the day of Pentecost, their understanding was transformed. In addressing the Jews in Jerusalem (2:14), Peter was delivering a message to the generation in that nation that had rejected the Messiah. This is stressed again when he said, "Men of Israel" (v. 22). He accused the nation of putting to death the Messiah: "You, with the help of wicked men, put him to death by nailing him to the cross" (v. 23). Peter authenticated the person of the Messiah by his resurrection, which had been prophesied by David (vv. 25–31), seen by many witnesses (v. 32), and verified by the ascension (v. 33), for his ascension and enthronement at the Father's right hand would have been impossible apart from his bodily resurrection. Peter's exhortation to that generation was, "Save yourselves from this corrupt generation" (v. 40). This exhortation shows that Peter viewed that generation under the physical, temporal judgment about which Christ had spoken so forcefully and clearly. What Jesus had warned them about earlier (Matt. 12:31–32) had come on them and was inescapable.

Peter's message was given to the nation under judgment to "let all Israel be assured of this: God has made this Jesus, whom you crucified, both Lord and Christ" (Acts 2:36). His hearers were convinced by Peter's message and were brought under conviction of their sin and recognized the justice of the judgment pronounced on them. In response they asked, "Brothers, what shall we do?" (v. 37). In response to their cry Peter first called on the nation to "Repent" (v. 38). Here Peter was dealing not with the question of personal sins, but rather with the sin of the nation in rejecting Christ (which has brought judgment upon them). Repentance after disobedience was a precondition to blessing (Deut. 30:1–6). Second Chronicles 7:14 explained what was involved in national repentance: Israel must "humble themselves," that is, acknowledge their sin; then they must "pray," that is, cast themselves in dependence on God. Further, they must "seek my face," that is, put faith in God. Finally, they must "turn from their wicked ways," that is, walk in obedience to him. When the nation does that, the covenanted and promised blessings will follow. This is the response of Peter to the nation that stands under judgment. The promised blessings will not be realized until there is repentance on the part of the nation.

Peter then turned from addressing the Jewish nation to address the need of individuals who, because they were a part of that nation, were individually under judgment. Evidently many in that assembled audience were penitent, had acknowledged their guilt, and cried out for deliverance from the judgment. Peter offered them hope in his invitation: "Save yourselves from this corrupt generation" (Acts 2:40). While judgment on the nation was inescapable, individuals could be delivered from it. Peter's answer was, "Be baptized, every one of you, in the name of Jesus Christ so that your sins may be forgiven," that is, they were no longer to participate in the repeated sin of the nation in rejecting Christ. The confession of their faith in Christ and of their identification with him by baptism would demonstrate their separation from the nation. They would be put out of the synagogue and lose all identity in the nation. Thus, by this separation they would individually not undergo the judgment on that generation since they ceased to be a part of it. Baptism did not save them. Only their faith in the One in whose name they were being baptized could do that. But baptism did terminate their identity with the nation so that they could escape its judgment.

Thus, it must be seen that Peter was preaching on the day of Pentecost in light of the certainty of a physical, temporal judgment coming on that generation. He was telling those brought under conviction by his preaching how they could escape this judgment. His message was not so much concerned about how to escape the eternal judgment passed on all sinners, but how to escape the judgment that was peculiar to that generation that rejected Christ as Messiah. This call in 2:22 to the "men of Israel" (cf. 3:12) is repeated in 3:19: "Repent, then, and turn to God, so that your sins may be wiped out, that times of refreshing may come from the Lord." This was addressed to the nation as a whole, not to individuals, so there is no reference to baptism as a way of escape from the coming eternal judgment.

Paul's Preaching on Physical Judgment on Israel

In the synagogue in Antioch of Pisidia Paul preached a message (Acts 13:41) strikingly similar to Peter's message in Jerusalem. Paul's message on that occasion was addressed both to the "men of Israel" and to God-fearing Gentiles (v. 16; cf. v. 26). In spite of God's faithfulness in dealing with the nation (vv. 17–23) the generation to whom the Messiah came rejected him (v. 28). His person was authenticated by his resurrection (vv. 30–37), and his death provided a basis for the justification of sinners (vv. 38–39). But then Paul sounded a warning: "Take care that what the prophets have said does not happen to you: 'Look, you scoffers, wonder and perish; for I am going to do something in your days that you would never believe, even if someone told you'" (vv. 40–41). Habakkuk 1:5, which Paul quoted here, refers to an invasion of Judah by a Gentile nation that would be used as God's disciplinary instrument to punish Judah for her disobedience. Paul evidently saw his generation in Israel under a similar disciplinary judgment. Paul's message, like Peter's was delivered to a generation in Israel under the judgment Christ had predicted.

Physical Judgment on Israel in the Book of Hebrews

The writer of the Epistle to the Hebrews was evidently anticipating this same judgment when he wrote, "you see the Day approaching" (10:25). Numerous references in the epistle suggest that the recipients were genuine believers (3:1; 4:3, 16; 5:12; 6:4–10; 10:10, 22–25). Having believed in Christ, they had been baptized in his name, thereby openly identifying themselves with him and disassociating themselves from the nation of Israel. (The confession referred to in 3:1; 4:14; and 10:23 was their baptism.) Because these Jewish believers had identified with Christ, they were experiencing persecution (10:34; 12:4; 13:3, 5). This persecution was not political, coming from Rome, but was religious, coming from Israel, the nation from which they had separated themselves by their baptism.

Seeking relief from the persecutions, they considered returning to the rituals of Judaism they had abandoned. Such a consideration on their part showed they had regressed spiritually (5:11–14). If they, without renouncing their faith in Christ, were seen in the temple at the appointed seasons, perhaps their persecutors would forget their baptism and the pressure would be alleviated. No wonder the writer warned them against not "meeting together" (10:25). Recognizing that they needed patience in their circumstances, the writer exhorted them, "let us draw near" (v. 22), "let us hold unswervingly to the hope we profess" (v. 23), and "let us encourage one another" (v. 25).

Why were they to have patient endurance in the face of intense persecution? Because "you see the Day approaching" (v. 25). Some understand this to refer to the day of the Lord's second coming when he will judge his enemies. However, it seems preferable to view this as referring to that day about which Christ had spoken frequently—the day in which Israel, which was then persecuting Jewish believers, would come under God's judgment. Rome would destroy Jerusalem and scatter the nation Israel. Because that judgment would thereby end Israel's persecution of Jewish believers, the writer encouraged them to endure patiently.

Physical Judgment on Israel in Peter's Epistles

In his epistles, Peter seems to have made several references to this judgment on Israel that came in A.D. 70. In 1 Peter 2:12 he wrote of a coming "day of visitation." Writing to pilgrims of the dispersion (1:1), that is, Jewish believers who had been scattered from their homeland, Peter recalled the response of his generation to the chosen and precious cornerstone (2:6). He was the One the builders "rejected" but whose person and claims were validated in that he had "become the capstone" (v. 7). Having been rejected by the "builders," he became to them "a stone that causes men to stumble and a rock that makes them fall" (v. 8), that is, as judge he will crush those who rejected him. In light of this coming judgment in A.D. 70, those who had found him precious because they believed (v. 7) were to lead godly, upright lives as a testimony to unbelievers (vv. 11–12), so that when judgment came the God whom they served would be vindicated and his name glorified.

In 2 Peter 2:4–9, Peter may have had in mind this coming physical judgment. The flood in Noah's day was a physical judgment on a generation that had rejected the witness of Noah to the righteousness of God and the fact of a coming judgment. When his testimony was finally rejected, God's judgment removed the unbelievers from the earth. This judgment was on "ungodly people" (v. 5).

Peter then referred to God's physical judgment on Sodom and Gomorrah. Lot exemplified God's righteousness before men by his life (vv. 7–9). The destruction of Sodom and Gomorrah was a warning to all ungodly men that God would not tolerate their ungodliness but would bring judgment on them (v. 6). Lot warned of a coming physical judgment if the people refused to repent (Gen. 19:14). That judgment came in the form of fire and brimstone that destroyed those two cities and their inhabitants (vv. 24–25). This event may have been the background for Peter's words of encouragement in 2 Peter 2:9: "The Lord knows how to rescue godly men from trials and to hold the unrighteous for the day of judgment." While "the day of judgment" could refer to the future final judgment of the wicked, in light of Peter's references to physical judgments in the days of Noah and of Lot, it seems better to see this judgment as the predicted judgment about to come on that generation. The expectation of such a judgment should produce godliness and patience in them as it did in Lot before them.

The same expectation of judgment could form the background of the problem passage in 1 Peter 3:18–22. Peter was concerned that the suffering saints to whom he was writing should maintain "a clear conscience" (3:16). Suffering for "what is right" (v. 14) would be the lot of all who identified themselves with Jesus Christ. Some, out of fear of suffering, were reluctant to identify with him openly by baptism. Peter referred to God's judgment in the flood to show the danger of not identifying with the One who offered them deliverance from judgment. This same Jesus, with whom they were being challenged to identify themselves by baptism, had preached to men in Noah's day through the Holy Spirit, offering them deliverance from the judgment of the flood. The ark was a way of escape from physical judgment. Those who identified themselves with the ark were delivered from the judgment. Those who refused to be identified with the ark are now "spirits in prison" (v. 19) because they rejected the invitation to enter into the safety of the ark. Peter applied the truth of this historical incident to the people of his generation who were under the sentence of a physical, temporal judgment. If they by baptism identified with the One who was pictured by the ark, they would be delivered from judgment. If they refused to identify with him, they would be swept away in the coming judgment. In this way baptism "saves" (v. 21). The physical act of water baptism did not deliver them from the coming judgment. Instead that which baptism signified, namely, identification with Christ, would deliver them. To identify openly with Christ in the face of persecution would result in "a good conscience" (v. 21), which was of greater value than an escape from suffering.

It is interesting to note that in Acts 2:22 and 3:12 Peter addressed the "men of Israel." In Antioch, Paul addressed those who had assembled in the synagogue (Acts 13:14). The writer to the Hebrews wrote to Jews. Peter wrote both of his epistles to the diaspora, that is, Jews who were living outside their homeland. In each of these instances in which the writer referred to a coming judgment, he was speaking or writing to Jews. The judgment Christ pronounced was on that nation, not on Gentiles, and the New Testament writers were conscious of such a judgment to come and gave exhortations in light of it.

Conclusion

The judgment Jesus pronounced on that generation fell when the Tenth Roman Legion under Titus invaded Jerusalem on the 14th of Nisan in A.D. 70. Fifteen days later the outer wall of the city fell. The inner wall fell on the twenty-fourth day of the siege, and the fortress of Antonia fell on the seventy-second day. All sacrifices ceased on the eighty-fourth day. The temple itself was destroyed 105 days after the attack. The destruction of the city continued to the 134th day, when the entire city was burned and even the foundations dug up to serve notice to the Jews that that area was under Roman domination. Jesus' prophecies of judgment on the city were literally fulfilled.

Jesus had told that generation, "When you see Jerusalem being surrounded by armies, you will know that its desolation is near. Then let those who are in Judea flee to the mountains, let those in the city get out, and let those in the country not enter the city. For this is the time of punishment in fulfillment of all that has been written" (Luke 21:20–22). When Rome attacked, many refused to heed Jesus' warning and were put to death. But many, like Lot so many centuries before, heeded the warning and were delivered.

In their preaching and writings, the apostles referred to this coming judgment on the city several times. This judgment was to come on that generation of Jews because they as a nation had rejected the Messiah. In light of this coming event the apostles gave a number of exhortations to believers and warnings to unbelievers. This understanding of the place and significance of Jesus' pronouncement of judgment on Jerusalem sheds light on many passages that have been much debated by expositors.

Tribute

Dr. Donald Campbell is to be counted worthy of "double honor" (1 Tim. 5:17) because of his dedication to Dallas Theological Seminary for forty years. He has purchased for himself the "excellent standing" promised to those who serve in their appointed place faithfully (1 Tim. 3:13).

Dependence and Duty: The Spiritual Life in Galatians 5 and Romans 6

Robert A. Pyne

In Galatians 5, Paul described an ongoing struggle between the "flesh" and the Spirit. Since this passage deals so directly with the believer's personal obedience and the universal temptation to sin, it has long been the focus of seminars and sermons on "victorious Christian living." The same may be said of Romans 6, which is often treated as a discourse on how to keep from sinning.

As we might expect, the high level of interest in these passages has resulted in a wide variety of interpretations. For example, some regard the "flesh" to be virtually synonymous with the "old nature," describing it as a power within, somewhat distinct from the "real" self, which compels us to sin.[1] Others see it not as a part of the individual, but as the whole.[2] How are we to understand Paul's terms? More pointedly, how are we to apply these passages to our own experience of the Christian life?

Galatians 5: The Nature of the Struggle

As Paul wrote to the Galatians, he was concerned that they were turning to the Jewish law following their conversion to Christianity. Apparently they had been led astray by false teachers (1:9; 5:10–12) who were telling them that they had to submit to the law in order to be justified before God (2:16–21; 5:4). From Paul's perspective an attempt to please God through obedience to the law would be a futile exercise undertaken independently of him. It would be a work of the flesh.

---

1. For example, W. Ian Thomas describes the flesh as "that perverted principle which perpetuates in man Satan's proud hostility and enmity against God" (*If I Perish, I Perish* [Grand Rapids: Zondervan, 1967], p. 21). Likewise, Ryrie argues that "frequently it is used in Scripture to indicate the sin nature" (*Balancing the Christian Life* [Chicago: Moody, 1969], p. 34).
2. *Theological Dictionary of the New Testament*, s.v. "σάρξ," by Eduard Schweizer, 7:134.

"Flesh" in the Context of Law and Grace

Paul's understanding of the role of the "flesh" in sanctification can only be understood by means of his most passionate concern—justification by faith. Righteousness before God comes only by grace through faith. It is based on the redemptive death of Jesus Christ and is applied through the agency of the Holy Spirit. As he wrote in Galatians 2:16, "a man is not justified by works of the Law but through faith in Christ Jesus, even we have believed in Christ Jesus, that we may be justified by faith in Christ, and not by works of the Law; since by the works of the Law shall no flesh be justified."

In this verse "flesh" refers simply to humankind.[3] As in Romans 3:20 and 1 Corinthians 1:29, where he stated that no flesh shall boast before God, Paul emphasized that humankind is under God's judgment and cannot escape through their own efforts.[4] As mere "flesh," humankind is unable to stand before God.

From this perspective it was amazing to Paul that some would trust in their own works to justify themselves before God. No flesh can boast before him, and no flesh can be justified before him by means of the law; yet Paul's opponents were apparently trusting in the flesh to earn or maintain a place of honor before God.[5] In response to those who likely trusted in their physical descent from Abraham, "our forefather according to the flesh" (Rom. 4:1), Paul argued in Galatians 3:14–16 that the blessing of Abraham (and the promise of the Spirit) does not come through fleshly inheritance, but through faith in Christ as Abraham's true "seed." Those who share Abraham's faith, not those who merely share his ethnicity, are those who find favor before God (Rom. 4:11–16; Gal. 3:29). That is why he referred to "Israel according to the flesh" in 1 Corinthians 10:18 and compared them to Ishmael in Galatians 4:29 as those who are "born according to the flesh" (while the church is "according to the Spirit"). Similarly in response to those who likely trusted their own adherence to the law, Paul argued that the law could not give life—

3. As in Galatians 1:16, it is a metonymy of the part for the whole (referring to an entire subject by a particularly distinctive element).

4. Paul's argument seems to be derived in part from Psalm 143:2, which makes this point of all the "living." The fleshly body is the most distinctive characteristic of this life (Schweizer, "σάρξ," p. 129).

5. It is difficult to know exactly what Paul's opponents believed about the nature of salvation. Sanders has argued that the Palestinian Jews of Paul's day were generally "covenantal nomists" who believed they were chosen by mercy as a nation and given the law as a means of maintaining their status before God. He emphasizes that the law was not seen as a means of earning salvation, but as a means of maintaining a relationship with God in the covenant (E. P. Sanders, *Paul and Palestinian Judaism: A Comparison of Patterns of Religion* [Philadelphia: Fortress, 1977], p. 422). Sanders supports this argument rather persuasively from a variety of texts, but the system he describes continues to place a heavy emphasis on works, even if the focus is on "staying in" instead of on "getting in." For Paul, the relationship began and continued in faith (Gal. 3:3). Cf. P. T. O'Brien, "Justification in Paul and Some Crucial Issues of the Last Two Decades," in *Right with God: Justification in the Bible and the World*, ed. D. A. Carson (Grand Rapids: Baker, 1992), p. 87.

it could only demonstrate our need for forgiveness through faith in Christ (Gal. 3:21–22).

Paul himself had at one time placed great confidence in the advantages and efforts of the flesh. From his perspective Paul had been fulfilling the conditions of the covenant with zeal and faithfulness.[6] He had been doing what was expected of a righteous servant of God, but discovered on the road to Damascus that he was diametrically opposed to God's purposes. His trust had clearly been misplaced. As Schweizer correctly observes, "These things are not bad in themselves, but trust in them is wrong. Hence the direct opposite of σάρξ [flesh] here is Χριστὸς Ἰησοῦς [Christ Jesus]."[7] To trust in inheritance or obedience instead of in Christ is fundamentally inadequate, as Paul's own experience demonstrated.

One who is "boasting according to the flesh" is speaking foolishly (2 Cor. 11:18), for such vain pursuits are nothing to be proud of. The false teachers desired to boast in the flesh of the Galatians; they were proud of the fact that they had persuaded the Galatians to trust in the flesh through works of the law instead of trusting in Christ through faith. Paul's own desire is that he would never make such a boast, but that he would only boast of the work of Christ on his (and their) behalf (Gal. 6:13–14).

One's devotion may be oriented toward the flesh (seeking righteousness by law as an expression of self-effort) or toward the Spirit (receiving righteousness by grace as an expression of faith). This orientation provides a fundamental distinction between believers and unbelievers. As Schweizer notes, "the decision to orientate one's life to the σάρξ [flesh] or to the Lord and His promise and Spirit is obviously not just the single decision of a moment but a fundamental decision which affects the whole of life."[8]

This is also the basis for the contrast between those who are "in the flesh" and those who are "in the Spirit" (Rom. 8:1–13). All believers are indwelt by the Spirit, for "if anyone does not have the Spirit of Christ, he does not belong to Him" (v. 9b). Those who are indwelt by the Spirit (believers) "are not in the flesh but in the Spirit" (v. 9a). If believers are "not in the flesh," then those who are "in the flesh" must be unbelievers.[9] It is impossible for

---

6. Sanders notes that the Jews under covenantal nomism did not expect that anyone would maintain the law perfectly, but overall devotion to its precepts and a basic intention to keep the covenant through repentance and atonement would be regarded as satisfactory (*Paul and Palestinian Judaism*, p. 180).

7. Schweizer, "σάρξ," p. 130.

8. Ibid., p. 131.

9. Some have attempted to distinguish between those who are "in the flesh" and those who "walk according to the flesh" in Romans 8. This does not appear to be justified. Paul shifted from one expression to the other without attempting to set up any contrast between them. In verse 4 he referred to those who "walk according to the flesh." In verse 5 he described them as "those who *are* according to the flesh." In verse 8 he wrote of "those who are in the flesh." The real contrast comes at each level between those who are oriented toward the Spirit and those who are oriented toward the flesh (C. E. B. Cranfield, *A Critical and Exegetical Commentary on the Epistle to the Romans*, International Critical Commentary, 2 vols. [Edinburgh: T. & T. Clark, 1975], 2:387).

such persons to please God (v. 8), a statement that recalls Galatians 2:16—by the works of the law shall no flesh be justified before God. It is impossible to obtain righteousness through self-effort.

The Flesh as the Source of Rebellion

This fleshly orientation is not just unproductive; it is also counterproductive. Since it is the opposite of faith in Christ, Paul described it as a self-centered mind-set that is in rebellion against God. "The mind oriented toward the flesh is hostile toward God, for it does not subject itself to the law of God, for it is not even able to do so" (Rom. 8:7). Thiselton summarizes this text well when he writes, "The outlook of the flesh is *the outlook orientated towards the self, that which pursues its own ends in self-sufficient independence of God.*"[10] By acting independently of God and pursuing one's own interests, the individual who walks according to the flesh rebels against God. A similar pattern may be observed in Galatians 5. Here the self-directed orientation of the flesh, which is directly opposed to the will of God (v. 17), expresses itself in sinful acts of rebellion (vv. 19–21).

This discussion suggests that the flesh should be regarded as a condition or orientation rather than as an entity. Ronald Y. K. Fung supports this idea when he writes, "'Flesh' denotes not merely the bodily passions and lusts, nor even strictly speaking a 'lower nature' contrasted with a 'higher nature' in a person, but rather the human individual in his or her sin and depravity apart from the redeeming grace of God and the sanctifying work of the Spirit."[11]

In verse 17, however, Paul personified the flesh, describing it as having desires that are set against the Spirit. This personification does not seem to suggest that the flesh is a component part of the individual. Instead it is a rather vivid way of saying that this state and the actions generated by it are directly opposed to the will of God. As Fung observes, "By presenting the flesh as lusting against the Spirit as much as the Spirit desires against the flesh, Paul gives the flesh an autonomy which properly belongs to it as that which stands for mankind in sin apart from the grace of God and the power of the Spirit."[12] Similarly Schweizer describes the flesh as an orientation that becomes a controlling power: "The norm σάρξ [flesh] by which a man directs his life becomes a power which shapes him."[13]

The point of such statements becomes clear in the context of Paul's overall argument. Against the false teachers who had evidently encouraged his read-

---

10. *New International Dictionary of New Testament Theology,* s.v. "Flesh," by A. C. Thiselton, 1:680.

11. Ronald Y. K. Fung, *The Epistle to the Galatians,* New International Commentary on the New Testament (Grand Rapids: Eerdmans, 1988), p. 244. Fung cites Barrett in adding the observation that Paul would not have believed in a "higher nature."

12. Ibid., p. 249.

13. Schweizer, "σάρξ," p. 132.

ers to submit to the law, Paul argued that the blessing of a righteous standing before God could come only through faith. Further, he warned that their fleshly efforts would result in sin, for they would be acts of independence instead of acts of faith. By contrast, trust in Christ yields righteousness in both position and practice through the agency of the Holy Spirit (5:22–24).[14] By turning to the law and the efforts of their flesh, the Galatians were making a foolish choice (Gal. 3:1–3).

"Flesh" in the Context of Spiritual Regeneration

Another Pauline theme that has some bearing on this discussion is the work of the Holy Spirit as the animating breath of the new creation. The Old Testament recognizes the Spirit as the source of physical life (Gen. 2:7; Job 27:3–4; 33:4; 34:14–15; Ps. 104:29–30; Ezek. 37:9–10), and this principle provides the context for the Spirit's role in spiritual regeneration.

According to Paul the Holy Spirit brings spiritual (and ultimately physical) life through his presence (Rom. 8:10–11; Titus 3:5–6). Unbelievers are regarded as spiritually "dead" (Eph. 2:1), for they remain alienated from God and devoid of his animating Spirit (Jude 19–20).[15] They remain mere "flesh" until the life-giving Spirit is imparted to them.

One would expect that unbelievers would live by the flesh, for that is all they are. For believers, however, to return to that manner of life would be a Spirit-less existence, a charade of the life made possible in Christ.[16] This is precisely what Paul was referring to in Galatians 5:25, "If we live by the Spirit, let us also walk by the Spirit." The Spirit has given believers life; therefore they ought not behave like lifeless flesh.

Conclusion

How then should the "flesh" in Galatians 5 be defined? Schweizer seems to be correct when he maintains that it is not "a part of man which he may put off or overcome. It is the man himself."[17] Stated simply, the flesh is the individual behaving independently of the Spirit.

Those who pursue righteousness apart from faith are acting in the flesh, independently of the Spirit. Unfortunately even believers often seek this kind of behavior through personal choices (v. 13), but such independence leads to slavery to both the law and sin (vv. 1, 17–21).

---

14. Paul reminded his readers in Galatians 5:24 that they had already decisively chosen faith in Christ over the flesh and its rebellious desires. This is based on the same principles as those in Romans 6, which is discussed in more detail below.

15. Dunn appropriately refers to this non-Pauline text as "very Pauline in character" (*New International Dictionary of New Testament Theology*, s.v. "Spirit," by James D. G. Dunn, 3:705).

16. Cf. Walter C. Wright, Jr., "The Source of Paul's Concept of Pneuma," *Covenant Quarterly* 41 (1983): 18; and Raymond Brown, "Diverse Views of the Spirit in the New Testament," *Worship* 57 (1983): 228.

17. Schweizer, "σάρξ," p. 134.

Ironically independence leads to slavery, but even more ironically dependence leads to freedom. Paul called on believers to keep in step with the Spirit (v. 16), walking in obedience to him and bearing fruit in dependence on God (vv. 22–23). This brings freedom from the law and from sin, a message that Paul emphasized further in Romans 6.

Romans 6: The Nature of the Believer's Obligation

In Romans 6–8, Paul addressed many of these same issues, beginning with the believer's relationship to sin. The focus of his discussion, particularly in chapter 6, is not on how to obey God and avoid sinning, but on why we should obey God.

In answer to the hypothetical question, "Shall we continue in sin, that grace might increase?" (6:1), Paul stated that believers "have died to sin" and should not continue to live in it (v. 2). Then in verses 3–7 he explained this idea of dying to sin: "Or do you not know that all of us who have been baptized into Christ Jesus have been baptized into His death? Therefore we have been buried with Him through baptism into death, in order that as Christ was raised from the dead through the glory of the Father, so we too might walk in newness of life. For if we have become united with Him in the likeness of His death, certainly we shall be also in the likeness of His resurrection, knowing this, that our old self was crucified with Him, that our body of sin might be done away with, that we should no longer be slaves to sin; for he who has died is freed from sin."

Those who have been baptized into Christ, that is, all believers (1 Cor. 12:13), have come to share in his death. Paul had argued in Romans 5 that the actions of the head of a race are applied to the members of that race. Through Adam's sin, all his descendants were made sinners (5:12, 19). Similarly through Jesus' death all his descendants were made righteous (v. 19). In each case the consequences of the one man's actions are applied not only to him, but also to his descendants.

In this context the believer is said to have died with Christ. Specifically the results of Christ's death are applied to the believer's account. In Romans 5 this consists of a declaration of righteousness, resulting in a present state of reconciliation with God and the confidence of future deliverance. In chapter 6, however, Paul took the concept a step further, describing more of the present implications associated with the believer's new relationship to God.

A New Dominion

As a result of having "died with Christ," believers are no longer under sin's dominion. "Knowing this, that our old self was crucified with Him, that our body of sin might be done away with, that we should no longer be slaves to sin; for he who has died is freed from sin" (Rom. 6:6–7).[18] Paul reminded his readers that sin should no longer be master over them, for they were no longer enslaved to it as a ruling power (vv. 14, 22). Since they were no longer in bondage to sin, they were to stop allowing it to control their lives (v. 12). Obviously it was still possible for them to "obey its lusts," but they were no longer obligated to do so.

Continuing his response to the question posed in verse 1, however, Paul also maintained that believers have a new obligation to God. They have been freed from sin, but at the same time they have been enslaved to God (vv. 16–18, 22). Just as they formerly were instruments of sin, so now they are to be instruments of righteousness in obeying God (vv. 13, 19). Believers have been delivered from one dominion and placed into another through Christ. Siber nicely summarizes this transfer.

> In Rom. 6 the partner in the Christ-event is related to the motif of a change of dominion *[Herrschaftswechsel]*, which sees salvation as the withdrawal of an individual from the evil forces of the world and as the placement of that individual under God and Christ as his new Lord. To die with Christ means in connection with this motif to become free from the powers, in which the individual dies to them and so becomes free from their lordship claim.[19]

Similarly Tannehill observes, "Dying and rising with Christ is here related to two dominions or aeons and their rulers, and indicates release from one and transfer to the other."[20]

The believer's deliverance from the rule of sin is a result of "dying with Christ." That is, when the benefits of Christ's death are applied to the believer at conversion, the penalty of sin is removed and its ruling power is broken. Conversely, the believer's new relationship to God is here described in terms of resurrection. For example, in verse 4 Paul wrote that believers have been made to share in Christ's death "in order that as Christ was raised from the dead through the glory of the Father, so we too might walk in newness of life." He continued the thought in verse 5, saying that since we have been united with Christ in the likeness of his death, "certainly we shall be also in the likeness of His resurrection."[21] Similarly Paul wrote in verse 8,

---

18. Fung rightly regards verse 7 as a "pregnant expression embracing both the thought of being declared to be in the right with regard to the guilt of sin in the past and that of being set free from bondage to the power of sin in the present" (Ronald Y. K. Fung, "The Relationship Between Righteousness and Faith in the Thought of Paul, as Expressed in the Letters to the Galatians and the Romans" [Ph.D. diss., University of Manchester, 1975], p. 463).

19. Peter Siber, *Mit Christus leben* (Zurich: Theologischer Verglag, 1971), p. 248 (author's translation).

20. Robert C. Tannehill, *Dying and Rising with Christ* (Berlin: Alfred Töpelmann, 1967), p. 7.

21. Though this statement is not found in its entirety in the Greek text, Cranfield comments correctly, "it is clear that σύμφυτοι τῷ ὁμοιώματι and αὐτοῦ have to be supplied in the apodosis from the protasis" (*Critical and Exegetical Commentary on the Epistle to the Romans*, 1:306).

"Now if we have died with Christ, we believe that we shall also live with Him." And in verses 10 and 11 he wrote, "For the death that He died, He died to sin, once for all; but the life that He lives, He lives to God. Even so, consider yourselves to be dead to sin, but alive to God in Christ Jesus." Then in verse 13 Paul urged the Roman believers to present themselves to God "as those alive from the dead." Believers have died with Christ and as a result are no longer slaves to sin. In the same way, being made alive with Christ renders them slaves to God.

Resurrection with Christ

The believer's resurrection is an important concept in Pauline theology, for resurrection is the consummation of salvation.[22] In several passages the apostle discussed the physical resurrection as a yet future event (Rom. 8:11, 18–25; 1 Cor. 15:12–58; 2 Cor. 5:1–10; 1 Thess. 4:13–18). At the same time he wrote of the believer's regeneration as a spiritual resurrection that occurs at the moment of conversion (Eph. 2:1–6; Col. 2:13).[23]

In Romans 6 Paul apparently made use of both principles. First, the physical resurrection is clearly part of the believer's future hope in verses 5 and 8, which describe the event in the future tense. Some interpreters argue on the basis of these verses that Paul gave no thought here to the idea of a spiritual resurrection at conversion.[24] However, that conclusion has been challenged by Moo, who argues that the future tenses in verses 5 and 8 should be understood in a "logical" sense instead of a temporal one. Citing "the flow of the text" for support, he summarizes, "union with Christ in his resurrection follows logically and inevitably upon union with him in his death."[25] While his suggestion regarding the tenses may carry the point too far,[26] Moo may be justified in seeing Paul's concept of spiritual resurrection in this passage.

22. Cf. Robert A. Pyne, "The Resurrection as Restoration: A Thematic Study in Paul's Theology" (Th.D. diss., Dallas Theological Seminary, 1990).

23. Some have argued that Paul himself never spoke of the resurrection as a past event and that Colossians and Ephesians represent purposeful revisions in his teaching in this area (e.g., A. J. M. Wedderburn, "Hellenistic Christian Traditions in Romans 6?" *New Testament Studies* 29 [1983]: 346–47). Harris argues that the idea of a past resurrection with Christ is present "at least in embryonic form" in Paul's earlier epistles as well, and he correctly cites Galatians 2:19; 5:24–25; 6:14–15; and 2 Corinthians 13:4 as examples of texts in which the believer is said to have been given new life in Christ (Murray J. Harris, *Raised Immortal* [Grand Rapids: Eerdmans, 1983], pp. 102–3). This seems to be a legitimate argument, particularly in light of the fact that Paul regarded the present experience of new life in the Spirit as the downpayment on the physical resurrection in the future (Rom. 8:11, 23; 2 Cor. 1:22).

24. Gerhard Sellin, "'Die Auferstehung ist schon geschehen': zur spiritualisierung apokalyptischer Terminologie im Neuen Testament," *Novum Testamentum* 25 (1983): 228.

25. Douglas Moo, "Romans 6:1–14," *Trinity Journal* 3 n.s. (1982): 216.

26. As Dunn observes, the idea of a future resurrection is "certainly the most obvious implication of the future tense" (James D. G. Dunn, *Romans 1–8*, Word Biblical Commentary [Dallas: Word, 1988], p. 318).

For example, in verse 4 Paul wrote that, following the pattern of Christ's resurrection,[27] believers are to walk in "newness of life." Several factors suggest that this is to be the present experience of the Christian. Paul used the same verb (*peripateō*) elsewhere to describe the manner in which believers are to conduct themselves (Rom. 8:4; 13:13; 14:15; 1 Cor. 3:3; 7:17; 2 Cor. 4:2; 5:7; 10:2–3; 12:18; Eph. 2:2; 4:1; etc.), and it seems likely that he intended it the same way here. In addition Paul's emphasis on the believer's expected change of lifestyle in the rest of the chapter strongly suggests that the "walk" spoken of here is not limited to the future. Since the believer's new "life" (*zōēs*) is contrasted burial with Christ at baptism[28] and is parallel to Christ's own resurrection, it is appropriate to speak of this as a spiritual resurrection with Christ along the lines of Ephesians 2 and Colossians 2.[29]

In Romans 6:9 Paul observed that death is no longer master over Jesus. The statement implies that he was once under its dominion, as indeed he was in subjecting himself to the penalty of humankind's sin. That penalty no longer has any power over him, for "He died to sin, once for all" (v. 10). Jesus' death, which paid the penalty of sin for all time, left Him no more under the domain of sin in that he will never again be subjected to it. As Cranfield observes,

> What is actually meant here by "dying to sin" has to be understood from what Paul says elsewhere about the relation of Christ's death to sin (e.g., 3:24–26; 4:25; 5:6–8; 8:3; 1 Cor. 15:3; 2 Cor. 5:21; Gal. 3:13). He died to sin, that is, He affected sin by His dying, in that, as the altogether sinless One who identified Himself with sinful men, He bore for them the full penalty of their sins and so—in the pregnant sense in which the words are used in 8:3—"condemned sin in the flesh."[30]

This death is "an event which was so utterly decisive and final that there can be no question of its being repeated."[31] Having been raised from the dead,

---

27. The idea of conformity to a pattern is established by Paul's use of *hōsper. . . outōs kai* (Cranfield, *Critical and Exegetical Commentary on the Epistle to the Romans*, 1:304; Dunn, *Romans 1–8*, p. 315).

28. Since at conversion the believer has died and been raised with Christ, the transaction is associated with the conversion-initiation rite of baptism here and in Colossians 2:12. Moo correctly avoids overemphasizing the actual ceremony of baptism in this context: "There is considerable evidence that faith, the gift of the Spirit and water baptism were closely associated elements of the single 'conversion-initiation' experience of the believer. In the present passage, then, Paul is to be viewed as referring to conversion with one (external) element of that experience, and one which focused on the identification with Christ so important here. Thus, our identification with Christ in the central redemptive events is appropriated by means of conversion" ("Romans 6:1–14," p. 218; similarly, see Fung, "Relationship Between Righteousness and Faith in the Thought of Paul," p. 458).

29. Dunn rightly comments here, "There is clearly implied a sharing in some degree in Christ's risen life" (*Romans 1–8*, p. 330).

30. Cranfield, *Critical and Exegetical Commentary on the Epistle to the Romans*, 1:314.

31. Ibid.

Jesus now forever "lives to God," restored to the glorious state he had temporarily set aside (Phil. 2:6–9).

The critical point for this discussion comes in verse 11: "In the same way consider yourselves to be dead to sin but alive to God in Christ Jesus." The phrase at the beginning of the verse, *houtōs kai humeis*, treats the experience of Christ as a pattern for believers. That pattern underscores the fact that dying to sin consists of a change of dominion—Christ is no longer under sin's power, and neither are believers. At the same time believers have been brought into a new relationship with God because they have shared not only in Christ's death, but also in his resurrection.[32]

In urging believers to consider themselves dead to sin and alive to God, Paul was not encouraging them to pretend this was true.[33] As in Romans 3:28 and 8:18, *logizomai* here in 6:11 introduces a settled judgment about reality.[34] Believers *are* dead to sin and alive to God, so they are to realize this and act accordingly.

The fact of the believer's resurrection with Christ is also evident in verse 13. Since a change of dominion has taken place in which believers have no more obligation to sin, but have a new obligation to obey God, Paul exhorted his readers to stop making their bodies instruments of sin. Instead, he encouraged them to present themselves to God "as those alive from the dead" (*hōsei ek nekrōn zōntas*).

All this is to say that Romans 6 looks back on spiritual resurrection while also looking forward to physical resurrection. New life in Christ is a present reality, carrying with it new privileges and obligations, but that life will not be realized in its fullness until the believer experiences physical resurrection in the future. As Cranfield notes, "the newness of life, of which Paul speaks here, is a foretaste of the final renewal."[35]

Dunn suggests that Paul was maintaining an "eschatological reservation" in this passage, guarding against an overrealized eschatology by carefully

---

32. Lincoln writes correctly: "That there is a present aspect of sharing in Christ's resurrection is seen also in 6:10, 11. Through his resurrection Christ now lives to God and since they are ἐν Χριστῷ Ἰησοῦ and identified with Christ in both his death and his life believers are also to consider themselves alive to God. Unless Paul thought of believers as already having been identified with Christ in his resurrection, this would simply be make-believe. The 'already' pole of his thought is clearly implicit in Romans 6" (Andrew T. Lincoln, *Paradise Now and Not Yet: Studies in the Role of the Heavenly Dimension in Paul's Thought with Special Reference to His Eschatology* [Cambridge: Cambridge University Press, 1981], p. 123).

33. As in F. F. Bruce (*The Epistle of Paul to the Romans*, Tyndale New Testament Commentaries [Grand Rapids: Eerdmans, 1963], p. 139), who comments on this passage, "In other words, live as though you had already entered the resurrection life."

34. Heidland refers to this as "the judgment of faith," and speaks of its "unconditional validity." His comments seem appropriate. "Thus the obedient apprehension of the reality of faith in λογίζεσθαι poses the demand that life should be subordinated to this reality" (*Theological Dictionary of the New Testament*, s.v. "λογίζομαι," by H. W. Heidland, 4:288).

35. Cranfield, *Critical and Exegetical Commentary on the Epistle to the Romans*, 1:305.

retaining the idea of a resurrection in the future.[36] The presence of this "eschatological reservation" along with the emphasis on new life as a present reality means that Paul addressed the subject of the believer's resurrection more thoroughly here than in his other letters, where his focus seemed to be on one aspect or the other.

In addition, the Pauline Epistles differ concerning the type of death that precedes the believer's resurrection. In Romans 6 believers are said to have died with Christ at conversion, whereas Ephesians 2:1, 5 states that unbelievers are already dead in trespasses and sins. Ephesians 2 looks on individuals as either dead or alive, while Romans 6 describes believers as both dead and alive. This difference has been the subject of considerable discussion, in which some have wrongly regarded the two approaches as contradictory.[37] In Colossians 2:12–13, Paul combined these ideas of death. "Having been buried with Him in baptism [the perspective of Romans 6], in which you were also raised up with Him through faith in the working of God, who raised Him from the dead. And when you were dead in your transgressions and the uncircumcision of your flesh [the perspective of Ephesians 2], He made you alive together with Him."

Since Paul used the idea of death in three different ways in three letters,[38] it is not surprising to see him use the same variety of approaches in his discussion of the resurrection. An explanation of these differences may be found in the differing pastoral purposes of the letters in question. In 1 Corinthians Paul placed a great deal of emphasis on the physical resurrection of believers as an event that has not yet been experienced. This seems to have been a direct response to the overrealized eschatology of the Corinthian believers.[39] His letters to the Colossians and the Ephesians did just the opposite, emphasizing spiritual resurrection as an accomplished fact. The occasion of the epistle to the Ephesians is difficult to determine, but Paul may have written

36. Dunn, *Romans 1–8*, pp. 316, 318.

37. Perkins argues that Romans 6 represents a modification of Ephesians 2 and Colossians 2 (Pheme Perkins, *Resurrection: New Testament Witness and Contemporary Reflection* [Garden City, N.Y.: Doubleday, 1984], pp. 273–74), while Stanley sees Colossians 2 as the perfection of the teaching found in Romans 6 (David M. Stanley, *Christ's Resurrection in Pauline Soteriology*, Analectica Biblica [Rome: Pontifical Biblical Institute, 1961], p. 212). Tannehill, on the other hand, questions the authenticity of the references in Ephesians and Colossians, arguing, "Passages in the Pauline homologoumena which use the motif of dying and rising with Christ with reference to the past always speak of dying as an event, and this is connected with the event of Christ's cross" (*Dying and Rising with Christ*, p. 48).

38. Romans 6 speaks of death *to* sin as a cutting off of one's obligation to it. Ephesians 2 speaks of death *in* sin as alienation from God. Colossians 2 combines both of these approaches (cf. Woodcock, "The Significance of the Resurrection of Christ in the Writings of Paul" [Ph.D. diss., Duke University, 1967], pp. 204–5).

39. Cf. A. J. M. Wedderburn, "The Problem of the Denial of the Resurrection in 1 Corinthians 15," *Novum Testamentum* 23 (1983): 229–41; Karl Plank, "Resurrection Theology: The Corinthian Controversy Reexamined," *Perspectives in Religious Studies* 8 (1981): 41–54; and Jack H. Wilson, "The Corinthians Who Say There Is No Resurrection of the Dead," *Zeitschrift für die neutestamentliche Wissenschaft* 59 (1968): 90–107.

the epistle to the Colossians at least in part to warn them about false teachers.[40] In their situation Paul reminded them of their great security in Christ,[41] and an emphasis on the past aspect of their resurrection with Christ was most appropriate. In Romans, several factors probably entered into the apostle's desire to maintain his "eschatological reservation," but two may be suggested here. First, the epistle likely was written while Paul was in Corinth,[42] and therefore he may have been particularly conscious of the problems caused by a denial of the future resurrection. Second, one of Paul's purposes in this letter seems to have been to state the content of his preaching in a clear and orderly fashion. Cranfield suggests a number of reasons why this may have been so,[43] but the relevant point here is that Paul was being particularly careful that he be properly understood. He presented his views in a more complete form here than in his other epistles, and as with the approaches taken elsewhere, this is appropriate to his pastoral purpose.

In Romans 6 Paul viewed the spiritual resurrection of believers as a past event with present and future consequences. He maintained that the new life imparted at conversion was to result in a transformed lifestyle that demonstrated one's deliverance from sin and new allegiance to the risen Lord. He was not interested in what "part" of believers "died" at conversion, but in the locus of their obligation. The fact that believers are now aligned with Christ explains why they cannot simply enjoy sin. They are not their own.

Conclusion

In the Pauline passages discussed in this essay the apostle was not describing different aspects of human nature that have been affected in various ways at conversion. He was arguing that regeneration constitutes a decisive break with the past—a break that brings about the transformation of the individual believer in totality. Though this transformation will not be consummated until the eventual physical resurrection of the believer, the apostle called on believers to live a life of faithful devotion, recognizing their new obligation to Christ and enjoying the freedom that comes from dependence and duty.

Tribute

It is hoped that the rather lengthy arguments of this essay reveal a fairly simple approach to spirituality. What has been labeled "dependence and

40. Donald Guthrie, *New Testament Introduction*, 3d ed. (Downers Grove, Ill.: InterVarsity, 1970), pp. 515, 550–51.
41. This theme is also prominent in Ephesians (1:4–14; 4:30; 6:10–17).
42. Cranfield, *Critical and Exegetical Commentary on the Epistle to the Romans*, 1:12.
43. Ibid., 2:817–20.

duty" may be summarized in the familiar phrase "trust and obey"—a particularly appropriate theme for this tribute to Don Campbell, who has consistently upheld "the simplicity and purity of devotion to Christ" in his teaching and in his lifestyle. In a personal testimony delivered at the Dallas Seminary chapel in 1987, Dr. Campbell spoke of the Sunday school teacher who was instrumental in his conversion as a youth. "I responded to the gospel in part because of what he modeled." For forty years, Don Campbell has himself been the model, and we who watch have been encouraged to live for Christ.

"The New Man" as Community in Colossians and Ephesians

Darrell L. Bock

American culture is obsessed with the individual. Individual rights arc the cornerstone of many cultural truths we hold dear. The image of the strong individual moving west of the thirteen original colonies to claim both land and a future is a powerful theme in early American history. "Rugged American individualism" is a phrase we learn at a young age. Commercials ring with the refrain "You deserve a break today" and other appeals focusing on the individual. Such an emphasis often permeates the way Christians, especially in America, view their religious commitment. It is a private affair, often separated from life in the secular realm and lived in the privacy of our own homes, often before the television set. Most of the Christian walk is defined in terms of God, the individual, and the personal transformation God brings within the believer's life. Just as often the doctrine of the separation of church and state has permeated down to the soul; believers often separate their spiritual lives from their social or business lives. To think corporately in spiritual terms hardly ever enters our minds. To see ourselves as bound to others and representing others rarely crosses our consciousness.

Such an individualized view is often carried over into the spiritual life and the interpretation of biblical texts. Many passages do treat the spiritual life in individual terms, but not all of them view it in exclusively private terms. One set of terms often viewed individually is "the old man" *(ton palaion anthrōpon)* and "the new man" *(ton kainon anthrōpon)*. Three passages that use either or both of these terms are Ephesians 2:15; 4:22–24; and Colossians 3:9–11. They indicate that a person's identity is somehow related to "the old man" and "the new man." An individualistic reading of this phrase argues that the "old nature" and the "new nature" is meant, or as the New American Standard Bible and the New Revised Standard Version translate the key phrase in question, the "old self" and the "new self." The spiritual life is cast in terms of a battle royal between these two selves vying for control of the believer's will, which stands pressured but neutral in the battle until one side or the other takes hold. The image is a powerful one that many identify with, especially when they are struggling to walk faithfully with God.

But is this an appropriate description of the force of these terms in these epistles? We wish to examine this phrase by taking a careful look at the Greek text and Paul's argument. In a day when detailed examination of the Scriptures is falling on hard times and is often considered irrelevant, it is important to show that sometimes "nothing beats observing the Greek text." After our exegetical examination, we will move into a more homiletical mode to expound the significance of what we discover. We will then uncover a corporate dimension of the spiritual life often ignored in the Christian community to our great peril. We conclude by examining the practical implications of what we discover. So we will discuss Colossians 3:9–11; Ephesians 2:15; and then Ephesians 4:22–24, before turning our attention to "putting on the new man." Believers may think of it as a check of our spiritual wardrobe, a look at the kind of clothes we wear spiritually. How do we see ourselves as we live in the "public square"?

Colossians 3:9–11

Paul saw the Colossian believers as a strong church community, whose testimony had grown steadily (Col. 1:3–7). In his letter to them he warned them about the threat of thinking that anything, even ascetic religious practices or a desire to go directly into God's presence and see the angels worship, could add to what they already had in Christ (2:4–3:4).[1] They had been buried and raised with Christ (2:12–15; 2:20–3:4). Their personal identity and new life were associated with the exalted Jesus. In other epistles Paul wrote of being crucified with Christ, so that life was no longer his own (Gal. 2:20); he wrote about being raised with Christ into the heavenly places (Eph. 2:1–7); and he spoke of belonging to a commonwealth of heaven (Phil. 3:20). Clearly Paul saw his personal identity and activity as inseparably connected at all times to Jesus Christ. Whatever individuality Paul possessed as a Christian, it was no longer Paul merely living for, representing, or serving himself.

In this context Paul wrote of "putting to death" certain practices. In the time of the Reformers and the Puritans, texts such as this led some people to speak of the doctrine of "mortification" when discussing the spiritual life. Believers were encouraged to mortify the flesh, to "put it to death." Even in those times, the doctrine was interpreted in individualized terms. Believers needed to put behind and be separated from the practices of fornication, impurity, passion, evil desire, covetousness, anger, wrath, slander, foul talk, and lying (Col. 3:5–6, 8–9).

---

1. For this understanding of the Colossian heresy, see P. O'Brien, *Colossians and Philemon*, Word Biblical Commentary (Waco, Tex.: Word, 1982), pp. xxx–xxxviii.

Now it is clear that the exhortation includes the individual, but the rationale for the exhortation is not individualized. The exhortations throughout these verses, including the positive ones in Colossians 3:12–17, are second-person plurals. The community and each one within it are addressed.

In fact, the rationale is even more corporate than that, as verses 9–11 show.[2] A look at the Greek of Colossians 3:9–11 shows that the key images are *ton palaion anthrōpon* (lit. "the old man") and *ton neon* (lit. "the new," which in context is "the new man" because of the contrast with v. 9). To what do these two figures refer?

Paul wrote that lying to one another should cease because believers have "put off the old man together with its practices and have put on the new." In addition, Paul stated that the new man "is being renewed in knowledge after the image of its Creator." This means that God is at work to make the new man more like himself. But the real surprise comes in verse 11. Rather than saying the new man is the new nature, Paul spoke of the new man as a place where there is "no Greek and Jew, circumcised and uncircumcised, barbarian, Scythian, slave, free, but Christ is all, and in all."[3] Obviously one's inner man is not inhabited by people of various nationalities and of various social standings! So the new man cannot be referring to something inside a person.

What this means is that the "new man," made up of peoples, refers to a social structure or community, not to an entity inside an individual. Some have said the new man is a reference to Christ, suggested by the end of verse 11. If this is so, the view must be stated carefully, so one does not misunderstand in what sense Christ is meant. Paul could not mean the individual Christ since that would make Paul's assertion that "Christ is all and is in all" (v. 11b) redundant.

So the new man is related to Christ and consists of peoples. In other words, it is Christ conceived of as a corporate entity, that is, Christ's body. Another way to say it is that the new man refers to the new community in Christ that he forms by joining people to himself as they are saved (i.e., "buried and raised with him," as Paul already declared in Colossians). An even simpler way to say it is that the new man is the church, the new community in Christ. This means that the "old man" is also a community that has certain practices associated with it. This would be the community of the world out-

---

2. The reader must bear in mind differences of translations. The RSV speaks of the "old nature" and the "new nature" here. The NASB and NRSV use "old self" and "new self," which is not much better, as we shall see. Only marginal notes in some of these versions, noting the literal phrase, give the English reader a chance at figuring out what is being presented by this image. This observation is not made to complain about these translations in general or to complain about their translation philosophy, but only to make a point about how this particular figure is rendered. In some cases it helps to interact directly with the Greek text, if one has the ability to do so. If one lacks such ability, then consulting a resource that interacts with the Greek may surface such an observation.

3. The key connective here is *hopou* ("where"). It is clear contextually that it refers back to the new man.

side of Christ, what some theologians have referred to as the "in Adam" community. The existence of this new community is why Paul said Christians should not lie and why they should put to death the practices of the old world they shed (like old clothes) when they came to Christ. In place of the former practices, new virtues should make up their everyday attire: compassion, kindness, lowliness, meekness, patience, forbearance, forgiveness, love, and the peace of Christ (vv. 12–15). These are the clothes of authenticity in the Christian life.

Ephesians 2:15

Ephesians was probably written to people in a region rather than in one locale.[4] In it, Paul reviewed the blessings that have come to the church in Christ, as well as giving praise to God for salvation, especially election, redemption, Jew-Gentile unity, and the indwelling of the Holy Spirit (1:3–14). In his prayer, Paul mentioned the exaltation of Christ over all spiritual forces, as well as the existence of Christ's authority as head of the church (1:15–23). Paul prayed that God would illumine believers about the power to which they have access in God, power like that which raised Jesus from the dead and gave him such total authority. Paul then turned his attention to the fact that believers are raised out of the realm of sin and exalted into the presence of Christ in the heavenlies, an act that is grounded in God's grace and that comes to the believer through faith, not works (2:1–10).

The point of the unit, which continues the prayer, is that God has already exercised great power on the believers' behalf when he saved them and gave them new life, raising them from the dead. The debate over the meaning of "and *this* is the gift of God" in 2:8–10 has obscured a parallelism between 1:15–23 and 2:1–10.[5] Just as Christ was exalted into the heavenlies by resurrection (1:20), so the believer is raised together with Christ in salvation (2:6). God has already acted to deliver sinners from the power of sin and to transform them into a people who sit next to the One with authority over sin and those forces that oppose humanity. Since all believers are raised *together,* Ephesians too speaks of a corporate context, just like Colossians. The corporate force in Ephesians is clear form the *syn* ("together") prefix affixed to each of the verbs in 2:5–6. It is not "me and my God" but "we and our God." The Lord enables believers to walk in "good works" (2:10).

---

4. The Greek text of Ephesians 1:1 is uncertain at the point where Ephesus is mentioned. Though it probably should be included in the verse, there are other factors that suggest a broader audience. Parts of the letter suggest that Paul did not know some of his audience (1:15; 3:1–6). If the audience had to hear about his ministry and Paul had to hear about their faith, then it seems that Paul had more in mind here than the community he founded in Ephesus (cf. Acts 18:24–19:41).

5. The debate is whether "this" *(touto)* refers only to faith or to the whole of salvation. The neuter demonstrative pronoun makes the latter more likely.

In 2:11–13 Paul asked the Gentile believers in the community to consider where they were before they came to know Christ. Then in 2:14–18, he stated that Christ is the source of peace between Jew and Gentile, as well as between themselves and God. Discussion of the removal of the barrier, the abolishing of the law, and the reconciliation of the two into one dominates these verses. At this point, Paul once again mentioned the new man.

Ephesians 2:15 speaks about Jesus creating in himself "one new man," so that in place of the two there is now one. Now contextually this cannot be a reference to some entity inside an individual. The context is once again thoroughly social and racial in nature. Jew and Gentile are reconciled into one new body, the church. Both Ephesians 2:13 and 17 make the point that those who were far away (Gentiles) have now been brought near by the blood of Jesus. When verse 14 says Christ is our peace, it means that Jesus is the source of restored relationships, not only between an individual and God but also between individuals. Now people form a new community, the household of God, which itself is compared to a holy temple, a sacred work of God (2:18–22). All of it is sacred. In fact, every part in it is sacred and the entire building is attached to Christ and to each other as Christ holds it together. The "new man" is something Christ has created within himself.

Ephesians 4:22–24

In the second half of Ephesians, Paul spelled out what believers are to do as a result of what God has done. They are to pursue unity (4:1–6). They are to engage in ministry as they are stimulated by those with teaching gifts to grow in love (4:7–16). This inevitably caused Paul to consider the issue of lifestyle and the two worlds. It is here that the old man/new man imagery has its most developed application.

Ephesians 4:17–19 speaks of the world of the Gentiles. It is the world outside of Christ and the description of this group of people is bleak. They have futile minds and darkened understandings, are alienated from God, are ignorant, have hard hearts, and are callous, engaged in all sorts of unrighteous practices. Paul related these attributes in a kind of descending spiral of effect to cause until verse 19, where he described the practical result of such a life in the former world. This is not how believers are to live.

In a heavily figurative section (4:20–24) Paul described how Christians are to live. He began by saying that they did not learn Christ in that manner, that is, in the manner in which the world lives. There is a personification in the verse, in which Christ himself represents what is learned from him about the walk with God. Not only did they learn about him, but they also became associated with him; so verse 21 says that they heard about him and were taught in him. Paul then mentioned that truth is in Jesus. The term "truth" (*alētheia*) is often understood as referring to doctrinal truth, but a check of the context and the Book of Ephesians shows that this is too narrow a way to take the term. In verse 24 the term reappears and it is related to "righteousness and holiness." In addition, in Ephesians 5:9 the term appears as part of the fruit of the light. In both cases the issue is the product of life, the ethical quality of truth or of authenticity. Paul was saying that in contrast to the way the world lives in selfish indulgence and darkness, believers have learned to live ethically in Christ in a different way. Details of this different walk are mentioned in Ephesians 4:25–6:9. Colossians 3:12–24 summarizes the characteristics of this new walk as well.

By stating in Ephesians 4:21 that ethical truth is in Jesus, Paul began a grammatical construction he completed in verses 22–24.[6] In this summary teaching Paul spoke of three actions: putting off the old man, renewing the mind, and putting on the new man. It is important to note that the first and third infinitives are in the aorist tense, a summary tense whose grammatical aspect is undefined. Both "put off" and "put on" are marked in an unspecified way. They do not look at the progress of an action; they merely summarize its presence. In contrast, reference to the renewing of the mind is in the present tense, thereby stressing the progress of the action. So while "putting off" and "putting on" have occurred, the process of renewing the mind is ongoing. Life in the new world of the new community involves both a transition and a process.

Observing the tenses helps us understand the passage, but it does not solve all the problems of interpretation. The three key actions are contained in three infinitives: "to put off" *(apothesthai),* "to be renewed" *(ananeousthai),* and "to put on" *(endusasthai).* The interpretive problem is that infinitives, unlike verbs, lack a grammatical marking for mood. So should these infinitives be read as indicative statements or as imperative exhortations? If they are indicatives, this would mean that the Ephesians put off the old man in the past, are being renewed in the mind now, and put on the new man in the past. If they are imperatives, then the passage is a call to respond "Put off the old man; be renewed in the mind; and put on the new man." Which of these options is better?

Either option is possible, can be defended, and makes sense. Those who prefer the indicative statements appeal to the parallel participles in Colossians 3:9–10, which clearly describe an event. They also argue correctly that Paul often moved from indicative fact to exhortation, so here he stated the indicative in verses 22–24 and then gave exhortations in verses 25–32.

But those who interpret these infinitives as imperatives can reply to these arguments. First, the possibility of an imperative in the parallel can be seen in Colossians 3:12, where the imperative "put on" appears in the continua-

---

6. Technically this construction is called an indirect discourse clause, since it summarizes the content of the teaching that came in Jesus.

tion of the old man/new man image, where the virtues of the new man are enumerated. Second, the imperative position can point to tighter logic. The logical flow of speaking of putting off the old man and putting on the new as positional truth interrupted by the call to renew the mind continually is awkward conceptually. If one had wanted to present positional truth, the more appropriate order would be "you put off the old man; you put on the new; be renewed continually in your mind." So it seems better to see these as imperatives. Paul exhorted the community to put off the ways of the old man, to be renewed in their mind, and to put on the new. This contrastive form of exhortation continues in the next section, where specific exhortations appear. Also positive exhortations frequently appear alongside calls not to do something followed by a rationale for the exhortation.

The need to renew the mind on a regular basis is not a difficult concept to grasp. It means walking with an eye toward God, being careful about how one walks, and seeking his wisdom, much as was mentioned in Ephesians 5:15–18. But what does it mean to shed the old man and put on the new? Assuming that the image of the new man and old man is consistent in the Prison Epistles with what we have seen in the other texts, how does one put off one community and put on another? Here is Paul's major rationale for his ethical exhortation in Ephesians. It is the central point in the content of his teaching about truth being in Jesus. What does it mean?

Spiritual Identity, Ralph Lauren, and the People of God

In Ephesians 4:22–24 Paul made a crucial point about the believer's personal identity with God and other believers. There is an "attached" character to identity in Christ in that no Christian is an island to himself or herself. The reality of this connection should influence not only how we see ourselves as believers, but also how we respond to the ethical choices in life. These connections serve to build authenticity through community, responsibility, and accountability. Perhaps a few illustrations will show the emotional, psychological power of this truth. The two illustrations cover both the indicative and imperative aspects of this teaching, combining what we saw in Colossians (indicative) and Ephesians (imperative).

My sister-in-law once made an interesting "theological" statement. It happened one day at my in-laws' home in Houston. She was separating her T-shirts into two stacks. One stack was filled with Ralph Lauren polo T-shirts and any other shirts made of 100 percent cotton. Any trace of polyester or any other less refined material qualified the T-shirt for the second, inferior stack. Meticulously she made two piles. When she was done, she took the stack of T-shirts that did not measure up and handed them to my wife, saying, "You can have these. I only wear Ralph Lauren T-shirts. I only wear 100 percent cotton."

She was saying, in essence, "I have a certain understanding of who I am, and I reflect that understanding by what I wear. Anything that does not fit the way I see myself is inappropriate for me. I will have nothing to do with it. It is beneath my perception of who I am. My behavior reflects how I see myself." Similarly Paul was saying that the believer is to see himself or herself as belonging to the new community, as having joined a second world. Certain activities of the old world (the old man) are not appropriate to that identity and to the association the individual now has in representing Christ and others who belong to him. So certain activities are to be shed; they are beneath the believer. Yet other virtues should be worn like new, fine clothes, since they reflect the character of the new community, not to mention the character of God.

Combining the perspective of Colossians and Ephesians, which involves both position and practice, we can add a second illustration. Picture a person living in Las Vegas, carrying out the array of activities followed by most visitors to Las Vegas. This might picture our association with the old world, being in Adam. But God in his grace reaches down and moves that person to the holy city, to Jerusalem. Now his or her entire environment, orientation, and personal ethos have changed. This is the positional shift. The move probably would also impact personal identity; the believer should see himself or herself as different in Christ, not sinless, but able to overcome sin by the power of the Spirit of God now present. This does not mean that a believer is perfect or that there is no longer struggle with sin, but that the process of transformation and growth into Christ-likeness has begun with an awareness of a relationship not only to God but with the new community. Now the believer should no longer do what he or she did in Las Vegas. The believer has moved into the new community, into the new world that comes in Jesus Christ. Now the believer represents and is attached to the holiness of being in the second city and shares that honor with others who share in that citizenship. One does not do as a citizen of Jerusalem what one did as a resident of Las Vegas. The activity of the old life is to be shed and the virtue of the new citizenship is to be worn in daily practice, because of the awareness that citizenship has changed; old things have become new in Christ. The illustration is hardly far-fetched; Ephesians 2:18–22 pictures the new community as a holy temple, being built and held together through the activity of Jesus Christ.

Practical Implications

The "new man" teaching has major implications for the spiritual life. First, the believer should not see the internal personality primarily as a battlefield, whose neutral will is pulled between two forces. Whether we illustrate this struggle as a battle between a good dog ("Spirit") and a bad dog ("flesh") inside the person, or depict the conflict in some other way, this struggle is secondary in Paul's mind to grasping who one is in Jesus. The child of God should see that God has introduced a transformation into his or her life that means that sin is no longer automatically the victor in the struggle (Rom. 6–8). The one who walks by the Spirit provided by God can have victory. But behind that realization is a more fundamental theological perception. It means recognizing that who we were on our own led us at one time into rebellion and sin. At that time we were driven by the bad dog (or dogs!), what Ephesians 2:2–3 calls the "course of this world, following the prince of the power of the air" and "the passions of our flesh," so that now we must rely on the One who can transform us. He has made us alive to live for him. To be born again also means to be born into newness of life with a capacity to please him, because he is at work in us. He has redeemed us for a purpose, and we know we are his (Eph. 2:4–10; 5:1–2). Paul's exhortation here is not unlike the Old Testament command, "You shall be holy, for I am holy" (Lev. 11:44; repeated in 1 Pet. 1:16).

Second, God does not renew us to turn us into "private" Christians. There is no ministry in solitary confinement. The Christian is not to withdraw, only to emerge for brief periods of corporate worship or periodic excursions into the holy huddles of a withdrawn believing community. The church should be a community of the committed who encourage one another and engage the world with a lifestyle that points to the possibility of living in the new world and in the reality that is Christ (Matt. 5:14–16).[7] The church needs to be in the public square revealing a contrastive way of life to that which directs others' lives. We are transformed to serve, but to serve means that others to be served are present. Our culture makes creating a sense of authentic community in our churches and Christian organizations very difficult. In fact, our cultural bent is antithetical to the corporate emphasis of Scripture. When a person exalts individual rights and a private religion, either he or she will seek to dominate the agenda through the exercise of power or through withdrawal. Neither of those routes reflects authentic community. A Christian

---

7. Stanley Hauerwas and William H. Williamson, *Resident Aliens* (Nashville: Abingdon, 1989), speak of the church by the metaphor of a "colony in the world." They see it as a colony of virtue that functions as light in the midst of the world, but that function is especially seen in corporate terms. See also Stanley Hauerwas, *The Peaceable Kingdom* (London: SCM, 1984), pp. 96–115, where he speaks of a "servant community" and a "community of virtue." The singular "virtue" is important, since it is character as a whole that is the point, not just a list of characteristics. The mark of such a community includes the ultimate test of spiritual success, namely, faithfulness to God. This is similar to the direction I called for in "The Son of David and the Saints' Task," *Bibliotheca Sacra* 151 (October–December 1993): 440–57, and in Spanish in *Kairos* 11 (1992). There I argued that the church's relationship to culture is tied to her relationship to Christ and that he is the "transformer of His community as a model for other cultures." Such a model allows the church to have her ministry to the world in a variety of structures and through a wide range of ministries. Of course, the ultimate goal of such ministry is to invite others to share in the benefits of belonging to the new community, which is uniquely enabled by his Spirit to reflect God's character.

cannot live an authentic Christian life without being part of an authentically functioning community.

Third, the new man teaching emphasizes that each believer represents Christ *and* the community. There is much talk in the church about being accountable. But this ignores one reality. The church as community *already is* accountable. Sin in the community does not stain merely the individual (as our culture might want us to believe); it stains the entire community. Scandal in the church does not reflect simply on those directly responsible; it also dims or destroys the testimony of those who have attempted to be faithful to their call. Every member of the church is accountable already. That does not mean that seeking to be accountable is a waste of time, but we should recognize that as members of the new community and as one in Christ, we "wear" Christ whether at work, at home, or in private.

Fourth, an authentic community is a relational community, not merely a cognitive one. It is no accident that when Paul defined truth in Ephesians 4:21–24, he not only did so ethically, but he also presented it in a heavily relational context. The specific applications Paul made in Ephesians 4:25–6:9 are relational, and some of them even deal with relationships in societal structures. Relationships take time and involvement. They require honesty, openness, bearing one another's needs and burdens, and sharing in one another's journeys of faith. Another danger in our society is that believers attend church on Sunday and then withdraw to the privacy of their homes without building meaningful relationships. Small groups are a way of attacking this individualized style of living that often also breeds a subtle type of loneliness, especially in a society in which the family structures that used to provide such bonds of support often no longer function as they did. The dynamics of relationship in the believing community require effort and patience as Christians relate to each other (Eph. 4:1–6, 30–32).

Conclusion

When God created humanity in his image, he desired that they function in the context of community.[8] Understanding this truth, Paul described people as belonging to one of two humanities, the old man or the new man. Authentic Christian existence takes place in the context of a renewed community that God is forming in Christ. Spiritual life is incomplete without this corpo-

---

8. Theologically the fact that God is a Trinity already suggests the potential for relationship when one speaks of being created in the image of God. In addition, the fact that God created humanity with the goal that they fellowship with him shows God's commitment to relationship. This relational focus is also why Jesus summarized the law by speaking of two relational levels: loving God and loving one's neighbor (Luke 10:27). The love Jesus called for made no distinctions; everyone was a neighbor to be loved (Luke 6:20–49; 10:25–37). In the Epistles this love is to be especially present within the church (Gal. 6:10; James 2:5–8; 1 Pet. 2:11–12; 3:8–17; 1 John 3:23).

rate dimension. Paul calls on believers not only to wear the T-shirt of virtue Christ provides, but also to recognize as one does so that any one believer represents not only his Lord but also other believers as they function in the public square. One is to draw strength from the recognition that he or she functions in the context of the presence and support of a community. No Christian is an island to himself or herself. Every believer is part of a colony in which each member is related to the other. The Christian life is not a matter of "me and my God" but of "us and our God."

Tribute

It is an honor to contribute to a festschrift for Dr. Donald Campbell. He has been an encourager ever since I arrived at Dallas as a student. He once took seventy-five minutes on a Monday evening to watch a green seminary student struggle his way through teaching the Old Testament to a Lay Institute class and offered much in instruction, wisdom, and support (something he did for other students as well). Since that time, I have known him as dean, president, and friend, and the encouragement still continues. No concern is greater to Donald Campbell than that faculty and students pursue the spiritual life eagerly and come to know God in his fullness. So this essay has looked at an issue that impacts how one views the spiritual life. It is but a small, meager offering of thanks to one who has given so much to so many and who has reflected the God he loves so visibly to those he has led and served.

Does James Give Believers a Pattern for Dealing with Sickness and Healing?

Wendell G. Johnston

Does James 5:13–16 exhort believers to seek healing? Does James call the elders of the church to pray for someone who is terminally ill? Does this passage support the concept that all Christians should be healed if the instructions are followed carefully? Is this passage a normative statement about sickness? Should Christians expect healing from every sickness when they pray? Does God hear the prayers of those who come to him in sincerity and trust?

Assuredly God does hear the prayers of his people when they pray, and he does have the power to raise the sick. However, nowhere does God promise that he will always heal sick people, even when church leaders anoint them with oil.

James 5:13–16 needs to be considered in the light of its context, including the beginning of James 4. Strife was present in the church, and Christians were living with anger and hostility. Much of this anger and strife seems to be related to the sins of the tongue. James stated earlier in his book that Christians should be "quick to hear, slow to speak, slow to anger" (1:19). Anger does not bring about the righteous life God desires (v. 20). Anger had affected the believers' prayer life, their communion with God, and their fellowship with each other. Christians were slandering and judging one another (4:11–12). They were also displaying a boastful attitude which James called "evil" (v. 16).

The church quarrels condemned by James were not an isolated incident. Paul and Timothy encountered the same sin in churches in which they ministered. Paul warned Timothy about "word" battles (2 Tim. 2:14–16, NASB). The term Paul used for "wrangling about words" is a compound form of the same word James used in 4:1 when he mentioned the quarrels and conflicts in the early church. Paul declared that such word battles led to ungodliness and were worldly and empty chatter. Envy, strife, abusive language, and evil suspicions would follow (1 Tim. 6:4, NASB). Paul claimed that the sins of the

168

tongue are not limited to gossip, slander, and evil remarks; they also include deception and deviation from the truth.

James 5 focuses on another problem: oppression by the rich. Believers were finding life intolerable because of the many injustices they faced. In light of these things James wrote that believers need to be patient. It is easy to react in anger, but this is not the Christian way of conduct. God had heard the cries of those who were experiencing this oppression (v. 4). This illustrates that God can and will sustain those going through difficult times if they seek his face. James then added that the coming of the Lord will correct all injustices, and that Christians are to stand firm until then (v. 8). James summarized his message by reminding his readers to be patient and to stop grumbling about each other (v. 9).

Having commanded his readers to be patient, James provided two examples of those who were patient in former years. The first example is "the prophets who spoke in the name of the Lord" (v. 10), and the second example is Job (v. 11). James singled out Job because Job's life is a good illustration of how God will correct injustice. Job was tempted by his wife to curse God and die. Job resisted and the Scripture says, "In all of this, Job did not sin in what he said" (Job 2:10). Perhaps still reflecting on the integrity of Job, James suggested that frustration could lead to unwarranted oaths, and he warned against them (James 5:12).

Although many commentators do not make any connection between James 5:13–16 and what was written before, there is no reason to detach the passage from its context. The context shows that James was suggesting how a Christian can face testing, injustice, frustration, and the problems within the church that had brought about quarrels and fighting.

James began this section with a series of questions that he then answered. "Is anyone in trouble?" Then that person should pray. The Greek word for "in trouble" *(kakopathēo)* is the verbal form of the noun *kakopathia* used in verse 10 to describe the trials suffered by the prophets. It certainly should be included in the "many trials" James said would come on believers (1:2). The believer's attitude toward these trials should not be to avoid them, but to endure them with God's grace and strength. As stated earlier in the epistle, perseverance leads to maturity (1:3–4). The exhortation to pray corresponds to the teaching in 1:5–7, where James already mentioned the importance of prayer. Prayer is the solution for those who lack wisdom (1:5).

James' second question focuses on the joy that can come from answered prayer. "Is anyone cheerful?" Then that person should sing praises. The response to trouble is to be prayer, and the response to joy is to be praise. In 5:14 James asked a third question: "Is any of you sick?" His answer has been discussed for centuries.

What about sickness? Is it not also a trial? Why is it singled out and a specific reference made concerning it? It would be wrong to assume that James was contradicting what he wrote in the early verses of chapter 1. Sickness is as much a trial as anything we encounter in life. Why does James give special attention to this trial? Can prayer deliver us from sickness but not from other trials? Should sickness not be endured? Was Paul wrong to assume that his sickness had a purpose in this life (2 Cor. 12:7–10)? Was God unfaithful to Paul? Would the result have been different if Paul had gone to the elders rather than directly to God? The answer has to be a resounding no! It is this fact that helps us understand what James had in mind.

Opinion differs on the meaning of the term "sick" used here. The verb James uses is *astheneō,* which basically means "to be weak." "Weakness embraces the full range of physical, emotional, social, economic and even spiritual incapacity."[1] The noun *astheneia* is the opposite of *sthenos,* "strength." The verb *astheneō,* the noun *astheneia,* and the adjective *asthenēs* "denote primarily bodily weakness, i.e. sickness."[2] This translation is also supported by Arndt and Gingrich.[3] In other words James was referring to having physical or bodily illness, which may include emotional sickness.[4]

In his study of this Greek word, *asthenia,* Black has shown that its common technical meaning is physical sickness.[5] He concludes that in the Pauline Epistles and also in classical Greek literature it refers to bodily illness.[6]

James 5:15 uses *kamnō,* a different word for sickness, which basically means to be weary from the effect of constant work.[7] Vine suggests the word is used here because "it is suggestive of the common accompaniment of sickness, weariness of the mind."[8] Mayor concludes that there is no reason to interpret this word any differently from *astheneia* in verse 13, since classical Greek writers used both words for bodily sickness.[9]

Understandably some believe James was speaking of emotional or spiritual exhaustion since the term can refer to either physical or nonphysical ailments. Physical illness often leads to emotional stress.[10] Many people become depressed because of physical sickness. And Christians often experience spiritual trials when they are suffering. Add to this the possibility of sin as men-

1. *New International Dictionary of New Testament Theology,* ed. Colin Brown (Grand Rapids: Zondervan, 1978), s.v. *"astheneia,"* by H.-G. Link, 3:993.
2. Ibid.
3. Walter Bauer, William F. Arndt, and F. Wilbur Gingrich, *A Greek-English Lexicon of the New Testament and Other Early Christian Literature,* 2d ed., rev. F. Wilbur Gingrich and Frederick W. Danker (Chicago: University of Chicago Press, 1979), p. 115.
4. D. Edmond Hiebert, *The Epistle of James* (Chicago: Moody, 1979), p. 318.
5. David Alan Black, *Paul, Apostle of Weakness* (New York: P. Lang, 1984), p. 8.
6. Ibid., p. 11.
7. W. E. Vine, *An Expository Dictionary of New Testament Words,* 4 vols. in 1 (Westwood, N.J.: Revell, 1940), 4:27.
8. Ibid.
9. Joseph B. Mayor, *The Epistle of St. James* (1913; reprint, Grand Rapids: Zondervan, 1954), pp. 173–74.
10. Vine, *Expository Dictionary of New Testament Words,* 4:27.

tioned in James 5:16 and the suffering becomes an even greater burden. The normal understanding of *astheneō* in verse 14 is that it refers primarily to someone who is sick with a physical illness. There is no reason to go to a secondary interpretation, as will be shown in the following explanation.

James commanded the one who is sick to call the elders of the church to pray over him and anoint him with oil (5:14). The normal practice in those days was for people to consult a physician if they were ill.[11] Why then would the elders of the church be called for sickness? It is reasonable to assume that special prayer for this sickness was appropriate. Apparently the sickness was related in some way to the corporate body of believers. Because of this the leaders of the church would be involved. The context strongly indicates that the sickness was the result of a believer's ungodly behavior in the church. James had already spoken about the fighting and quarreling that had gone on in the church (4:1–2). The misuse of the tongue was shown to be a devastating problem (3:1–12). At the beginning of his letter James urged Christians to be "quick to hear and slow to speak and slow to anger" (1:19) as though anger were a serious problem with which his readers were struggling.

The anointing with oil is not to be considered an element contributing to one's healing. Though some interpreters see the oil as medicinal, the language of the passage does not support this and the evidence is inconclusive.[12] At best the oil could only be symbolic of the cleansing work of the Holy Spirit since healing is said to result from the prayer offered in faith and thus is ultimately from God.[13] In that case the oil was probably used to provide tangible anticipation of the healing similar to what the Lord did on several occasions (Mark 7:33; John 9:6).[14] The ceremony would have a lasting impression on the people who participated. To make the anointing with oil determinative in any way is beyond the purpose of the passage and detracts from the results of the prayer.

Another aspect of James 5:13–16 is intriguing. Why should a believer ask someone else to pray for him when James had already pointed out in 1:5 that the way is open for every Christian to approach the Lord in prayer? The answer may be that the sick believer was out of fellowship with God. James had written that a "double-minded" believer will not "receive anything from the Lord" (1:7–8). Also the person who prays with the wrong motives will not receive affirmative answers from God (4:3). This is also what Jesus taught about prayer during his earthly ministry. He indicated that an unforgiving spirit could hinder a believer's prayers from being answered (Matt.

11. Ludwig Edelstein, "Temple Medicine," in *Asclepius: A Collection and Interpretation of the Testimonies* (Baltimore: Johns Hopkins University Press, 1945), 2:139.

12. Hiebert, *Epistle of James*, p. 321.

13. Charles R. Erdman, *The General Epistles* (Philadelphia: Westminster, 1941), p. 48.

14. E. H. Plumptre, *The General Epistle of St. James with Notes and Introduction* (Cambridge: University Press, 1899), p. 103.

6:9–15; 18:21–35; Mark 11:22–25). The fact that James raised the question of sin (5:15) adds support to the possibility that the sickness he wrote about is related to sin in the believer's life.[15]

Can people be sick as a result of wrong attitudes and actions? The answer is yes. Illness brought on by tension, stress, or other emotional or behavioral problems is not unusual. James wrote that the people "kill and covet" (4:2)—strong language indeed! Interestingly the Lord connected the word "murder" to "anger" in his Sermon on the Mount (Matt. 5:21–22).

The specific Greek construction used by James in 5:15 indicates that sin was a strong factor in this situation. The statement "If he has sinned, he will be forgiven" is a third class conditional sentence,[16] which suggests the probability of sin being related to the sickness. This would explain why the readers were to confess their sins to each other (v. 16). It seems that Christians had sinned against each other in strife, and physical sickness was the result. It is important to note that confessing sins is not to be a public confession before the church but private confession to the offended party.[17]

The next phrase in verse 16 adds weight to the argument that the prayer for healing is related to sickness that resulted from sin. James wrote "the prayer of a righteous man avails much." Those who had sinned against each other were acting in an unrighteous way. Human anger does not bring about the righteousness of God (1:20). The anger they were expressing by the wrong use of the tongue, which resulted in fighting and quarrels, was an expression of unrighteousness. Once sins were confessed, cleansing from unrighteousness followed (1 John 1:9). Then their prayers would be effective and powerful.

James used Elijah as an example of how effective the prayers of the righteous can be. Elijah was a righteous man, who stood out among the unrighteous Israelites. After seeing all that James wrote about unanswered prayer and unrighteous conduct, this positive statement about a righteous man's prayers stands as a bright beacon.

The incident James selected from the life of Elijah seems to substantiate the view that James was dealing with physical sickness resulting from unrighteous behavior. To support his statement that Elijah's prayer was powerful and effective, James referred to a specific incident from Elijah's life. To be effective an illustration must correspond to the statement or point being made. Otherwise it is superfluous. James was keenly aware of Elijah's prayer life, and he deliberately chose *not* to select Elijah's prayer that brought heal-

15. Walter W. Wessell, "James," in *The Wycliffe Bible Commentary,* ed. Charles F. Pfeiffer and Everett F. Harrison (Chicago: Moody, 1962), p. 1439.

16. Fritz Rienecker, *A Linguistic Key to the Greek New Testament,* ed. Cleon L. Rogers, Jr. (Grand Rapids: Zondervan, 1980), p. 714.

17. R. V. G. Tasker, *The General Epistles of James,* Tyndale New Testament Commentaries (Grand Rapids: Eerdmans, 1956), p. 135.

ing and life to the widow's son in Zarephath (1 Kings 17:7–24). This incident had all the ingredients to fit James' argument. The woman felt that the illness and death of her son were directly related to her sin (v. 18), and she confessed this to Elijah, God's prophet and a spiritual leader in Israel. This would substantiate the teaching of James, if he were intending to teach the power of prayer to raise up the sick. The fact that the Spirit of God did not lead James to use this example is significant and must be considered in a consistent interpretation of the passage.

The incident James did select focused on Ahab and is found in 1 Kings 17–18. Elijah prayed that it would not rain on the earth because of the wickedness of the people of Israel. Moses had declared in Deuteronomy 28:15, 23–24, that when the people of Israel failed to obey God, he would judge them by holding back rain. Only when they humbled themselves and turned back to God and prayed could they expect to receive rain from heaven. The unrighteousness of the people was forgiven because of their heart response to God. Likewise James was dealing with sickness that resulted from sinful behavior toward others. Thus, they needed to repent and call the elders of the church to pray for them. The issue is not one of healing; rather it pertains to discipline.

James' final statement in the book gives added weight to this interpretation. It is a fitting climax to the entire section: "My brethren, if any among you strays from the truth, and one turns him back, let him know that he who turns a sinner from the error of his way will save a soul from death, and will cover a multitude of sins" (James 5:19–20, NASB). Obviously James was addressing believers who go astray for he referred to "my brethren" and "any among you." This view is supported by, among others, Blue,[18] Ryrie,[19] Erdman,[20] and Plumptre.[21] Those who wander from the truth are not unbelievers who have rejected the gospel message; rather, they are believers who have been deceived.

Earlier in his letter James had warned believers about the dangers of being deceived, tempted, and drawn away (1:13–16). Christians needed to stop talking about each other and be reconciled to one another. Rather than judge each other, the exhortation was to love and care for others. Peacemakers who sow in peace will see a harvest in righteousness (3:18).

The seriousness of the situation among the believers is alluded to in the closing words in the epistle. Believers in the church were in danger of death—physical death—because of the way they were treating each other. God does

---

18. J. Ronald Blue, "James," in *The Bible Knowledge Commentary, New Testament,* ed. John F. Walvoord and Roy B. Zuck (Wheaton, Ill.: Victor Books, 1983), p. 835.

19. Charles C. Ryrie, *The Ryrie Study Bible* (Chicago: Moody, 1978), p. 1863.

20. Erdman, *General Epistles,* p. 50.

21. Plumptre, *General Epistle of St. James with Notes and Introduction,* p. 106.

not look lightly on unrighteous behavior. It has a devastating effect on individuals as well as on an entire church.

How do Christians get into a situation like the one James mentioned in chapter 5? Often it is by ignoring the truth of the Word of God, that is, by failing to hear and apply God's instruction (1:19–25). Believers need to treat each other in true wisdom, which James described as pure, peace-loving, considerate, and submissive (3:15–16). This attitude will enable people to be helpful and bring reconciliation.

The truth of James 5:13–16 is applicable for believers today. James was not discussing sickness in general, nor necessarily severe illness that doctors cannot heal. Rather he was speaking of sickness that is the result of unrighteous behavior. James did not write to give a definitive statement on the healing of all sickness for Christians. The passage sheds light on God's dealing with those in the early church whose actions were not pleasing to him. This text speaks about individuals who sin against the Lord and, in light of the context of the book, especially those who sin with their tongues. If church members today took this passage seriously, it would bring about significant results, just as did Elijah's prayer. When Christians recognize sinful attitudes and wrongful behavior and turn to the Lord, the result is forgiveness and restoration and, in specific cases in which sickness is the result of a particular sin, there can be physical healing.

Tribute

It has been my privilege to know Donald K. Campbell for more than thirty-nine years; he has been my teacher, friend, and partner in the ministry. For the past seven years I have served in an administrative role under his leadership. He is admired because of his godly character—a delightful blend of kindness, graciousness, and thoughtfulness with integrity, humility, and a strong sense of justice. His ministry has been marked by faithfulness to the Lord and loyalty to those who have served with him. The term "man of God" is a fitting tribute to one who has consistently modeled the Christian life.

Peter's Instructions
to Husbands in 1 Peter 3:7

James R. Slaughter

It seems natural for a husband to love his wife, expressing his tenderness toward her and his affection for her in ways that meet the longing of her heart. But many men find it difficult to love their wives in a deeply meaningful way. Is it because their efforts become entangled in a web of self-centered attitudes and actions? Recent data reveal that goals in marriage have shifted from a posture of other-centeredness or commitment to one of self-centeredness focused on objectives of personal happiness and contentment.[1] With this paradigm shift it is little wonder that a wife finds herself questioning whether her husband is more concerned about meeting his own needs than hers. Peter and Paul address this issue in their instructions to husbands, which indicates that the problem of a husband's self-centered concerns may not be so current a phenomenon as modern analysts assume.

Though Peter and Paul both enjoin husbands to sacrifice self for the benefit of their wives (sacrificial love, Eph. 5:25; living with wives in accord with knowledge, rendering them honor, 1 Pet. 3:7), the apostles' messages contain different emphases that must be understood if their instructions are to be interpreted properly and applied accurately. Peter did not simply echo Paul's words in Ephesians 5. Instead he arranges a combination of themes, words, and phrases to communicate a particular idea in his own style, carefully chosen to achieve his objectives. To understand Paul is not to understand Peter. Their messages are complementary, not identical. Peter focused on a particular motif Paul did not emphasize, namely, enduring unfair circumstances in marriage. Paul instructed husbands to love their wives (Eph. 5:22, 25). Peter carried the instruction a bit further by enjoining husbands to honor their

---

1. Larry Crabb, *Men and Women: Enjoying the Difference* (Grand Rapids: Zondervan, 1991), p. 28; Randy Cirner and Theresa Cirner, "Is Christian Marriage Any Different?" in *Husbands and Wives*, ed. Howard Hendricks and Jeane Hendricks, with LaVonne Neff (Wheaton, Ill.: Victor Books, 1988), pp. 19–20; and Jack O. Balwick and Judith K. Balwick, *The Family: A Christian Perspective on the Contemporary Home* (Grand Rapids: Baker, 1989), p. 81.

wives even when wives create hardship or frustration for their husbands (1 Pet. 3:7). Paul stated the basic exhortation; Peter narrowed it to a particular situation.

In today's culture, which stresses so strongly the defense of personal rights, Peter's message to husbands is extremely crucial. The world is hostile toward the concept of deference in the face of unfairness because individuals naturally tend to resist giving up their rights. But Peter's instructions to behave with a spirit of deference in an encounter with unfair circumstances emphasizes a biblical truth. The apostle's reference to it in the context of marriage places a husband's responsibility in a new light, which must be understood clearly if harmony in marriage is to be achieved.

The Argument of 1 Peter in Relation to Peter's Instructions to Husbands

When taken together, the motifs of 1 Peter[2] embody a message that may be expressed as follows. When a believer encounters unfair circumstances, his or her behavior should reflect a spirit of deference[3] in all relationships as that person follows Christ's example and anticipates future glory. The apostle extends greetings to believers encountering unfairness in their circumstances (1:1–2), assuring them of future glory as a way of encouraging them during their unjust trials (1:3–2:10). Peter expects believers who face unfair circumstances to behave with a spirit of deference (2:11–5:11). Believers are to behave righteously before Gentile neighbors who persecute them (2:11–12), and to behave with deference when they face unfair circumstances in legal affairs (2:13–17), domestic affairs (including marriage) (2:18–3:7), civil affairs (3:8–4:19), and church affairs (5:1–9). After encouraging these believers (5:10–11), the apostle closes his letter with a final charge, greeting, and blessing (5:12–14).

In seeking to understand Peter's instructions to husbands, we must read them with the author's argument in mind. From a literary perspective it would be unreasonable for Peter to give husbands directives independent of his purpose and structure. The reader must seek to interpret Peter's words to husbands in light of the argument that controls the epistle's elements. Husbands, just like Christian household slaves and Christian wives, are to render

2. Peter constructed the message of this epistle by weaving together five primary motifs: (1) the believer's behavior, (2) the believer's unfair treatment, (3) the believer's deference, (4) the believer's motivation by Christ's example, and (5) the believer's anticipation of future glory. He emphasizes these themes by the use of a broad vocabulary, and by their occurrence throughout the document.

3. The word "deference" conveys the idea of thoughtful consideration of another person's desires or feelings; it also suggests the courteous, respectful, or ingratiating regard for another's wishes. A spirit of humility is consistent with deferential behavior. "Respect" may be the closest synonym. Deference does not necessarily connote acquiescence, agreement, or passivity, though it does rule out retaliation.

deference to those responsible for their unfair circumstances. In this context the object of the husband's deference is his wife.

Peter's Use of "in the Same Way"

The word *homoiōs* ("likewise," "in the same way") near the beginning of 1 Peter 3:7 reveals Peter's dependence on his argument for the instructions to husbands. Though some expositors take the adverb as a simple connective in Peter's train of thought,[4] many interpret it as contributing to the flow of his argument, especially as it relates to the issue of deference. Wand relates *homoiōs* to 2:13, "Submit yourselves . . . to every authority instituted among men," suggesting that the marriage state is a mutual contract involving obligations for both parties.[5] On the other hand, Bigg links *homoiōs* to 2:17 and the honor due to all.[6] In light of the honor due every person, husbands are to honor their wives.

The view that *homoiōs* relates to a broader, previous concept, and is not simply a connective, lends better support to the author's argument as it flows from one section of the letter to another. As with Peter's instructions to wives in 3:1, this use of the adverb focuses on the spirit of deference that encourages Christians to render honor to all, even when it may be difficult to do so. Clark points out the reciprocal responsibilities of husbands and wives regardless of the performance of the other.[7] Such reciprocal responsibilities do not include submission *(hypotassō)* of the husband to his wife, but an expression of deference through other attitudes and actions.[8] His part is represented by deferential behavior toward his wife, which demonstrates his unconditional, sacrificial love for her and his unreserved honor of her as a mutual heir of the grace of life.

Peter's Use of the Words "Live Together"

Peter gives instructions to husbands regarding their living together *(synoikountes)* with their wives in marriage. This use of *synoikountes* includes

---

4. J. Ramsey Michaels, *1 Peter*, Word Biblical Commentary (Waco, Tex.: Word Books, 1988), p. 167.
5. J. W. C. Wand, *The General Epistles of St. Peter and St. Jude* (London: Methuen, 1934), p. 93.
6. Charles Bigg, *A Critical and Exegetical Commentary on the Epistles of St. Peter and St. Jude*, International Critical Commentary (Edinburgh: T. & T. Clark, 1902), p. 154.
7. Stephen B. Clark, *Man and Woman in Christ* (Ann Arbor, Mich.: Servant Books, 1980), p. 90.
8. Regarding the view that Paul in Ephesians 5:22–33 did not require mutual submission, see F. F. Bruce, *The Epistles to the Colossians, to Philemon, and to the Ephesians*, New International Commentary on the New Testament (Grand Rapids: Eerdmans, 1984), pp. 381–84. In addition, Foh's treatment of the concept of mutual submission and the differences between the responsibilities of husbands and wives is extremely helpful (Susan T. Foh, *Women and the Word of God* [Phillipsburg, N.J.: Presbyterian and Reformed, 1979], pp. 200–201).

much more than the sexual connotation suggested by Demarest[9] and Kelly.[10] Because of the broad use of the term historically there is no need to read into it a special sexual nuance here in 1 Peter 3:7. The word is used in the papyri and in the Septuagint of husbands and wives in marriage,[11] but it is sometimes used of siblings living together.[12] The noun can refer to a lodging house where a variety of people may dwell together.[13] The New Testament uses *synoikountes* only in this verse. It seems best to relate the word to all aspects of a husband and wife's participation together in domestic life, including the sexual relationship, but not focusing exclusively on it. Davids translates it simply, "live together."[14] This broader sense fits well with 1 Peter 3:7, encompassing all relationships between husband and wife in marriage, including the sexual.

The Meaning of "in Accordance with Knowledge"

Peter tells husbands to live with their wives "in accordance with knowledge" *(kata gnōsin)*. Because of its apparent vagueness, "in accordance with knowledge" has invited disagreement among interpreters. But in seeking to interpret the phrase correctly, the reader must ask, What is the object of the *gnōsis* of 3:7—knowledge of what? How does knowledge of something, or of someone, produce godly behavior of a husband toward his wife? "Some identify God as the object of this knowledge. Husbands then are to live with their wives as their knowledge of God would require them, or lead them to live."[15] But the New Testament uses *gnōsis* more to express obedient knowledge of the will of God rather than in reference to the knowledge of God himself.[16] The compound *epignōsis* is used in a more technical sense for the decisive knowledge of God in conversion to the Christian faith.[17] Thus, when referring to the saving knowledge of God or of the Lord Jesus Christ, Peter prefers *epignōsis* (2 Pet. 1:2–3, 8; 2:20). But when he refers to knowledge of the Scriptures or to one's understanding of God's will or plan, Peter uses *gnōsis* or *ginōskō* (see 2 Pet. 1:5–6, 20; 3:3).

9. John T. Demarest, *A Translation and Exposition of the First Epistle of the Apostle Peter* (New York: John Moffatt, 1851), p. 152.

10. J. N. D. Kelly, *A Commentary on the Epistles of Peter and Jude* (Grand Rapids: Baker, 1986), p. 132.

11. James Hope Moulton and George Milligan, *The Vocabulary of the Greek New Testament* (Grand Rapids: Eerdmans, 1930), s.v. "*synoikeō*," p. 611. Cf. Gen. 20:3; Deut. 22:13; 24:3; 25:5b; and Isa. 62:5 in the Septuagint.

12. Ibid.

13. Ibid.

14. Peter H. Davids, *The First Epistle of Peter*, New International Commentary on the New Testament (Grand Rapids: Eerdmans, 1990), p. 142.

15. Francis Wright Beare, *The First Epistle of Peter* (Oxford: Basil Blackwell, 1947), p. 131.

16. *Theological Dictionary of the New Testament*, s.v. "γινώσκω," by Rudolph Bultmann, 1:707.

17. Ibid.

In his first epistle Peter did not use the noun *epignōsis* or the verb *ginōskō*, and the noun *gnōsis* occurs only once. Therefore a clear pattern in 1 Peter is impossible to obtain. But from the New Testament use of *gnōsis* and *epignōsis*, and from Peter's application of the words in his second epistle, it seems preferable not to interpret "knowledge" in 1 Peter 3:7 as saving knowledge of God.

Another interpretation of *kata gnōsin* in verse 7 is that Peter refers to husbands' knowledge of their wives. Swindoll interprets it in the following way: "Knowing your wife includes those things about her that others don't and won't know. Her deep fears and cares. Her disappointments as well as her expectations. Her scars and secrets and also her thoughts and dreams. That's knowing your wife."[18]

However, *gnōsis* does not ordinarily appear in the New Testament as knowledge of another person.[19] This fact tends to weaken the position that knowledge in this passage is knowledge of the wife. In addition to this, the argument that controls the instructions in Peter's letter suggests Peter was not instructing husbands to understand their wives, but *how to act when they do not understand their wives.*

Instead of referring to the knowledge of God or of the wife, Peter may have meant knowledge of principles from the Scriptures that dictate a husband's behavior in marriage. Lenski calls this "Scripture knowledge."[20] Hiebert believes that it refers to "an understanding of Christian principles directing the marriage relationship."[21]

As noted, New Testament writers rely on the word *gnōsis* when they speak of knowing or understanding God's will, or understanding spiritual truth. This is likely the meaning of *gnōsis* in 1 Peter 3:7, which refers to a husband's knowledge of principles revealed in the Word of God to which he is accountable. In 2 Peter the author uses *gnōsis* ("knowledge") and *ginōskō* ("to know") to refer to an awareness of and understanding of God's Word (e.g., knowledge of God's promises, 1:4; knowledge of the coming of mockers in the last days, 3:2–3; knowing that those who distort the Scriptures incur destruction on themselves, 3:16–17; etc.).

Within the context of his household instruction (1 Pet. 2:18–3:7) and the summary statement following it (1 Pet. 3:8–12), Peter inserted two Old Testament passages to support his teaching about Christian behavior in unfair circumstances. One passage is Isaiah 53:9, which describes the Messiah's behavior when he suffered unjustly—"[Christ] had done no violence, nor

18. Charles Swindoll, *Strike the Original Match* (Portland, Oreg.: Multnomah, 1980), p. 52.
19. The verb *ginōskō* is used of sexual intercourse in Matt. 1:25 and Luke 1:34, but it is not used with regard to knowing another person's traits or understanding a person's behavior.
20. R. C. H. Lenski, *The Interpretation of the Epistles of St. Peter, St. John and St. Luke* (Minneapolis: Augsburg, 1961), p. 138.
21. D. Edmond Hiebert, *First Peter* (Chicago: Moody, 1984), p. 193.

was any deceit in his mouth." Peter's readers are to discern from their understanding of Isaiah 53:9 what their own responsibility is to be when they are in similar situations. Christ becomes the husband's example for living out the instructions of 1 Peter 3:7.

Peter used a second Old Testament text, Psalm 34:12–16, to exhort his readers to "seek peace and pursue it" (1 Pet. 3:11). The apostle developed this theme throughout his epistle as he taught how believers are to respond to others, especially those who oppose them or treat them unfairly. This behavior is to be deference on the part of Christians who encounter hard, unfair circumstances.

Therefore, *gnōsis* in 1 Peter 3:7 is best interpreted as knowledge of the Word of God. The husband's knowledge of the message of Isaiah 53 and Psalm 34 (and other Old Testament texts used by Peter) reveals his responsibility to follow the example of Christ in his relationship with his wife. Peter's message implies that some husbands were experiencing unfair circumstances in relationship to their wives. At times the husbands may have been unfairly burdened, deprived, or otherwise inordinately stressed by situations brought on by their wives. They might even have been maligned by their spouses. In such cases the husbands are to follow the example of Christ in Isaiah 53 and the precepts of David in Psalm 34. A husband is not to commit sin against his wife nor speak deceitfully to her; if she reviles him, he is not to revile in return or threaten her. A husband is to "keep his tongue from evil and his lips from deceitful speech." Though he might be tempted to blame her for her part in his dilemma, and react with a spirit of retaliation, he is instead, as God's Word requires, to "turn from evil and do good, . . . seek peace and pursue it" (1 Pet. 3:11). He is to render honor to his weaker feminine partner.

The Meaning of the "Weaker Vessel"

Unfair circumstances encountered by a Christian husband are, at least in part, caused by his wife's being the weaker of the two partners, literally, "weaker vessel" *(asthenesterō skeuei tō gynaikeiō)*. The word "vessel" is used here for the wife as a person and represents more than just her body.[22] It is best understood as "person," or in the context of the passage, "[marriage] partner."

Peter qualified "vessel" in this verse with the adjective *gynaikeiō* ("feminine"), a reference to the wife. Kelly understands "feminine vessel" as "female sex,"[23] and Reicke suggests it means "female element."[24] Bauer,

22. Edward G. Selwyn, *The First Epistle of St. Peter* (London: Macmillan, 1946), p. 187; Kelly, *Commentary on the Epistles of Peter and Jude,* p. 133.

23. Ibid.

24. Bo Reicke, *The Epistles of James, Peter, and Jude,* Anchor Bible (Garden City, N.Y.: Doubleday, 1964), p. 102.

Arndt, and Gingrich suggest the adjective means "feminine," stating that authors often use it as a periphrasis for "woman" or "wife."[25]

More attention has been given by expositors to the other adjective modifying "vessel," namely, *asthenesterō* ("weaker"). The word *asthenēs* ("weak") is used in the literal sense to refer to someone who is sick (Matt. 25:43; Acts 4:9), or physically without strength (Hos. 9:1–2), or more generically, of any weakness, such as weakness of the flesh that gives up easily (Matt. 26:41), of an unimpressive personal appearance (2 Cor. 10:10), or ineffective, elementary principles (Gal. 4:9). Figuratively the word is used of less important parts of the human body (1 Cor. 4:10), moral deficiency including sinfulness (Rom. 5:6), and an inability to understand Christian liberty (1 Cor. 8:7, 9–10). Various translations of the term in 1 Peter 3:7 have been suggested, including "more fragile vessel,"[26] "more vulnerable sex,"[27] and "more delicate element."[28] Whatever the wife's weakness in 1 Peter 3:7, there is no implication that the wife is inferior to her husband. The comparative form *asthenesterō*, "weaker," highlights the fact that both husband and wife are weak vessels. First Peter 3:7 simply focuses on the weakness of the wife.

Though a common interpretation of "weaker feminine vessel" views the statement as a reference to physical strength,[29] more likely Peter has in mind a combination of female traits. This is because of *skeuos*, which often stands for the whole person. Current research indicates that at least three basic female traits exist by which a woman may be perceived as weaker than the male. She tends to be less physically powerful, less aggressive, and less objective. Characteristic of the male is a greater muscle mass than his female counterpart, and a greater thickness and density of bone.[30] The male tends to be taller, larger boned, and more muscular. The female tends to be shorter and smaller, and to have less muscle tissue.

In addition to these physical characteristics the presence of the male hormone (testosterone) accounts for much of the increased levels of aggression in men.[31] This difference apparently plays a role in emotional response. Men have more distance from their emotions, and a greater capacity to detach themselves from immediate reactions. Women respond to situations more

---

25. Walter Bauer, William F. Arndt, and F. Wilbur Gingrich, *A Greek-English Lexicon of the New Testament and Other Early Christian Literature*, 2d ed., rev. F. Wilbur Gingrich and Frederick A. Danker (Chicago: University of Chicago Press, 1979), p. 167.

26. Andre S. Bustanoby, "Love, Honor and Obey," *Christianity Today*, June 13, 1969, p. 804.

27. Davids, *First Epistle of Peter*, p. 122.

28. Reicke, *Epistles of James, Peter, and Jude*, p. 103.

29. Beare, *First Epistle of Peter*, p. 132; Bigg, *Critical and Exegetical Commentary on the Epistles of St. Peter and St. Jude*, p. 155; Alan M. Stibbs, *The First Epistle General of Peter*, Tyndale New Testament Commentaries (Grand Rapids: Eerdmans, 1974), p. 127.

30. Arthur C. Guyton, *Textbook of Medical Physiology* (Philadelphia: W. B. Saunders, 1966), p. 1128.

31. Interview with Howard Lang, Bedford, Tex., October 1986.

immediately and spontaneously, finding it harder to distance themselves from the way they feel. Thus, a man more readily reacts to a situation with a response that is more purely mental or physical.[32] The tendency to be less aggressive may make the female less confrontational in her behavior toward her husband and children, and toward those outside the family. In light of such considerations Grudem concludes:

> There may also be [another] sense of "weakness" which would fit the context [of 1 Pet. 3:7] . . . namely, a greater emotional sensitivity. While this is something which is also a great strength, it nonetheless means wives are often more likely to be hurt deeply by conflict. . . . Knowing this, Christian husbands should not be "harsh" (Col. 3:19) or fill their marriage relationships with criticism and conflict, but should rather be positive and affirming.[33]

The words "weaker feminine partner" may also refer to the tendency of the female to be less objective than the male. Neuroscience research has established that the two hemispheres in the brain make different contributions to what a person knows and how a person acts, though complex activity requires the entire brain.[34] Left-half cognition involves formal logic and conveys the appearance of an objective reality. Right-half cognition combines bodily perception and active imagination, creating patterns of mosaics of meaning by a leap of imagination.[35] People who utilize a more equal portion of right and left brain hemispheres are more dependent and are more sensitive to their surroundings.[36] The male mind discriminates, analyzes, separates, and refines. The feminine mind knows relatedness, has an intuitive perception of feeling, and has a tendency to unite rather than separate.[37]

While one pattern of cognition does not have more value than the other, it does suggest that those who are cognitively right brain-oriented (usually women) find it more difficult to make decisions based on objectivity. Women therefore may find themselves more vulnerable to intimidation than men, and more vulnerable to emotional pressure and appeals applied by others. It may be that this vulnerability constitutes a part of what the apostle meant by "weaker feminine vessel," though he lacked awareness of the scientific basis for his observations.

The argument of 1 Peter suggests there will be times when these differences between a husband and his wife place him in an unfair circumstance or

---

32. F. J. J. Buytendijk, *Woman, a Contemporary View* (New York: Newman, 1968), p. 140.
33. Wayne Grudem, *1 Peter,* Tyndale New Testament Commentaries (Grand Rapids: Eerdmans, 1988), p. 144.
34. James H. Ashbrook, "Ways of Knowing God: Gender and the Brain," *Christian Century,* January 1989, p. 14.
35. Ibid.
36. Ibid.
37. Judith Bardwick, *Psychology of Women* (New York: Harper and Row, 1971), p. 100.

perhaps at an awkward disadvantage. The apostle is instructing Christians regarding their behavior when they encounter unfair circumstances. First Peter 3:7 addresses husbands who encounter such circumstances because of the tendencies of their wives who are "weaker feminine partners," weaker presumably in that they ordinarily are less strong, less aggressive, and less objective than their husbands. Some husbands might find themselves inordinately burdened by additional household labors because of their wives' lesser muscular strength. They might have to live with uncomfortable situations brought on by decisions made on the basis of a wife's more subjective criteria for judging. Some husbands might have to take unusual steps to protect their wives or their homes against outsiders who might persuade or intimidate, and who might seek to gain a foothold because of a wife's tendency to be less aggressive. Within the home a husband might be judged by his wife as harsh or insensitive when on occasion he takes a more objective approach to problem solving.

In such circumstances the husband might be tempted to become defensive, self-justifying, and retributional toward his wife. He might argue with her, raise his voice, or otherwise try to intimidate her, accuse her, threaten or belittle her. However, Peter's instructions clearly reveal the husband's responsibility in such circumstances: he is to behave with respect, kindness, and understanding, taking into consideration her feelings and wishes, that is, to reflect a spirit of deference. Specifically he is to render his wife honor, even if she has been responsible for his hardship.

The Husband's Responsibility toward His Wife

In 1 Peter 3:1–6 Christian wives are instructed to behave with deference as they encounter the difficulties of living with an unbelieving husband. Similarly in verse 7 Christian husbands are told to honor their wives in unfair circumstances brought about by the wife's being the weaker vessel. An accurate translation of the phrase would be "rendering honor [to them] as to the weaker feminine partner" *(hōs asthenesterō skeuei tō gynaikeiō aponemontes timēn)*. "As" *(hōs)* simply introduces the characteristic quality of the wife, that is, the fact she is the weaker vessel. In effect, "rendering honor" *(aponemontes timēn)* is an elaboration of how husbands are to live together with their wives in accord with knowledge.[38]

Aponemontes, appearing only here in the New Testament, means "to assign, show, or pay."[39] It is used in the papyri of an officer who is commended for giving to his soldiers their just dues.[40]

---

38. Hiebert, *First Peter,* p. 194.
39. Bauer, Arndt, and Gingrich, *Greek-English Lexicon of the New Testament and Other Early Christian Literature,* p. 96.
40. Hiebert, *First Peter,* p. 194.

When a Christian husband encounters unfair, unduly stressful circumstances because of his wife's weaknesses, he is not to respond harshly to her, berate her, or demean her, but is to behave in accord with the principles of God's Word, which require him to honor her. Though "honor" *(timē)* is sometimes equated with "respect," the word may carry the stronger nuance of "reverence."[41] Peter combined it with "praise" *(epainos)* in 1 Peter 1:14, and uses the adjectival form in 1:19 to describe the blood of Christ. In the latter verse *timē* is often translated "precious."

The husband is to respond to his wife in such a way as to acknowledge her preciousness to him (and to God), her special nature, and her praiseworthiness. He is to exhibit no arrogance, no overbearing attitude; nor is he to assume superiority or a domineering attitude. He is not to accuse, castigate, or intimidate her. He is not to treat his wife rudely, patronizingly, or contemptuously, nor is he to represent her to others in such a way. Instead, he is to render her honor, which would include kind and affirming words both privately (with her) and publicly (with others).[42] He is to make the best of his encounters with unfair circumstances, even when they are the fault of his wife, without blaming her or reminding her of her weaknesses. Though he might confront in a loving way, he is to be forgiving, accepting, and unwilling to hold a grudge.

In addition to rendering honor to their wives as the weaker feminine partners, husbands are to honor them as "heirs together with them of the grace of life" *(hōs kai synklēronomois charitos zōēs). Synklēronomois* is literally "inheriting together with." Christian husbands are to honor their wives, for they enjoy spiritual standing and privilege equal to that of their husbands. With this statement in 1 Peter 3:7 Peter emphasized the important fact that wives share with their husbands in the great salvation so eloquently described in 1:3–9 (cf. "inheritance," *klēronomia*).

Husbands and wives will inherit together "the grace of life" *(charitos zōēs)*. In light of Peter's eschatological focus this life probably refers not to physical life, but to eternal life. It is best to take "life" as appositional to "grace." Peter has already said his readers have an eternal inheritance awaiting them in heaven. The grace to be inherited is eternal life.

The Effect of the Husband's Behavior

Husbands' behavior toward their wives directly affects their relationship to God. If they fail to honor their wives as heirs with them of eternal life, their prayer life may be in jeopardy: "so that your prayers may not be hindered"

41. Bauer, Arndt, and Gingrich, *Greek-English Lexicon of the New Testament and Other Early Christian Literature*, p. 825.
42. Grudem, *1 Peter*, p. 143.

(eis to mē egkoptesthai tas proseuchas hymōn). Eis to with the infinitive may denote purpose, but here it more likely indicates a contemplated result.[43] Other New Testament passages affirm that relational disturbances with others will hinder one's relationship with God, including one's prayer life (Matt. 5:23; 6:12, 14–15; 1 Cor. 11:33–34; James 4:3). The verb "hinder," used here as a present passive infinitive, denotes the work of impeding, arresting, or putting up an obstacle. It is used of soldiers digging trenches to slow a pursuing enemy.

Peter did not specify the nature of the hindrance to prayer. He may have had in mind an unwillingness on God's part to answer the prayers of a husband who refuses to honor his wife. Or he may have been referring to the unwillingness of husbands and wives to pray together because of their unhealthy relationship. Probably "your prayers" *(tas proseuchas hymōn)* refers to the prayers of husbands since the passage is addressed to them initially.

Conclusion

How should a husband love his wife? He is to love her sacrificially, with other-centered attention and affection, not a self-serving preservation of his own rights, goals, or even feelings. He is to treat her with honor, demonstrating her preciousness to himself and to God. He is to render her honor because she is his spiritual equal, an heir together with him of the gracious gift of eternal life. This is to be his response even when he may experience difficult, unfair circumstances precipitated by her characteristics as a woman. Even then he is to honor her, never threatening her, demeaning her, or blaming her. If he insists on treating her dishonorably, he runs the risk of an interrupted prayer life, as his *relationship to God is intimately affected by his relationship to his wife.*

Peter's message must be understood and practiced by husbands in their efforts to represent Christ to their wives. Otherwise the marriage dynamic is weakened by the absence of a crucial biblical element. Only with the consistent application by Christian husbands of Peter's instructions in 1 Peter 3:7 can marriage truly be all God intends it to be.

Tribute

I admire and give thanks to Dr. Campbell who taught me the Pentateuch, and who provided an example of excellence as teacher, administrator, and friend. His able leadership has been an inspiration to those of us who remain here at Dallas Seminary to carry on the tradition he has so nobly advanced. May the Lord continue to bless him with every success.

---

43. Hiebert, *First Peter,* p. 195; Bauer, Arndt, and Gingrich, *Greek-English Lexicon of the New Testament and Other Early Christian Literature,* pp. 228–29.

The New Covenant

John F. Walvoord

Introduction

General Considerations

The concept of divine covenants in the Bible has long been a subject for theological discussion and biblical exegesis. From the early centuries of the Christian era and probably before, a number of God's promises in the Bible are referred to as biblical covenants. From Genesis to Revelation there is constant reference to covenants, some of them by name, as in the case of Noah, and others in the form of general and sweeping promises, as in the case of Adam and Eve. It is rather obvious that when God promises something, whether it is in the form of a covenant or not, it becomes an important consideration in understanding biblical revelation.

A survey of the literature in the field reveals that this subject has been discussed for centuries, and it would be a major undertaking even to summarize all the writings on it from the time of the early church until now. Unfortunately, the variety of subjects and premises involved has led to theological confusion rather than theological clarity, and it is important to ask basic questions about what the Bible actually teaches and what the principles that govern its interpretation are.

Major Issues

In a preliminary way certain major issues emerge in the study of biblical covenants. One such issue is the distinction advocated by Augustine of Hippo that biblical covenants are of two major kinds. First, there are biblical covenants in which God pronounces promises in a formal way, which continue to govern his relationship to humankind throughout the centuries. Second, there are moral covenants or legal requirements that may or may not be directly connected with the covenants but whose connections are often implied. The distinction between covenants, which God promises in a sovereign way, and moral covenants, which are often conditional on the part of humankind, is most important to observe in the study of the subject.

Prominent features of God's covenants with humanity are his righteousness that governs his moral requirements and his mission of grace for human beings and their sin. These two lines of thought should not be confused, even though they are often related.

When examining covenants relating to God's moral requirements for humankind, progressive revelation in the various dispensations of God's government must be observed. The concept of progressive revelation is essential to any coherent view of the Bible since obligations in different periods are not the same. This is illustrated particularly in the Mosaic period when God instituted more than six hundred laws to govern Israel's behavior.

In connection with moral covenants, it should be observed that human thinking is inherently legalistic. This is illustrated in heathen religions in which worshipers attempt to please God and curry his favor. It is important to separate this from the Christian concept of grace in which God alone is able to forgive in spite of humanity's lack of merit. Grace is a peculiarity of the Scriptures.

In connection with the gracious element of God's covenant with humanity, two major covenants are often distinguished. One is the covenant of redemption, which embraces the work of God in Christ's death on the cross, making possible our forgiveness. The other is the covenant of grace, which is usually considered as humanward, in contrast to redemption, which is Godward. In this covenant God promises grace to human beings who are without merit and who in no way deserve God's grace.

In the consideration of the covenants, attention should also be paid to the increased clarification on this subject in the New Testament in contrast to the less clear revelation of the Old Testament.

The Biblical Covenants

In the Old Testament the term *bĕrît* is used of a covenant. In the New Testament the word *diathēkē* is used. The first reference to a covenant in the Bible is in God's relationship to Noah (Gen. 6:18). Some have suggested, however, that other covenants preceded this one, though they are not called covenants.

The Edenic Covenant

Before Adam and Eve fell into sin, God made a proposition to them that some have regarded as a covenant, as stated in Genesis 1:26–31 and 2:16–17. God gave Adam authority over the creatures of the world, commanded him to be fruitful, and gave him permission to eat from every green plant.

The only restriction was that Adam and Eve not eat of the tree of the knowledge of good and evil, for if they did so they would surely die (2:16–17). Basically, the covenant was conditional, requiring obedience; but it also declared God's purpose to elevate humanity to a place of authority and prominence, ultimately fulfilled by Christ.

The Adamic Covenant

Adam and Eve failed, however, to observe the restrictions of the Edenic covenant. Innocence was lost and conscience was born. The result was also that God would judge the world, as stated in his word to Adam (3:14–15) and to Eve (3:16). Adam was told that the ground was cursed and that he would find food with difficulty (3:17–19).

Having failed under the Edenic covenant, human beings were then faced with the provisions of the Adamic covenant. That covenant was unconditional in the sense that Adam and Eve's descendants would be unable by human effort to escape the consequences of sin. God judged not only Adam and Eve but also Satan (Gen. 3:14; Rom. 16:20; 2 Cor. 11:3, 14; Rev. 12:9).

A ray of light is provided, however, in the Adamic covenant because God promised that a redeemer would come. As stated briefly in Genesis 3:15, God promised to crush the head of Satan, though Satan would be allowed to strike the heel of the woman's seed, a reference to Christ. This is the introduction of the great theme of grace and redemption found in the Scriptures.

The Adamic covenant continues to be fulfilled in human history as individuals struggle to earn food, and as life ends in sorrow and death (3:19). Unless tempered by the grace of God and changed by subsequent promises, people continue to the present time to labor under the provisions of the Adamic covenant.

The Noahic Covenant

In dealing with Noah and the preflood period, God made certain promises that are declared to be in the form of a covenant (Gen. 6:18; 9:9–16). After stating his purpose to wipe out the human race because of its sin, except for Noah and his family, God gave Noah instructions on how to build the ark in anticipation of the time when the flood would cause everyone except those in the ark to perish. God established this whole situation as a covenant: "But I will establish my covenant with you, and you will enter the ark—you and your sons and your wife and your sons' wives with you" (6:18).

In making a covenant with Noah, God illustrated a very important point. While covenants between individuals are normally a matter of compromise between two parties who are equals, in God's covenants the parties to the covenant are unequal, for God is sovereign and all-powerful and humankind is weak and helpless. The covenant with Noah is entirely unconditional rather than a conditional covenant, as in the Edenic situation. The certainty of the fulfillment of the covenant with Noah rested entirely with God and not with Noah. As this point is somewhat obscured in current discussion on the covenants of Scripture, it is important to distinguish covenants that are conditional from those that are unconditional. Conditional covenants depend on the recipients meeting the conditions imposed by God. Unconditional covenants declare that God's purpose will be fulfilled regardless of an individual's response. The fact that the covenant is one-sided—from God to humankind—does not mean that there is no response on the part of humankind. But the point is that the response is anticipated and does not leave the fulfillment of the covenant in doubt.

The covenant with Noah is amplified in the period after the flood, as recorded in Genesis 9:9–17. In this statement God declared in his covenant with Noah and the entire creaturely world that he would never again destroy the world with a flood. In keeping with this promise, he established the rainbow as "the sign of the covenant between me and the earth" (9:13). The unconditional nature of this covenant is clear, even though Noah failed God by getting drunk (9:20–23) and his three sons became the progenitors of a sinful race. The promise is nevertheless sure and unconditional, unrelated to human worthiness.

The Abrahamic Covenant

Covenants preceding Abraham dealt with the entire human race, though because of the flood their fulfillment is limited to Noah and his three sons. Beginning with the covenant with Abraham, God selected certain individuals and groups to inherit promises that were not for the entire human race. In the discussion of the Abrahamic covenant, major disagreements emerge regarding the premises and fulfillment of these covenants. This is caused partly by the different approach of Calvinists and Arminians, but more particularly by the premillennial versus the amillennial and postmillennial interpretations of eschatology. All branches of theology find it necessary to consider the Abrahamic covenant and how its provisions relate to their theological presuppositions.

The Abrahamic covenant involves promises along several lines. First, God promised Abraham that he would become a great man and would be the father of a great nation (Gen. 12:1–2). Second, God promised that Abraham's progenitors would produce a great nation, referring to Israel (v. 2). Later Abraham became the father of more than the nation Israel, including some of the Arabs who descend from Abraham. A third major provision, however, is that God would bless all peoples of the earth through Abraham (v. 3). This is generally interpreted to refer to the salvation and grace that come through Christ.

As these promises have already been literally fulfilled, it does not allow much freedom to interpret them other than in their literal sense. These promises that God has made are certain of fulfillment regardless of human response. Important in all these promises, however, is the fact that they do not govern the whole race, as some of them relate only to Israel, though the whole race is promised to be blessed through Abraham. Even this general promise, however, is limited to fulfillment to those who come to God in faith.

The provision that God will bless those who bless Abraham and curse those who do not (Gen. 12:3) introduces a conditional element that figures largely in Israel's history. Not only was Israel blessed or cursed in accord with her obedience to God in the Old Testament, but this also extended to other nations as well and their relationship to Israel. As history has graphically demonstrated, every nation that has persecuted Israel has paid a price for it in subsequent history.

The major area of theological conflict, however, is in the promise of God to Abraham, "To your offspring I will give this land" (12:7). This promise is so transparently a reference to the land to which God had directed Abraham after he left Ur of Chaldees that it would seem almost impossible to question its intent. A number of interpretive problems surface, however. Amillenarians and postmillenarians do not believe that Israel will ever inherit the land. This contrasts with the premillennial interpretation, which holds that this promise will be fulfilled in the millennial kingdom after the second coming of Christ. Amillenarians offer several alternative solutions. The most common view is that the promise is about heaven, not a literal land. Postmillenarians also offer this view. This nonliteral interpretation, however, has no scriptural support since every reference to the land in Scripture refers literally to the land of Israel. A more modern explanation is that its promise is literal but conditional on Israel's obedience.

The problem is further amplified by the fact that even though the ultimate fulfillment seems certain, any given generation of Israel could enjoy the land only if obedient to God. In the Old Testament period as well as in the New, Israel was not allowed possession of the land unless she deserved it. Accordingly, while the Israelites went down to Egypt and left the land as God promised in Genesis 15:13, they were also promised blessing if they went back to the land, as recorded in Exodus and later books of the Old Testament. In their return, however, Moses stated specifically in Deuteronomy 28 that their possession of the land depended on their obedience to God. If they were obedient, God would bless them physically and in other ways. If they disobeyed, they would be driven out of the land and would be subject to frightful persecutions. This has tragically been fulfilled in history in the Babylonian and Assyrian captivities and in the worldwide dispersion that occurred after the destruction of Jerusalem in A.D. 70.

In view of these difficulties, in what sense is the Abrahamic covenant unconditional? The point here, which has often been misunderstood, is that *while the fulfillment of any particular generation of Israel depended on obedience to God, the ultimate possession of the land is promised unconditionally to Israel even though she does not deserve it.* Scripture prophesies that a godly remnant of Israel will be the ultimate possessors of the land at the second coming (Ezek. 20:33–38).

Premillenarians hold that the Abrahamic covenant is unconditional in the sense that its ultimate fulfillment is absolutely certain and is specifically predicted in the Old Testament. It depends on God's faithfulness and grace rather than on the merit of the people of Israel.

Most significant, Jeremiah in the midst of Israel's apostasy predicted their return from Babylon and Assyria and in addition promised their ultimate return to the land subsequent to the second coming of Christ (23:5–8; 31:4–11). Further, Ezekiel predicted the partition of the land to the twelve tribes of Israel after the second coming (chaps. 47–48).

This is based on divine grace rather than Israel's worthiness. This is supported by many promises of the glorious kingdom on earth, which will follow the coming of the Messiah King that premillenarians relate to his second coming. Obviously the Abrahamic covenant is a covenant of grace that depends on God's faithfulness and promise. Humankind's enjoyment of it prior to its ultimate fulfillment, however, is conditioned on the faith of any particular generation. But the ultimate fulfillment is absolutely certain.

The Mosaic Covenant

The covenant with Moses occupies most of the Old Testament because, beginning in the Book of Exodus and continuing throughout the rest of the Old Testament, the Mosaic covenant was the dominant factor affecting Israel's history.

This covenant related only to the people of Israel, not the entire human race. This factor is often overlooked. Though the Mosaic covenant did reveal God's moral nature and his will concerning moral issues, the Mosaic covenant was not the basis of judgment on the surrounding nations. To some extent the Mosaic covenant was a partial outgrowth of the Abrahamic covenant because it described the application of this earlier covenant during the entire period of the Old Testament.

The major difference between the Mosaic covenant and the Abrahamic covenant is that the former was conditional and also was *ad interim,* that is, it was a covenant for a limited period, beginning with Moses and ending with Christ. Basically it was a sovereign covenant in which God declared his will for Israel. Though Israel did indicate a preliminary willingness to obey it, they certainly failed, as history records.

In contrast to the other covenants, the Mosaic covenant, though it had provisions for grace and forgiveness, nevertheless builds on the idea that obedience to God is necessary for blessing. While this to some extent is true in every dispensation, the Mosaic covenant was basically a works covenant rather than a grace covenant. The works principle, however, was limited to the matter of blessing in this life and was not related at all to the question of salvation for eternity.

The ultimate application of the Mosaic covenant is stated in Leviticus 19:2: "Be holy because I, the LORD your God, am holy."

Basic to the covenant idea, however, is the fact that this covenant was imposed by God whether or not the people of Israel accepted it. It is therefore a sovereign series of promises as to what God would do under varied circumstances according to Israel's response.

Israel's experiences under the Mosaic covenant were intended by God to be an illustration of how God deals with the people he considers holy to himself. Both her punishments and blessings are related to this basic principle. The limitations of the Mosaic covenant also should be emphasized. The covenant did not relate to eternal life and was not a basis for grace. Instead, compliance meant that God would bless Israel, much as a father would bless a child who is obedient.

The Davidic Covenant

Both the Abrahamic and Mosaic covenants had a certain group of people as their objects, though part of the Abrahamic covenant had worldwide relevance. The Davidic covenant, however, selected a particular family, that is, the descendants of David. God's covenant made certain promises to David's descendants that by their nature affect Israel, but nevertheless do not extend to the entire human race. The basic statement of the covenant is found in 2 Samuel 7, with details also given in 1 Chronicles 17. Confirmation of the Davidic covenant is also found in Psalm 89. This psalm reiterates the fact that the Davidic covenant will be fulfilled regardless of human response. As the promises of the Davidic covenant go far beyond what David deserved, it is obviously a gracious covenant that in its ultimate fulfillment is unconditional.

The provisions of the Davidic covenant were, first, that God would provide through David and his physical posterity a person who would sit on the throne of the kingdom forever (2 Sam. 7:13). God promised that under no circumstances would this covenant ever be rescinded (vv. 15–16). Even David recognized that this was an unusual covenant because it was everlasting, based entirely on God's promises and not on human worthiness.

All conservative interpreters of the Bible recognize that the promise has its ultimate fulfillment in Christ. Again the amillennial and premillennial differences in explaining eschatology come to the fore, however. The amillennial position is that Christ is now on the throne of David in heaven, equating the heavenly throne with the earthly throne of David, whereas the traditional premillennial view is that the Davidic throne will be occupied at the second coming of Christ when Christ assumes his rule in Jerusalem.

As in the case of David, Christ was appointed heir to the throne of David long before he will occupy it. The throne should not be considered a physical chair but a sphere of rule that cannot in the nature of the case be fulfilled until God has restored Israel as a nation and established Christ as king on the earth. Again the major issue is whether the details of a covenant are to be understood in their normal and literal sense or whether they are to be spiritualized, given another meaning, or made conditional and therefore never fulfilled.

Amillennial interpreters affirm that the promises in the Davidic covenant cannot be taken literally or, if taken literally, are conditional. Neither of these assertions, however, is supported by the facts. Premillenarians, however point to the many passages that not only reiterate that the Davidic throne will be on earth in Jerusalem and will continue forever, but also to the fact that this is related to the second coming of Christ at which time he will establish his millennial reign on earth, a situation that is not true at the present time. This is supported in such passages as Psalm 72, Jeremiah 23:5–8, and the many passages that speak of Israel's ultimate regathering, as in Ezekiel 39:25–29 and Jeremiah 30:5–9, and the New Testament confirmation of a millennial kingdom in Revelation 20. A literal fulfillment of the Davidic covenant necessarily presumes a second coming of Christ, the restoration of Israel, and the establishment of God's authoritative rule on earth.

The New Covenant

The issues raised in the eschatological interpretation in the preceding covenants come to a head in the prediction of a new covenant in both the Old and New Testaments. Here there is diversity of opinion among amillenarians and premillenarians.

The Contrast Between the Old and New Testaments

One of the most obvious differences in Scripture is the division of the Bible into the Old and New Testaments, or Old and New Covenants. This division recognizes that the covenants of the Old Testament will be climaxed by a new covenant, which will have its ultimate fulfillment in the New Testament. In contrast to the Mosaic covenant, which had a legalistic emphasis and was temporary, the new covenant is unconditional and is clearly a result of the grace of God that has its full manifestation in Christ in history and in prophecy.

The New Covenant Contrasted
to Previous Biblical Covenants

The new covenant is far-reaching in its divine revelation of God's purpose to bestow his grace on humanity. The Mosaic covenant dominated the Old Testament and was a temporary covenant to be superseded by the new covenant. The Mosaic covenant was legalistic in contrast to the essential feature of the new covenant, which is grace.

The new covenant is God's affirmation of his intention to extend grace and blessing to those who do not deserve it. The new covenant is basically a unilateral agreement in which God pronounced what he will do even though there is failure and lack of merit on the part of the human race. A predominant feature of the Old Testament was God's revelation of his faithfulness to his promises, whether of judgment or of mercy. The new covenant is a gracious declaration of God's mercy to those who put their trust in him but are otherwise unworthy of blessing.

The Old Testament revealed that it was possible for individuals to gain favor with God (but not salvation) by obedience to the law. By contrast, the new covenant offers grace and blessing apart from legal justification in human acts. This is stated clearly in passages such as Romans 3:21–24. Even though salvation was impossible by the keeping of the law, Paul revealed the great principle of justification by faith. Paul wrote, "But now a righteousness from God, apart from law, has been made known, to which the law and the prophets testify. This righteousness from God comes through faith in Jesus Christ to all who believe. There is no difference, for all have sinned and fall short of the glory of God, and are justified freely by his grace through the redemption that came by Christ Jesus."

Righteousness comes not from works but through faith in Christ, and believers are justified, declared righteous, without cost because of the grace of God that has come through the redemption provided by Christ Jesus. This redemption was accomplished when Christ died on the cross for the sins of the world.

This is further stated in Romans 3:25–26: "God presented him as a sacrifice of atonement, through faith in his blood. He did this to demonstrate his justice, because in his forbearance he had left the sins committed beforehand unpunished—he did it to demonstrate his justice at the present time, so as to be just and the one who justifies those who have faith in Jesus."

Old Testament believers were forgiven and saved on credit, as it were, and this debt had to be paid by Jesus Christ when he died as the Redeemer. So in the death of Christ God demonstrated his justice in that he recognizes that Christ is the Sin-bearer and the Sin Offering. Therefore, God is just in declaring a believer righteous because he sees the individual in the person and work of his Son.

This same truth of redemption through Christ is stated in other passages such as Ephesians 2:4–7: "But because of his great love for us, God, who is rich in mercy, made us alive with Christ even when we were dead and seated us with him in the heavenly realms in Christ Jesus, in order that in the coming ages he might show the incomparable riches of his grace, expressed in his kindness to us in Christ Jesus." This grace of God is manifested in the present age. Also in eternity believers in Christ who have been justified by the grace of God will be illustrations of what the grace of God can accomplish.

It is obvious that this is not through works but through faith in Christ, as stated in Ephesians 2:8–10: "For it is by grace you have been saved, through faith—and this not from yourselves, it is the gift of God—not by works, so that no one can boast. For we are God's workmanship, created in Christ Jesus to do good works, which God prepared in advance for us to do."

The gospel message, of course, based on the new covenant, is the message that people in spite of their best efforts are not acceptable to God apart from the righteousness that comes through faith in Jesus Christ. Salvation is not something earned, deserved, or attained, but is a gift of God to those who place their trust in Christ. Believers in Christ are "God's workmanship," heirs of all the blessings that belong to a child of God.

The New Covenant as Revealed in the Old Testament

One of the principal Old Testament passages on the new covenant is Jeremiah 31:31–37:

The "time is coming," declares the LORD, "when I will make a new covenant with the house of Israel and with the house of Judah. It will not be like the covenant I made with their forefathers when I took them by the hand to lead them out of Egypt, because they broke my covenant, though I was a husband to them," declares the LORD. "This is the covenant I will make with the house of Israel after that time," declares the LORD. "I will put my law in their minds and write it on their hearts. I will be their God, and they will be my people. No longer will a man teach his neighbor, or a man his brother, saying, 'Know the LORD,' because they will all know me, from the least of them to the greatest," declares the LORD. "For I will forgive their wickedness and will remember their sins no more." This is what the LORD says, he who appoints the sun to shine by day, who decrees the moon and stars to shine by night, who stirs up the sea so that its waves roar—the LORD Almighty is his name: "Only if these decrees vanish from my sight," declares the LORD, "will the descendants of Israel ever cease to be a nation before me." This is what the LORD says: "Only if the heavens above can be measured and the foundations of the earth below be searched out will I reject all the descendants of Israel because of all they have done," declares the LORD.

Certain salient features stand out in this covenant:

1. The new covenant will be made with the house of Israel and the house of Judah.
2. The new covenant will be in contrast to the covenant made with Moses.
3. The new covenant will not be written on tables of stone but in the hearts of believers.
4. It will have its fulfillment as far as Israel is concerned at a time when everyone from the least to the greatest will know the Lord.
5. The major provision is that God will forgive Israel's wickedness and not remember their sins.
6. The covenant is irrevocable and does not depend on human response.
7. As a result, Israel will be a nation forever.
8. The absolute certainty of the new covenant is compared to the impossibility of measuring the heavens or the foundations of the earth.

Though there have been many attempts to apply this covenant in a general way to those other than Israel, it is obvious that the particulars of the covenant require a special situation that has never occurred. Accordingly, the covenant has not yet been completely fulfilled.

Further revelation of the new covenant is given in Isaiah 61:8–9, which states essentially that Israel will be recognized as a people blessed by God.

Jeremiah again took up this theme in Jeremiah 32:27–41. God declared that Israel will "be my people, and I will be their God. I will give them singleness of heart and action, so that they will always fear me for their own good and the good of their children after them" (vv. 38–39). As in Jeremiah 31, this passage again asserts that this covenant is everlasting.

Ezekiel gave an extended discourse on the new covenant. In addition to repeating some of the facts given to Jeremiah, other promises were made. God declared, "I will take the Israelites out of the nations where they have gone. I will gather them from all around and bring them back into their own land. I will make them one nation in the land, on the mountains of Israel" (Ezek. 37:1–22). This requires fulfillment in an earthly millennium.

God promised, according to Ezekiel, that Israel will be one nation with one king and will never again be divided as they were in the kingdoms of Israel and Judah (37:22). Further, God will keep them from sinning against him by worshiping idols and backsliding (v. 23). A new factor is introduced in verse 24: "My servant David will be king over them, and they will all have one shepherd. They will follow my laws and be careful to keep my decrees." This is reinforced in verse 25: "They will live in the land I gave to my servant Jacob, the land where your fathers lived. They and their children and their children's children will live there forever, and David my servant will be their prince forever."

The fulfillment of God's promise requires the resurrection of David at Christ's second coming. As in other references to the new covenant, Ezekiel declared that this covenant will be everlasting. In addition, God promised to put his sanctuary among them (v. 26) and to dwell with them (v. 27). As in the other passages, all nations will know that Israel is considered holy before God.

These passages indicate that the promises are directed to Israel, not to Gentiles, and therefore cannot be made universal in their application.

Because amillenarians generally deny a future for Israel, which these passages require, it is necessary for them to accommodate this passage in prophecy either by making the church the inheritor of Israel's promises, which the Bible never does, or to make these promises conditional on Israel's obedience, which is also foreign to these passages. All these promises were sovereignly given and will be fulfilled in God's time. Premillenarians point out that these passages imply and demand a kingdom after the second coming in which these promises will have their literal fulfillment.

New Testament References to the New Covenant

In the New Testament the new covenant takes on extended meaning. The best known reference to this, of course, is in the record of Lord's Supper, which celebrates the death of Christ. As stated in Luke 22:20, Christ said, "This cup is the new covenant in my blood, which is poured out for you." Here the new covenant is clearly applicable to the church, a fact that is supported by other references, such as Matthew 26:28 and Mark 14:24. In 1 Corinthians 11:25 Paul wrote that in reference to the cup at the Lord's Supper, Christ said, "This cup is the new covenant in my blood; do this, whenever you drink it, in remembrance of me."

In these references to the new covenant in relation to the church, however, there is no detail that connects it with the new covenant with Israel, and this has created a diversity of opinions even among premillenarians.

Premillennial Interpretations of the New Covenant

In the theology of the church, whether premillennial or otherwise, there has been considerable confusion as to how the new covenant relates to different classes of believers. Amillenarians tend to make the church the fulfiller of God's promises to Israel. This is not universally held by amillenarians, however, because while the church may inherit some blessings similar to Israel's, they do not inherit Israel's curses, and one cannot be separated from the other.

Among premillenarians there is also diversity in understanding of the new
covenant as it relates to Israel. Some insist that the new covenant is exclusively for Israel, but that the church inherits the blessings of the blood of the
new covenant. A popular view is that while the new covenant is preeminently
for Israel as revealed in the Old Testament, the church receives an oblique
application of it. The problem here is that the Bible seldom blurs the promises to Israel and the church even though some of these promises may be similar. Lewis Sperry Chafer held that there were two new covenants—one for
Israel and one for the church.

This diversity of explanation, however, is resolved, in this author's view,
by making a distinction between the covenant of redemption and the covenant of grace. The covenant of redemption involves the promise that Christ
would redeem many by his death on the cross, and the covenant of grace provides that God will extend grace on the basis of this sacrifice to those who
trust in Christ as their Savior. This concept of salvation through redemption
in Christ is probably the key to understanding this whole doctrine.

If it is understood that Christ by his death on the cross provided grace,
then it can be understood that this grace of God is extended to various classes
and individuals. In fact, everyone who is saved from Adam on was saved by
the grace of God, not by human works, and the covenant of grace to that
extent provides the salvation of all who trust in the Lord.

The prominence of the new covenant in the prophecies concerning Israel
in the Old Testament arises from the obvious fact that God has a special plan
and purpose for Israel that has its culmination, according to premillenarians,
in the future millennial kingdom following the second coming. Accordingly
the Old Testament promises, detailed as they are, will be literally fulfilled in
that period. In the New Testament, in which the new covenant is related to
the church, it is the grace of God as it applies to the church. While none of
the major features of the covenant for Israel are repeated, nevertheless the
church has a new covenant in contrast to her former estate in Adam, just as
Israel has a new covenant in contrast to her former position under the
Mosaic covenant.

Other References to the New Covenant in the New Testament

One of the principal passages that has often been misinterpreted is
Hebrews 8:8–12. Here in the discussion with Hebrew Christians, the promise found in Jeremiah 31 is repeated in detail. Amillenarians seize on this passage as proof that the covenant with Israel in Jeremiah 31 applies to the
church. A careful reading of the passage, however, does not reveal support
for this.

The argument of Hebrews 8 is that Christ is superior to Moses, and that the promises given to the church are superior to the promises given to Israel. This is stated in Hebrews 8:6: "But the ministry Jesus has received is as superior to theirs as the covenant of which he is mediator is superior to the old one, and it is founded on better promises." In the verses that follow, the argument is made that if the Mosaic covenant had been sufficient, God would not have promised a new covenant. This is why Jeremiah 31 is quoted. The point is that even the Old Testament anticipated the temporary character of the Mosaic covenant. So Jews who clung to the Mosaic covenant were informed that even the Old Testament anticipated the Mosaic covenant would pass away and the new covenant for Israel would be installed. This was proof that the Mosaic covenant was only temporary and insufficient.

No statement is made in Hebrews 8 to the effect that the new covenant of Jeremiah is applied to the church. The only application is made in Hebrews 8:13: "By calling this covenant 'new,' he has made the first one obsolete; and what is obsolete and aging will soon disappear." In other words, the promise of the new covenant makes clear that the Mosaic covenant in time would become obsolete and would be done away with. So here as well as in other references in Hebrews to the new covenant (10:16, 29; 12:24; 13:20), there is no evidence that the church is ever regarded as fulfilling the many details of the new covenant in the Old Testament relating to Israel.

The Major Features of the New Covenant in Relation to Salvation

As previously stated, the major point of the new covenant as revealed in the New Testament is that salvation is not by works but by grace. This is true for the church. It is also true for Israel. It is true for every child of God, regardless of the dispensation.

Not only is salvation not by works, but it is entirely by grace as a gift of God. Though works are recognizable and will be judged at the judgment seat of Christ for Christians, works are never made the basis for salvation in any dispensation, for salvation has always been by the grace of God.

Also the new covenant makes clear that human effort is not the point in securing salvation, but rather the act of one's will in trusting God's promises of salvation results in the individual becoming a child of God. As stated in John 1:12–13, a child of God becomes such not by any work of merit or effort on his or her part, but by the grace of God. This also leads to the fact that once a person is saved he or she is saved forever as it is a work of God, a work of spiritual resurrection, a work of new birth, a work of new creation.

Few doctrines of Scripture are more important or more central to understanding the Scriptures than the new covenant. Properly understood, the doctrine of grace extends to the church, to Israel, and to every child of God in every dispensation. Its full revelation, however, was made in the New Testament, and its further revelation will be in eternity as God points out the wonders of his grace.

Tribute

Donald K. Campbell is an accomplished administrator, educator, and expositor of Scripture. His long career is worthy of admiration and commendation. His contribution to Dallas Theological Seminary as academic dean, professor of Bible exposition, and president of Dallas Seminary has been beyond estimation. His ministry will be perpetuated in the lives of hundreds of students at Dallas Seminary who have shared one way or another in his contribution to the work of the Lord.

Dispensational Definitions
of the Kingdom

Mark L. Bailey

When one begins to discuss the definition of the kingdom among dispensationalists, the observation of Robert Saucy is immediately apparent:

> Any discussion of contemporary dispensationalism must recognize at the outset that there exists within this broad theological school a considerable variety of interpretive opinion. From specific interpretation of the Sermon on the Mount to the relation of the Church age to the Old Testament Messianic promises and many lesser issues those who fall within "dispensationalism" arrive at differing exegetical conclusions.[1]

Mentioning the term "kingdom" raises a number of questions. Which kingdom is being referred to? The Old Testament kingship within Israel? The kingdom that was "near" in the preaching of John the Baptist, Jesus, and the disciples? Did the kingdom arrive then? Was it postponed? Is there a kingdom in the present age? Was the concept of the kingdom reinterpreted for its fulfillment in the church? What will be the final form of its manifestation? And if it is to be on the earth, will both the church and the nation of Israel participate? If so, how? Will those two relationships change in eternity? All these questions are relevant for dispensationalism as a system of interpretation.

This essay isolates the various ways in which the concepts of the kingdom of God and the kingdom of heaven have been defined by key contributors to the modern dispensational position. It is recognized that many defenders of dispensational premillennialism could be cited who, in other significant ways, have shaped the thinking of dispensationalism as a system. But since it was not their purpose to refine or advance the study of the nature of the kingdom, they have not been included in this study. While a multiplicity of

---

1. Robert L. Saucy, "Contemporary Dispensational Thought," *Tyndale Student Fellowship Bulletin* (March–April 1984): 10.

related issues bear on an understanding of dispensational theology, this essay is intentionally restrictive and has been narrowed to definitional concerns and not the supporting arguments or ancillary discussions. The survey is organized into three somewhat arbitrary divisions of modern interpretation: the formulative era, from Darby to Gaebelein; the crystallization era, from Scofield to Chafer; and the present era, from McClain to contemporary contributions.

The Formulative Era

John Nelson Darby

Ample evidence in the writings of John Nelson Darby shows that his ecclesiology affected his eschatology. In various letters to Professor Tholuck of Halle, Darby reiterated two basic truths that were to form the background and backbone of his system of interpreting the Scriptures:[2] (1) the believer's heavenly positional standing in Christ, and (2) a future dispensation when the Holy Spirit will be poured out on the Jewish nation and reign in righteousness. Thus the distinction of the church from Israel became the central tenet of what came to be known as dispensationalism.

Implicit in Darby's views was the belief that the Bible was to be interpreted literally. With the Napoleonic wars having recently ended and given the desperate state of the Church of England, prophetic writings about the future of the church, the coming of the Lord, and the future of the nation of Israel found a ready and waiting audience for Darby's dispensational emphasis, first in England and then in America. He has been credited with being the father of modern dispensationalism, though many writers have demonstrated that the early church already recognized various economies in which God has governed and will govern his program on earth. As a system of interpretation, however, Darby's is a logical starting point for the present discussion.

Darby's definitions of the kingdom of God and the kingdom of heaven were to affect the discussions of the kingdom for over one hundred years. "The kingdom of God is the exercise or exhibition of the ruling power of God under any circumstance in the wisdom of God. The kingdom of heaven is the kingdom of God in its heavenly character."[3] According to Darby, the

---

2. "In my retreat, the 32nd chapter of Isaiah taught me clearly, on God's behalf, that there was still an economy to come of his ordering; a state of things in no way established yet. The consciousness of my union with Christ has given me the present heavenly portion of that glory, whereas this chapter clearly sets forth the corresponding earthly part. I was not able to put those things in their respective places or arrange them in order, as I now can; but the truths themselves were then revealed of God, through the action of the Holy Spirit by reading His word" (John N. Darby, *Letters of J. N. D.*, 3 vols. [Kingston Row, Thames: Stow Hill Bible and Tract Depot, n.d.], 3:299).

3. J. N. Darby, "The Dispensation of the Kingdom of Heaven," in *The Collected Writings of J. N. Darby*, ed. William Kelly, 34 vols. (reprint, Sunbury, Pa.: Believer's Bookshelf, 1972), 2:55.

throne of God on earth had ceased at the time of the captivity and from the time of Daniel there was an emphasis on the God of heaven.[4] While the prophecies as contained in the law and the prophets were to be accomplished, the departure of God from Israel and his ultimate return take on "immense importance."[5]

Three major emphases make Darby's contribution to kingdom theology worthy of note. First, according to Darby, the kingdom of heaven as preached by Jesus was not the earthly, Davidic kingdom. The kingdom that was "near" in the preaching of John, Jesus, and the disciples was the present dispensation. "The King was there in an adverse world, and in the midst of a people which was going to reject Him. But the kingdom of the heavens *could not take place*. For this the King was to go up to heaven; for the kingdom of the heavens is the kingdom of God, while the King and the government are in heaven."[6]

Second, what would become a major distinctive for almost a century of dispensational argumentation was that the kingdom of heaven was distinguished from the kingdom of God. Darby's articulation differs somewhat from those who followed him. He stated: "Since the Son of God was present on earth the kingdom of God (the ruling power of God) was there. The kingdom of heaven, as a development of God's purpose on the earth, would result from His departure as a result of His rejection."[7]

Third, Darby is to be remembered for his divisions of the spheres of the kingdom in their final manifestation.

These kingdoms are the full development of that which now rests in an anomolous [*sic*] and ambiguous state (glorious and blessed, indeed, but still ambiguous as regards the manifested results), to wit, "the kingdom of God's dear

---

4. Ibid., 11:477.
5. Ibid.
6. Darby, *Notes on the Gospel of Matthew* (London: G. Morrish, n.d.), p. 20.
7. Darby, *Collected Writings of J. N. Darby*, 2:54–55. "'The kingdom of God' is a distinct expression from 'the kingdom of heaven,' although in many respects so identified, that the same things could be affirmed about it. Thus it could be said that the kingdom of God was at hand: that was most true; as it could be said also, that the kingdom of heaven was at hand. But at the same time they were of very distinct import; for it was a matter of faith to know that 'the kingdom of God was come amongst them.' (See Gr., Luke 11:20; ch. 17:21.) So the Lord makes the expressions never used of the kingdom of heaven—to know that the kingdom of heaven was not, but was 'at hand' (Matt. 4:17, Gr.); whereas the same evangelist, or rather the Spirit of God by him, in speaking of the kingdom of God, immediately changes his phrase to the one noticed in Luke (Gr., Matt. 12:28). The kingdom of God was necessarily there when the Son of God was there—in a word, when God was there. The kingdom of heaven, as a development of God's *purpose*, could not be there while He was there; it resulted from the Lord's going away into heaven. The kingdom of God is the exercise or exhibition of the ruling power of God under any circumstance in the wisdom of God. The kingdom of heaven is the kingdom of God in its heavenly character. In *dispensation* this is set up by the *rejection of the King of God's kingdom by the world*. . . . The kingdom of God, therefore, was amongst the Jews when He, the Son of God, Jesus was there—and they ought to have known it—and the kingdom of heaven was at hand."

Son," the kingdom of the Son of God as sitting upon the Father's throne. This is not the kingdom of the Son of man; it is not the kingdom of the Father, but the kingdom of the Son of God sitting on His Father's throne; the lamb rejected, slain, sitting on the right hand of God, or in the midst of the throne. I believe this to be the great mystery of the present order of the kingdom, the promise to be, "To him that overcometh will I grant to sit down with *me* on my throne, even as I overcame and am set down with my Father on His throne," where no saint ever sat, none but He whose right it is.[8]

Thus for Darby the kingdom of God's dear Son is presently taking place, while the kingdom of the Son of Man will take place in the future. Likewise the Father's kingdom and the kingdom of the Son of man are to be contrasted as to location, the former being in the heavens during its future kingdom manifestation, while the latter is the reign of the Son of man in his kingdom during that same period of time on earth.

William Kelly

Probably no one was as familiar with Darby as was William Kelly, who edited the thirty-four volumes we now have available from the former's writings. While continuing to distinguish between the kingdom of heaven and the kingdom of God, Kelly taught two additional concepts. One relates to his expansion of the kingdom of heaven to a two-stage manifestation rather than confining it to one as did his predecessor. Of the kingdom of heaven, Kelly wrote, "It may be applied, as it often is to what is going on now, or as sometimes, to what will go on when the Lord comes in glory, and brings His rule in a manifested form to bear upon the earth."[9] What is of interest is his explanation of the "postponement" of the originally announced kingdom.

> And we shall find subsequently that for the rejection of Jesus by the Jews, John was not at all prepared. This too it was that led to the twofold form taken by the kingdom of heaven. While the old Jewish view of the kingdom established by power and glory as a visible sovereignty over the earth is postponed, the rejection of Jesus on earth and His ascension to God's right hand lead to an introduction of the Kingdom of heaven in a mysterious form; which is, in point of fact, going on now. Thus it has two sides. When Christ went up to heaven and took His place as the rejected [One] here, but the glorified One there, the Kingdom of heaven began.[10]

A second concept presented by Kelly relates to his understanding of the kingdom as separate from the church. As opposed to the true church, which

8. Ibid., 2:57.
9. William Kelly, *Lectures on the Gospel of Matthew*, rev. ed. (New York: Loizeaux Brothers, 1868), p. 236.
10. Ibid., p. 51.

is made up of only regenerate believers, the kingdom of heaven is the whole scene of Christian profession. While this view was shared by Darby, who came before him, and many who followed, Kelly defines the entrance factor into that kingdom of heaven as the rite of baptism.[11] For the two-stage development of the kingdom of heaven, together with the postponement theory, and for his unique baptismal requirement for entrance into the kingdom of heaven, Kelly set a new direction in this formulative period of dispensationalism.[12]

Arno C. Gaebelein

With the arrival of Arno C. Gaebelein came a more clearly defined discussion of the way the phrase "kingdom of heaven" is used in Matthew. His delineations are summarized in his two "one-word" statements of explanation. He defines the kingdom before Matthew 13 this way: "In one word, the kingdom of the heavens is the literal fulfillment of all the prophecies and promises contained in the Old Testament, which the Lord gave to the seed of Abraham, and the blessings of the nations of the earth to come after the kingdom is set up."[13] Following the turn of events he sees in Matthew 12, the kingdom is defined differently: "In one word the kingdom of the heavens in Matthew is equivalent with 'Christendom.' It includes the whole sphere of Christian profession saved and unsaved, so-called Romanists and Protestants, all who are naming the name of Christ. Therefore the church is not the kingdom of the heavens, though the church is in the kingdom of the heavens."[14] Therefore with Gaebelein an understanding of the various contexts

11. "But the 'kingdom of heaven' embraces every one that confesses the name of Christ. This was begun by preaching and baptizing. When a man is baptized he enters 'the kingdom of heaven,' even if he should turn out to be a hypocrite. He will never be in heaven, of course, if he is an unbeliever; but he is in 'the kingdom of heaven.' He may either be a tare or real wheat in the kingdom of heaven; an evil or a faithful servant; a foolish virgin or a wise one. The kingdom of heaven takes in the whole scene of Christian profession" (ibid., p. 333). As he put it elsewhere, "Thus Greeks, Copts, Nestorians, Roman Catholics, as well as Protestants, are in the kingdom of heaven; not believers only, but all who outwardly profess Christ's name" (ibid., p. 275).

12. James H. Brookes deserves mention as one of the formative dispensationalists, although his writings added no new developments to the understanding of the kingdom. He is most noted for his defense of the rapture of the church (James H. Brookes, *Till He Come* [Chicago: Gospel, 1891], pp. 58–96).

13. Arno C. Gaebelein, *The Gospel of Matthew: An Exposition* (Neptune, N.J.: Loizeaux Brothers, 1910), p. 60.

14. Ibid., pp. 262–63. "That it can no longer mean the kingdom as it is revealed in the Old Testament, as it is promised to Israel, and as He offered it to the people, is evident. For in the first place, the offer was made and rejected. The preaching of Him and the messengers He sent out was, 'The kingdom of heaven it [*sic*] at hand, repent.' Not a word do we hear of this in the thirteenth chapter, nor after this chapter. And in the second place, if our Lord had had the Old Testament kingdom promised to Israel in view, when he says here 'The kingdom of the heavens is like,' He could not have said that He uttered things hidden from the world's foundation, for the kingdom in the Old Testament is not a mystery, but clearly revealed" (ibid., p. 260).

in which the kingdom of heaven appears in Matthew gives rise to the language of postponement during the mystery period.

In summary, the formulative era was grounded in the conviction that the destinies of the church and of Israel are to be understood as separate and distinct. A literal interpretation of the promise to Israel demanded an earthly explanation for the manifestation of the kingdom. Much of the polemics and apologetics of this era was an attempt to deal with the pervading influence of postmillennialism and the trend toward apostasy in the organized church. The time frame for the kingdom of heaven expanded in definition from only this dispensation (Darby) to include the present age and the age to come (Kelly), until in Gaebelein the threefold division was made that became popular in *The Scofield Reference Bible*. To articulate the interruption of the Davidic promise and its fulfillment in the consummation, the terminology of a postponement was employed to explain how it could be "near" in the ministry of Christ but yet future when it became obvious that the church would be built between the two advents of Christ.

The Crystallization Era

As has been stated by others,[15] with Scofield, dispensationalism entered its "scholastic period" in which it was defended in and disseminated by *The Scofield Reference Bible* (1917) and later by Lewis Sperry Chafer's *Systematic Theology* (1948). Much of the attacks against dispensationalism in this era came from covenant theologians reacting to the reference notes of the Bible and the codification of Scofieldian dispensationalism in Chafer's theology. These two works contained the teachings of dispensationalism in a readable and understandable form, which accounted for its rapid growth and acceptance by so many. The outlines and definitions pertaining to the kingdom were no exception.

C. I. Scofield

For the purpose of this discussion, three notes of Scofield are worth highlighting. In his note on Matthew 6:33 Scofield makes five contrasts between the kingdom of heaven and the kingdom of God. The kingdom of God is universal, entered only by the new birth, encompasses the earthly sphere of the kingdom of heaven, is primarily internal and spiritual, and will culminate with the merger of the kingdom of heaven and its deliverance to the Father at the end of history. The kingdom of heaven is the promised messianic mediatorial kingdom of David that in this age includes the sphere of profession of

---

15. John D. Hannah, "The Early Years of Lewis Sperry Chafer," *Bibliotheca Sacra* 144 (January–March 1987): 17–18.

both the true and the false, and in the future will be manifested on the earth before it ultimately merges into the kingdom of God before being delivered up to the Father.[16]

In other notes Scofield defines the kingdom of heaven according to the background of Daniel 2 and 7 as the earthly Davidic kingdom that is to be set up on the earth after the destruction of the Gentile world system. This follows the tradition of Gaebelein in suggesting a three-stage usage of the phrase "the kingdom of the heavens" in Matthew. These three stages include the time it was "at hand" from the beginning of the ministry of John the Baptist to the rejection, the mysteries of the kingdom including parables that have to do with the sphere of Christian profession (he does not give guidelines on how to determine this), and the prophetic aspect of the kingdom to be set up at the return of Christ.[17]

Finally, for Scofield, "at hand" was not a promise of immediacy but immanency. "'At hand' is never a positive affirmation that the person or thing said to be 'at hand' will immediately appear, but only that no known or predicted event must intervene."[18]

---

16. "(1) The kingdom of God is universal, including all moral intelligences willingly subject to the will of God, whether angels, the Church, or saints of past or future dispensations (Lk. 13. 28, 29; Heb. 12. 22, 23); while the kingdom of heaven is Messianic, mediatorial, and Davidic, and has for its object the establishment of the kingdom of God in the earth (I Cor. 15. 24, 25). (2) The kingdom of God is entered only by the new birth (John 3. 3, 5–7); the kingdom of heaven, during this age, is the sphere of a profession which may be real or false (Mt. 13. 3; 25. 1, 11, 12). (3) Since the kingdom of heaven is the earthly sphere of the universal kingdom of God, the two have almost all things in common. For this reason many parables and other teachings have spoken of the kingdom of heaven in Matthew, and of the kingdom of God in Mark and Luke. It is the omissions which are significant. The parables of the wheat and the tares, and of the net (Mt. 13. 24–30, 36–43, 47–50) are not spoken of the kingdom of God. In that kingdom there are neither tares nor bad fish. But the parable of the leaven (Mt. 13. 33) is spoken of the kingdom of God also, for, alas, even the true doctrines of the kingdom are leavened with the errors of which the Pharisees, Sadducees, and the Herodians were representatives. (4) The kingdom of God 'comes not with outward show' (Lk. 17. 20), but is chiefly that which is internal and spiritual (Rom. 14. 17); while the kingdom of heaven is organic, and is to be manifested in glory on the earth. (5) The kingdom of heaven merges into the kingdom of God when Christ, having 'put all enemies under His feet, shall have delivered up the kingdom to God, even the Father' (1 Cor. 15. 24–28)" (*The Scofield Reference Bible* [Oxford: Oxford University Press, 1909], note on Matthew 6:33).

17. "(1) The phrase, kingdom of heaven (lit. of the heavens), is peculiar to Matthew and signifies the Messianic earth rule of Jesus Christ, the Son of David. It is called the kingdom of heaven because it is the rule of the heavens over the earth (Mt. 6. 10). The phrase is derived from Daniel, where it is defined (Dan. 2. 34–36, 44; 7. 23–27) as the kingdom which 'the God of heaven' will set up after the destruction by the 'stone cut without hands' of the Gentile world-system. It is the kingdom covenanted to David's seed (2 Sam. 7. 7–10); described in the prophets (Zech. 12. 8, note) and confirmed to Jesus Christ, the Son of Mary through the angel Gabriel (Lk. 1. 32, 33)" (ibid., p. 996, n. 1).

"(2) The kingdom of heaven has three aspects in Matthew: *(a)* 'At hand' from the beginning of the ministry of John the Baptist (Mt. 3. 2) to the virtual rejection of the King, and the announcement of the new brotherhood (Mt. 12. 46–50); *(b)* In seven 'mysteries of the kingdom of heaven,' to be fulfilled during the present age (Mt. 13. 1–52), to which are added the parables of the kingdom of heaven which were spoken after those of Matthew 13, and which have to do with the sphere of Christian profession during this age; *(c)* The prophetic aspect—the kingdom to be set up after the return of the King in glory (Matt. 24. 29–29. 46; Lk. 19. 12–19; Acts 15: 14–17)" (ibid., p. 996, n. 2).

18. Ibid., p. 998, n. 3.

Lewis Sperry Chafer

Probably no dispensational leader in this crystallization period is better known than Lewis Sperry Chafer. The influence of Scofield is seen in Chafer's explanations of the kingdom distinctions. For Chafer, the kingdom of heaven refers to the rule of God on earth, whereas the kingdom of God is the rule of God throughout the bounds of the universe.[19] He chides those expositors who fail to recognize the "wide differences" that exist between these concepts and concludes, "the real difference between that which these designations represent is to be discovered in connection with the instances where they are not and cannot be used interchangeably rather than in the instances where they are interchangeable."[20]

Again, following Scofield, Chafer uses a series of arguments to support his definition. The righteousness of Matthew 5:20 is legal righteousness in contrast to imputed righteousness. Sons of the kingdom are said to be cast out (Matt. 8:12; 24:50–51; 25:28–30). Neither of these truths could apply to the kingdom of God, as Chafer interprets these passages. In addition, the evil that is associated with the tares and the bad fish in the parables referred (as it did in all three eras of dispensational development) to the kingdom of heaven as the sphere of profession instead of reality.[21] Chafer concludes his discussion of the contrasts by saying, "Such contrasts might be cited to great lengths, but the important objective has been gained if it has been made clear that there is an eschatology of Judaism and an eschatology of Christianity and each, though wholly different in details, reaches into eternity."[22]

A final and somewhat subtle thought is observable in Chafer as he expands the duration of the kingdom of heaven to seven periods of development, thus developing the synthesis of the kingdom beyond that of Darby, Kelly, and Scofield, whose schemes included one, two, and three dispensations, respectively.[23] The seven stages are outlined as follows:

> The kingdom of heaven, since it embraces the rule of God in the earth, is subject to various modes of manifestation in Israel's history and that of the world. (1) The theocracy of the Old Testament was a form of divine rule in the earth,

19. Lewis Sperry Chafer, *Systematic Theology*, 8 vols. (Dallas, Tex.: Dallas Seminary Press, 1948; reprint [8 vols. in 4], Grand Rapids: Kregel, 1992), 4:173. "A study of the passages involved will reveal there is a wide difference between the kingdom of God and the kingdom of heaven. This will be seen to be the extent of government which is implied in each. The term 'kingdom of God' it will be found, is employed when there is nothing stated that would limit its authority over all the universe. The term 'kingdom of heaven,' it will also be found, is used when the divine government is considered limited to the earth" (Lewis Sperry Chafer, *The Kingdom in History and Prophecy* [Chicago: Bible Institute Colportage Association, 1936], p. 52).

20. Chafer, *Systematic Theology*, 4:26–27.

21. Ibid.

22. Ibid.

23. Ibid., p. 976. However, in his note on Zechariah 12–14, he outlined the dominion of God in the Old Testament under the themes of dominion, theocracy, and the Davidic covenant.

and hence an aspect of the kingdom of heaven. (2) The covenant with David is the kingdom of heaven in covenant form. (3) Prophecy concerning the scope and character of the kingdom of heaven is that rule in prophetic form. (4) The announcing of that kingdom by John the Baptist (Matt. 3:1–2), by Christ (Matt. 4:17), and by His disciples (Matt. 10:5–7) was the kingdom of heaven offered. (5) The subsequent rejection and postponement of the kingdom of heaven became a phase of that kingdom. (6) The present age, though so wholly without comparison, with that which went before or with that which follows, does, nevertheless, include a form of divine rule in the earth. . . . (7) The final form of the kingdom of heaven is that which will yet be set up in its full manifestation in the earth and in compliance with all that God has spoken.[24]

Both Scofield and Chafer maintained the distinctions between Israel and the church. The church was not to be identified with the present form of the kingdom, which was again associated with professing Christendom. A major development in this era was the expansion of the concept of the kingdom of heaven to include whatever God might be accomplishing on earth during the periods comprising most of the history of the Old and New Testaments. This no doubt laid the groundwork for the theodicies of both Alva McClain and J. Dwight Pentecost.

Present Era

Alva J. McClain

A corner was turned in the study of kingdom theology in American dispensationalism with the works of G. N. H. Peters, J. Dwight Pentecost, and Alva J. McClain. The influence of Peters on the other two is noted in the quotations within their books. Because many of the critics of dispensationalism deny that Peters could be labeled a dispensational premillennialist, we have not included him in the present discussion. However, for a thorough and comprehensive argument for premillennialism, his work deserves continued study.[25]

In his comprehensive work *The Greatness of the Kingdom*, McClain attempts an inductive approach to the concept of the kingdom. He suggests that a kingdom must have three elements: "A general survey of Biblical materials indicates that the concept of 'a kingdom' envisages a total situation containing at least three essential elements: first, a *ruler* with adequate authority and power; second, a *realm* of subjects to be ruled; and third, the actual exercise of the function of *rulership*."[26]

24. Ibid., 4:326–27.
25. George N. H. Peters, *The Theocratic Kingdom*, 3 vols. (reprint, Grand Rapids: Kregel, 1952).
26. Alva J. McClain, *The Greatness of the Kingdom* (Winona Lake, Ind.: Brethren Missionary Herald Books, 1968), p. 17.

Understanding that the kingdom of God is eternal and yet within time, universal as well as local, directly and mediatorially ruled, present as well as future, unconditional and yet covenanted, he opts for the words "universal" and "mediatorial."[27]

The universal kingdom exists throughout all time (Ps. 145:13) and space (1 Chron. 29:12), is generally providential (Ps. 148:8), but is sometimes miraculous (Dan. 6:27), exists efficaciously (regardless of the attitude of its subjects, Dan. 4:35), is administered through the eternal Son (Col. 1:17), and is to be distinguished from the mediatorial reign that is to come.[28]

The mediatorial kingdom is defined as it relates to the earthly purposes of God's reign: "On the basis of mediatorial redemption it must 'come' to put down at last all rebellion with its train of evil results, thus finally bringing the Kingdom and will of God on earth as it is in heaven, when this purpose has been fully accomplished, the mediatorial phase of the kingdom will disappear as a separate entity, being merged with the Universal Kingdom of God."[29] "The Mediatorial Kingdom may be defined tentatively as (a) the rule of God through a divinely chosen representative who not only speaks and acts for God but also represents the people before God; (b) the rule which has especial reference to the earth, and (c) having as its mediatorial ruler one who is always a member of the human race."[30] For McClain, "the mediatorial idea began to take shape in Abraham,[31] but was established in kingdom terminology with Moses and the chosen nation of Israel."[32]

Because of these definitions and the fact that the mediatorial rule is primarily limited to Israel, the only kingdom God himself ever established, the present age is viewed as an "interregnum" of God's rule on the earth.[33] While he does mention the kingdom in mystery form, for him "interregnum" is a better description of what is presently going on. This is essentially the view espoused by Stanley Toussaint.[34] The church exists within this period but the interregnum began with Jesus' death and extends beyond the church to Christ's return to the earth after the Tribulation.

Dispensationalists owe much to McClain for one of the first comprehensive treatments of the kingdom as it is developed throughout history. The writings of both McClain and Pentecost were also helpful as an attempt to

27. Ibid., p. 21. He concludes, "In seeking for terms which might best designate these two things, I can find nothing better than the adjectives 'universal' and 'mediatorial.' The first refers to the extent of rule and the latter to the method of rule."
28. Ibid., pp. 22–37.
29. Ibid., p. 35.
30. Ibid., p. 41.
31. Ibid., p. 50.
32. Ibid., p. 53.
33. Ibid., p. 321.
34. Stanley D. Toussaint, *Behold the King* (Portland, Oreg.: Multnomah, 1980), pp. 172–76. He holds that the term "kingdom" always relates to the future thousand-year reign of Christ on earth.

refute the charges that dispensationalists hold a pessimistic view of history and lack a unifying plan with which to understand the Scriptures.

Erich Sauer

The English translation of Erich Sauer's works on biblical theology[35] demonstrates an early modification of classical dispensationalism which, as it has turned out, anticipated much of the modern discussion of dispensationalism discussed later in this essay.[36] Perhaps his physical distance from the scene of American dispensationalism has resulted in his works often being unnoticed as a credible presentation and defense of dispensational theology.

Sauer is thoroughly dispensational in distinguishing Israel from the church and in his defense of the earthly millennial kingdom as "the only and necessary means of carrying forward human history from its present stage on to its goal in the eternal kingdom of the Father."[37] Sauer preceded American dispensationalists in identifying the kingdom of heaven with the kingdom of God.[38] Advocating an inaugurated eschatology, Sauer rejects the concept of the offer and postponement of the kingdom in the Gospels.[39]

For him there is no difference between the gospel of the kingdom and the gospel for the church.[40] He advocates only one new covenant, which is and will be the fulfillment of both the Abrahamic and Davidic covenants.[41] Especially anticipatory is his view that the Davidic covenant has a spiritual fulfillment in the church before its earthly consummation.[42] Also, while maintaining the historical distinction between Israel and the church, Sauer allows for a single people of God with a common destiny and inheritance for all eternity.[43] Only future dispensational developments will reveal the extent of Sauer's premonitions on dispensationalism.

Charles C. Ryrie

In the writings of Charles Ryrie, one can see some of the most significant

---

35. Erich Sauer, *Das Morgenrot der Welterlösung: ein Gang durch die alttestamentliche Offenbarungsgeschichte* and *Der Triumph des Gekreuzigten: ein Gang durch die neutestamentliche Offenbarungsgeschichte.* The works, published in 1937, were originally one book translated and published in English as two: *The Dawn of World Redemption: A Survey of Historical Revelation in the Old Testament,* trans. G. H. Lang (Grand Rapids: Eerdmans, 1951), and *The Triumph of the Crucified: A Survey of the Historical Revelation of the New Testament,* trans. G. H. Lang (Grand Rapids: Eerdmans, 1952). In addition he wrote *From Eternity to Eternity* (Grand Rapids: Eerdmans, 1954).

36. See the excellent discussion by Russell H. Bowers, "Dispensational Motifs in the Writings of Eric Sauer," *Bibliotheca Sacra* 148 (July–September 1991): 259–73.

37. Sauer, *Triumph of the Crucified,* p. 144.

38. Ibid., p. 23, n. 1.

39. Sauer, *From Eternity to Eternity,* p. 174.

40. Ibid., pp. 25–26.

41. Ibid., pp. 91–92.

42. "The continuing humanity of Christ in resurrection is thus the fulfillment in principle of the prophecy of the kingdom as given to David" (ibid., p. 45).

43. Sauer, *Triumph of the Crucified,* p. 64.

changes in the dispensational view of the kingdom. Ryrie originally defended the definitional distinctions of the traditional view of the kingdom of heaven and the kingdom of God.[44] However, in response to the charges of George E. Ladd against the dispensational premillennial position, Ryrie aptly diverts the discussion to the central issues of dispensationalism. He writes: "In other words, the issue is not the labels but the present form of the kingdom. If it is the Church, then dispensationalism is unwarranted. If the present form of the kingdom is not the Church, and if the future form is the Davidic kingdom on earth, then dispensational premillennialism is the only answer."[45] Ryrie is often quoted for his statement that communicates what many view as the basic tenet of dispensationalism: "The issue is whether or not the Church is the kingdom, and the distinctives of the Church in this age as recognized by dispensationalists is a *sine qua non* of the system."[46]

Like his mentors, Ryrie affirmed and wrote one of the best defenses for Jesus' bona fide offer of the Davidic kingdom and reverses the argument against those such as Ladd and others who would see in the Gospels an offer of only the spiritual kingdom of God.[47]

Furthermore, in analyzing the framework of Matthew, he advances that "there is no better way to express God's purposes concerning the Messianic kingdom than with the word *postponed*."[48] The references to the kingdom in the Epistles, which affirm a present experience of the kingdom, are expressions of the spiritual kingdom. He even believes the kingdom of the Son in Colossians 1:13 has always existed and "believers in every age are part of this spiritual kingdom."[49] Ryrie concludes, "Therefore, when a dispensationalist says the kingdom is postponed, he is speaking of the Davidic kingdom, but

44. "The characteristics of the two are different. The kingdom of heaven is characterized by religious profession; the kingdom of God by a new birth (John 3:3). It follows that there are nonbelievers in the kingdom of heaven and nowhere is a separation of unbelievers out of the kingdom of God spoken of. Both the kingdom of heaven and the kingdom of God experience abnormal growth in the world (Mark 4:30–32), and both include a saved remnant of Israel and the Church. In brief, there are significant distinctions between the two that make it erroneous to equate the terms; on the other hand, the similarities pose no problems" (Charles C. Ryrie, *The Basis of the Premillennial Faith* [Neptune, N.J.: Loizeaux Brothers, 1953], pp. 98–99). In his Study Bible notes, those distinctions are not stressed (Charles C. Ryrie, *The Ryrie Study Bible* [Chicago: Moody, 1976], p. 1448).
45. Charles C. Ryrie, *Dispensationalism Today* (Chicago: Moody, 1965), p. 171.
46. Ibid., p. 173.
47. In commenting on the relationship of the kingdom to the church, he says that "if one's concept of the kingdom is a spiritual one, then the Church can easily be assumed to be the form of the kingdom today. If Jesus preached and offered the Davidic Kingdom, it was obviously postponed, for it simply has not been established according to the picture of the Old Testament promises." He notes along with Alva McClain that "if it [the kingdom preached by Jesus] were the spiritual kingdom Christ was offering, then such an announcement would have had no special significance whatever for Israel, for such a rule of God has *always* been recognized among the people of God" (ibid., pp. 172–73). Cf. McClain, *Greatness of the Kingdom*, p. 303.
48. Charles C. Ryrie, *Biblical Theology of the New Testament* (Chicago: Moody, 1959), p. 88.
49. Ryrie, *Dispensationalism Today*, p. 172.

he also affirms the continuing presence of the universal kingdom and the spiritual rule of God in individual hearts today."[50]

Ryrie's works reflect the developing decline of the importance of what was once considered a basic distinction within dispensationalism, namely, the clearly defined bifurcation of the kingdom of heaven and the kingdom of God. In the last three decades few dispensationalists make such a diverse distinction the deciding factor of their system as was advanced by earlier writers within the movement.[51] One of the first to abandon that particular aspect of early dispensationalism was J. Dwight Pentecost.

J. Dwight Pentecost

J. Dwight Pentecost has been renowned for his interest and expertise in the study of biblical prophecy. Taking the lead from McClain, he developed the concept of the kingdom as a theodicy under the terminology of the "eternal" and "theocratic" kingdoms. He contends: "Premillennialists are accustomed to designating the eternal kingdom as the kingdom of God and the earthly as the kingdom of heaven. Such a categorical distinction does not seem to be supported by Scriptural usage."[52]

Pentecost defines the eternal kingdom as "God's kingly rule and sovereignty over all intelligences in heaven or on earth who are willingly subject to God in the exercise of sovereignty."[53] This includes a subtle but significant change from McClain in that the latter saw the universal ("eternal" for Pentecost) kingdom as effectively and efficaciously ruling over even the rebellious, whereas with Pentecost it is only those willingly subject who are said to be a part of the eternal kingdom of God.

The outworkings of the theocratic program may be summarized as follows:

> From the outset of God's program to manifest His sovereignty by His rule in this earthly sphere until the consummation of that program, when universal

50. Ibid., p. 173.

51. Clarence Mason, Jr., *Prophetic Problems with Alternative Solutions* (Chicago: Moody, 1973), pp. 102–3. Toussaint states that they are "essentially synonymous" and says both refer to the future millennial kingdom (Stanley D. Toussaint, "The Kingdom in Matthew's Gospel," in *Essays in Honor of J. Dwight Pentecost*, ed. Stanley D. Toussaint and Charles H. Dyer [Chicago: Moody, 1986], p. 23).

52. J. Dwight Pentecost, *Things to Come* (Grand Rapids: Zondervan, 1958), p. 434. He also notes that both phrases, "kingdom of heaven" and "kingdom of God," are used for the eternal kingdom, the future millennial kingdom, as well as the present form of the kingdom (ibid., pp. 433–34). "In regard to the terms kingdom of God and the kingdom of the heavens it is to be observed that, while not synonymous, they are used interchangeably. What distinctions there are not inherent in the words themselves, but in their usage in the context. Both of these terms are used to designate the millennial kingdom, the spiritual kingdom, and the mystery form of the kingdom. While we recognize the distinctions between the earthly and the eternal aspects of the kingdom program, we must guard against making the terms kingdom of God and the kingdom of the heavens absolute. Only the context can determine the meaning intended to be conveyed by the terms" (ibid., p. 144).

53. Ibid., p. 430.

sovereignty is acknowledged (1 Cor. 15:24), there has been one continuous, connected, progressive development of that program. While there might be various phases of that program and different media through which that sovereignty was exercised, it has been the development of one program. This whole program may be called the theocratic kingdom.[54]

Because of the challenge of Satan, God instituted the theocratic program to manifest his right to rule through a divinely chosen representative. This approach demonstrates a unity to the Scriptures for which the dispensational position has been so often maligned. The unity is doxological and theocentric.

Against the traditions of the dispensational heritage, Pentecost brings two important developments to the subject of the kingdom. The first concerns the phrases "the kingdom of God" and "the kingdom of heaven." He states, "In regard to the terms kingdom of God and kingdom of the heavens, it is to be observed that, while not synonymous, they are used interchangeably. What distinctions there are are not inherent in the words themselves, but in their usage in the context."[55] The second coordinates with the optimistic view of the theocracy represented above. Pentecost no longer (a change since the original publication of *Things to Come*) views certain parables of Matthew 13 as the false profession of the present dispensation, which has been the traditional approach to the parables of the tares, mustard tree, leaven, and the dragnet. In contrast, the parables, he says, were given to reveal the form and characteristics with which the theocratic kingdom will manifest itself in the interadvent age. Although the church age fits within this span of time, the parables do not primarily reveal truth about the church, but rather the interadvent age of God's kingdom program of which the church is a part.[56]

John F. Walvoord

While the distinctions between the meanings of the kingdom of heaven and kingdom of God have almost entirely fell beside the way, John F. Walvoord is one who continues to maintain the historic position even in his most recent writings.[57] In all fairness, however, as early as 1953, the relevancy of such distinctions were minimized in a review of George Ladd's book, *Crucial Questions about the Kingdom of God*.[58]

54. Ibid., p. 433.
55. Ibid., p. 144.
56. J. Dwight Pentecost, *The Parables of Jesus* (Grand Rapids: Zondervan, 1982), p. 49.
57. John F. Walvoord, "The New Testament Doctrine of the Kingdom," *Bibliotheca Sacra* 139 (July–September 1982): 206. He takes his clue from Earl Miller, *The Kingdom of God and the Kingdom of Heaven* (Meadville, Pa.: Author, 1950), pp. 60–64.
58. "Another major confusion in this discussion is the mistaken notion commonly held by nondispensationalists that a distinction often affirmed between the kingdom of God and the kingdom of heaven is essential to the dispensational argument. Actually one could maintain this distinction and be

With regard to the present session of Christ in heaven and the Davidic throne, Walvoord throws down the following gauntlet:

> A search of the New Testament reveals that there is not one reference connecting the present session of Christ with the Davidic throne. While this argument is, of course, not conclusive, it is almost incredible that in so many references to David and in so frequent reference to the present session of Christ on the Father's throne there should not be one reference connecting the two in any authoritative way. The New Testament is totally lacking in positive teaching that the throne of the Father in heaven is to be identified with the Davidic throne. The inference is plain that Christ is seated on the Father's throne, but that this is not at all the same as being seated on the throne of David.[59]

This is not to say that there is not a present form of the kingdom today. He has affirmed, "While premillenarians continue to insist that Old Testament prophecies concerning a kingdom on earth will be fulfilled literally, most premillenarians recognize that there is a present form of the kingdom which is spiritual. In a sense God is reigning; but that is not fulfilling the Old Testament prophecies."[60]

With the exception of a few articles and popular treatments, dispensationalists have not been pursuing the discussions of the nature of the kingdom. However, with the rise of dominion theology, Christian reconstructionism,

---

an amillenarian or deny it and be a dispensationalist. The distinction as usually presented is between the kingdom of heaven as an outward sphere of profession and the kingdom of God as a sphere of reality including only the elect. . . . As far as affecting the premillennial or dispensational argument, in the opinion of the reviewer it is irrelevant. The issue is not whether the kingdom of heaven is postponed but whether the Messianic kingdom offered by the Old Testament prophets and expected by the Jewish people in connection with the first advent was offered, rejected, and postponed until the second advent. We believe the author is therefore incorrect in building this dispensational doctrine of a postponed kingdom on the distinction between the kingdom of God and the kingdom of heaven. It depends rather upon the distinction between the present form of the kingdom and the future form of the kingdom, which is an entirely different matter" (John F. Walvoord, "Review of *Crucial Questions about the Kingdom of God*, by George Eldon Ladd," *Bibliotheca Sacra* 110 [January–March 1953]: 6).

59. John F. Walvoord, *The Millennial Kingdom* (Grand Rapids: Zondervan, 1959), p. 203.

60. "As used in the New Testament, 'the kingdom of God' always speaks of a realm of spiritual reality (that may include holy angels), but it never includes unsaved men. In contrast, 'the kingdom of heaven' seems to refer to men alone and to include some who are merely professing Christians. This is illustrated in Matthew 13 where the kingdom of heaven is compared to a field with both wheat and tares, with wheat representing the saved and the tares seemingly representing a sphere of profession without reality. Likewise, the kingdom of heaven is compared to a net which includes both good and bad fish. These parables are never used in the other Gospels to refer to the kingdom of God. Accordingly, the view that the kingdom of heaven refers to the spirit of profession including true believers while the kingdom of God includes only holy angels and true believers has some support in the Gospel of Matthew. As such, the kingdom of heaven can refer either to the present form of the kingdom as it does in Matthew 13, or in eschatological form to the kingdom which will follow the Second Advent. In both cases there is a sphere of profession as contrasted to the sphere of reality composed only of those who are elect men or angels" (John F. Walvoord, "The New Testament Doctrine of the Kingdom," *Bibliotheca Sacra* 130 [July–September 1982]: 207).

and the kingdom apologetics of the Vineyard movement, the subject of the kingdom has again become a focus of attention and discussion.

Furthermore, increasing interaction has begun to take place within dispensationalism, which is bound to give rise to more and better articulation of the distinctives. Two recent contributors to this dialogue are Robert L. Saucy and Darrell L. Bock.

Robert L. Saucy

Seeking to draw a contrast with traditional dispensational thinking, Saucy describes a contemporary form of dispensationalism that argues for a greater continuity in the plan and purpose of God's kingdom program:

> Some dispensationalists, however, have come to see a greater unity in the historical program of God centered in the Messianic kingdom. Without giving up the fulfillment of the promises for the nation of Israel when Christ returns to reign openly in glory, this form of dispensationalism agrees with non-dispensational premillennialism that it is preferable to interpret this age as the first phase of the fulfillment of the one promised Messianic kingdom. The present age involves the spiritual aspects of that Messianic kingdom, that is, the blessings of the New Covenant (i.e. regeneration, the indwelling spirit, etc.). The remainder of the promises including those concerning Israel and the nations will find their fulfillment following the second advent.[61]

According to Saucy, this form of dispensationalism sees a present "power" of the messianic kingdom in fulfillment of the Old Testament prophecies, especially in the realm of salvation, and yet retains the distinctive understanding of the relationship of the church and Israel. It continues to affirm a future salvation for the nation of Israel in relation to other nations in the millennial kingdom.

In another article Saucy advocates a "mediating position" between traditional dispensationalist and nondispensationalist understandings of God's plan for history. Reacting to the terms "parenthesis"[62] and "intercalation,"[63] which have often been used to describe the present age, he advocates a historical unity while preserving the distinctive between Israel and the church.[64] In the present age the power of God's kingdom is present to save and transform,[65] but the coercive force involved in the domination of

61. Saucy, "Contemporary Dispensational Thought," p. 11.
62. Walvoord, *The Millennial Kingdom*, pp. 227–30.
63. Chafer, *Systematic Theology*, 4:41.
64. Robert L. Saucy, "The Crucial Issue Between Dispensational and Nondispensational Systems," *Criswell Theological Review* 1 (1986): 149–65.
65. Robert L. Saucy, "The Presence of the Kingdom and the Life of the Church," *Bibliotheca Sacra* 145 (January–March 1988): 44.

hostile powers awaits the arrival of the King for its general and universal application.[66]

Darrell L. Bock

Another dispensationalist, Darrell L. Bock, has argued for an initial and an inaugural rule of Jesus in the present age. His position can be seen in the following summary:

> What emerges is a picture of a career that comes in stages as different aspects of what the Old Testament promised are brought to fruition at different phases of Jesus' work. One might characterize these phases as the "already" and "not yet" of Jesus' career or, by reference to the kingdom, as the invisible and visible kingdom of God. The descriptions *invisible* and *visible* do not characterize the kingdom as ineffective or secret now, versus powerful later. Rather the terms are intended Christologically to describe the nature of Jesus' rule. In the current period, he is not visible, though he sits in heaven and reigns from the right hand of God through the work of the Spirit in his disciples. In the future period, he will reign visibly on the earth. The kingdom is present in both periods. The kingdom is the powerful manifestation of God's activity in the world but the King's visibility differs between the two periods.[67]

Drawing from the Old Testament quotations and allusions in Acts 2, Bock argues that the resurrection and seating of Christ at the Father's right hand are linked to the promises of the Davidic covenant (Ps. 132) and the sending of the Spirit is linked with the promises associated with the new covenant: "Jesus' rule is present in the salvation benefits he bestows in conjunction with the initial fulfillment phase of his rule. The kingdom is invisible in the sense that he rules not over man directly, but in those who share in the benefits he offers, especially the provision of the Spirit. Those who share the Spirit show the influence of God in the world and reflect his work on earth."[68]

From Acts 3, Bock strongly affirms and argues for a future visible kingdom on earth in which all the promises of the Old Testament prophets will be fulfilled as God restores the role of Israel on the earth. Contrasting the "periods of refreshing" (Acts 3:19) and "the time of restoration" (1:6; 3:21), the argument is advanced for a two-stage program of fulfillment:

> In other words the last days of fulfillment have two parts. There is the current period of refreshing, which is correlated to Jesus' reign in heaven and in which a person shares if he or she repents. Then at the end of this period Jesus will come to bring the restoration of those things promised by the Old Testament.

---

66. Ibid., pp. 45–46. Saucy's recent book, *The Case for Progressive Dispensationalism* (Grand Rapids: Zondervan, 1993), was received too late to be consulted in the writing of this essay.

67. Darrell L. Bock, "The Reign of the Lord Christ," in *Israel, the Church and Dispensationalism*, ed. Craig A. Blaising and Darrell L. Bock (Grand Rapids: Zondervan, 1991), p. 46.

68. Ibid., p. 53.

Peter does not predict when Jesus comes, but with his return will come the second period of fulfillment, the times of restoration. This is a time when promises made to Israel are completed, as the linkage between Acts 1 and 3 shows.[69]

Bock argues against a "postponement" theory in favor of a program that was not postponed but was always seen as coming in two phases:

> However, the appearance of delay does exist, since the ultimate culmination does not come in the current phase. When it became clear through the New Testament revelation that Jesus would accomplish God's program in two stages, not one, the appearance of parenthesis could not be avoided, since the Old Testament placed these events side by side. The expectation had been that the Chosen One would bring all fulfillment in one coming. But one of the promises not integrated into the current expectation, not even by the disciples, was that the Messiah-Servant would be rejected by his own people. When one pulls apart what had appeared together, the gap in between the two parts inevitably looks like a parenthesis. Having made this caveat on parenthesis and delay, we nevertheless should be clear that Jesus was always coming with the kingdom, as an early passage such as Luke 4:14–30 makes clear (note also vv. 42–44). The offer of the kingdom came. . . . The offer was not withdrawn, but it did have heretofore unannounced elements in it as certain parables make clear. The kingdom program of God was progressively revealed, and some of that progress came in the life and ministry of Jesus and in the period of the apostles. In this revelation what the Old Testament meant was made clear and some new elements of the program were introduced.[70]

Concluding Observations

Based on this descriptive survey, the following observations and questions are offered.

First, dispensationalists have been unanimous in advancing a premillennial eschatology that advocates that Israel is the covenant nation of God, retaining her identity throughout both the historical and prophetic portions of the Scriptures. The result will be her salvation and restoration to the land to fulfill those promises of the future millennial kingdom on this earth prior to eternity.

Second, there has been a progressive expansion in the understanding of the earthly concept of the kingdom. From the early days of Darby's confinement of the kingdom of heaven to one dispensation to an understanding of a unified plan of history centered in a theocratic or mediatorial development of God's kingdom, it may be concluded that there has never really been "a dispensational view" of the doctrine of the kingdom other than the insistence

---

69. Ibid., p. 57.
70. Ibid., pp. 60–61.

on a final earthly phase of Davidic fulfillment. Further work needs to be done in the articulation of the concept of theocracy before the establishment of the nation of Israel. Can it really be said that Noah, Abraham , or even Moses was God's earthly ruler?

Third, the distinction between the kingdom of heaven and the kingdom of God, though held today by some, has all but vanished as a necessary tenet of dispensationalism. What was once considered an indispensable part of the system has been effectively eliminated as a necessary corollary.[71] However, the traditional explanation for Matthew's preference for substituting the kingdom of heaven for the kingdom of God out of deference to Jewish sensitivity with regard to the name of God, does not explain why Matthew uses the term "God" almost fifty other times in the book. The answer is rather to be found more in the connection of the name with the concept of the kingdom. With a Jewish readership in view, Matthew seems to have made a strong appeal to Danielic imagery of the heavenly Son of Man in order to authenticate Jesus as the Christ who would be King over Israel. Further, the parables that were customarily utilized to defend the traditional view of the kingdom of heaven as Christendom (mustard seed, leaven, dragnet) have been interpreted differently throughout the history of dispensationalism and therefore need to be reexamined along with the other kingdom parables for their contribution to an understanding of the kingdom and dispensationalism.

Fourth, until recent days the "offer-rejection-postponement" model has been a generally accepted explanation of the Gospel passages that teach a present manifestation as well as a future consummation of God's kingdom purposes with Israel. This interpretation had the value of preserving the distinction between the present age, which includes God's purposes for the church, and God's future purpose for the nation of Israel. Recent challenges to the traditional view have been in response to a larger context of eschatological debate. As Turner has stated, "the central question seems to revolve around the nature of the kingdom of God in Jesus' teaching as being either present/imminent or future/transcendent. Today it is customary to merge the present and future views in an 'already but not yet' inaugurated or proleptic eschatology."[72]

Some remaining questions need to be answered or articulated from the dispensational perspective. Does the New Testament sufficiently redefine or expand the Davidic covenant to include a reign by the Seed of David in absentia from the earth over a non-Israel realm and which does not overtly control the activities of man on the earth? Must the references in Acts 2 to

---

71. Chafer, *Systematic Theology,* 5:316. Feinberg also states, "these distinctions are vital and must be made to harmonize the Word of God" (Charles L. Feinberg, *Millennialism: The Two Major Views* [Chicago: Moody, 1980], p. 253).

72. David L. Turner, "The Continuity of Scripture and Eschatology: Key Hermeneutical Issues," *Grace Theological Journal* 6 (1985): 283.

the seating of Christ on the Father's throne be taken as the direct fulfillment of Old Testament promises? Or, to put it another way, can the references to the Davidic promises in Acts 2 be viewed as a vindication of the royalty of Jesus as both Lord and Christ, in authenticating the mission of the church and the demonstration of the righteous judgment that has come on Israel? Would this not better explain the resultant judicial delay of the Davidic fulfillment until after the present age? How does the present manifestation of God's kingdom differ from other ages when God was or will be providentially ruling the affairs of the earth at times when there is no visible earthly kingdom? If it can be demonstrated from the New Testament that there is Davidic rule already present that is to be associated with what God is doing in and through the church, what will be the manifestation of that rule after the rapture of the church during the tribulation?

Most though not all dispensational scholars would state that the sine qua non of dispensationalism is the distinction between Israel and the church. As Saucy has pointed out, there are significant differences as to the extent of such a separation as represented in various works published within the last decade of dispensational dialogue.[73] These differences are reflected not only in their respective place in the plan of history,[74] but also in the question of their destiny. The early dispensational distinctive of two peoples of God who remain separate in time and eternity has been challenged by dispensationalists of late in favor of a common destiny in both the millennium and eternity.[75]

A reexamination of the differences between the saved of Israel, the church, and those coming to salvation outside or beyond those institutions in other

73. Kenneth L. Barker, "False Dichotomies Between the Testaments," *Journal of the Evangelical Theological Society* 25 (March 1982): 3–16. Also see Craig A. Blaising, "Development of Dispensationalism by Contemporary Dispensationalists," *Bibliotheca Sacra* 145 (July–September 1988): 254–80; Earl D. Radmacher, "The Current Status of Dispensationalism and Its Eschatology," in *Perspectives on Evangelical Theology,* ed. Kenneth S. Kantzer and Stanley N. Gundry (Grand Rapids: Baker, 1979), pp. 163–76; and Blaising and Bock, eds., *Israel, the Church and Dispensationalism.*
74. Saucy, "Contemporary Dispensational Thought," pp. 10–11.
75. Cook has written, "Contrary to some dispensational teaching which makes a firm distinction between Israel as God's earthly people and the Church as God's heavenly people, which distinction is to be maintained throughout eternity, the Biblical evidence seems to show a progressive blurring of such distinctions as history moves toward its climax. Beginning with the time of the rapture and resurrection of the saints these groupings, which during the outworking of God's historical purposes are legitimate to a certain degree, become less and less important. It should be observed that most passages dealing with the rapture and resurrection of the saints in the New Testament relate to individuals rather than to entities such as Israel or the Church. Beginning with the Millennium and continuing on into the Eternal Kingdom of God there is an inter-penetration of time and eternity, heaven and earth. During the Millennium saints with glorified bodies will relate to the people of earth. In the final form of the Kingdom, as set forth in Revelation 21:1ff., such an inter-penetration is clearly set forth (see especially verses one to seven, nine and ten) as the heavenly city comes down out of heaven to, or at least proximate to, earth. Thus it would appear that sharp distinctions between groups of saints in eternity is not Biblically warranted and tends to lead to an unnecessary and potentially divisive elitism" (W. Robert Cook, *The Theology of John* [Chicago: Moody, 1979], pp. 226–41). Also see Sauer, *From Eternity to Eternity,* pp. 81–96.

periods of God's dealings with humankind needs to be made. This is needed to help determine whether those differences are confined strictly to eras in which each group was saved or whether the sphere and share of their ultimate inheritance should be at all distinguished whether in the millennium or in eternity.

Tribute

My introduction to Donald K. Campbell was in my first doctoral course I took at Dallas Theological Seminary. His love for the Word and skill in its exposition made me an immediate fan. His heart for application and his skill in exposition make the title of this honorary volume even more appropriate for me.

As with many professors-turned-administrators, the demands of such activities too often steal one away from what has been a significant contribution through their classroom teaching in the lives of their students. While I have had the privilege to work for Dr. Campbell on the Dallas Seminary campus, minister together with him at conferences, and travel overseas with him and other colleagues together with our wives, I am blessed to have profited from his exposition of the Bible. Under Dr. Campbell's presidential leadership, many innovations and advancements have been achieved. I have personally appreciated his encouragement, counsel, and friendship over these recent years.

The Contingency of the Coming of the Kingdom

Stanley D. Toussaint

Generally dispensationalists have taught that the Lord Jesus in his earthly ministry not only presented himself to Israel as their promised Messiah, but also in that presentation tendered the promised kingdom if Israel would accept him. In other words, Christ offered the kingdom (by way of the cross) if Israel would repent. Some dispensationalists, however, have disputed this, saying there was no offer of the kingdom.[1] The reasons for this objection to a kingdom proposal will be discussed later.

The Importance of the Problem

For Accuracy in Exegesis and Exposition

Hermeneutics always operates in a cycle or preferably a spiral. Students of Scripture study a passage using a synthesis and analysis cycle. That is, they test an overview (synthesis) by the details of the passage and then examine an analysis by synthesis. Hermeneutics is to be a spiral because as we study we are constantly growing in our understanding of the passage. The same is true of theology and exegesis. Does Scripture validate the doctrine one holds or does theology help in interpreting the Bible? Actually, both are involved in interpretation and that becomes the issue in this discussion. What is meant by the often-recorded announcement, "Repent for the kingdom of God (heaven) has drawn near" (Matt. 4:17)? Or, "Therefore I say to you, the kingdom of God will be taken away from you, and be given to a nation producing the fruit of it" (Matt. 21:43)? And what is meant by Peter's words in Acts 3:19–21? Those who hold to the doctrine of the contingency of the coming of the kingdom will interpret the passages differently than if they do not;

---

1. One example is Erich Sauer, *From Eternity to Eternity* (Grand Rapids: Eerdmans, 1954), pp. 175–76.

at least the verses will take on different nuances of thought. The issue of contingency, then, becomes important in exegesis and exposition.

For Confirming or Correcting an Element of Traditional Dispensationalism

Dispensationalism over time has been modified in a number of areas.[2] For instance, it was common at one time for dispensationalists to make a distinction between the kingdom of God and the kingdom of heaven.[3] The Sermon on the Mount was usually said to be a definition of millennial ethics.[4] Normative dispensationalism taught that the Jews were God's earthly people and the church was God's heavenly people.[5] Few contemporary dispensationalists would hold to these distinctives. In other words, dispensationalism has been refined and continues to develop.

The question being discussed here is whether traditional dispensationalism is correct in teaching an offer of the kingdom to Israel. It must be noted that the basic theses of dispensationalism do not rise or fall on the answer to that question. One of these theses is the distinction between Israel and the church, a doctrine that can be held even if one denies the tender of the kingdom to Israel in the Gospels and Acts. However, if the Scriptures do teach an offer of the promised earthly reign of Christ, the distinction between Israel and the church is even more clearly seen. No such offer was made to the apostolic church. But the primary justification for this study is the pursuit of accurate exegesis within the ranks of dispensationalism.

A Definition of Two Key Terms

The term "kingdom" is now being considered within the parameters of dispensationalism. All dispensationalists agree on the doctrine of a coming earthly millennium followed by the eternal state. This millennium is the

2. Craig A. Blaising, "Doctrinal Development in Orthodoxy," *Bibliotheca Sacra* 145 (April–June 1988): 133–40; idem, "Development of Dispensationalism by Contemporary Dispensationalists," *Bibliotheca Sacra* 145 (July–September 1988): 254–80.
3. Earl Miller, *The Kingdom of God and the Kingdom of Heaven* (Meadville, Pa.: Author, 1950), pp. 63–64; Charles L. Feinberg, *Premillennialism or Amillennialism?* (Wheaton, Ill.: Van Kampen, 1954), pp. 298–99; C. I. Scofield, ed., *The Scofield Reference Bible* (New York: Oxford University Press, 1917), p. 1003.
4. Donald Grey Barnhouse, *His Own Received Him Not, But . . .* (New York: Revell, 1933), p. 47; Lewis Sperry Chafer, "The Teachings of Christ Incarnate," *Bibliotheca Sacra* 108 (October–December 1951): 410; E. Schuyler English, *Studies in the Gospel According to Matthew* (New York: Revell, 1935), p. 51; A. C. Gaebelein, *The Gospel of Matthew*, 2 vols. (Neptune, N.J.: Loizeaux Brothers, 1910), 1:10; William Kelly, *Lectures on the Gospel of Matthew* (New York: Loizeaux Brothers, n.d.), pp. 103–6; and William L. Pettingill, *Simple Studies in Matthew* (Findlay, Ohio: Dunham, n.d.), p. 58.
5. Lewis Sperry Chafer, *Systematic Theology* (Dallas, Tex.: Dallas Seminary Press, 1948; reprint [8 vols. in 4], Grand Rapids: Kregel, 1992), 4:33–35, 47, 52, 142.

future Davidic kingdom in premillennial dispensationalism.[6] A considerable debate is being carried on within dispensationalism as to the nature of Christ's kingdom in this age.[7] This present essay does not deal with the present existence or nature of Christ's kingdom.

When dispensationalists discuss the contingency of the kingdom, they are talking about a kingdom that is earthly and literal, and is the fulfillment of the Old Testament promises, covenants, and prophetic predictions for Israel. However, it must be understood that dispensationalists who may not believe in the contingency of the kingdom agree with other dispensationalists that ultimately Israel's promises will have an earthly fulfillment in the future millennium. No matter what their view of Christ's present kingdom, dispensationalists still believe in a coming earthly reign.[8]

The term "contingency" means that seen from the human side, the coming of that kingdom is conditional, depending on Israel's response to Jesus as its Messiah. According to traditional dispensationalists the Lord Jesus, along with the presentation of himself to Israel as Messiah, also offered the kingdom promised in the Old Testament.[9] Because Israel rejected Christ, the kingdom did not come and was in fact postponed to a future date. During this intercalation the Lord is building his church. In other words, the coming of the kingdom depended and depends on Israel's response to the Lord Jesus. This is the fundamental concept in the expression "the contingency of the coming of the kingdom."

It should be noted that the term not only looks back to the apostolic age of the New Testament; in its fullest sense it also looks ahead to the future. The coming of the kingdom in the future still depends on Israel's response to Christ.

Is Contingency in the Scriptures?

A Determinative Question

The question of contingency is crucial because if contingency is not found in the Scriptures in connection with other matters, the problem is probably solved. It would be possible for contingency to exist for the coming of the kingdom even if contingency could not be found in connection with anything else; however, it would be highly improbable. On the other hand, if contin-

6. Cf. Sauer, *From Eternity to Eternity*, p. 176.

7. For a recent discussion of this issue from the standpoint of "progressive dispensationalism," see Craig A. Blaising and Darrell L. Bock, eds., *Dispensationalism, Israel and the Church* (Grand Rapids: Zondervan, 1992).

8. For a defense of this view of the coming kingdom, see Alva J. McClain, *The Greatness of the Kingdom* (Grand Rapids: Zondervan, 1959), pp. 274–303; and J. Dwight Pentecost, *Things to Come* (Findlay, Ohio: Dunham, 1958), pp. 65–128, 476–77.

9. McClain, *Greatness of the Kingdom*, pp. 304–20; Pentecost, *Things to Come*, pp. 452–56.

gency can be shown in other areas of theology, especially in parallel concepts, then it is possible and even probable for it to be a factor in the coming of the kingdom.

To make other situations parallel to the idea of an offer of the kingdom during the apostolic era, certain factors must exist. First, the contingency must involve a divine offer or statement. The tender of a condition cannot be between two humans. Second, the offer must have in mind a human response. In other words, the contingency must be vertical, with a human or humans responding to a statement from God.

The question of contingency does not void God's decree. Whether something is accepted or rejected in an immediate situation does not annul what God has ultimately decreed will come to pass. If Israel rejected a proffer of the kingdom during Christ's ministry, it does not mean the promised kingdom will never arrive. This principle is only mentioned here because of parallels where the contingency by man's refusal forever shuts off the possibility of repentance. In such a case an offer will never be made again (Heb. 12:17). This is not true in Israel's situation (Rom. 11:15, 26–27, 30–32).

Contingency Stated Explicitly in the Scriptures

A number of passages state the concept of contingency explicitly. One example is Jeremiah 18:7–10:

> At one moment I might speak concerning a nation or concerning a kingdom to uproot, to pull down, or to destroy it; if that nation against which I have spoken turns from its evil, I will relent concerning the calamity I planned to bring on it. Or at another moment I might speak concerning a nation or concerning a kingdom to build up or to plant it; if it does evil in My sight by not obeying My voice, then I will think better of the good with which I had promised to bless it.

Here the response of a nation to God's prophecy may affect its future.

Another example of an explicitly stated contingency is 1 Kings 11:38. Ahijah the prophet promised Jeroboam that he would have a house as enduring as David's if he would walk in the ways of the Lord. This spectacular offer is especially interesting because of God's foreknowledge and eternal decree. Certainly Jeroboam's intense apostasy was no surprise to the Lord. Nevertheless this was an offer with contingency depending on Jeroboam's response.

The contingency stated in Exodus 19:5–6 is significant because it indicates an unconditional promise may be individually conditional and temporarily contingent. Certainly Israel will be God's special treasure,[10] a holy nation,

---

10. The term *sĕgūllāh* was used of a private treasure belonging to royalty (1 Chron. 29:3).

and a kingdom of priests (Deut. 7:6–10; Isa. 61:6). However, individual participation in these promises depended on one's personal relationship with the Lord; national blessing is a matter of repentance by the people as a whole. God promised that this will take place (Zech. 12:10; Rom. 11:26). This concept of national blessings for Israel being conditioned on the nation's repentance is common in the Old Testament (Deut. 28:1–68; Josh. 23:11–16; 2 Chron. 7:13–18; etc.). In fact, the ringing outrages of the prophets against Israel were based on the doctrine of Deuteronomy 28. On the other hand, the words of eschatological comfort spoken to Israel by the prophets were premised on the promises given to the patriarchs and David. At any rate, contingency is affirmed directly in the Bible.

Contingency Implied in the Scriptures

If blessings and promises are explicitly conditional, it would be logical to assume there may be instances in which contingency is only implied. And there are such cases. A classic example is that of Jonah, who warned that Nineveh would be overthrown in forty days. Because Nineveh repented, God spared the city. An implied condition was contained in Jonah's proclamation—a fact that was painfully clear to Jonah (Jon. 3:10–4:2).

When Hezekiah was deathly ill, Isaiah told him, "Set your house in order, for you shall die and not live" (2 Kings 20:1). However, Hezekiah prayed and was granted fifteen more years of life. The prophecy of Isaiah, like Jonah's, appeared to be without condition; however, Hezekiah's pathetic pleas to God changed the prognostication. This is totally in keeping with the statements of Jeremiah 18:7–10. Indeed conditionality is a part of the warp and woof of the fabric of divine-human relationships until eternity.[11] It was so in the garden of Eden and has been so ever since. Salvation depends on

---

11. If conditionality is implied in certain prophetic pronouncements, how can anyone know if unconditional promises exist? Can contingency vitiate any and all promises? Peters, who was aware of this problem, sets forth eleven marks of unconditional prophecies and promises:

> It may be proper to give some marks by which we may distinguish predictions that will finally be fulfilled from those that are merely conditional. They are the following: 1. Predictions that are bound up with the Divine Plan of Redemption, as e.g. those refering [*sic*] to Christ's birth, life, death, etc. 2. Those which are confirmed by solemn affirmations or by an oath, as e.g. Numb. 14:20, 28, Heb. 6:17, etc. 3. Those that are incorporated in the Covenants, as e.g. the Abrahamic and Davidic covenants. 4. Predictions which expressly declare that they will take place irrespective of what man will do, as e.g. Dan. chs. 2 and 7, the Apocalypse, Ps. 89:33, 34, etc. 5. Predictions that form the basis of succeeding ones and of promises, as e.g. Nathan to David, 2 Sam. 7:5–17 (this at first sight might seem an exception, but in another place its due fulfillment will be proven). 6. Those that are illustrated by a parable, as e.g. parable of the tares, net, nobleman, etc. (the parable enforces, or takes the fulfillment for granted). 7. Predictions relating to the destiny of the good, whoever they may be. 8. Those referring to the destiny of the wicked, whoever they are. 9. Prophecies given to the Jews respecting other nations, and not to those nations themselves for purposes of repentance, as e.g., Babylon, Tyre, etc. 10. Those that relate to the establishment of the Kingdom of God, being a revelation of God's will and pleasure respecting redemptive ordering. 11. Those that describe the final restoration of

faith in accord with God's revelation, and blessing for believers is conditioned on obedience. All God's dealings with humans are conditioned on their response to his revelation.

Unconditional Promises and Contingency

If God has made unconditional covenants and has given irrevocable promises to certain individuals and peoples, how can contingency be involved? This of course raises the age-old problem of God's sovereignty and human responsibility. It is a theological conundrum and antinomy. In illustrating the same tension, Packer uses the analogy of light.[12] Evidence exists that light is comprised of light waves and light particles, an apparent contradiction; yet physicists work with both principles. Likewise God's sovereignty is a fundamental doctrine of the Scriptures but human responsibility is also taught alongside the doctrine of sovereignty.

In a matter of unconditional promises the issue must ultimately go back (as in all cases, including divine election and human responsibility) to the sovereignty of God. He will pour out his Spirit on Israel and bring about repentance in Israel. He will resurrect the Old Testament saints to bring them into their promised inheritance. He will accomplish his will in his time. However, this does not negate contingency as is seen in the previous sections regarding conditionality in the Scriptures. An offer of the gospel is a legitimate one whether it is given to an elect or a nonelect person.

The Contingency of the Coming of the Promised Kingdom

As suggested earlier, when dispensationalists discuss the question of the contingency of the coming of the kingdom, they are dialoguing about the potentiality of the promised Davidic kingdom coming to earth if Israel had responded favorably to Christ at his first coming. In fact, more than potentiality is involved; the question is, do the Scriptures teach that along with the presentation of himself Jesus was also offering the promised millennial kingdom? Is the coming of the eschatological kingdom contingent on Israel's response? Was the kingdom postponed because Israel as a nation rejected Jesus as her Messiah? Of course, this "postponement" is from a human perspective and involves the question of contingency. It is the thesis of this essay that the coming of the promised kingdom was contingent on Israel's response and remains so to this day.

---

the Jewish nation, this being (as will be fully shown hereafter) essential to secure the manifestation of the Kingdom and the Salvation of the Gentiles (George N. H. Peters, *The Theocratic Kingdom*, 3 vols. [1884; reprint, Grand Rapids: Kregel, 1972], 1:177).

12. J. I. Packer, *Evangelism and the Sovereignty of God* (Downers Grove, Ill.: InterVarsity, 1961), p. 19.

The Significance of Acts 3:19–21

The context of this passage is Peter's sermon to a Jewish audience that had assembled after the spectacular miracle of the healing of the man born lame. After accusing Israel of rejecting her Messiah, who is now glorified, Peter called on them to repent. The repentance is emphasized by his use of two synonymous aorist imperatives, *metanoēsate* and *epistrepsate*. The *eis to* with the infinitive construction[13] which follows probably indicates purpose, although result is also possible.[14] For the purpose of this discussion it does not matter. In either case, those who repented would receive the wiping away or removal[15] of their sins.

The significant issue in this discussion is the meaning of the next clause and its relationship to the imperatives to "repent" and "turn." The *hopōs an* clause almost certainly indicates purpose.[16] This clause contains two subjunctive verbs. Are these two verbs referring to simultaneous acts or are they sequential? In other words, does the time of the "seasons of refreshing" occur simultaneously with the arrival of the Messiah or do the "seasons of refreshing" precede the return of the Messiah by some time?

First, the answer to this problem can be seen in the relationship of the purpose clauses to each other. The second purpose clause appears to be a more remote purpose than the first. Peter commanded Israel to repent for the remission of their sins in order for "seasons of refreshing" to arrive and so that the Lord might send the Messiah to them. The removal of the sins precedes the "seasons of refreshing" and the return of Jesus. The way the sentence is constructed implies that the coming of "seasons of refreshing" and the sending of the Messiah are simultaneous. If the coming of the Messiah were to follow the "seasons of refreshing" at a later time, it would seem a separate clause would have introduced the coming of Christ. It is evident

---

13. Manuscripts ℵ and B have *pros to*. The difference in meaning is inconsequential.

14. F. Blass and A. Debrunner, *A Greek Grammar of the New Testament and Other Early Christian Literature* (Chicago: University of Chicago Press, 1961), p. 207; Nigel Turner, *Syntax: A Grammar of New Testament Greek* (Edinburgh: T. & T. Clark, 1963), 3:143. Moulton says the use of *eis to* with the infinitive in this case is "with final force fairly certain" (James Hope Moulton, *Prolegomena: A Grammar of New Testament Greek* [Edinburgh: T. & T. Clark, 1908], 1:218). Green says that in Acts 3:19 it can indicate only purpose (Samuel S. Green, *Handbook to the Grammar of the Greek Testament*, rev. ed. [New York: Revell, n.d.], p. 322). Green's work is old and shows no awareness of *eis to* and the infinitive as it relates to the Hebrew infinitive construct. Cf. Nigel Turner, *Grammatical Insights into the New Testament* (Edinburgh: T. & T. Clark, 1965), pp. 11–12; and William Douglas Chamberlain, *An Exegetical Grammar of the Greek New Testament* (New York: Macmillan, 1941), p. 108.

15. Walter Bauer, William F. Arndt, and F. Wilbur Gingrich, *A Greek-English Lexicon of the New Testament and Other Early Christian Literature*, 2d ed., rev. William Gingrich and Frederick W. Danker (Chicago: University of Chicago Press, 1979), p. 272.

16. Ibid. p. 580; Blass and Debrunner, *Greek Grammar of the New Testament and Other Early Christian Literature*, pp. 186–88; Chamberlain, *Exegetical Grammar of the Greek New Testament*, p. 186; C. F. C. Moule, *An Idiom Book of New Testament Greek* (Cambridge: University Press, 1959), p. 138.

Peter intended to relate the "seasons of refreshing" to the return of the Lord Jesus. The two form a sort of hendiadys.

Second, the phrase "seasons of refreshing" looks ahead to the promised eschatological Davidic kingdom on this earth. Not all agree with this interpretation. Actually some five interpretations are made of this phrase. (1) Some say it looks at present-day spiritual blessings, and the coming of Christ takes place in a person's heart when that person trusts in him.[17] (2) Others see the entire *hopōs* clause as looking to the future when it is fulfilled in an amillennial sense.[18] (3) "The seasons of refreshing" are taken by others to be present-day blessings for believers, but the sending of the Messiah refers to the second coming of Christ when he will bring great spiritual blessings.[19] (4) Others say "the times of refreshing" refer to present-day blessings whereas the sending of the Messiah is yet future when the Old Testament prophecies regarding a literal earthly kingdom will be fulfilled.[20]

A number of writers take a fifth position, maintaining that the "seasons of refreshing" and the sending of Jesus are totally eschatological, referring to the coming of the promised Davidic kingdom.[21] That this is the best view is confirmed by a number of factors.

The two clauses that follow *hopōs* go together. In other words, "that the times of refreshing may come from the presence of the Lord" must be taken with the words "and that He may send Jesus." As Haenchen puts it, "But the two promises are complementary statements about one and the same

17. Joseph Addison Alexander, *Commentary on the Acts of the Apostles* (reprint, Grand Rapids: Zondervan, 1956), p. 115; Kirsopp Lake and Henry J. Cadbury, *The Beginnings of Christianity* (reprint, Grand Rapids: Baker, 1965), p. 37.

18. I. Howard Marshall, *The Acts of the Apostles*, Tyndale New Testament Commentaries (Grand Rapids: Eerdmans, 1980), pp. 93–94. Marshall sees this as the fulfillment of the Old Testament promises.

19. William Barclay, *The Acts of the Apostles* (Philadelphia: Westminster, 1955), p. 32; and Robert J. Karris, *Invitation to Acts* (Garden City, N.Y.: Image Books, 1966), pp. 52–53.

20. Darrell L. Bock, "The Reign of the Lord Christ," in *Dispensationalism, Israel and the Church*, ed. Craig A. Blaising and Darrell L. Bock (Grand Rapids: Zondervan, 1991), pp. 55–61. Bock seems to be unaware of the relationship and significance of the two purpose clauses because he does not mention them. Cf. William Neil, *Acts*, New Century Bible Commentary (Grand Rapids: Eerdmans, 1973), pp. 85–86.

21. Charles F. Baker, *Understanding the Book of Acts* (Grand Rapids: Grace Bible College Publications, 1981), pp. 29–32; Donald Grey Barnhouse, *Acts* (Grand Rapids: Zondervan, 1979), p. 38; Hans Conzelmann, *Acts of the Apostles*, Hermeneia (Philadelphia: Fortress, 1987), pp. 7, 29; W. A. Criswell, *Acts: An Exposition*, 3 vols. (Grand Rapids: Zondervan, 1978), 1:140; Ernst Haenchen, *The Acts of the Apostles* (Oxford: Basil Blackwell, 1971), p. 208; Everett F. Harrison, *Acts* (Chicago: Moody, 1975), p. 76; A. J. Mattill, Jr., *Luke and the Last Things* (Dillsboro, N.C.: Western North Carolina Press, 1979), pp. 50–51; John B. Polhill, *Acts,* New American Commentary (Nashville: Broadman, 1992), pp. 134–35; Richard Belward Rackham, *The Acts of the Apostles* (London: Methuen, 1901), pp. 53–54; Charles Caldwell Ryrie, *The Acts of the Apostles* (Chicago: Moody, 1961), p. 31; *Theological Dictionary of the New Testament*, s.v. "ἀνάψυξις," by Eduard Schweizer, 9:664–65. This list is only partial, but it represents a wide spectrum of views, from ultradispensationalists to critical scholars.

event."[22] Nothing grammatically separates the promises; in fact, they are joined together by the connective *kai*.

The noun *anapsuxis*, translated "refreshing," is a New Testament hapax legomenon. It is used in Greek literature in various forms to refer to "cooling by blowing, refreshing, relieving, resting."[23] It occurs in the Septuagint only in Exodus (in 8:15 in the English text; 8:11 in LXX), where it refers to Egypt's relief from the plague of frogs. Schweizer correctly observes, "The context makes sense only if the 'times of refreshing' are the definitive age of salvation. The expression is undoubtedly apocalyptic in origin. . . . The reference, then, is to the eschatological redemption which is promised to Israel if it repents."[24]

Furthermore, the plural *kairoi*, translated "times" in Acts 3:19, parallels the plural noun *chronōn*, meaning "seasons" or "times" and translated "period" in the New American Standard Bible in verse 21. The two terms refer to the same era. The plurals simply emphasize duration. The context makes it clear that the synonyms refer to the future kingdom age, with the one emphasizing time in its concept of quality and the other the duration of time.

Therefore, it is concluded that in Acts 3:19–21 Peter was discussing the eschatological age promised in the Old Testament.

But having come to this conclusion, was Peter saying that if Israel repented the kingdom would come? Was he offering the kingdom to Israel? The answer must be in the affirmative.

Peter had just said that removal of their sins was contingent on their repentance (v. 19). If contingency exists here, then certainly conditionality is present in verses 20–21.

Furthermore, there was a common teaching in Israel that if Israel would repent, the promised eschatological era would arrive. This doctrine has some basis in the Old Testament. Certainly God's blessings on Israel were conditioned on obedience with a proper heart attitude. This is taught often enough (e.g., Deut. 28–31; 2 Chron. 7:14). This doctrine of the coming of the Messiah being associated with national repentance is seen quite clearly in Zechariah 12:10; it is also implied in Malachi 4:5–6. Peter's commands with the promises attached fit well with Jewish expectations of that time. Yes, Peter was saying that if Israel repented the kingdom would come and the Messiah would return.[25]

22. Haenchen, *Acts of the Apostles*, p. 208; cf. Conzelmann, *Acts of the Apostles*, p. 29.
23. *Theological Dictionary of the New Testament*, s.v. "ἀνάψυξω," by Albert Dihle, 9:664.
24. *Theological Dictionary of the New Testament*, s.v. "ανάψυξις," by Eduard Schweizer, 9:664–65.
25. Baxter, who strongly defends the idea of a kingdom offer in Acts 3, believes the entire Book of Acts revolves around the offer of the kingdom to Israel. This offer, in Baxter's view, comes to a climax and conclusion in Acts 28. He, of course, also believes Matthew describes an offer of the kingdom (J. Sidlow Baxter, *Explore the Book*, 6 vols. [Grand Rapids: Zondervan, 1960], 5:161–62; 6:17–35).

The Significance of the Nearness of the Kingdom

A statement that is highlighted in the Synoptic Gospels is, "The kingdom . . . has drawn near."[26] Much has been written about the meaning of the verb *ēngiken*, normally translated "has drawn near." This term is taken by some to mean "here" or "present."[27] Others insist it means, "has drawn near." The majority of English translations take it this way as do the greater number of commentaries.[28] Bock takes the verb to mean "here" in the sense of "arrival."[29] He argues from the fact that the verb is used with *epi* in Luke 10:9 and also from other New Testament usage. The construction of *ēngikeō epi*, a phrase occurring only in Luke 10:9 (but see Luke 11:20), can easily be explained. It occurs not because the kingdom was present but because the kingdom is always said to come from above (cf. Acts 3:19).[30] Interestingly, none of the illustrations used by Bock to support the meaning of "arrival" are in the perfect tense. Admittedly it is difficult at times to make a distinction between arrival and close proximity. If someone is at the front door, the common expression is, "He is here." However, James used the same concept and the verb *ēngiken* to convey nearness (James 5:8–9). The illustrations used by Bock to support the meaning of "arrival" (Luke 12:33; 15:1; 18:40; 22:47; 24:15, 28; Acts 21:33) may all be disputed. Lane concludes, "The linguistic

---

Robinson says Acts 3 is very primitive, more so than Acts 2 (John A. T. Robinson, "The Most Primitive Christology of All?" *Journal of Theological Studies* 7 [1956]:177–89). He asserts this because in Acts 2 Jesus is now the Messiah, whereas in Acts 3 he will become Christ in the future. Furthermore, Christ is viewed as absent in Acts 3, but in Acts 2 he is present in the Holy Spirit. For a brief rebuttal, see C. F. D. Moule, "The Christology of Acts," in *Studies in Luke–Acts*, ed. Leander E. Keck and J. Louis Martyn (Philadelphia: Fortress, 1966), pp. 166–69.

26. The clause is found in Matthew 3:2; 4:17; 10:7; Mark 1:15; and Luke 10:9, 11. The nearness of the kingdom is not proclaimed in John's Gospel.

27. Some who assert this is the meaning in this construction are Paul J. Achtemeier, *Invitation to Mark* (Garden City, N.Y.: Image Books, 1966), p. 38; Joseph Addison Alexander, *The Gospel According to Mark* (reprint, Grand Rapids: Baker, 1980), p. 15; John Martin Creed, *The Gospel According to St. Luke* (New York: Macmillan, 1930), pp. 146, 161; E. Earle Ellis, *The Gospel of Luke*, Century Bible (Camden, N.J.: Thomas Nelson and Sons, 1966), pp. 13, 161, 202–3; Robert H. Smith, *Matthew*, Augsburg Commentary on the New Testament (Minneapolis: Augsburg, 1989), p. 70. Phillips' paraphrase renders it "has arrived" (J. B. Phillips, *The Gospels* [New York: Macmillan, 1952]).

28. A sampling of those who take it with this meaning are the following: Willoughby C. Allen, *A Critical and Exegetical Commentary on the Gospel According to S. Matthew*, International Critical Commentary (Edinburgh: T. & T. Clark, 1912), p. 23; Hugh Anderson, *The Gospel of Mark*, New Century Bible (Grand Rapids: Eerdmans, 1976), p. 86; William F. Arndt, *The Gospel According to St. Luke* (St. Louis: Concordia, 1956), p. 282; Francis Wright Beare, *The Gospel According to Matthew* (San Francisco: Harper and Row, 1981), p. 89; David Hill, *The Gospel of Matthew*, New Century Bible (Greenwood, S.C.: Attic, 1972), p. 90; Alan Hugh McNeile, *The Gospel According to St. Matthew* (1915; reprint, Grand Rapids: Baker, 1980), p. 25; Alfred Plummer, *A Critical and Exegetical Commentary on the Gospel According to S. Luke*, International Critical Commentary (Edinburgh: T. & T. Clark, 1922), p. 275.

29. Bock, "Reign of the Lord Christ," pp. 40–41.

30. For further discussion, see Plummer, *Critical and Exegetical Commentary on the Gospel According to S. Luke*, p. 275.

232 Stanley D. Toussaint

objections to the proposed rendering 'has come' are weighty, and it is better to translate 'has come near.'"[31]

If *ēngiken* in the announcement "The kingdom of God has drawn near" means "near," what was its practical significance to the hearers? It meant at least two things. First, the hearers were to repent so that they could enter the kingdom when it arrived. This is clearly the emphasis of John's preaching in Matthew 3:7–12 (cf. Luke 3:7–17). They were to repent *for* the kingdom had drawn near. Mark's expression "preaching a baptism of repentance for the forgiveness of sins" (Mark 1:4) implies the same emphasis. Those who expected to enter the future kingdom had to be prepared spiritually by repentance (cf. Ezek. 20:37–38).

A second reason existed for the necessity of repentance: it was necessary for Israel to repent for the kingdom to come. The fact that national repentance to allow the kingdom to come is also involved in these proclamations is clear from a number of passages. It is seen in the Lord's pronouncements of judgment on the cities of Chorazin, Bethsaida, and Capernaum (Matt. 11:20–24; Luke 10:13–15). The reason? They did not repent. In Matthew 12:41 Jesus said, "The men of Nineveh shall stand up with this generation at the judgment, and shall condemn it because they repented at the preaching of Jonah; and behold, something greater than Jonah is here" (cf. Luke 11:32). Because Israel did not repent, the kingdom could not come; instead the nation was doomed for judgment. Repentance is involved in and necessary for the coming of the kingdom (cf. Deut. 28:1–30:20; 2 Chron. 7:14; Ezek. 36:31; Hos. 5:14–15; 6:1–3; Zech. 12:10–14; Mal. 4:5–6). In addition, the concept of contingency in the proclamation of the proximity of the kingdom is clearly implied by other factors.

First, why was the message of the nearness of the kingdom confined to Israel? "These twelve Jesus sent out after instructing them, saying, 'Do not go in the way of the Gentiles, and do not enter any city of the Samaritans; but rather go to the lost sheep of the house of Israel. And as you go, preach, saying, "The kingdom of heaven is at hand"'" (Matt. 10:5–7). The same point is made in Matthew 15:24. The clearest and most pointed answer to this exclusiveness is found in conditionality. The coming of the kingdom depends on Israel's response. This explains Paul's statement to his Jewish hearers in Acts 13:46, "It was necessary that the word of God should be spoken to you first." The whole world could turn to Christ, but until Israel accepts Jesus as her Messiah, the millennial kingdom will not come.

Second, why is there a cessation to the announcement that the kingdom has drawn near? After Christ's opponents accused him of casting out demons

---

31. William L. Lane, *The Gospel According to Mark*, New International Commentary on the New Testament (Grand Rapids: Eerdmans, 1974), p. 65, n. 93. For a more thorough defense of the meaning "near," see A. J. Mattill, Jr., *Luke and the Last Things*, pp. 70–77.

by the power of Satan, the kingdom is no longer said to be near (Matt. 12:24–32; Mark 3:22–30; Luke 11:14–26). Because the Lord was meeting such antagonism, the kingdom was no longer near in the sense of its coming. The amazing feature in all this is that the Lord predicted the kingdom of God will once again be near in the future during that great time of stress known as the Tribulation. In Luke 21:31 he prophesied, "Even so you, too, when you see these things happening, recognize that the kingdom of God is near." This is important because it indicates the kingdom is not now near. It was near; then it ceased to be near; in the future it will be near again. This strongly suggests the kingdom was offered to Israel, but because the nation rejected its Messiah the kingdom was and is no longer near.

It should be noted that this does not mean Christ stopped presenting himself to Israel as its Messiah. He did this, particularly in his so-called triumphal entry, but the die had already been cast. The kingdom was no longer near; Israel's tragic decision had actually been made much earlier.

That the kingdom was offered to Israel is clearly seen in the pathetic laments of the Lord Jesus over Jerusalem (Matt. 23:37–39; Luke 13:34–35; 19:41–44). The gathering of the young fowl probably is a figure to describe God's care of Israel in the coming kingdom. Schweizer says, "The Old Testament speaks of God in the imagery of a bird protecting its young (Deut. 32:11; Isa. 31:5; Ps. 36:7). Converts to Judaism were also described as having been taken 'under the wings of the Shekinah [the presence of God].'"[32] It was the desire of the Lord Jesus to bring Israel into its promised blessings, and the nation refused. It must be noticed that Jesus' lament was addressed to Jerusalem, the city of the great King (Matt. 5:35).[33] That city with its "house" (probably the temple; cf. 1 Kings 9:7–8; Jer. 12:7; 22:5), would be left to Israel as a desolate place until Israel repents (Matt. 23:38–39). It is clear that the ensuing pronouncement of judgment is not on a few individuals; this expression of grief is national in scope. Christ came to Israel to bring the kingdom and regather the nation, but Israel refused; consequently judgment followed. However, he will return and Israel will repent.

It is not without significance that when the Lord approached Jerusalem for the last time he wept over it and referred to his ministry in Israel as "the time of your visitation" (Luke 19:44). The restrictive attributive construction makes it a most definite event. Judgment was to fall on Israel because they did not properly interact with the triumphal entry. In the Old Testament the verb *pāqad* ("to visit") simply means "to give attention to"; the verb is neutral and may be used of a judgment or of a blessing.[34] It was used of God's

---

32. Eduard Schweizer, *The Good News According to Matthew* (Atlanta: John Knox, 1975), p. 444.
33. The repetition of the name "Jerusalem" shows deep emotion.
34. The verb always has a view to action. See R. Alan Cole, *Exodus,* Tyndale Old Testament Commentaries (Downers Grove, Ill.: InterVarsity, 1973), p. 71.

concern for Israel (Exod. 3:16; 4:31; Ruth 1:6; Ps. 80:14). The exodus itself was a time when God visited Israel (Gen. 50:24–25; Exod. 13:19). Jeremiah used the word to anticipate God's deliverance of Israel from the Babylonian captivity (Jer. 27:22; 29:10). Most significant, the verb describes God's visiting his people to bring the anticipated and promised coming kingdom (Zeph. 2:7;[35] Zech. 10:3[36]). This is undoubtedly what is referred to in Zechariah's prophecy in Luke 1:68, "Blessed be the God of Israel, for he has visited us." The context of that prophecy looks to the Messiah's coming deliverance of his people Israel as predicted in the Old Testament.[37] The "time of your visitation" in Luke 19:44 then must be a reference to the Lord's presentation of himself as Messiah with the promised deliverance contingent on Israel's response (in fact, the passage says, "If you had known in this day," that is, the day of the so-called triumphal entry [v. 41]). This was the official offer of the Lord Jesus. The process of Christ presenting himself, Israel's acceptance of him, and the coming of the promised blessings including the kingdom were wrapped up in the phrase *ta pros eirēnēn,* "the things that make for peace." Israel was responsible as is clear from the emphatic *kai su,* "even you." It should be translated, "If you, even you, had known in this day the things that make for peace." The laments over Jerusalem show an offer, a rejection, a postponement of the millennial kingdom, and the coming of that kingdom when Israel repents.

The Significance of the Parables of Rejection

The parables involving Christ's rejection also show the conditionality of the coming of the kingdom. This is seen in a parable that is so crucial to the arguments of the Synoptics that it is found in all three (Matt. 21:33–46; Mark 12:1–12; Luke 20:9–18): the parable of the vineyard and the landowner. Because of Israel's rejection the kingdom was taken from Israel (Matt. 21:43; Mark 12:9; Luke 20:16). That the hearers understood the significance of the story is seen in their response, *mē genoito* (Luke 20:16). The kingdom was no longer near for Israel.

The parable of the spurned invitation to the wedding banquet (Matt. 22:1–10; cf. Luke 14:16–24) is another case in point. This marriage feast is an illustration of the coming kingdom (cf. Matt. 8:11; Isa. 25:6). In the Luke account the parable is told in response to the statement, "Blessed is everyone who shall eat bread in the kingdom of God." Most certainly the banquet is

35. Richard D. Patterson, *Nahum, Habakkuk, Zephaniah,* Wycliffe Exegetical Commentary (Chicago: Moody, 1991), p. 343.

36. Charles L. Feinberg, *God Remembers* (Portland, Oreg.: Multnomah, 1965), pp. 183–84; and Merrill F. Unger, *Zechariah* (Grand Rapids: Zondervan, 1963), pp. 176–77.

37. Creed, *Gospel According to St. Luke,* pp. 25–26; H. K. Luce, *The Gospel According to S. Luke,* Cambridge Greek Testament (Cambridge: University Press, 1933), p. 94.

the kingdom.[38] Some "had been invited" (Matt. 22:3); this looks at the Old Testament promises, covenants, and prophecies given to Israel. When the feast was almost prepared, the call to those who had been invited was issued (Matt. 22:3). This call probably portrays the ministries of John the Baptist and the Lord Jesus. But Israel was "unwilling to come." The next spurned invitation to the nation was by the apostles both before and after the Lord's crucifixion. The call to go to the main highways refers to the message going to the Gentiles.

This parable of the spurned invitation teaches several crucial truths with regard to contingency. First, if Israel had responded favorably to the invitation, the banquet would have taken place. In other words, the kingdom had been near. Second, because Israel rejected the call to come, the kingdom was no longer near and there was a postponement of the kingdom. The call to Gentiles is going on during the present time of postponement.

The parable of Luke 19:11–27 involving the investment of the minas by ten of the king's slaves speaks to the same issue. In Luke 10:9, 11, the seventy were told to preach that the kingdom of God had drawn near. But here the parable was told in order to forestall the disciples' expectation that the appearance of the kingdom was close at hand (Luke 19:11). Significantly, the kingdom was no longer near. This is in contrast with Luke 10:9, 11. Once again the rejection of the Lord by Israel is illustrated by the words of the citizenry, "We do not want this man to reign over us" (v. 14). But this parable teaches more than Jewish rejection; it affirms the Lord's followers have responsibilities to fulfill *in the interim* while he is gone. What had happened? Israel had rejected the King; the kingdom was postponed so that it was no longer at hand. One day the King will return to judge and to establish his kingdom on earth. These parables teach, at least by implication, an offer of the Davidic kingdom, rejection by Israel, and the postponement of that kingdom.

Objections to the Contingency of the Coming of the Kingdom

Sauer, an able defender of dispensationalism, objects to the doctrine of an offer to Israel by Christ to set up the messianic earthly kingdom. He gives

---

38. One of the few who disagrees is Morris. He says, "the application to the end time must be seen as uncertain" (Leon Morris, *The Gospel According to Matthew* [Grand Rapids: Eerdmans, 1992], p. 548). On the other hand, Tasker asserts, "The present parable is concerned with the extension of the offer of the kingdom of God, here thought of as a royal wedding feast, to others than those who were originally invited, because the latter when the moment arrived were unwilling to come" (R. V. G. Tasker, *The Gospel According to St. Matthew*, Tyndale New Testament Commentaries [Grand Rapids: Eerdmans, 1961], p. 206). Tasker, not a premillennialist, sees the banquet as an analogy to the kingdom.

three reasons for not holding to such an offer.[39] First, he refers to "the silence of the Bible."[40] He says, "In the whole Bible there is no single place which speaks distinctly of such an 'offer.' . . . Rather do all the explanations related to this idea rest upon inexact attention to the wording of certain passages of Scripture or upon inferences drawn from them."[41] It seems, however, that Sauer has not carefully considered Acts 3:19–21. If language means anything, this passage is teaching contingency, as the earlier part of this discussion indicates.[42] It is true, the word "offer" is not used in the Gospels in connection with the kingdom, but as has been explained in the preceding section, it is a necessary implication from the Lord's words. The temporary nearness of the kingdom, the national judgment because of lack of repentance, the laments of Christ, and the parables of judgment all teach this doctrine.

Sauer voices a second objection. "An offer of and setting up of Messiah's kingdom before Golgotha was simply not possible. For no kingdom of glory could come without the forgiveness of sins. But forgiveness of sins was possible only on the ground of the substitutionary atoning death of Christ."[43] Clearly, Christ never meant to bypass the cross. He came to die as a ransom (Matt. 20:28; Heb. 10:5–10). The answer to this objection is found in a basic concept and doctrine. The Lord Jesus came to offer the kingdom *by way of the cross.*[44] In no way does the offer of the kingdom exclude the cross.

Sauer's third objection has already been considered in a previous section. Sauer states, "They did not say, '*If* you repent *then* the kingdom will draw near.' The repentance of man was not the condition for the coming of the kingdom, but the coming of the kingdom was the ground of the demand for repentance."[45] These two ideas are not mutually exclusive. The people of Israel were to repent in order for them individually to enter the kingdom, but they were also to repent for the kingdom to come.

One may object that the offer of the kingdom was not valid because God had foreordained Israel's rejection. In fact, the Old Testament predicted Israel would reject her Messiah (cf. Isa. 53:1–10; Dan. 9:26; Zech. 12:10). Since God's eternal purposes determine Israel's actions, some may object that the offer was not valid. McClain answers this charge: "Those who cavil at

39. Sauer, *From Eternity to Eternity,* pp. 175–76.

40. Ibid., p. 175.

41. Ibid.

42. Cf. Baxter, *Explore the Book,* 6:19–20. He writes, "What can this mean but a renewed offer of the Messiah-King Jesus and the Kingdom of heaven to the Jews? And is it not equally clear that these words of Peter utter the promise that the Lord Jesus would return, and the times of restoration set in, without delay, upon the repentance of Israel?"

43. Sauer, *From Eternity to Eternity,* p. 175; cf. Oswald T. Allis, *Prophecy and the Church* (Philadelphia: Presbyterian and Reformed, 1945), p. 234.

44. For a defense of this, see Stanley D. Toussaint, *Behold the King* (Portland, Oreg.: Multnomah, 1980), pp. 63–65.

45. Sauer, *From Eternity to Eternity,* p. 176.

the idea of an offer which is certain to be rejected betray an ignorance, not only of Biblical history (cf. Isa. 6:8–10 and Ezek. 2:3–7), but also the important place of the legal proffer in the realm of jurisprudence."[46] It parallels an invitation to trust in Christ for justification to a nonelect person.

Some may protest that an offer of the kingdom destroys the doctrine of imminency. Some reason that if Israel must repent before Christ returns, then the Lord's appearance is not imminent. If such an objection should be made, the answer is found in the distinction between the rapture of the church and Christ's return to establish his kingdom. The rapture is imminent; however, a number of events must take place before the Lord Jesus will return to reign: the appearance of the Antichrist and his false prophet, the ten-kingdom confederation, the signing of a covenant with Israel by the man of sin, and others. Likewise, Israel must repent before the millennial kingdom will be established.

Conclusion

Conditionality in divine-human relationships is clearly taught in the Bible. It is a factor in such a basic doctrine as justification by faith. Individuals are justified when they meet the condition of placing faith in Jesus Christ as Savior. If contingency is so fundamental in justification, why is it strange that it be a part of God's program with regard to Israel? Acts 3:19–21 teaches it very pointedly. It is a clear inference from the pronouncement of the nearness of the kingdom with its restriction to Israel. The Lord's parables teach such an offer. A principle of the Scriptures is that God's blessings for Israel rest on her repentance. The contingency of the coming of the kingdom, then, is clearly based on Israel's repentance.

Tribute

It has been a privilege and honor to work with Dr. Donald K. Campbell for many years as he has served in various capacities at Dallas Theological Seminary—as registrar, academic dean, president, and, above all, as a friend. In all these positions he has carried out his responsibilities with graciousness, affability, and skill. May the Lord grant him many more years of health and ministry.

---

46. McClain, *Greatness of the Kingdom*, p. 344.

Reformed Theology, Covenant Theology, and Dispensationalism

Stephen R. Spencer

Covenant theology and dispensationalism figure prominently in contemporary theological discussions, particularly in evangelicalism where they often appear dominant.[1] This essay addresses two errors that often occur in those discussions.

First, both covenantal and dispensational writers[2] use the terms "covenant theology" and "Reformed theology" interchangeably. If these terms are equivalent, then to espouse Reformed theology necessarily involves the espousal of covenant theology and vice versa. If that is the case, then it is as appropriate to contrast Reformed theology with dispensationalism as to contrast covenant theology with dispensationalism. This would make the incompatibility between Reformed theology and dispensationalism as strong as that between covenant theology and dispensationalism. A person could not consistently advocate both Reformed theology and dispensationalism.

---

1. See the bibliographical references on covenant theology in David Weir, *The Origins of the Federal Theology in Sixteenth Century Reformation Thought* (Oxford: Clarendon, 1989), pp. 160–95; Charles S. McCoy and J. Wayne Baker, *Fountainhead of Federalism: Heinrich Bullinger and the Covenantal Tradition* (Louisville: Westminster/John Knox, 1991), pp. 149–70; John S. Feinberg, ed., *Continuity and Discontinuity: Perspectives on the Relationship Between the Old and New Testaments: Essays in Honor of S. Lewis Johnson, Jr.* (Westchester, Ill.: Crossway Books, 1988); and Stephen R. Spencer, "Francis Turretin's Concept of the Covenant of Nature," in *Later Calvinism: An International Perspective,* ed. W. Fred Graham (Kirksville, Mo.: Sixteenth Century Essays and Studies, 1994). For dispensationalism, see the bibliographical references in Craig A. Blaising and Darrell L. Bock, eds., *Dispensationalism, Israel and the Church* (Grand Rapids: Zondervan, 1992); and Robert L. Saucy, *The Case for Progressive Dispensationalism* (Grand Rapids: Zondervan, 1993); Craig A. Blaising and Darrell C. Bock, *Progressive Dispensationalism* (Wheaton, Ill.: Victor Books, 1993); Larry V. Crutchfield, *The Origins of Dispensationalism: The Darby Factor* (Lanham, Md.: University Press of America, 1992), pp. 219–31; and Jeffrey J. Richards, *The Promise of Dawn: The Eschatology of Lewis Sperry Chafer* (Lanham, Md.: University Press of America, 1991), pp. 211–43.

2. Michael A. Harbin makes the same observation, although his attempt at clarification is not entirely successful ("The Hermeneutics of Covenant Theology," *Bibliotheca Sacra* 143 [July–September 1986]: 247).

The second error is to consider covenant theology and dispensationalism as the only available options, particularly for ecclesiological and eschatological matters. Consequently to refute dispensationalism is to establish covenant theology or vice versa. This error perhaps is more commonly found in dispensational writings, but it occurs in covenant works as well.[3] This results in a narrowed focus and a misconstrual of the significance of the contrast between these two points of view.

This study attempts to correct both of these common errors, clarifying the meaning and relationship of Reformed theology, covenant theology, and dispensationalism, and placing them in the larger context of alternative theological positions. It suggests that Reformed theology is larger than covenant theology and that a person may align with Reformed theology without aligning with covenant theology. Furthermore, dispensationalism (particularly earlier forms) may be placed within the Reformed tradition. This of course is not always true. One may be dispensational and *not* be within the Reformed tradition.[4] Nor should dispensationalism per se be linked with Reformed theology. There is no more reason *necessarily* to associate dispensationalism with Reformed theology than necessarily to contrast them. The purpose of this essay is descriptive, not polemical. It is not proposing that dispensationalism *must* be associated with Reformed theology. It is arguing for their logical and theological compatibility.

This essay also proposes that an individual need not be either covenantal or dispensational and that most of the church has been and is neither. Nevertheless covenant theology has significant commonalities with dominant traditions in the church, though covenant theologians' critiques of dispensationalism's "novelties" have not always correctly identified these shared characteristics. Likewise dispensational critiques of covenant theology usually overlook the links between the covenant tradition and the historically typical teachings of the church.[5]

---

3. See, for example, Renald E. Showers, *There Really Is a Difference! A Comparison of Covenant and Dispensational Theology* (Bellmawr, N.J.: Friends of Israel Gospel Ministry, 1990), p. 6; and Charles C. Ryrie, *Dispensationalism Today* (Chicago: Moody, 1965), pp. 15–21 (he seems to imply this, at least within nonliberal Christianity; see p. 10). Oswald T. Allis, *Prophecy and the Church* (Nutley, N.J.: Presbyterian and Reformed, 1947), pp. vi–vii, 47–48, 165–66, is a covenantal example.

4. See Douglas A. Oss, "The Hermeneutics of Dispensationalism within the Pentecostal Tradition," paper presented to the Dispensational Study Group, 1991, pp. 2–5.

5. A common source for a dispensational critique of covenant theology is C. Fred Lincoln, "The Covenants" (Th.D. diss., Dallas Theological Seminary, 1942). Also see his article "The Development of the Covenant Theory," *Bibliotheca Sacra* 100 (1943): 134–63; and the series "The Biblical Covenants," *Bibliotheca Sacra* 100 (1943): 309–23, 442–49, 565–73. His treatment of covenant theology is unfortunately inaccurate at numerous points and therefore is not a reliable guide. Similar to Lincoln, Ryrie's *Dispensationalism Today* criticizes covenant theology's recency (pp. 178–83, 190–91). See the Allis passages cited above (n. 3) for the corresponding failure to acknowledge the distinctiveness of covenant theology.

Reformed Theology

Though sometimes used interchangeably with "Calvinism,"[6] the term "Reformed theology" more accurately designates a broader, more complex tradition that antedates Calvin by approximately fifteen years and includes a variety of theologians, some of whom differ significantly from Calvin and even opposed him.[7] "Reformed theology" designates the tradition of doctrine and churches that stems from the Swiss Reformation beginning with Huldrych Zwingli in Zurich in 1519 and extending to other Swiss cantons. Guillaume Farel launched the Reformation in Geneva in 1532 and in 1536 convinced John Calvin to join him. Calvin thus is not the originator of Reformed theology. In fact, he was preceded as well by Zwingli's successor in Zurich, Heinrich Bullinger, who had been leading the Reformed church there since Zwingli's death in 1531.

There clearly are sufficient commonalities among Zwingli, Bullinger, and Calvin (to take only these early leaders) to warrant grouping them under one theological umbrella, namely, "Reformed." It also is clear that, overall, Calvin has been the most influential theologian of that tradition, though he has not been the most influential in every period or place.[8] Nevertheless on matters such as church/state relations, the Lord's Supper, church discipline, predestination and grace, depravity, and others, significant disagreements occurred within the Reformed tradition. When the larger circle of theologians is included (such as Bucer, Vermigli, Zanchi, Ursinus, Beza, Perkins, Ames, and others), many additional variations—and additional topics of disagreement—appear.[9]

6. This can be seen in popular treatments such as Paul Enns, *The Moody Handbook of Theology* (Chicago: Moody, 1989), p. 475, as well as in more standard scholarly sources such as John T. McNeill, *The History and Character of Calvinism* (New York: Oxford University Press, 1954), p. viii. Calvinism itself, of course, should be defined broadly as the theology of Calvin and his followers, not merely or even primarily as the teachings of the *Canons of Dort*.

7. See, for example, Philip Schaff, ed., *Creeds of Christendom,* 3 vols. (New York: Harper and Brothers, 1877; reprint, Grand Rapids: Baker, 1977), 1:358–59; and William Stacy Johnson and John H. Leith, eds., *Reformed Reader: A Sourcebook in Christian Theology,* vol. 1, *Classical Beginnings 1519–1799* (Louisville: Westminster/John Knox, 1993), pp. xvi, xix–xx; *New Dictionary of Theology,* s.v. "Reformed Theology," by R. W. A. Latham, p. 571; *Evangelical Dictionary of Theology,* s.v. "Reformed Tradition," by W. S. Reid, p. 922; *Westminster Dictionary of Church History,* s.v. "Reformed Church," p. 698; and Richard A. Muller, *Post-Reformation Reformed Dogmatics,* vol. 1, *Prolegomena to Theology* (Grand Rapids: Baker, 1987), pp. 20–22. See John H. Leith, *Basic Christian Doctrine* (Louisville: Westminster/John Knox, 1993), pp. 9–13, for an extensive list of Reformed theologians, confessions, and catechisms.

8. See, for example, Patrick Collinson, "England and International Calvinism 1558–1640," in *International Calvinism 1541–1715,* ed. Menna Presturch (Oxford: Clarendon, 1985), pp. 214–15.

9. For surveys, see the older works by Heinrich Heppe, *Reformed Dogmatics,* rev. and ed. Ernst Bizer, trans. G. T. Thomson (London: George Allen and Unwin, 1950; reprint, Grand Rapids: Baker, 1978); McNeill, *History and Character of Calvinism;* and John Leith, *Introduction to the Reformed Tradition* (Louisville: John Knox, 1977). Also see the more recent works such as Richard A. Muller,

Reformed Theology and Covenant Theology

Covenant theology may be understood in at least two senses. It can designate a theology in which the concept of covenant plays a significant or even central role, so that it is basic to the understanding of Scripture and the program of redemption. It also can designate a theology in which covenant is the explicit structural principle around which a theological work is written. Both of these uses are appropriate but they are not equivalent. A theology obviously may be covenantal in both senses, or it may be covenantal in the first meaning, but not the second.

Like Reformed theology, covenant theology antedates John Calvin. Though there are some significant patristic antecedents and a late medieval version that was particularly influential, within the Reformed tradition covenant theology can be traced to Heinrich Bullinger's *A Brief Exposition of the One and Eternal Testament or Covenant* (1534),[10] "the first independent study of the covenant ever produced in the history of the church."[11] Even before this, however, Zwingli's understanding of the church/society/state relationship, the sacraments, and the relationship between the Old and New Testaments was firmly rooted in a clearly articulated theology of covenant.[12]

Though some have suggested that Calvin, unlike the Zurich theologians, did not espouse a covenant theology, in fact he too fits well into the stream of early covenantal thought, as Osterhaven has shown:

> While the doctrine of the covenant does not receive treatment in Calvin's earliest writings, the second edition of the *Institutes of the Christian Religion*, published in 1539, devotes a chapter to the relation of the old and new covenants, the *Commentary on the Epistle to the Romans*, published the same year, makes numerous references to the covenant in the exposition of the ninth chapter, the later commentaries and sermons discuss or refer to the covenant at appropriate times, and the last edition of the *Institutes*, published in 1559, has

Post-Reformation Reformed Dogmatics, 2 vols. (of 3 projected) (Grand Rapids: Baker, 1987, 1993); Donald K. McKim, ed., *Encyclopedia of the Reformed Faith* (Louisville: Westminster/John Knox, 1992); idem, ed., *Major Themes in the Reformed Tradition* (Grand Rapids: Eerdmans, 1991); Johnson and Leith, eds., *Reformed Reader*, vol. 1, *Classical Beginnings 1519–1799*; vol. 2, *Contemporary Trajectories 1799–Present*, ed. George Stroup (Louisville: Westminster/John Knox, 1993). Also see David F. Wells, ed., *Reformed Theology in America* (Grand Rapids: Eerdmans, 1985) and the literature cited there.

10. Translated in McCoy and Baker, *Fountainhead of Federalism*, pp. 99–138. See J. Wayne Baker, *Heinrich Bullinger and the Covenant: The Other Reformed Tradition* (Athens, Ohio: Ohio University Press, 1980). For annotated selections regarding covenant theology, see Johnson and Leith, *Reformed Reader*, 1:115–31.

11. Peter Alan Lillback, "The Binding of God: Calvin's Role in the Development of Covenant Theology" (Ph.D. diss., Westminster Theological Seminary, 1985), p. 183.

12. Jack Warren Cottrell, "Covenant and Baptism in the Theology of Huldreich Zwingli" (Th.D. diss., Princeton Theological Seminary, 1971).

three chapters on the relation of the old and new testaments [*sic*] of Scripture
to each other and makes frequent mention of the covenant in the discussion of
the sacraments. It is not a dominant theme in the reformer's writings. . . . It is
nevertheless an important theme which, one suspects, Calvin had ever in
mind.[13]

After Calvin, theologians such as Zacharias Ursinus, Caspar Olevianus,
Robert Rollock, Dudley Fenner, and Thomas Cartwright used the covenant
concept as a fundamental unifying theme for understanding Scripture.[14] By
the end of the sixteenth century, the divine promise of gracious redemption
was often complemented by a "covenant of nature" (or "life") by which God
had pledged his fidelity to his promise to Adam to bless him for his loving
obedience to divine commands.[15]

Enshrined in the Westminster Standards (1647), covenant theology was
later developed in new and distinctive ways by Johannes Cocceius and Herman Witsius.[16] Cocceius especially used the covenants to oppose scholastic
theology, which he accused of being rationalistic, static, and unhistorical.
Later still, Francis Turretin included a less idiosyncratic and elaborate covenant theology in his *Institutio Theologiae Elencticae*.[17]

For the next two centuries covenant theology's development slowed,
though the variety persisted in the number and names of covenants and in
the prominence of the covenants in the structural pattern of individual the-

13. M. Eugene Osterhaven, "Calvin on the Covenant," *Reformed Review* 33 (1980): 136. Also
see Anthony A. Hoekema, "Calvin's Doctrine of the Covenant of Grace," *Reformed Review* 15
(1962): 1–12; idem, "The Covenant of Grace in Calvin's Teaching," *Calvin Theological Journal* 2
(1967): 133–61. For an extended discussion of the centrality of covenant in Calvin's theology, see Lillback, "Binding of God," pp. 219–487, esp. pp. 219–42.

14. See Douglas Andrew Stoute, "The Origins and Early Development of the Reformed Idea of
the Covenant" (Ph.D. diss., Cambridge University, 1979); Weir, *Origins of the Federal Theology*;
Gottlob Schrenck, *Gottesreich und Bund im älteren Protestantismus vornehmlich bei Johannes Coc-
cejus* (Gutersloh: C. Bertelsmann, 1923; reprint, Darmstadt: Wissenschaftliche Buchgesellschaft,
1967); Heinrich Heppe, *Geschichte des Pietismus und der Mystik in der Reformirten Kirchen* (Leiden:
E. J. Brill, 1879; reprint, DeGroot-Goudriaan, 1979), pp. 205–40; Michael A. McGiffert, "Grace and
Works: The Rise and Division of Covenant Divinity in Elizabethan Puritanism," *Harvard Theological
Review* 75 (1982): 463–502; idem, "From Moses to Adam: The Making of the Covenant of Works,"
Sixteenth Century Journal 19 (1988): 131–55; and John Von Rohr, *The Covenant of Grace in Puritan
Thought* (Atlanta: Scholars, 1986).

15. See the bibliography in Spencer, "Francis Turretin's Concept of the Covenant of Nature."

16. Cocceius, *Summa Doctrinae de Foedere et Testamento Dei* (1648); Schrenck, *Gottesreich und
Bund im älteren Protestantismus*, pp. 82–147, 190–299; Charles Sherwood McCoy, "The Covenant
Theology of Johannes Cocceius" (Ph.D. diss., Yale University, 1957); idem, "Johannes Cocceius: Fed-
eral Theologian," *Scottish Journal of Theology* 16 (1963): 352–70; McCoy and Baker, *Fountainhead
of Federalism*, pp. 63–79; and Herman Witsius, *The Economy of the Covenants Between God and
Man: Comprehending a Complete Body of Divinity* (1677; reprint, Escondido, Calif.: The den Dulk
Christian Foundation, 1990).

17. Spencer, "Francis Turretin's Concept of the Covenant of Nature." See *The Encyclopedia of
Christianity*, s.v. "Covenant Theology," by John Murray, 3:203–4, 208, 211–13, for Turretin's for-
mulations and his relative distinctiveness and representativeness.

ologies. With the advent of biblical theology in the late nineteenth century and later the impact of research into ancient treaty formularies after the 1950s, covenant theology again underwent development.[18]

Covenant theology clearly has occupied the central place in the Reformed tradition, if by "covenant theology" one means a theology in which covenant is a significant concept for understanding the program of redemption and the relationship between the Old and New Testaments. On the other hand, covenant was not ordinarily the structural principle of individual theologies. Coccceius and Witsius were notable exceptions. Turretin's three-volume *Institutio*, which served as a textbook until the late nineteenth century, did not follow them in this regard. Though covenant was fundamental to Turretin's theology, the work is divided into twenty-two *loci*, only two of which explicitly address the covenants. Later theological textbooks nearly all followed Turretin in using some structural principle other than covenant, as earlier Reformed theologians and confessional statements had done.

A second qualification is necessary. Reformed theologians widely used the covenant concept but they did not all include the covenant of nature (or "life," or, more commonly in Britain in contrast to the Continent, "works") or the covenant of redemption. The former covenant may appear implicitly in Calvin (though that is widely contested)[19] but appears in Olevianus[20] and Ursinus and then became a common feature by the end of the sixteenth century[21] and is included in the Westminster Standards, from which it passed to

---

18. Geerhardus Vos was one of the earliest occupants of a chair of biblical theology, at least in the United States (Princeton Theological Seminary, 1893). See his *De verbondsleer im de gereformeerde theologie* (Grand Rapids, 1891; translated as "The Doctrine of the Covenant in Reformed Theology," trans. S. Voorwinde and Willem VanGemeren, in *Redemptive History and Biblical Interpretation: The Shorter Writings of Geerhardus Vos*, ed. Richard B. Gaffin [Philipsburg, N.J.: Presbyterian and Reformed, 1980], pp. 234–67); and Gerhardus Vos, *Biblical Theology* (Grand Rapids: Eerdmans, 1948).

For the treaty formulary research, see G. E. Mendenhall, *Law and Covenant in Israel and the Ancient Near East* (Pittsburgh: Biblical Colloquium, 1955); D. R. Hillers, *Covenant: The History of a Biblical Idea* (Baltimore: Johns Hopkins University Press, 1969); and D. J. McCarthy, *Treaty and Covenant*, 2d ed. (Rome: Pontifical Biblical Institute, 1978). John Murray, *Covenant of Grace: A Biblico-Theological Study* (London: Tyndale, 1954) was an important recasting of covenant theology. See Klaus Baltzer, *The Covenant Formulary*, trans. D. E. Green (Oxford: Basil Blackwell, 1971 [German original, 1960]). Also see Edward J. Young, *The Study of Old Testament Theology Today* (Westwood, N.J.: Fleming H. Revell, 1959), pp. 61–78; J. Barton Payne, *The Theology of the Older Testament* (Grand Rapids: Zondervan, 1962), esp. pp. 71–119; and Meredith G. Kline, *The Treaty of the Great King* (Grand Rapids: Eerdmans, 1963) for early appropriations by covenant theology. See also O. Palmer Robertson, "Current Reformed Thinking on the Nature of the Divine Covenants," *Westminster Theological Journal* 40 (1977–78): 63–76.

19. See Spencer, "Francis Turretin's Concept of the Covenant of Nature," p. 77, n. 15 for a selected bibliography of interpretive options.

20. For the most extensive discussion of Olevianus's contribution, see Lyle D. Bierma, *German Calvinism in the Confessional Age: The Covenant Theology of Caspar Olevianus* (Durham, N.C.: Labyrinth, 1993).

21. See Weir, *Origins of the Federal Theology;* and McGiffert, "From Moses to Adam."

most later Reformed theologies.[22] The covenant of redemption appeared in Cocceius,[23] but there also were earlier references in Olevianus. It never became as common as the other two covenants.[24]

Two factors suggest that Reformed theology and covenant theology are separable, not only conceptually but in fact.[25] The first is seen in the example of two ecclesiastical groups that embraced the Reformed theology of the Presbyterian churches but with varying modifications. Congregationalism, derived from the English Puritan tradition (primarily in its Dissenter or Independent form), endorsed the Westminster Confession (1647) for its Cambridge Platform (1648), except for certain portions of chapters 25 ("Of the Church"), 30 ("Of Church Censures"), and 31 ("Of Synods and Councils").[26] In the preface, the platform presents "our professed and hearty assent and attestation to the whole confession of faith (for substance of doctrine) which the Reverend assembly presented to the Religious and Hononrable [sic] Parlemet [sic] of England: Excepting only some sections in the 25, 30 and 31."[27] Walker states, "They had put the churches of New England by formal declaration, where they had always been in fact, at one in doctrine with the Puritan party in England, whether Presbyterian or independent."[28] The 1658 Savoy Declaration is substantially a word-for-word reproduction of Westminster with occasional additions, deletions, or modifications, for the distinctive polity portions.[29]

22. See Benjamin B. Warfield, *The Westminster Assembly and Its Work* (New York: Oxford University Press, 1931; reprint, Grand Rapids: Baker, 1981), pp. 56–57; John H. Leith, *Assembly at Westminster: Reformed Theology in the Making* (Louisville: John Knox, 1973), pp. 91–95. Leith gives a qualifying estimation of the significance of covenant theology in the Westminster Confession.

23. McCoy and Baker, *Fountainhead of Federalism*, p. 73; *Encyclopedia of Reformed Faith*, s.v. "Federal Theology," by Dewey D. Wallace, p. 137. On Caspar Olevianus's earlier use, see Richard A. Muller, "The Spirit and the Covenant: John Gill's Critique of the *Pactum Salutis*," *Foundations* 24 (1981): 4; Schrenk, *Gottesreich und Bund in älteren Protestantismus*, p. 61; and especially Lyle D. Bierma, "Covenant or Covenants in the Theology of Olevianus?" *Calvin Theological Journal* 22 (1987): 230–35, 249–50.

24. Murray, "Covenant Theology," p. 212.

25. A third factor could also be included. The espousal of forms of covenant theology by Jacob Arminius and the Remonstrants as well as the later English "Arminians" is additional evidence that Reformed theology and covenant theology are separable. See Richard A. Muller, "The Federal Motif in Seventeenth Century Arminian Theology," *Nederlands archief voor Kerkgeschiedenis* 62 (1982): 102–22; and Cornelius Lettinga, "Covenant Theology and the Transformation of Anglicanism" (Ph.D. diss., Johns Hopkins University, 1987). On the question of whether Arminius warrants classification as a Reformed theologian, see Carl Bangs, *Arminius: A Study in the Dutch Reformation*, rev. ed. (Grand Rapids: Zondervan, 1985) for an affirmative answer, and Richard A. Muller, *God, Creation, and Providence in the Thought of Jacob Arminius* (Grand Rapids: Baker, 1991) for a negative answer.

26. See *The Creeds and Platforms of Congregationalism*, ed. Williston Walker (1893; reprint, with new introduction by Elizabeth C. Nordbeck, New York: Pilgrim, 1991), pp. 194–237.

27. Ibid., p. 195.

28. Ibid., p. 185.

29. Ibid., pp. 354–408.

Likewise the Baptist churches in London aligned themselves with the Reformed churches in their First (1644) and Second (1689) Confessions.[30] The prefatory letter to the reader of the 1689 Confession explicitly announces that they followed the Congregationalists in adapting the Westminster Confession, not only "in the same order," but also "in making use of the very same words . . . in those articles (which are very many) wherein our faith and doctrine is the same with theirs."[31]

While both these groups concurred with the Reformed doctrine expressed in the Westminster Confession, they did not agree with each other regarding the covenant theology of Westminster. The Savoy Declaration retains the references to covenant from the Westminster Confession, even adding some. For instance, the Savoy Declaration adds a phrase about "a Covenant of Works and Life" at the beginning of chapter 6 on the fall of humanity, while the Westminster Confession waits until chapter 7 ("Of God's Covenant with Man") to introduce that covenant.

The 1689 London Baptist Confession retains references to the "covenant of grace" but makes no mention of the "covenant of works" (though there are instances of generic references to "covenant" at points parallel to Westminster's more explicit references to the "covenant of works").[32] Moreover, the covenant functioned differently in that the church was defined by Baptists as composed of believers, not "believers and their seed" (i.e., their physical, "covenantal" children),[33] as both Presbyterianism and Congregationalism defined it.

The second factor that works against seeing Reformed theology and covenant theology as equivalent is the voices within the Reformed tradition that call into question various aspects of covenant theology. A. A. Hodge omitted the covenant of redemption,[34] and Henry B. Smith and Thomas M. Lindsay criticized covenant theology (especially in its Cocceian and Witsian forms) for the systematic elaborateness and structural prominence of covenant in its theology.[35] Recently theologians such as Herman Hoeksema, John Murray, Anthony Hoekema, Fred Klooster, I. John Hesselink, Willem VanGemeren, and especially James Torrance have challenged aspects of more traditional

30. W. L. Lumpkin, *Baptist Confessions of Faith*, rev. ed. (Valley Forge, Pa.: Judson, 1969), pp. 144–71, 241–95.

31. Ibid., p. 245.

32. For example, chapter 7.1 (ibid., p. 259).

33. Chapter 26.2, 6; cf. the Westminster Confession 25.2; the Savoy Declaration 29.4; and the Cambridge Platform 3.2.

34. A. A. Hodge, *Outlines of Theology*, rev. ed. (1879; reprint, Grand Rapids: Zondervan, 1972), pp. 369–71.

35. Henry B. Smith, *System of Christian Theology*, 4th ed. (New York: A. C. Armstrong and Son, 1892), pp. 377–78; and Thomas M. Lindsay, "The Covenant Theology," *British and Foreign Evangelical Review* 28 (1879): 521–38.

forms of covenant thought.[36] The covenants of nature/life/works/creation
and of redemption are the most frequently criticized elements, though the
character and significance of covenant per se have been given substantial
attention as well. Torrance has made the most sweeping criticisms, charging
that developed "Federalism" was flawed from early in its history (though his
reading of the tradition has been seriously called into question).[37] To cite
these divergencies is not to pass judgment on their accuracy or value, but
merely to note the varying status of covenant theology within the Reformed
tradition.

One further observation is in order. It is important to note that Reformed
theology can be a historical term; it designates a group of churches and theologians who developed a specific relationship to Roman Catholic or
Lutheran churches, opposing certain things and embracing others, and it
marks out the descendants of those churches. It thus is a broad term referring
to an entire theological perspective (or complex of perspectives). On the

36. Herman Hoeksema, *Reformed Dogmatics* (Grand Rapids: Protestant Reformed, 1966), pp.
214–26, 285–336; idem, *Believers and Their Seed,* (Grand Rapids: Protestant Reformed, 1971), pp.
13, 66–71; Murray, *Covenant of Grace,* esp. pp. 4–5, 8; idem, "Adamic Administration," in *Collected
Writings of John Murray,* 4 vols. (Carlisle, Pa.: Banner of Truth, 1977), 2:47–59; A. A. Hoekema, *Created in God's Image* (Grand Rapids: Eerdmans, 1986), pp. 117–21, 161; Fred Klooster, "The Kingdom
of God in the History of the Christian Reformed Church," in *Perspectives on the Christian Reformed
Church,* ed. Peter DeKlerk and R. R. DeRidder (Grand Rapids: Baker, 1983), pp. 203–24; idem, "Cov-
enant Theology Today," *The Messenger* 51 (January 1980): 6–9; idem, "The Biblical Method of Sal-
vation: A Case for Continuity," in *Continuity and Discontinuity,* pp. 131–60; I. John Hesselink, *On
Being Reformed,* 2d ed. (New York: Reformed Church Press, 1988), pp. 57–58, 135–36; Willem
VanGemeren, "Israel as the Hermeneutical Crux in the Interpretation of Prophecy," *Westminster
Theological Journal* 45 (1983): 132–44 and 46 (1984): 254–97; idem, "Systems of Continuity," in
Continuity and Discontinuity, pp. 37–62; idem, "The Spirit of Restoration," *Westminster Theological
Journal* 50 (1988): 81–102; idem, *The Progress of Redemption: The Story of Salvation from Creation
to the New Jerusalem* (Grand Rapids: Zondervan, 1988); James B. Torrance, "Covenant or Contract?
A Study of the Theological Background of Worship in Seventeenth-Century Scotland," *Scottish Jour-
nal of Theology* 23 (1970): 51–76; idem, "The Covenant Concept in Scottish Theology and Politics
and Its Legacy," *Scottish Journal of Theology* 34 (1981): 225–43; idem, "Strengths and Weaknesses of
the Westminster Theology," in *The Westminster Confession in the Church Today,* ed. A. I. C. Heron
(Edinburgh: Saint Andrews Press, 1982), pp. 40–57; and idem, "Calvin and Puritanism in England and
Scotland—Some Basic Concepts in the Development of 'Federal Theology,'" in *Calvinus Reformator:
His Contribution to Theology, Church and Society* (Potchefstroom: Potchefstroom University for
Christian Higher Education, 1982), pp. 264–89. For a brief summary of changes, see Vern S. Poyth-
ress, *Understanding Dispensationalists* (Grand Rapids: Zondervan, 1987), pp. 39–52.

37. Torrance emphasizes the distinction between "covenant" and "contract." He says the first is
gracious and unconditional, the second is legal and conditional. "Federal theology" is said to be characterized by a "contract" orientation rather than a "covenant" perspective. For articulation of this
interpretation, see Leonard J. Trinterud, "The Origins of Puritanism," *Church History* 20 (1951): 37–
57; Jens G. Møller, "The Beginnings of Puritan Covenant Theology," *Journal of Ecclesiastical History*
14 (1963): 46–67; and Richard L. Greaves, "The Origins and Early Development of English Covenant
Thought," *The Historian* 31 (1968): 21–35. For critiques, see Michael McGiffert, "William Tyndale's
Conception of Covenant," *Journal of Ecclesiastical History* 32 (1981): 167–84; Lyle Bierma, "Federal
Theology in the Sixteenth Century: Two Traditions?" *Westminster Theological Journal* 45 (1983):
304–21; and idem, "The Role of Covenant Theology in Early Reformed Orthodoxy," *Sixteenth Century Journal* 21 (1990): 453–62.

other hand, covenant theology specifically designates a perspective on the program of redemption as it unfolds historically and a perspective on the relationship of the Old and New Testaments (and thus on related matters such as Israel and the church, law and gospel, and, to some extent, on the church and society or culture).

Both terms, of course, have acquired a range of meanings as they have been used in various ways, in various contexts. Moreover, each involves multiple elements, which are separable so that various "degrees" of applicability are possible. Nevertheless, it seems that the terms themselves "pick out" different types of referents; they do not seem to be equivalent terms, interchangeable with each other.

Reformed Theology and Dispensationalism

In light of the preceding discussion, it seems that "Reformed theology" and "dispensationalism" are not mutually exclusive terms, but are (or can be) mutually compatible. If Reformed theology and covenant theology, for various reasons, are not strictly equivalent, it is at least possible that an individual could be consistently aligned with both Reformed theology and dispensationalism. Two lines of evidence support this observation.

First, the early emergence of dispensationalism, in both Great Britain and North America, involved churches, movements, and individuals associated in one way or another with the Reformed tradition. The Brethren churches were Calvinistic in commitment.[38] For instance Hoffecker describes J. N. Darby's "basic theological assumptions" as "compatible with traditional Calvinism."[39] Elmore characterizes Darby as "a moderate Calvinist."[40] This seems generally true of the larger movement as well.

Moreover, dispensationalism has its roots in two conference traditions: the prophecy conferences, especially Niagara,[41] and the British "higher life" conferences, especially Keswick.[42] The latter in particular had Calvinistic inclinations. Keswick was distinguished from the larger holiness tradition by

38. For histories of the Brethren, see Harold H. Rowdon, *The Origins of the Brethren* (London: Pickering and Inglis, 1967); and Roy Coad, *A History of the Brethren Movement* (Exeter: Paternoster, 1968).

39. *Evangelical Dictionary of Theology*, s.v. "Darby, John Nelson," by W. A. Hoffecker, p. 293.

40. Floyd Saunders Elmore, "A Critical Examination of the Doctrine of the Two Peoples of God in John Nelson Darby" (Th.D. diss., Dallas Theological Seminary, 1990), p. 256, n. 33. Elmore cites *The Collected Writings of J. N. Darby*, 1:252–53. There Darby criticized the "rigid Calvinist" and the "Arminian" as extremes, and advocated a mediating position.

41. For dispensationalism's relationship to the Niagara Bible Conference, see Ernest R. Sandeen, *The Roots of Fundamentalism: British and American Millenarianism, 1800–1930* (Chicago: University of Chicago Press, 1970; reprint, Grand Rapids: Baker, 1978), pp. 132–61; also see Larry D. Pettigrew, "The Historical and Theological Contributions of the Niagara Bible Conference to American Fundamentalism" (Th.D. diss., Dallas Theological Seminary, 1976).

42. See Steven Barabas, *So Great Salvation: The History and Message of the Keswick Convention* (Westwood, N.J.: Revell, 1952); and John C. Pollock, *The Keswick Story* (Chicago: Moody, 1964).

its rejection both of perfectionism as a possibility in this life and of the erad-
ication of sinfulness in this life.[43] Though some Reformed theologians (most
notably B. B. Warfield) were sharply critical of Keswick's views on sanctification and the Christian life,[44] Keswick clearly fell on the Reformed side of
the divide, at least in the rejection of Wesleyan perfectionism.

Numerous early dispensationalists belonged, by ecclesiastical association
and doctrinal affirmation, to the Reformed tradition. Anglican/Episcopalian,
Presbyterian, and Congregational churches were the most common denominations among early dispensationalists. James Brookes and Samuel Kellogg
(Presbyterian), James M. Gray and W. H. Griffith Thomas (Episcopalian),
C. I. Scofield (Congregational), and Lewis Sperry Chafer (Congregational
and, later, Presbyterian) are examples. William M. Anderson, one of the
founders of Dallas Theological Seminary, pastored the First Presbyterian
Church in Dallas, and Donald Grey Barnhouse and John F. Walvoord,
among others, also were Presbyterians. Walvoord's departure from the Presbyterian Church, U.S.A., seems to have had more to do with his conservative
theological convictions than his dispensationalism.[45]

Numerous statements in early private correspondence of the founders of
Dallas Seminary as well as the school's published material explicitly asserted
the Reformed orientation of the new school and its theology.[46] Chafer
described it as "in full agreement with the Reformed Faith" and "strictly Calvinistic," "definitely Calvinistic," and "four square on the great vital truths
embodied in that marvelous document 'The Westminster Confession of
Faith.'"[47] A 1934 *Bibliotheca Sacra* advertisement for the school declared
that it was "A Standard Calvinistic Seminary, Denominationally Unrelated."[48] Chafer's review of Lorraine Boettner's *The Reformed Doctrine of
Predestination* heartily commended it as "a worthy restatement of the writings of the great Calvinistic teachers of past generations."[49]

None of this establishes that dispensationalism is *necessarily* Reformed;
and there is no lack of examples of individual dispensationalists, past and
present, who do not desire to, and could not plausibly, be categorized as

43. See, for example, Melvin Easterday Dieter, *The Holiness Revival of the Nineteenth Century*
(Metuchen, N.J.: Scarecrow, 1980), pp. 187–88; and Donald W. Dayton, *Theological Roots of Pen-
tecostalism* (Grand Rapids: Zondervan, 1987), pp. 100–106.

44. B. B. Warfield, "Review of *He That Is Spiritual*, by Lewis Sperry Chafer," *Princeton Theological Review* 17 (1919): 322–27. Also see B. B. Warfield, *Perfectionism*, 2 vols. (New York: Oxford
University Press, 1931; reprint, Grand Rapids: Baker, 1981), 2:463–611.

45. See the account in Timothy Gale Mink, "John F. Walvoord at Dallas Theological Seminary"
(Ph.D. diss., North Texas State University, 1987), pp. 65, 170–77, 226–28.

46. See John David Hannah, "The Social and Intellectual Origins of the Evangelical Theological
College" (Ph.D. diss., University of Texas at Dallas, 1988), pp. 199–200, for an extended list of references.

47. Ibid., p. 200.

48. *Bibliotheca Sacra* 91 (October 1934): back cover.

49. *Bibliotheca Sacra* 94 (January 1937): 104.

Reformed. Dispensationalism is widely held in Pentecostal and charismatic circles, where some variant of Wesleyan theology is a typical theological perspective. Furthermore the denominational associations of some early dispensationalists were matters of convenience, to greater or lesser extent, reflecting the interdenominational patterns of frontier Christianity and of revivalism more generally.[50]

Yet with all the appropriate qualifications it remains true that there is a long history of varying types and degrees of interconnections between Reformed theology and dispensationalism. For the present purposes, it need only be argued that the two are compatible, not that they are necessarily or even commonly linked.

Another support, very interesting and perhaps somewhat surprising, for the compatibility between Reformed theology and dispensationalism comes from the at least qualified acceptance of some aspects of covenant theology by leading dispensational theologians. Chafer, for instance, stated that the covenant of redemption, though it "rests upon but slight revelation," is "sustained largely by the fact that it seems both reasonable and inevitable."[51] Later he wrote, "It is certain that . . . an agreement existed between the Persons of the Godhead concerning the part to be executed by each."[52] Chafer defined the covenant of works as "the theologian's designation for those blessings God has offered men and conditioned on human merit."[53] Repeated references to a covenant of works or a covenant of grace occur in Chafer's discussion of the various covenants that Scripture records God as entering into with humans at various times in history.[54]

These references designate the character of these covenants as being "works" or "gracious," but they do not identify the *name* of any of them as the covenant of works or the covenant of grace. The resemblance between Chafer's "Edenic Covenant" and the covenant of nature/life/works is intriguing.[55] Chafer was sharply critical of covenant theology at several places in his

50. On the nonsectarian and interdenominational patterns of revivalism, see Timothy L. Smith, *Revivalism and Social Reform* (New York: Abingdon, 1957), pp. 83–85. For a case study involving those patterns, see George M. Marsden, *The Evangelical Mind and the New School Presbyterian Experience* (New Haven, Conn.: Yale University Press, 1970). For Lewis Sperry Chafer's and C. I. Scofield's denominational relationships, see Hannah, "Social and Intellectual Origins of the Evangelical Theological College," pp. 105–8, 121, 140–43. For this nonsectarian impulse as characteristic of American dispensationalism's earliest stage, see Craig A. Blaising, "Dispensationalism: The Search for Definition," in *Dispensationalism, Israel and the Church*, pp. 17–20.

51. Lewis Sperry Chafer, *Systematic Theology*, 8 vols. (Dallas, Tex.: Dallas Theological Seminary, 1948; reprint [8 vols. in 4], Grand Rapids: Kregel, 1992), 1:42. For a similarly qualified assessment, see Enns, *Moody Handbook of Theology*, p. 510.

52. Chafer, *Systematic Theology*, 5:27–28; cf. 7:97.

53. Ibid., 1:42.

54. For example, ibid., 1:43; 4:211–12, 228–33, 246–47.

55. Ibid., 1:42; 7:97; and Lewis Sperry Chafer, *Major Bible Themes* (Findlay, Ohio: Dunham, 1926 and 1953), p. 104. Albertus Pieters previously noted the "resemblance" in his *A Candid Examination of the Scofield Bible* (Swengel, Pa.: Bible Truth Depot, n.d.), p. 6.

Systematic Theology, but he acknowledged that it is a "part-truth."[56] It is almost trivially true, he judged, that divine redemption is always gracious, but, he said, to build a theology on that alone and to assert the continuity of Israel and the church and of all the stages of redemptive history on that continuing principle is incorrect. In other words, Chafer acknowledged at least some of the biblical data underlying covenant theology but found their significance to be erroneously interpreted by that viewpoint.

John F. Walvoord, though insisting, as did Chafer, on a distinction between Israel and the church and on fundamental dispensational discontinuities in redemptive history (unlike covenant theology), nevertheless repeatedly uses at least some elements of covenant theology, but without the emphasis on continuity and unity.[57] In a discussion of the "work of the Son of God in eternity past," Walvoord mentions the covenants of grace and redemption as means proposed to help understand the eternal decree of God.[58] He associates the covenant of grace with the view that "the work of God in saving the elect is therefore made the major undertaking of God in time and eternity," an unduly narrow perspective, in Walvoord's judgment. He is less critical of the covenant of redemption, finding it more fully supported in Scripture and thus less objectionable.[59]

In Walvoord's revision of Chafer's *Major Bible Themes*, he added a discussion of "The Theological Covenants" at the beginning of Chafer's chapter on "The Covenants," which covered eight biblical covenants. Walvoord identifies the covenant of works, grace, and redemption. Regarding the covenant of works, he observes, "This covenant is based almost entirely on inference and is not called a covenant in the Bible, and for this reason is rejected by many students of Scripture as having an insufficient ground."[60] By contrast the covenant of redemption "has more support in Scripture,"[61] from passages in which "it is clear that God's purpose is eternal. That a formal covenant was entered into between God the Father and God the Son is inferred from the fact that God's purpose is also a promise."[62] Though the covenant of grace "also is an inference from the eternal plan of salvation, it tends to emphasize the gracious character of God's salvation."[63] Walvoord

---

56. For criticisms, see Chafer, *Systematic Theology*, 4:156–57; 7:97. The "part-truth" reference occurs on 4:156.

57. For criticism of the covenant emphasis on continuity and unity, see Walvoord, "Review of Louis Berkhof, *Systematic Theology*," *Bibliotheca Sacra* 99 (1942): 375, where he states that Berkhof "unduly presses the covenant theory, which is characteristic of reformed theology."

58. John F. Walvoord, *Jesus Christ Our Lord* (Chicago: Moody, 1969), pp. 33–35.

59. Ibid., pp. 34–35.

60. Chafer, *Major Bible Themes*, rev. John F. Walvoord (Grand Rapids: Zondervan, 1974), p. 140. Walvoord follows Chafer (and Scofield) in affirming a prefall Edenic covenant (ibid., p. 142).

61. Ibid., p. 140.

62. Ibid.

63. Ibid.

then concludes that these last two covenants "have some scriptural basis and are more acceptable to most students of the Bible than the concept of the covenant of works, which has no scriptural support."[64] He immediately qualifies this endorsement:

> A problem has arisen, however, in that those who are adherents of these theological covenants often make the plan of God for salvation His primary purpose in human history. . . . While it is true that God's plan of salvation is an important aspect of His eternal purpose, it is not the total of God's plan. A better view is that God's plan for history is to reveal His glory, and He does this not only by saving men but by fulfilling His purpose and revealing Himself through His dealings with Israel, with the church, and with the nations.[65]

Walvoord concludes this section on the theological covenants by distinguishing covenant theologians and dispensationalists. The former "emphasize the theological covenants" while the latter "emphasize the biblical covenants" that "reveal the distinctions in the various stages in human history which are revealed in the dispensations."[66] This makes the distinction between covenant theology and dispensationalism a matter of emphasis (continuity via the theological covenants versus discontinuity via the biblical covenants), rather than a matter of separate and exclusive assertions. That Walvoord's discussion overlooks the variations within the covenantal tradition and finds most acceptable the covenant that has had the least support within that tradition (i.e., the covenant of redemption) should not detract from the significance of this addition to Chafer's chapters. More recently, Walvoord has affirmed the covenant of grace:

> There is one new covenant, commonly recognized as the covenant of grace in systematic theology, which stems from the death of Christ. . . . This one covenant of grace, however, has a wide application. . . . Accordingly the concept of one covenant of grace with many applications serves to provide an intelligent understanding of the various provisions of the covenant in both the Old and New Testaments and preserves the distinction that should be observed between God's purpose and plan for Israel and God's purpose and plan for the church.[67]

Are Covenant Theology and Dispensationalism the Only Options?

If Reformed theology, covenant theology, and dispensationalism relate to each other in the preceding ways, how do covenant theology and dispensa-

---

64. Ibid., pp. 140–41.
65. Ibid., p. 141.
66. Ibid.
67. John F. Walvoord, *Major Bible Prophecies* (Grand Rapids: Zondervan, 1991), p. 189; also see idem, *The Prophecy Knowledge Handbook* (Wheaton, Ill.: Victor Books, 1990), p. 140.

tionalism relate to other alternatives? Are there alternatives? Or is covenant theology descriptive of all nondispensationalists?

Walvoord's above-noted contrast between covenant theology and dispensationalism can be used to illustrate both the popular misconception and a more accurate assessment. The dispensational emphasis underscores the discontinuity of the advances and changes in God's administration of history. The covenant theology emphasis on the unity of the covenant of grace underscores the unity of God's program. Both views argue for *progressive* revelation, each at times accusing the other of neglecting that truth. Such accusations are mistaken on both sides and overlook the distinctive ways in which the phrase is used. "Progressive" for covenantal theologians means progress within an overall unity.[68] "Progressive" for dispensationalists typically has meant progress with change and significant alteration.[69] The different meanings highlight the distinctive perspectives of the two traditions.

The continuity/discontinuity contrast has led some in both covenant and dispensational circles to see these as the only two choices. What else is there but to emphasize continuity *or* discontinuity? Even if that contrast is taken as exhaustive, it is incorrect to see the covenantal and dispensational perspectives as the only two choices.

The distinctive of covenant theology is that it uses the concept of divine covenants as the central rubric for interpreting Scripture. Its distinctive is not its emphasis on continuity, but rather its use of covenant as the means of emphasizing continuity. It belongs, as it were, to the genus of continuity theologies, but is a distinct species within that genus. Dispensational theology belongs to a different genus (discontinuity theologies), not just a different species (to continue the analogy).

Covenant theologians correctly point out dispensationalism's distinctiveness from the traditional viewpoint. It would be incorrect, however, to suggest that the covenantal viewpoint is the traditional view of the church. Covenant theology, as a continuity theology, is part of the traditional view, but, as covenantal, it is distinctive. Continuity theologies, emphasizing the unity of the Testaments and of Israel and the church, have predominated since the second century, but covenant theology originated in the Reformed wing of the Protestant Reformation. Alternative continuity theologies would include, among others, the Lutheran law/grace dialectic,[70] Roman Catholic

---

68. See, for example, Vos, *Biblical Theology*, pp. 5–6. More recently, and indebted to Vos, is VanGemeren, *Progress of Redemption*.

69. See, for example, Ryrie, *Dispensationalism Today*, pp. 19–20, 33–36, 42–43; and idem, *Basic Theology* (Wheaton, Ill.: Victor Books, 1986), pp. 114–15.

70. For a comparison of Luther and Bullinger on their "exegesis of the covenant in Genesis 17," see Lillback, *Binding of God*, pp. 183–218; for Calvin's treatment see, ibid., pp. 268–73. Lillback terms that passage "the hermeneutical watershed between Wittenberg and the Swiss Reformations" (ibid., p. 183).

theology, and the Eastern Orthodox Church. Anabaptist theologies are discontinuity in character as is much of Baptist theology (at least insofar as it advocates a "believer's church" view).[71] Some theological traditions are not necessarily committed to either "continuity" or "discontinuity." Anglicans hold to "noncovenantal continuity" (especially "Anglo-Catholics"), or to "covenantal continuity" (e.g., J. I. Packer and a significant portion of the Puritan movement, namely, the non-Dissenter, non-Presbyterian, non-Congregational wing), or to "discontinuity" (e.g., W. H. Griffith Thomas).[72] The Methodist Episcopal tradition, derived from the Anglican, is similarly variable.[73]

Conclusion

According to Campbell, Chafer's *Systematic Theology* should be placed "within the limits of Reformed theology," though with the addition of several matters often omitted from theological textbooks, including "the distinctive divine programs for Israel and the Church" and "the content of premillennialism."[74] This accurately characterizes Chafer's theology, and as this essay has shown, it accurately characterizes the theology of many dispensationalists as well. There are many (Wesleyan dispensationalists, Pentecostal dispensationalists, and others) whose theology cannot be placed in the Reformed tradition, but dispensational theology has long and deep associations with Reformed theology, by denominational affiliation and individual conviction. It must be concluded, then, that it is incorrect to contrast Reformed theology and dispensational theology as necessarily mutually exclusive.[75] In particular cases, such a contrast may be accurate, but it is not a reliable generalization.

Zwingli, Bullinger, and Calvin, the founding Reformed theologians, all taught a covenantal form of a continuity theology. If Reformed theology must be restricted so that it embraces the whole of the thought of these men,

71. For Anabaptism, see William Klassen, *Covenant and Community: The Life and Writings of Pilgrim Marpeck* (Grand Rapids: Eerdmans, 1968), pp. 124–30. More generally, see Donald Durnbaugh, *Believers' Church: The History and Character of Radical Protestantism* (New York: Macmillan, 1968). Also see Paul K. Jewett, *Infant Baptism and the Covenant of Grace* (Grand Rapids: Eerdmans, 1978). Note the first and second London Confession's alterations of the Westminster Confession.

72. See W. H. Griffith Thomas, *The Principles of Theology: An Introduction to the Thirty-Nine Articles* (Grand Rapids: Baker, 1977), p. 17, esp. pp. 87, 134–41, for discussion of relevant topics. Also note J. I. Packer's comments in the preface to that edition on p. 8 (pages are unnumbered).

73. See the *Methodist Articles of Religion* (1784), in Schaff, *Creeds of Christendom*, 3:802–13.

74. Donald K. Campbell, "Foreword," in Lewis Sperry Chafer, *Systematic Theology: Abridged Edition*, ed. John F. Walvoord, Donald K. Campbell, and Roy B. Zuck, 2 vols. (Wheaton, Ill.: Victor Books, 1988), 1:18.

75. As John Gerstner does in his *Wrongly Dividing the Word of Truth: A Critique of Dispensationalism* (Brentwood, Tenn.: Wolgemuth and Hyatt, 1991).

then dispensational theology cannot qualify. However, this is not how it has been used, historically, nor is it plausible to suggest that Reformed theology is monolithic or "indivisible." The Reformed tradition has seen numerous forms and is capable of being adopted to a greater or lesser degree. The discontinuity emphasis of dispensationalism places it outside the predominant covenant theology of the Reformed tradition, but does not preclude dispensationalism from being articulated in a way that draws significantly from Reformed theology.

The relationship between dispensationalism and covenant theology is clarified by seeing both as versions (or "species") of other, more basic categorizations of Christian theology, which address the overall perspective on Scripture's historical/redemptive disclosure of the divine glory as either unity and continuity or distinctives and discontinuity. Even so, dispensationalism may embrace significant elements of covenant theology (though giving them a different significance) while covenant theology generally recognizes "dispensational" or "administrative" distinctives in the various "economies" of God's program.[76]

Tribute

Dr. Donald K. Campbell has modeled sacrificial service in his forty years of leadership at Dallas Theological Seminary. His commitment to excellence in the training of those who serve the church around the world leaves a rich legacy. His presidency has been marked as well by the concern for faithful cooperation with other evangelicals in ministering the Word of God to a needy world. For all of this, we offer thankful praise to the Triune God for this servant.

---

76. See, for example, John Calvin, *Institutes of the Christian Religion*, ed. John T. McNeill, trans. F. L. Battles (Philadelphia: Westminster, 1960), Book 2, chaps. 9–11; Turretin, *Institutio Theologiae Elencticae*, Locus 12; Cocceius, *Summa Doctrinae de Foedere et Testamento Dei*, chaps. 10–12. The terms "administration," "dispensation," and "economy" (or their cognates) occur constantly in covenant theology literature, especially before the appearance of dispensationalism when the connotation changed. See Allis, *Israel and the Church*, p. 54; and Pieters, *Candid Examination of the Scofield Bible*, p. 14, for indications of this commonness (significant especially because of the polemical nature of those two works).

Part 2

Skillfulness of Hands
Essays in Christian Leadership

The Heart and Vision of Spiritual Leadership

Peter V. Deison

Spiritual leadership at its deepest core is leadership from the *heart*. Spiritual leadership at its widest impact is leadership from *vision*. Heart and vision make leadership authentic and dynamic, when combined with God-given skill. And we find these characteristics in the unique leaders of every generation. Such a leader was David who "shepherded them with integrity of heart; with skillful hands he led them" (Ps. 78:72, NASB). In Acts 13:36 Paul spoke to a Jewish audience, reminding them that David served God's purpose in his own generation before he died. David was a man with heart and vision for his times, and he exercised leadership skillfully, thus fulfilling his God-given purpose.

The heart of a leader is the necessary starting point for spiritual leadership. This is the place where God begins with every leader and he begins there early in life. In 1 Samuel 13 Saul acted from a self-centered heart when he disobeyed the Lord's command. Samuel then informed Saul that his kingdom would not endure. "The LORD has sought out for himself a man after his own heart and the LORD has appointed him as ruler over His people, because you have not kept what the LORD commanded you" (v. 14). Samuel first emphasized the fact that the Lord had sought a leader. God's "seeking" is always based on one criterion—a like-minded heart. When Samuel went to Jesse's family in Bethlehem to anoint a new king, he was about to choose the wrong man. Samuel was not thinking about God's criteria. In warning Samuel against anointing David's oldest brother, Eliab, God said, "Do not consider his appearance or his height, for I have rejected him. The LORD does not look at the things man looks at. Man looks at the outward appearance, but the LORD looks at the heart" (1 Sam. 16:7). The account emphasizes this point as seven fine young men were passed over, while the youngest was selected. The amazing thing is not so much that David was the youngest, but that God was examining hearts at that age. The heart of a spiritual leader is watched

257

thoroughly by God. There was something different about young David's heart, and he had it from an early age.

What kind of heart is God is looking for? Obviously not a perfect heart because no one is perfect. When we examine David's life, we see a courageous heart, evidenced in his facing Goliath. And yet later he had a lusting heart in seeking out Bathsheba. What was God looking for? The answer is found most clearly in Paul's description of David: "And after He [God] had removed Saul, He raised up David to be their king, concerning whom He also testified and said 'I have found David, the son of Jesse, a man after My heart, who will do all my will'" (Acts 13:22).

The Willingness to Follow God

The first measure of a heart that is like-minded after God's heart is the willingness to follow the Lord. Any leader needs to ask, Am I willing to do whatever God wants done? Am I willing to serve his purposes in my generation?

Willingness to Face Challenge

From the very beginning David displayed a willingness to face challenge. As a shepherd he faced the lions and bears that threatened his flock (1 Sam. 17:34–35). The first public example of this willingness was his decision to face Goliath. This was a big test, but David willingly volunteered when everyone else was paralyzed by fear. David was willing to face Goliath not because the task was easy, but because his heart was right with God. When David arrived in the camp and saw Goliath challenging the army of Israel, he viewed the situation from God's perspective. His first response was, "Who is this uncircumcised Philistine, that he should taunt the armies of the living God?" (1 Sam. 17:36). This response was a rebuke to Israel. The Israelites were afraid because they did not see themselves as the army of the living God. In contrast David saw himself as a servant of the living God. That is why David was willing to respond to Goliath's challenge. When David approached Goliath, he boldly proclaimed that he had come not in his own strength but in the name of God. This was David's confidence. And it stood in sharp contrast to the soldiers of Israel. David was willing to face the challenge as God's servant, while Israel was not. He had a willingness to do whatever God wanted him to do.

Where does such a heart come from? As in David's case, it stems from a relationship with God that is developed long before crises arise. Only when one has developed such a relationship with God can he or she face challenges that require courage. Such a relationship helps people move into difficult circumstances with ease. But few understand the process and struggle that helped prepare these individuals to face adversity. These individuals rise to the challenge because they first developed a heart relationship with God. This is the source of their willingness to face challenges for God.

Willingness to Wait

Besides being willing to face Goliath, David was also willing to wait to become king. The exact length of time David had to wait before assuming the throne is unknown. David was a teenager when he was anointed, possibly as young as thirteen or fourteen years of age. From that time he waited at least ten years to become king. Twice David had the opportunity to kill Saul, but his heart attitude gave him the patience to wait for God's timing. Most leaders are not overnight successes, and they do not get where they are by accident.

David went through God's training process. Yet even when he had the opportunity to seize the throne—and could have done so with everyone's approval—he waited. He recognized that God had his own timetable, and he did not become impatient as he waited on God to remove Saul.

God has a plan, and future leaders must see themselves in God's hands and in his training school.

Willingness to Face Sin

In the latter part of his life David displayed another characteristic of a willing heart—the willingness to face sin. Experiencing a dark time in his life, he realized his heart was not filled with obedience. He had to deal with his pride, lust, and evil passions. Though his heart was willingly given to God, he still had to undergo a painful refining process. At some point in his or her life every leader will face an experience God will use to show up sinfulness. This is where the individual learns to understand and appreciate God's grace. A proper response enables the leader to develop greater insight into the heart of God. It was not David's sin but his *response* to his sin that marked David as a man after God's own heart. David's cry in Psalm 51 vividly portrays his awareness of the depth of his sin and shows his desire to experience God's forgiveness.

In recent years a number of Christian leaders have fallen into sexual immorality. Leaders are needed who will examine their hearts as deeply as David did and express the same anguish over their sin. While genuine repentance for sin is the mark of a godly leader, so is the desire for holiness that leads one to reject immorality. The leader who is willing to face his or her sin should begin with David's prayer in Psalm 139:23–24, "Search me O God, and know my heart . . . and see if there is any hurtful way in me."

Focused on Others

A second dimension of David's heart is that it was focused on others. The theme verse of this tribute to Dr. Campbell is Psalm 78:72, which states that

God chose David from tending the sheep to be the shepherd of his people and that David shepherded them with a heart of integrity and with skillful hands. The word integrity means "wholeness" or "completeness." David shepherded others with a heart that was complete. Integrity also implies consistency. A heart of integrity is one that is consistent with God's will and ways. And God's heart is focused on his people. David's shepherding heart was focused more on helping others than it was on expanding his own kingdom. We see this in the way David treated his servants, in the way he got along with Jonathan, in the way he cared for his warriors, and even in the way he respected Saul. With a shepherd's heart he was willing to reach out to love, to heal, and to help others, even the downtrodden.

When David first fled from Saul, all the people who were in distress, in debt, or discontented gathered around him. These are the "followers" God gave him. David began his shepherding by caring for the "bottom of the barrel." These are hardly the nucleus most leaders look for to help them start their work! Yet David endeared himself to these people, and they loved him to the end. He saw them with a shepherd's heart. A group of these men from his army became known as "David's mighty men." They followed his example as they killed giants and performed mighty deeds. They were willing to risk their lives for this man who loved them and led them because they knew his heart was focused on them. A heart that is focused on others inspires and motivates.

Loving Worship

A third dimension of David's heart is that it was focused on loving God through worship. David was Israel's "singer of psalms" (2 Sam. 23:1), and believers through the ages have worshiped God by reading the psalms of David. These psalms record his devotional life and the thoughts he had about the God he loved and worshiped. By means of the psalms readers peer into David's heart and experience his pains, aches, struggles, joys, anguish, doubts, worries, and, most of all, worship.

After establishing his kingdom, one of David's first acts was to bring the ark of the covenant to Jerusalem. He wanted to make God the focus of his government and rule. He also desired to build a temple to God, but the Lord only allowed him to prepare for it, not actually to build it. The honor of building the temple went to David's son, Solomon. A spiritual leader's heart is so deeply in love with God that he wants everyone to know his God as he does. When God measures the worth of an individual's life, he does so by measuring the size of his heart, not his head. A leader increases the size of his or her heart by focusing on loving others and on loving God through worship.

A Leader's Vision

It is also from the heart that godly vision emerges. Vision is seeing the future the way God sees it and working to develop plans that please him. Perhaps David's vision began to form when he first moved into Saul's palace as a young commander in his army. As David conquered surrounding kingdoms, he must have noticed the great places of worship that crowned these earthly kingdoms. At some point in David's life he conceived a vision of building a great house of worship to honor the God of Israel. This desire is clearly apparent in David's first actions as king. First, he solidified the kingdom by securing his control over the northern and southern tribes of Israel (2 Sam. 5:1–5). Second, he established Jerusalem as his capital (2 Sam. 5:6–10). Third, he built himself a palace (2 Sam. 5:9–12). Fourth, he brought the ark to Jerusalem and established the place of worship (2 Sam. 6:1–10). As soon as David secured his kingdom, he told Nathan the prophet that he wanted to build a house for God that would serve as a place of worship (2 Sam. 7:1–2). Where did this desire come from? God never commanded David to build him a temple, but the desire to honor God had been growing in David's heart.

Instead of allowing David to build him a temple, God told the king he would bless him and his family (2 Sam. 7:14–16). This involved the establishing of the Davidic covenant. However, this only increased David's desire to honor his Lord. David's vision intensified, but now he faced a dilemma. On the one hand he continued to have a burning desire and vision to do something for God. On the other hand God specifically prohibited him from building the temple. Only toward the end of David's life did he explain to his officials why he was not allowed to build it: God wanted it built by a "man of peace" but God had called David to serve him as a warrior or "man of blood." However, designing it, accumulating materials to build it, training temple servants and singers, raising money for it, and motivating the people to support Solomon in its construction—all these, David said, God had placed in his mind (1 Chron. 28:12, 19). (Nearly six hundred years later Nehemiah used almost the same words to describe how God had placed in his mind and on his heart the desire to rebuild the walls of Jerusalem [Neh. 2:12].) Apparently God responded to David's vision by directing him in this way.

David's final enthusiasm and vision for the kingdom were greater than at first. He motivated the people to great acts of sacrifice and service for God. A person with a heart like God's heart enthusiastically does God's will. David willingly did all God wanted him to do. This attitude enabled David to focus on his people as God intended. And this attitude enabled David to think God's thoughts as the Lord gave him a vision for the future.

These are two key components of spiritual leadership: a *heart* that loves both God and his people, and a *mind* that is in tune with God's desires and seeks to accomplish his purpose.

Tribute

It has been my privilege to be associated with Dr. Donald Campbell for the past nineteen years. Like David, he loves God and his people. He is a man who has envisioned a great future for Dallas Seminary. Thank you, Dr. Campbell, for having, like David, a heart of love and a mind with vision.

Learning to Lead Like the Lord

Kenneth O. Gangel

As the decade of the 1990s approaches midpoint, the United States boasts 325,000 local congregations. That means one church for every 550 adults, a better ratio than McDonald's, Sears, or the United States Postal Service. Americans tend to be a religious lot. Four out of five consider themselves Christians, but only one out of five has any understanding of the gospel. With all the sociological analysis of church and culture, the danger in modern Christianity may well be to deemphasize its distinctives in order to make it more palatable to the multitudes.

Those 325,000 congregations are only as effective as the leaders who serve them. Incidentally, according to Schaller, "The 350,000 employed ministers in the United States in 1990 were outnumbered by 1.6 million registered nurses, 600,000 electrical and electronic engineers, 1.2 million high school teachers and 5 million secretaries and typists."[1] In Callahan's interesting book, *Effective Church Leadership,* he states that church leaders must take an entirely different posture for the 1990s because of changes in the American culture. Callahan claims that "1. The value of the church is not among the major values of the culture; 2. a substantial number of persons are not seeking out churches on their own initiative; 3. by and large, persons live life through as though the church could not substantially matter."[2]

Evangelicals tend to absorb the sociological assessment of culture and church and then turn to the sociological analysis of what kind of leadership best meets that situation. It is the premise of this essay that such a pattern will always be destructive, perhaps even fatal, because the church and church leadership must always be countercultural. Perhaps we see this most dramatically in Matthew 12:15–21, a passage of Scripture not commonly utilized in leadership studies.

1. Lyle E. Schaller, "Three Passing Parades," *Church Management,* August 1991, p. 47.
2. Kennon L. Callahan, *Effective Church Leadership* (New York: Harper and Row, 1990), p. 3.

Aware of this, Jesus withdrew from that place. Many followed him, and he healed all their sick, warning them not to tell who he was. This was to fulfill what was spoken through the prophet Isaiah: "Here is my servant whom I have chosen, the one I love, in whom I delight; I will put my Spirit on him, and he will proclaim justice to the nations. He will not quarrel or cry out; no one will hear his voice in the streets. A bruised reed he will not break, and a smoldering wick he will not snuff out, till he leads justice to victory. In his name the nations will put their hope."

This passage applies to church leaders at two levels: pastoral staff and lay leadership.

The Leader's Appointment

Matthew 12 deals with Sabbath controversies. The opening verses (vv. 1–14) address the question of working and healing on the Sabbath. In the closing verses (vv. 22–45), Matthew recorded two additional confrontations Jesus had with the Pharisees. The editors of the New International Version have titled verses 15–21 "God's Chosen Servant," pointing to the fact that Matthew linked Jesus' healing ministry (vv. 9–13, 15) with the Suffering Servant motif of Isaiah 42:1–4. This highlights the dramatic contrast between the religious leaders who attacked Jesus and the servantlike conduct of God's Son. The passage quoted from Isaiah 42 presents a pattern for all those appointed by God to a ministry that is both distinctive from and alien to the culture in which it must be carried out.

The servant was chosen by God (Matt. 12:18). The words, "Here is my servant whom I have chosen," underscore the fact that for Christian leaders a sense of divine calling is foundational to serving God. Maxwell wrote about the entry level of leadership, which he names "position." He says, "When a person gains authority through position, he lays hold of the title by right. People follow him because they have to. Do not falsely assume when you are 'voted' into a church that you have earned the congregation's following and allegiance."[3] Maxwell then discusses five other levels of leadership—permission, production, personal development, and personhood. Professional growth in leadership is a process; leaders move through these levels as they grow spiritually and as they gain professional experience.

Verse 18 also affirms that *God loves his chosen Servant and delights in him.* That love relationship is seen between God the Father and God the Son and in Jesus' relationship to his disciples. Similarly Christian leaders today persevere in the face of difficulties, knowing they are loved by God and that he delights in them. Heidebrecht discerns three phases in the Lord's ministry

3. John C. Maxwell, "Practices of Leadership in the Context of Pastoral Leadership," *Christian Education Journal* 20 (Autumn 1991): 59.

with his disciples: he was with them, he sent them, and he gave them authority.[4] So today leaders can delight in knowing that the Lord delights to be with them and has given them his authority. "Even as Christ put Himself under the Father's authority, and thus was empowered to do the whole will of God, so we as a *church full of ministers* need to follow that model."[5]

A third element in verse 18 affirms that the *chosen servant is endowed with God's Spirit*. Christian leaders are effective only to the extent that they minister in the power of the Holy Spirit and not in their own strength (Zech. 4:6). And yet, as Nouwen claims, many leaders are unable to function satisfactorily as spiritual leaders. "Most of them are used to thinking in terms of large-scale organizations, getting people together in churches, schools, and hospitals, and running the show as a circus director. They have become unfamiliar with, and even somewhat afraid of, the deep and significant movements of the Spirit."[6]

Success in ministry comes not with self-advancement and high visibility, but through patient service to others. Christian leaders can face whatever comes their way if they lay hold of the central truths that God has chosen them for ministry; that he loves and delights in them and their service; and that he will provide the power of his Spirit to fulfill any assignment.

The Leader's Assignment

Matthew 12:19–20a points up five characteristics one will *not* find in God's chosen servant. In other words *Christian leaders are marked primarily by their difference from the world around them*, not by how well they measure up to its standards. For example, Christian leaders *do not quarrel*. The word *erizō* appears only here in the New Testament in verbal form, but Paul used the noun *erithia* five times in his epistles (Rom. 2:8; 2 Cor. 12:20; Gal. 5:20; Phil. 1:17; 2:3) and James employs it twice (3:14, 16). In each case it carries the negative idea of contention. Interestingly the NIV translates it in Galatians 5:20; Philippians 1:17; 2:3 and James 3:14, 16 by the words "selfish ambition."

Perhaps the positive corollary to quarreling is *meekness*. Paul wrote of this in Romans 12:3: "For by the grace given me I say to every one of you: Do not think of yourself more highly than you ought, but rather think of yourself with sober judgment, in accordance with the measure of faith God has given you." Jesus displayed meekness by mingling with the poor, by "putting up with" the disciples; and by his nonretaliatory spirit while on trial in Pilate's hall.

4. Vern Heidebrecht, "Affirming the Laity for Ministry," *Direction* 19 (Fall 1990): 48–49.
5. Ibid., 49 (italics added).
6. Henri Nouwen, *The Wounded Healer* (Garden City, N.Y.: Image Books, 1979), pp. 37–38.

Second, the Christian servant *does not "cry out"* (Matt. 12:19). The word *kraugazō* simply means loud noise. John used it to describe the screaming of the murderous crowds at the crucifixion (John 19:12). Christian leaders should not be loud, boisterous people whose public behavior brings shame to their ministry. They are to function in *dignity,* a second positive quality that follows right along with meekness.

Third, committed Christian leaders *do not make a public spectacle of themselves.* "No one will hear his voice in the streets" (Matt. 12:19b). This does not mean he is silent, because the servant obviously proclaims justice (vv. 18, 20). But it does portray humility. At the May 1991 Dallas Theological Seminary Commencement service Joseph Stowell quoted a *USA Today* list of what it called "The 10 Sleaziest Vocations in America." Number one was drug pushing; number two, prostitution; and number three, television evangelism. We need not agree with that list to admit that ministry is more difficult in the 1990s because a few Christian leaders have made public spectacles of themselves.

Fourth, Christian leaders, functioning in the pattern of Jesus, *will not break "a bruised reed"* (v. 20). To meekness, dignity, and humility may be added *gentleness.* This is the opposite of the leadership style of communism:

> The Communist system produces worship of the leader as a snake produces poison. The leader's authority embodies the wisdom of the Party that knows the secret of history and the path to Paradise and is an inescapable and essential element of the system. . . . (This philosophy was clearly articulated in 1919 by Lenin.) We must establish the principle of personal authority, of the moral authority of the individual person whose decisions have to be obeyed without long debates.[7]

Fifth, spiritual leaders *do not snuff out a "smoldering wick."* Instead they exercise *patience.* They do not advance their ministries with such callousness, especially to the weak and inarticulate, that they forget they must serve the weak, not be served by them. These five characteristics contrast sharply with a society that is not servant-friendly.

The Leader's Achievement

As Matthew wrote, God's servant "leads justice to victory" and gives the nations "hope," obvious paraphrases of Isaiah 42:3–4. The Old Testament prophet referred here to the Lord's ultimate redemption of his people and his reign over the entire world. The practical application cannot be missed: like Jesus, the Lord's servants practice affirmation of other people. Their ministry

---

7. Mikhail Heller, *Cogs in the Wheel: The Formation of Soviet Man* (New York: Knopf, 1988), pp. 66–67.

assures that even the weakest are not trampled, but offered justice and hope. For such a Messiah, Israel was hardly prepared. For such church leaders late-twentieth century Americans are no more prepared.

In one of the best articles ever published in *Search*, Rose talked about servant leadership. "Affirmation is a servant leader's way of saying to followers how important their ministries are in giving a needed endorsement, providing support, and entering the celebration."[8] And, it may be added, all of this is to be done from proper other-oriented motivation, without manipulating people to become involved in the leaders' programs.

As the Lord said to his own, so Christian leaders should seriously say to those with whom they work, "You will do what I have been doing and you will do even greater things than these" (John 14:12).

Conclusion

In the fall 1991 issue of *Christian Education Journal,* I attempted to pull together fifteen dimensions of godly leadership seen in the Old and New Testaments. Several of these are evident in Matthew 12:18–21. Pooled together in a narrative paragraph they look like this:

> Biblical leadership takes place when divinely appointed men and women accept responsibility for obedience to God's call. They recognize the importance of preparation time, allowing the Holy Spirit to develop tenderness of heart and skill of hands. They carry out their leadership roles with deep conviction of God's will, clear theological perspective from His Word, and an acute awareness of the contemporary issues which they and their followers face. Above all, they exercise leadership as servants and stewards, sharing authority with their followers and affirming that leadership is primarily ministry to others, modeling for others and mutual membership with others in Christ's body.[9]

How, then, can Christian leaders today "learn to lead like the Lord"? How can they exhibit the same qualities of servant leadership he displayed? Consider the following suggestions:

1. Ask God's Spirit to replace natural selfish ambition with a burning desire to serve others.
2. Measure everything you read and hear about leadership by the standards of God's Word.
3. Determine by God's grace that the unbiblical leadership style of others will not unbalance your efforts to emulate the biblical pattern.

8. Morton F. Rose, "Steps Toward Servant Leadership," *Search* 20 (Spring 1990): 19.
9. Kenneth O. Gangel, "Biblical Theology of Leadership," *Christian Education Journal* 20 (Autumn 1991): 30.

4. Acknowledge in your heart and publicly that your achievements are the result of God's grace spread like a sheltering blanket over your life, your family, and your ministry.

Christ, God's chosen Servant, evidenced ideal qualities for leadership, as described by Isaiah. Similarly, today's Christian leaders are God's chosen servants. When they function in accord with New Testament guidelines, especially those that describe the ultimate Model, then they have learned to lead like the Lord.

Tribute

During his many years of leadership at Dallas Seminary, Dr. Campbell has exemplified the kind of leadership described in this essay. Amid the constant turmoil of major administrative posts, he demonstrates a gentle blend of vision, mission, and care for people.

A Vision for Personal
and Leadership Development

William D. Lawrence

George Bernard Shaw, the English atheist, infidel, essayist, and playwright, once wrote:

> This is the true joy of life, the being used for a purpose recognized by yourself as a mighty one; the being a force of nature instead of a feverish selfish little clod of ailments and grievances complaining that the world will not devote itself to making you happy.
>   I want to be thoroughly used up when I die, for the harder I work the more I live. I rejoice in life for its own sake. Life is no "brief candle" to me. It is a sort of splendid torch which I have got hold of for the moment, and I want to make it burn as brightly as possible before handing it on to future generations.[1]

Life is a splendid torch. But what is there about life that makes it a splendid torch for pastors or college and seminary professors? It is the privilege God has given us of being leaders and of training others to be leaders.

This splendid torch is the glory of the indwelling presence of the Lord Jesus Christ in us, shining forth from us as leaders in his body under *the* Leader. The splendid torch is the glory of Christ reflected through the service of life-change leaders, those who measure their impact not in terms of babies, budgets, books, and buildings, but in terms of the life changes the glory of Christ makes in the followers of their followers. It is the brilliant light of love and truth in action that calls others to follow its visionary way to greater heights than they ever thought possible.

Our task as pastors and professors is to develop such "life-change leaders" who serve as clear, brilliant reflectors of *the* Life-change Leader, the Lord Jesus Christ.

---

1. Cited in Warren Bennis and Burt Nanus, *Leaders: The Strategies for Taking Charge* (New York: Harper and Row, 1985), p. 32.

What must be the primary mark of the men and women we develop as leaders? Some would say *knowledge;* they assert that those "in the know" should be "in the lead." While it is true that leaders must lead thoughtfully, knowledge alone is not enough. It is becoming increasingly evident that the cerebral model of leadership has been tried and found wanting.

Others, especially in today's world, would say the primary mark of life-change leaders must be *know-how.* Those with the know-how should be in the lead. To these people, leaders must have skills, unique abilities to influence others, to inculcate in them the capacities they must have to induce change in others.

Yet is anything more dangerous than know-how without knowledge? Nothing is more likely to produce heresy in the name of Jesus Christ than this deadly combination. Such leaders may be experts in making paths, but they will have very little idea where they are going nor will they realize when they have gone off the cliffs of confusion and contradiction.

Leadership development is caught in a tug-of-war between knowledge and know-how. But must we make this choice? Is there really a choice to make? Can anyone lead without the balance of knowledge and know-how? Is this really the primary issue? Obviously, knowledge is the one hand of leadership and know-how the other.

The real issue is, What is the heart of leadership, the missing link that connects these two? The heart of leadership is an integrity that characterizes a life integrated around the healthy identity of Christ within us. It is this integrity that cleanses the reflecting surface of the leader's heart and enables that leader to shine with the brilliant luminescence of the Light of the World.

Our vision in fulfilling the responsibility of personal and leadership development is to aim for two-handed leaders with heart. Such leaders possess the knowledge of Christ's Word in the one hand, and the know-how of Christ's works in the other, while in their hearts they grow in the integrity of Christ's will. Pastors and teachers are called to develop leaders for the body of Christ, leaders who define themselves by their impact in the lives of others. Our task is not to develop institutional leaders but personal leaders who bring character, ethics, and integrity to the institutions in which they serve.

The development of such leaders involves three specific steps.

Understanding the Unique Needs of Our Times

We send leaders into a secularized society. On the cover of Chuck Colson's *Against the Night,* we read:

> The sun is setting on western civilization. Ominous shadows fall across politics, family life, and education. We live with a growing sense that things are winding down—that somehow freedom, justice, and order are slipping away.

Scandals and scams are commonplace as men and women trade character for cash and sacrifice commitment on the altar of selfishness. Divorce, drugs, and easy sex create an environment of abuse for much of our youth. . . . We stand on the brink of a new dark age.

The barbarians of the new dark age are pleasant and articulate men and women. They carry briefcases, not spears, but their assault on culture is every bit as devastating as the barbarian invasion of Rome. We have bred them in our families and trained them in our schools. Their ideas are persuasive and subtle, and very often they undermine the pillars upon which our civilization was founded.[2]

The fact that we send leaders into a secularized society means we live in a new era and face a new war, a war that is being fought on a new battlefield. In the past we fought on a cerebral battlefield in a war over absolutes. Once the dragons with which we had to contend were intellectual leviathans, the recognized issues of right and wrong. In those days there were the two antagonists, liberalism and fundamentalism. The issues in that battle concerned right and wrong, truth and accuracy, and they were settled largely on the basis of who had the best proof in the opinions of the evaluators. The focus was on the accuracy of the Bible, which was commonly accepted by all to have some valid authority. The concern centered on facts—facts about how the Bible came into being, why it is true, and how to interpret it—and the truth, objectively stated and cerebrally assimilated, was the key issue.

Our approach among those who share our faith with us has been to assume we are addressing a motivated audience who want to know the Bible and therefore are ready and willing to listen. We assumed we had an informed and motivated audience who would listen to us and respond in obedience once we made the truth clear to them. So we focused on training leaders to know the Word and transmit it in such a way that others would both come to know the Word and obey it once they understood it. Our appeal was intellectual and cerebral, and it worked well on the cerebral battlefield.

Today we fight on a new battlefield, an emotional battlefield, which assumes there are no such things as absolutes. The battle is now secularism versus biblicism. In the past the concern was on such things as the validity of miracles, the historicity of biblical records, and the accuracy of the biblical text. Now the irrelevance of these debates is assumed. The war has moved past these concerns to deny all they supported, the moral absolutes of the holy God.

Because secularism denies absolutes on any basis, let alone the biblical, it lessens the intellectual and heightens the emotional. Reality is not determined and defined by right and wrong, but by good and bad, that is, good and bad feelings rather than truth and error.

---

2. Charles Colson, *Against the Night* (Ann Arbor, Mich.: Servant Publications, 1989).

This can be illustrated by the issue of abortion. There is nothing rational or logical about the arguments for abortion. Everyone knows that a fetus is a form of human life, and to cut it off is to destroy that life and all the potential it represents. Bad logic creates a false dichotomy between embryonic human life and birthed human life; but capable, intelligent people do it every day because the battlefield of our day is not cerebral but emotional. It is not a matter of right and wrong, but of what one wants to do because of what he or she feels. Students who come to Christian colleges and seminaries are not immune to this kind of "feel/think." The people to whom they will minister in the local church are totally controlled by it. In view of this, schools cannot teach truth merely through the mind gate. To continue to do so will make the educational process increasingly irrelevant in the eyes of the generation whose attention we seek to attract.

Of course, we had the emotional before and we need the intellectual now. Previous generations were never devoid of emotional responses, and current generations are not devoid of intellectual perspective. The difference is that the value base was formerly cerebral whereas now the value base is emotional. This is a major difference, and the awareness of this needs to be part of our personal and leadership development process.

What we must understand is that today's leaders and followers enter life with a totally different sense of need than that of previous generations. Churches and schools must prepare life-change leaders in light of this. In today's world the key question with which many students come to college and seminary is not, "What can I learn?" but "Will what I learn fix my problems?" The primary issues for today's students are issues of self-image and self-worth. These are restricting, self-centered reactions, not releasing, self-sacrificing responses. These are paralyzing reactions that bring harm and loss rather than health and love. Nonetheless these are the real issues of today, and we must face them if we are to make a difference in our world. However, most schools of higher education are not prepared to relate to such concerns.

Understanding the Unique People of Our Times

We send leaders into a cynical, apathetic generation. We face two new groups: baby boomers and baby busters. Baby boomers are defined as those born between 1945 and 1964, and baby busters are those born between 1965 and 1984. They are a cynical lot, radically different from the generation preceding them. Anderson summarizes these differences well. He says the generation of the 1920s and 1930s was bonded by the Great Depression, the rise of Hitler, Pearl Harbor, World War II, and the longest presidency in history.[3]

---

3. Leith Anderson, *Dying for Change* (Minneapolis: Bethany House, 1990), p. 64.

There was no television and far less mobility, which meant that local culture and mores prevailed as the defining context of life.

On the other hand, the boomer generation is bonded by television, prosperity, peace, Vietnam, and rock-and-roll music. On top of all of this, every national institution has failed these people in their minds: the ideals and security of the nation through assassination of national heroes such as John F. Kennedy, Robert F. Kennedy, and Martin Luther King; the presidency through Watergate; the family through divorce; business through the internment of the wealthiest prisoners in history; and Congress through its check kiting and post office scandals.

As a result of all of this, baby boomers have neither trust nor confidence in most forms of leadership. They expect leaders to fail them and are not surprised when they learn of some other new scandal or shame. They are cynical about government, the church, and leaders. Perhaps this helps us understand much of what is happening in the media who chronicle this lack of trust and cynicism in daily headlines and nightly telecasts. Their ideals have been shattered; they simply cannot trust those in authority.

If baby boomers are cynical, baby busters are apathetic. Twenty-somethings long for authority in their lives but fear to make commitments.

Older adults have led the way in refusing to make commitments, choosing instead to sacrifice their families for their own pleasure, thinking nothing of putting their children and grandchildren into overwhelming national debt due to their own lack of discipline. But busters have matched and raised the older generation, making lack of commitment an art form. Yet they seek the security of a life-giving authority in response to the certainty that someone cares enough to give them direction in life and provide them with wisdom and truth.

I saw this recently when I watched Barbara Walters interview four women and three men, all in their twenties. Though nearly all of them were from broken homes, they were bright, capable, and pursuing careers. One was a single welfare mother who had graduated from high school after giving birth to a son. She was trying to make it on her own and get off the welfare treadmill.

They had hope, hope that someday they would make something of their lives. Only one was married; none of the others seemed to feel ready for marriage. They did believe in romantic love and longed to find that one right man or woman. Only one of them had a sense of direction in life. Only one of them was pro-life. All of them had a college degree except for the welfare mother. Several of them had master's degrees. Only one of them, the married one, had some sense of direction, though he did not have great assurance that he would attain his goal of having his Ph.D. within ten years. None of them had any interest in politics. They simply did not care. None of them seemed to have any sense of the American dream or the hope of seeing it come true. Virtually all of them were seeking a sense of identity.

One young woman in particular struck me as struggling to find herself. She had a master's degree in literature, yet she served with seemingly little concern doing grunt work for a nursery. Her strongest drive in life seemed to be reading, searching for herself, attempting to bring wholeness into her heart out of her parents' divorce and the pain it brought her.

It was singularly painful to watch them struggle. I felt they were unable to trust but longing to trust. All this was because they had no consistent authority in their lives to give them a sense of identity, a self-respect that produced in them the discipline, courage, and confidence necessary to commit to other people and causes. They were simply apathetic! It is into these cynical and apathetic generations that we send the life-change leaders we develop.

Besides sending leaders into a cynical, apathetic generation, *we also send leaders into a fatherless generation.*

The fracturing of the family means the failure of fathering. The vast majority of fathering is being done by mothers in our society, even when a father is present in the home.

> Since 1970 the rate of marriages has dropped 30 percent while the number of divorces is up 50 percent. More than one million American children witness their parents' divorce each year, and ten million children now live in one-parent homes. The illegitimacy rate has doubled; over half of inner-city children are born out of wedlock . . . the family has all but disappeared from America's inner cities.[4]

Fathers are the missing link in the modern family, yet this seems to be a surprise to many. As Wallerstein states:

> Amazing as it may seem, developmental psychology has only recently become aware of the vital role that fathers play in the lives of their children. For many years, child psychology was preoccupied with the mother-child relationships, as if fathers were secondary figures whose primary role psychologically was to help their sons consolidate a sexual identity.
>
> Our research is part of a growing body of knowledge that puts this lopsided view of child development back into perspective. Fathers exert a critical influence on their sons and daughters throughout childhood and adolescence, helping to shape their characters, values, relationships with other people, and career choices. . . . Children do not dismiss their fathers just because there has been a divorce. Indeed, it is the children of divorce who taught us very early that to be separated from their father was intolerable. The poignancy of their reactions is astounding, especially among the six-, seven-, and eight-year-olds. They cry for their daddies—be they good, bad, or indifferent daddies. I have been deeply struck by the distress children of every age suffer at losing their fathers.[5]

4. Colson, *Against the Night,* p. 73.
5. Judith Wallerstein and Sandra Blakeslee, *Second Chances* (New York: Ticknor and Fields, 1989), p. 234.

Furthermore, we all know that fathering at home does not necessarily mean fathering in the heart; therefore, many who come from whole families still feel the deficiency of failed fathering. This may be the most significant reality of all in thinking through a vision for personal and leadership development. Certainly the absence of fathering is one of the major contributing factors to our last step, the step we must take to meet these needs.

Creating New Ministry Training Structures That Meet the Needs of the People of Our Times

New ministry training structures must minister to the hands and the heart as well as the head. They must put the knowledge of Christ's Word, the know-how of Christ's works, and the integrity of Christ's will into the hands and the hearts of those whom we develop as human beings and as leaders. We must also develop structures that meet the needs of our times. This means we have to bridge a bigger river than we have been bridging, a river with three distinct currents.

The Emotional Current

We must first bridge the emotional current. Before we can get to the level of significant life change, we must meet the emotional needs that keep this from happening. No self-focused individual can help others gain release from themselves. Such a person will never be able to lead without becoming truly free from the bondage that self-focus brings.

How do we go about meeting the emotional needs first? By modeling *true* identity and integrity in the intensity of small-group community relationships. Modeling demands a vulnerability and authenticity that enable others to see us in the process of growing from our own self-centeredness to a Christ-centeredness that releases us to others-centeredness. In doing this, we show how our lives are being changed, we teach others how their lives can change, and we help them find the courage to make the changes needed to produce life-change leaders.

Vulnerability means sharing Christ's strength through our weakness. It is the appropriate disclosure of an older brother or sister's pilgrimage that focuses on Christ in his conviction, faithfulness, grace, and blessing in such a way that attention turns to him and the developing leader is encouraged, released from sin, and motivated to grow in confidence and impact. Leadership development is impossible without such vulnerability.

Authenticity means consistent integrity.[6] It is the integration of both character and behavior around the security of one's identity in Christ so there is

---

6. Bradley Laws Smith, *Authenticity* (Dallas, Tex.: Center for Christian Leadership, Dallas Theological Seminary, 1992).

a consistency of holiness that is real and true according to the temperament, experience, age, and gifts of the leader developer. It comes across as a relational style that expresses love as measured by God's truth that radiates from the inner person as a kind of a "see-through" quality in which there is neither fold nor spot.

Along with modeling we can help meet emotional needs by ministering to the feeling level. Vulnerability shows our own emotional needs and the way we have seen the Lord meet them. This gives us the freedom to touch the emotions of those who respond to us so they can focus these emotions and face them in ways they have not done before. We help them define their feelings and realize how futile it is to hide them, either from themselves or from others, which will enable them to touch these deep needs through the healing power of the Word of God.

The Intellectual Current

Once we have bridged the emotional segment of the river, we turn to the intellectual current. We must move from the relational to the informational by showing those who follow us how the Bible meets these emotional needs, how theology renews the mind, breaks the world's mold, and brings the mercies of God to bear on the paralyzing pain of life. Never has there been a time in which hermeneutics, exegesis, theology, and Bible knowledge have been more needed.

The Bible must be taught out of the vulnerability and sincerity of life, not just the accuracy of word. The Bible with its depth of truth about the holy God, the sin of man, and the cross of Christ must be our essence. We have to turn from the popular Christian culture of our day in which we are focused on solving problems with a never-ending collection of shallow how-to's that never release us from the grip of personal pain and problems. Such language as John Owen's, "the mortification of the flesh," may not be on today's wavelength, but the concept has to be translated so that Madonna freaks and David Letterman lovers can grasp its liberating reality. As difficult as it is, we must teach these generations to move past their emotional needs to the health God's revealed truth brings. Only the Holy Spirit can actually accomplish this, but our responsibility is to seek to create avenues by which He can move.

The Spiritual Current

The third current we must bridge is the spiritual one. This demands that we recast our understanding of spiritual issues in order to relate more effectively to the needs of our times. The primary issues of men and women today are issues of identity that affect integrity. We in leadership development are deluged with the task of developing men and women who have distorted identities and diluted integrity. Because of this lack of healthy identities the people we train may be unable to get in touch with their feelings and to relate on the emotional level with those whom they seek to develop. They may be unable to be open to others, so they must maintain control over them with their minds and superior knowledge (an inevitable result of academia unless it is consciously and consistently resisted). The people we train may be locked in struggles with insecurity, which makes them subjective and defensive. And they may use their gifts to advance themselves in the name of Jesus Christ under cover of the glory of God.

These marks of a distorted identity lead to a diluted integrity. The people we train may keep their appointments on time; they may follow through on their commitments; they may keep their word. Their integrity issues show up on a much deeper level than this. While they do many of the things we normally associate with integrity, more significant deficiencies have a much greater impact on identity than we may realize. For example, they may act as if everything is fine in a relationship when inwardly they are immensely angry. Or they may be unable to feel what their sheep feel, so they lack significant sensitivity. Or they may use their college or seminary training to maintain a position of impeccability to cover up great feelings of inadequacy. Or they may use their gifts to promote themselves in the name of Jesus Christ.

These problems may sound like psychological problems because the language of self-worth, self-esteem, and identity are psychological terms. However, these are spiritual issues, not psychological ones. Long before Freud had a dream or Jung rendered an opinion or Rogers uttered a restatement, the Bible was dealing with these issues. Identity is the essence of the sanctification process. We were made in the image of God (Gen. 2–3). But sin marred and scarred our identity. All humans are on an identity search, as Paul demonstrated through his vulnerability in Philippians 3. Identification with Christ and the resulting new identity are the keys that bring release from sin as seen from Romans 6. The ultimate issue in all this is not the psyche but the flesh. The flesh keeps us and our followers in bondage to the fears of self-centeredness and insecurity, not the psyche, and we must approach the development of life-change leadership in the light of this darkness.

As Lovelace writes, "Most congregations of professing Christians today are saturated with a kind of *dead goodness*, an ethical respectability which has its motivational roots in the flesh rather than in the illuminating and enlivening control of the Holy Spirit."[7] This reality has a terribly destructive impact on the church. "Much of the church's warfare today is fought by blindfolded soldiers who cannot see the forces ranged against them, who are buffeted by invisible opponents who respond by striking one another."[8]

7. Richard F. Lovelace, *Dynamics of Spiritual Life* (Downers Grove, Ill.: InterVarsity, 1979), p. 92.
8. Ibid., p. 18.

278   *William D. Lawrence*

We also realize how difficult our task is when we remember that "human depravity, like the mule, is reluctant to move even when it is given a hard shove; but it will sometimes at least shift its weight from one foot to another."[9] Sometimes the spiritual current appears to be placid, but we discover that any effort to plumb its depths will rapidly suck us unto an undertow that will challenge us beyond anything else we ever attempt.

We must build personal/leadership development structures that bridge this three-current river. We can do this only when we accept the limits of current academic structures. There are advantages to current academic structures such as efficiency in learning, the advancement of study and scholarship, the flow of research and writing that benefits the body of Christ, and the credentialing of all who participate.

On the other hand, there are fatal limits in current academic structures. Discipling does not occur naturally in current academic structures; ministry skills development does not occur naturally in current academic structures; leadership skills cannot be adequately developed in current academic structures; personal character issues are not deeply touched in current academic structures.

These limits in current academic ministry leadership training are not news to anyone who knows the field. Ferris's work, *Renewal in Theological Education*, shows these to have been well known facts back in the early 1930s. At that time a study under the direction of William Adams Brown of Union Theological Seminary concluded that a seminary curriculum should be dictated by ministry practice rather than research interests, although the participants provided no guidelines to implement their conclusions.[10] More recently Glenn T. Miller, professor of church history at Southeastern Baptist Theological Seminary, reached a similar conclusion:

> *Readiness* was the high point of professionalism in theological education. Yet, the program's 1976 inauguration marked the beginning of a season of discontent in American theological education. The worry was whether professionalism produced leaders. In and outside theological education, thoughtful people noted that the churches did not have effective people at their head. At least part of the reason was that the seminaries did not educate people to take charge. . . . Professional training had little to do with what was actually happening in the seminaries. Much of the study of theology was conducted on the model of the university arts and sciences. The profession that, for example, church historians pointed students to was church history. The same is true of Hebrew Scripture, New Testament, systematic theology, and other "theological" disciplines.
> The practical fields suffered from many of the same problems. The theory used by practical theologians was the theory of that specific discipline. Thus,

9. Ibid., p. 54.
10. Robert W. Ferris, *Renewal in Theological Education* (Wheaton, Ill.: Billy Graham Center, 1990).

religious education had its own body of theory and its own body of practice. Moreover, the relationship between theology and social science in these disciplines was ambiguous. . . . The more one examined the identification of professional education and ministerial preparation the less substance the concept had. The mountain on the horizon was a column of smoke. The problem was . . . a profession in the modern sense did not correspond to what faith demanded of a Christian leader. . . . The clergy should have been pathfinders. But ministers were only pathminders. At best the pastors kept their churches on the well-worn older trails.

The modern minister was scarcely in the godly fellowship of prophets, apostles, and reformers.[11]

All this leads Miller to conclude, "The only way forward is beyond the professional school."[12] The question is, What lies beyond the professional school?

Our current academic ministry training structures fail to meet both personal and leadership development needs. Graduates can leave our campuses without ever having led in the real sense of the word. For many, the first time they ever find themselves in a board meeting may also be the first time they find themselves in the sights of a contrary deacon or elder. Even in a friendly situation they may be utterly unprepared to provide the leadership needed because of inadequate training that failed to go beyond theory to real experience. Often this leads to a response of anger and resentment because these leaders thought they were being well prepared in the academic setting even though any thoughtful individual knows there is no way mass education prepares a person to lead. Seminaries tend to be passive places of listening, thinking, interacting, and drawing conclusions, a most appropriate set of disciplines. Ministry leadership, however, is an active place of listening, thinking, interacting, drawing conclusions, communicating vision, organizing around that vision, and acting on the conclusions drawn to accomplish the vision in such a way as to earn the trust of followers because good things happen. In the one place, thinking is the primary element changed; in the other, lives are the primary element changed. Each in its place is essential, but one does not always prepare for the other. That is, the academic approach to personal and leadership development does not necessarily prepare for the actual demands of ministry leadership. This is why current ministry training structures are not as well received as they once were by practitioners. This is also why their existence is threatened by some very powerful forces.

The megachurches of today respect seminaries less and less. Often structured around the ministry of one individual, many times self-made, mega-

11. Glenn T. Miller, "The Virtuous Leader: Teaching Leadership in Theological Schools," *Faith and Mission* 9 (Fall 1991): 27–28.
12. Ibid., p. 32.

churches tend to question the value of the classroom. The questions they raise of the academic approach to personal and leadership development are often valid, but they are not as able to produce balanced leadership education as they think. No one person in ministry or in the team has the balance needed to prepare any other one man or woman for the demands of ministry leadership. In the next decade it is possible that megachurches will make a determined effort to replace seminaries because they regard this structure as irrelevant and ineffective. Because of the charisma of their ministry and the amount of money they control, megachurches can make a major impact on the viability of seminaries. Though this is not why seminaries should respond to their challenge, it may be the one thing that gets attention and forces change. If megachurches are successful in replacing seminaries, the body of Christ will lose much that is essential to its ongoing well-being. Depth of thought, theological precision, exegetical excellence, and biblical balance may be lost. Those called by Christ to serve him to whom he has not given "megapersonalities" and gifts will get lost in the shuffle, and major parts of our culture will miss out on essential training for ministry. This says nothing of the potential loss to international leaders, many of whom benefit greatly from training in the United States. These realities demand that those engaged in the current academic model of personal and leadership preparation must seriously consider making the changes needed to prepare this generation of unique and fatherless men and women for service to the King.

Our problems are equally significant on the personal level, with the result that we turn out leaders who are sometimes tragically unaware of their own flaws. As a result, many men and women enter ministry leadership held in the grip of "invisible shackles." They receive the threefold foundation for ministry provided by seminaries—biblical knowledge, theological perspective, and communication skill—but the subfoundation of personal struggles and issues remains untouched. The inevitable result is that when the pressures of ministry are placed on top of the foundation we build into them, the subfoundation collapses and all we have done as well as all they have done comes crashing down. A vision for personal and leadership development cannot ignore this undeniable reality.

As Anderson has observed,

> The church of the twenty-first century promises to place a premium on performance rather than on credentials. There is less concern over degrees, accreditation, ordination, and other credentials, but an increased asking of the practical question, "Can he or she do the job?"
>
> Anticipate a growing division between scholarship and practice. It has already affected most professions and will have a growing impact on clergy education. . . .

Traditional seminary education is designed to train research theologians, who are to become parish practitioners. Probably they are adequately equipped for neither. . . .

The institutions will change. They must. Few schools have the resources to train both. We will need comparatively few graduate schools of theology and comparatively more professional schools of ministry. Both must move away from the traditional notion of education being time and place, but this switch must especially apply to the preparation of practitioners. They want to be (and the church wants) men and women who can *do* something, not know everything.[13]

Anderson also states,

There is a growing realization that classical theological education has not appropriately prepared men and women for leadership in late twentieth-century American churches. . . .

Much theological education is based on the "academy model" of classical European universities. Students are trained to be scholars. They are given the tools for research and analysis, and then are trained to be theoretical theologians. Certainly there is a need for such specialized training. Without careful scholarship the Christian church would probably repeat the heresies of earlier eras within a generation.

The rub comes when graduates face the realities of parish ministry. There is little time for the more leisurely life of scholarship. People aren't asking for academic alternatives, they are expecting practical answers to life's problems. Too often the pastor is like an emergency-room physician trained in genetic research but surrounded by patients with gunshot wounds.[14]

The need is evident: seminaries and churches must join together in new structures of formal relationships to develop leaders. Here is one view of what personal and leadership development for ministry could look like in the future. Whether the approach suggested here is the best one, we *must* change or we shall lose much of our influence in the body of Christ.

First, seminaries must maintain a core of residential specialists who serve as scholarly resources. Academic instruction, methodology, and discipline have a strategic role in personal and leadership development. However, this role can be neither exclusive nor dominant. Throughout church history, God has given great minds to love him and serve him by helping others grasp truth more accurately and effectively. God will continue to do this, and these gifted thinkers and teachers must be honored and given an essential place in personal and leadership development. Leaders must lead thoughtfully or they will lead their followers into the chaotic darkness of untruth.

13. Leith Anderson, *A Church for the 21st Century* (Minneapolis: Bethany House, 1992), pp. 46–47.

14. Ibid., pp. 74–76.

Second, seminaries must serve as study resource centers that include library facilities and resident scholars, and provide instruction in theological study and thinking. A place for focused instruction, research, and reflection is essential. Without this, the God-given thinking of the past as well as insight into the present and future will be lost, and leaders will be subject to every theological wind that blows.

Third, seminaries must employ practitioners associated with local churches who serve as ministry skill developers and personal disciplers. Professors of Christian education and pastoral ministries may function in place as practitioners of their disciplines in the local church. A "skeleton crew" could direct the study resource center and teach introductory courses in each discipline to prepare the students for further development, but most such education will occur more effectively in its natural habitat. The key to all this is to find enough dedicated practitioners to be the personal disciplers needed to develop our future leaders.

A practitioner functions in the ministry workplace as a leader of men and women serving God through local or parachurch structures. He or she has fully developed all the skills necessary in such a setting. Unfortunately many practitioners have not learned how to train others in the most effective way possible. They function according to innate intuitive drives and do not know how to transfer their skills to others. They can take others who are like them in gift and temperament and help them grow, but they often lack an adequate understanding of the divine shape in others, the giftedness and temperament that God gives to people who are different from them. As a result they are unable to implement the processes that enable them to transfer their skills to others. In other words, they are effective practitioners but ineffective professors.

For this role we need men and women who are effective practitioners and are also skilled in the knowledge needed to train others in ministry. The purpose of the practitioner/professor is not to do the work of the ministry nor to train laymen and laywomen to do the work of the ministry, but to train the "trainers of trainers" so they can "teach others to teach others" to do the work of the ministry. This cannot be done in the classroom, but must be done in the laboratory of life.

Undoubtedly the best word for this concept is "mentor," but the term must have a focused meaning in this context since it is the key to making this proposal work. Since "mentor" is too general a term the concept of "practitioner/professor" helps bring essential focus.

Fourth, seminaries must require preseminary ministry experience in order to prove fitness and call to the ministry. Declared preseminary students must be tested, not only in terms of call and giftedness, but also in terms of heart, virtue, and character. Seminaries must determine whether these students belong in a seminary program that will lead to ordination by the body of

Christ as servant-leaders on his behalf. Too often in today's structure, we accept and graduate students no one ever truly gets to know.

Fifth, seminaries must formally accept students into a ministry training program that is jointly approved by the local church and the seminary. The application and acceptance process should be conducted jointly by the involved local churches and the seminary. Those who know the applicant well should have major input in determining acceptance in a formal personal and leadership development program. In today's process a paper standard becomes determinative rather than a personal one, and applicants who look like reincarnations of the prophets on paper turn out to be troubled and confused people whom the recommender thought seminary might be able to help. We need less of this.

Sixth, seminaries must maintain formal accreditation that demonstrates measurable quality in the program but that does not limit it to the academic model as we now know it. The accreditation process is a searching and grueling one that adds to the excellence of the training given. Educational institutions are the only structures in our society that are forced to face such a demanding test, and this discipline is an affirming and cleansing one. Such an advantage should not be lost.

Seventh, seminaries must state both the minimum and the maximum length of time required in the formal program. Personal and leadership development takes time, yet this time needs to be defined so progress can be monitored and both the developer and the developing leader know how far along in the process they are.

Eighth, seminaries must balance the number of hours required in formal classroom instruction with the number of hours in evaluated ministry training/experience. This is another helpful way of providing guidance and measurement along the path to development. Both instructional and experiential progress needs to be measured and evaluated. Stated hours serve effectively as a tool to help measure this progress.

Ninth, seminaries must continue to charge tuition for ministry training hours both in the study resource center and in the local church. Since the professor/practitioners must be specialists in their own right, able to both minister and mentor, there must be a way to fund their service apart from the local church in which they serve. This is necessary because of the time it will take for these specialists to serve developing leaders, which will be more than a local church can afford. Professors at the study resource centers would be funded as professors as in the current model of seminary education.

Tenth, seminaries must allow pastors, mentors, and other practitioners to have a stronger voice in determining curriculum together with the professors at the main campus. For far too long those who do the work of the ministry and who understand best what training is needed in seminary have had much too small a voice in determining the seminary curriculum. Academic instruction is essential for ministry training, but those in academics must act as servants and not as masters, or they will lose any major role in such training.

As already stated, virtually all hands-on ministry training will occur in the local or parachurch setting under the guidance and evaluation of those who actually are responsible to accomplish the ministry. This means that virtually all pastoral, educational, and missiological instruction will occur in the setting where such ministry takes place rather than being taught in isolation in the classroom.

Conclusion

We must have leaders with heart—leaders with knowledge, know-how, and integrity. Unique needs force us to fight a new war on a new battlefield. Unique people force us to bridge a new river with deep and dangerous currents. The combination of these elements forces us to face one more reality: to achieve our dreams as educators of personal and leadership development, we must establish new and more effective training structures.

Today we face financial strictures that may be due to more than a poor economy. Could they be due to questions about the value of the structures we represent? Will it become increasingly difficult for seminaries to show the relevance of academia to ministry training? Have we reached a generational fault that will introduce a seismic blow to the structures in which we serve? Can it be that we are beginning to feel the difference between the generation dominated by the Great Depression and the one distorted by the disasters of the 1960s and 1970s? Will their desire to give only to those ministries that directly serve them become a barrier to fund-raising among them? Does all this mean that it will become increasingly difficult for us to show the relevance of academia to ministry training?

These are difficult questions to face as well as to answer. No one can respond to these issues with certainty, but seminaries cannot refuse to face and consider them if we want to preserve the values that drive us. Whatever we do, we must not allow the luster of the shining torch of the glory of Christ in those whom we develop as leaders to tarnish, darken, and fail in its reflection of Christ's light. Instead we must give all we have to minister to the hands and the heart as well as the heads of those whom we serve for such a wonderful and overwhelming purpose. So we strive to send them out with the knowledge of Christ's Word in one hand, the know-how of Christ's works in the other, and the integrity of Christ's will in their hearts.

Tribute

It has been my privilege to serve under the leadership of Dr. Donald K. Campbell for thirteen years, and I am thankful to God for his encouragement as the president of Dallas Theological Seminary in all that I have undertaken for the Lord during this time. Without his support and willingness to take risks in establishing and maintaining the Center for Christian Leadership, I would have neither the opportunity or the growth that has come to me through my ministry at the Seminary. I am grateful to Dr. Campbell for his faithfulness to our Lord during his long and effective service.

The Leader as Visionary

Aubrey M. Malphurs

A Christian leader is a godly person (character) who knows where he or she is going (vision) and has followers (influence). Thus, vision is one of the three critical components of a leader.

Leaders must be able to articulate what God has called them to do. To be unable to do so is to invite ministry disaster. When people follow a professed leader who does not know where he or she is going, they all wind up in the proverbial ditch. Also, without a clear target a leader is unable to develop a plan to implement his or her ministry.

In the Bible a number of leaders modeled a clear ministry focus. Moses demonstrated his acute knowledge of God's direction for the people of Israel when he appeared before Pharaoh and demanded their release from bondage to the Egyptians (Exod. 5–7). Joshua took the baton from Moses and completed the vision by leading Israel into the promised land. Nehemiah demonstrated that he knew precisely where he was going when he presented his vision to King Artaxerxes (Neh. 2:5).

Schaller illustrates the importance of vision in his book *The Seven-Day-a-Week Church*. He directs attention to the large number of rapidly growing churches that have emerged in America whose churchgoers were born after World War II. In presenting the main reason why these churches have become so large, he uses the word "vision" three times and "visionary" once:

> The number-one reason is not location or favorable demographics or seven-day-a-week programming or a particular theological stance. The number-one factor, as was pointed out in the introduction to this book, is transformational leadership by a *visionary* pastor who knows how to rally people in support of a cause. To be more specific, these transformational leaders are completely convinced that people's lives can be transformed by the power of the Gospel. That is the number-one distinctive characteristic of these senior ministers.
>
> In addition, these transformational leaders (1) can conceptualize a *vision* of a new tomorrow, (2) can articulate that *vision* so persuasively that people rally in support of it, and (3) know how to turn that *vision* into reality.[1]

1. Lyle E. Schaller, *The Seven-Day-a-Week Church* (Nashville: Abingdon, 1992), p. 58 (italics added).

Some suggest that this concept of vision is what the writer of Proverbs is addressing in Proverbs 29:18. The word translated "vision" in the King James Version is better translated as "revelation" in the New International Version. It is explained in the second line of the verse as "the law." So the "vision" referred to in this passage is a revelation or word from God and cannot be *limited* to an institutional vision as many suggest. However, it certainly *includes* it because ultimately an institutional ministry vision must come from God as found in his Word. Robinson writes, "Since our vision must be God's vision, we must gain it from the Scriptures."[2]

The Definition of Vision

Vision in leadership and ministry exists on both a personal and an institutional level. Personal ministry vision focuses directly on a leader's unique design, which helps in determining and guiding that leader's future ministry direction. It comes as the result of discovering his or her divine design from God (Ps. 139:15–16; Isa. 49:1, 5; Jer. 1:5; Luke 1:15; 1 Cor. 12:18; Gal. 1:15). This unique design consists of spiritual gifts, natural talents, passion, temperament, and leadership style. The discovery of personal ministry vision helps in mobilizing laypeople within the ministry. It also assists leaders in determining their place of ministry within the body of Christ.[3]

Institutional vision relates directly to the ministry of a particular Christian organization, whether church or parachurch. Once leaders have determined their personal ministry vision, they should seek to identify with a ministry organization that has an institutional vision that aligns itself closely with their personal vision. An institutional vision can be defined as a clear and challenging picture of the future of a ministry as its leadership believes it can and must be.[4] This definition consists of six important facets.

It Is Clear

A ministry cannot flourish if no one understands the vision. A ship cannot set sail if the captain and crew do not know where they are going. The leadership must understand the vision. If they cannot articulate the dream for themselves, they should not be surprised when no one follows them.

2. Cited in Aubrey Malphurs, *Developing a Vision for Ministry in the Twenty-first Century* (Grand Rapids: Baker, 1992), p. 9.
3. The concept of personal ministry vision is developed more fully in chapters 5 and 6 of the present author's *Planting Growing Churches for the Twenty-first Century* (Grand Rapids: Baker, 1992). Chapter 5 explains the divine design concept in the context of personal ministry assessment. Chapter 6 takes the reader through the assessment process to help him or her actually discover a personal ministry vision.
4. For an expanded discussion of this concept and how to develop a vision for one's ministry, see Malphurs, *Developing a Vision for Ministry in the Twenty-first Century*.

The people who make up the ministry must clearly comprehend where they are going. Even if the leadership has a clear vision, people cannot possibly follow unless they too have clarity of vision. Consequently, an important aspect of leadership is vision-casting. Leaders must articulate the dream for their people.[5] Scripture provides several models of men who led in this manner.

A prime example of a clear vision caster is Nehemiah. He made known to all that God's vision for the distressed remnant in Israel was to "rebuild the wall of Jerusalem" (Neh. 2). This is a concrete version of a more abstract vision concerning the restoration of Israel to a place where they could glorify God. A second example of a clear vision caster is Moses. He clearly caught God's vision for Israel and communicated it to approximately 2 million people. The vision was simple and precise: through the leadership of Moses, God was about to liberate Israel from Egyptian bondage and take them into a land "flowing with milk and honey" (Exod. 3:8).

It Is Challenging

A good vision serves as a catalyst and energizes people. If the leaders of a ministry are not challenged by the vision, it will not move those who follow them. For example, a church board may attempt to arrive at a ministry vision on a weekend retreat. However, a weekend usually is not enough time to develop a good vision statement and to challenge first the leaders and then others. The result is a premature product that excites only a few, and the statement may die a quick death in a file buried in some cabinet.

Nehemiah was challenged by God's vision to restore and rebuild the walls of Jerusalem. Otherwise he would not have risked communicating the dream to King Artaxerxes and requesting his help in accomplishing the vision. Moses was challenged by God's vision to lead Israel out of Egypt into the promised land. Had this not been so, then he would not have stood up to powerful Pharaoh or resisted the armies of Egypt.

It Is a Mental Picture

After the completion of Disney World someone remarked, "Isn't it too bad that Walt Disney didn't live to see this!" Mike Vance, creative director of Disney Studios replied, "He did *see* it—that's why it's here."[6] Vision is a "seeing" word. Stott says that vision "is an act of seeing—an imaginative perception of things, combining insight and foresight."[7] He adds, "We see what is—but do we see what could be?"[8] A good vision challenges the imag-

5. Chapter 5 in *Developing a Vision for Ministry in the 21st Century* discusses various creative ways for leaders to communicate their visions.

6. Malphurs, *Developing a Vision for Ministry in the 21st Century*, p. 11.

7. John R. W. Stott, "What Makes Leadership Christian?" *Christianity Today*, August 9, 1985, p. 24.

8. Ibid., p. 25.

ination and creates exciting pictures in people's minds of what can be. They begin to see things and dream great dreams for God.

Visionary leaders carry in their mental wallets a picture of what their future ministries look like. No doubt Nehemiah carried with him a mental picture of the rebuilt wall from the time God gave him the vision until the wall was in place. Most likely when Moses led the people of God in the wilderness he had a picture in his mind of a promised land "flowing with milk and honey."

It Is the Future of the Ministry

The leader always articulates a significant vision in terms of the future. It is a mental picture of what tomorrow will look like. It is a view of all the exciting possibilities of a ministry's future.

A scholar who had studied for a Ph.D. at Cambridge University in England told of a history professor who not only studied the past but mentally lived in the past. Visionary leaders think in the opposite direction. They not only think about the future; they spend time living in the future. In doing so they play a significant role in determining their futures. By cultivating institutional visions, leaders have a vital part in inventing and influencing the future of their ministries. They know precisely the kind of ministry they want and where they are going with that ministry and press on toward the accomplishment of their goals.

This does not mean that visionary leaders ignore the present or the past. They use the present as a platform to launch their ministries into the future. They accomplish this by pointing to the inadequacies of the present ministry situation, thus creating dissatisfaction with the status quo. Then they cast the vision of a better tomorrow and rally people toward it. Visionaries learn from the past but do not live in the past. An example is Paul who wrote, "But one thing I do: Forgetting what lies behind and reaching forward to what lies ahead, I press on toward the goal" (Phil. 3:13–14).

It Can Be

A good vision has solid potential. It rests firmly on the bedrock of reality. While it often tests the limits of the possible, a good vision remains within the realm of the feasible. Visionary leaders believe they are involved in something big for God. They possess a sixth sense (intuition) that tells them God is about to do something special and plans to use them in the process. It simply is a matter of time before what can be becomes what is.

Because of Nehemiah's vision he had confidence in what God would do. Therefore he could assure the people, "The God of heaven will give us success" (Neh. 2:20).

It Must Be

Besides believing that their vision *can* become a reality, visionary leaders are convinced that it *must* be. A critical sense of urgency dominates these leaders' lives. This is true for several reasons.

First, they believe God is the source of their dream. They are convinced that they are on a mission for God. Nehemiah expressed an awareness of this divine involvement when he said, "I did not tell anyone what my God was putting into my mind to do for Jerusalem" (Neh. 2:12).

Second, visionary leaders believe that God will use them in some way to accomplish the vision. They view themselves as in a position to impact their generation much as David served God's purpose in his own generation (Acts 13:36).

Third, leaders with vision understand that the vision will benefit people. Leaders care about others and are convinced that they will be better off because of this dream. This includes such benefits as eternal life, spiritual renewal, the reconciliation of a relationship, and much more. Nehemiah demonstrated his heart for people when he said, "You see the bad situation we are in, that Jerusalem is desolate and its gates burned by fire. Come, let us rebuild the wall of Jerusalem that we may no longer be a reproach" (Neh. 2:17).

A Single, Clear Vision

An effective leader's vision must be clear. Without a carefully articulated vision an organization will quickly plateau into a maintenance mode. If this is not corrected, there follows a downward spiral that may ultimately result in the demise of the ministry. Many churches fall into one of three problematic categories of ministry direction. Either they have no vision, multiple visions, or the wrong vision.

No Vision

The largest category consists of churches with little or no vision. If you were to visit one of these churches on a Sunday morning and ask some lay members what they envision the church to be like in five or ten years, most would shrug their shoulders and look puzzled. If you ask elders or deacons the same question, they may respond in a similar way. The pastor too may be unable to state the church's overall goals, and so may direct you back to an elder or deacon. This is the ecclesiastical "hot potato" routine. Like football, everyone keeps punting to another player.

The awful truth is that without vision these churches are not going anywhere. Many are part of the 80 to 85 percent of churches in America that have either plateaued or are in decline. They have three characteristics: they are maintenance-minded, they fear change, and they cling to the status quo. Maintenance churches become ministry black holes. The few people who are involved in ministry spend most of their time bailing out water to keep the ship afloat. This leaves little time to set a course and sail out of the port.

Another characteristic is fear of change. The primary problem is that in a decade of quantum change churches that desire to impact their generation for the Savior will face only one choice: change or perish.[9] Without a clear, significant vision for the future how will churches be able to make critical adjustments and address the spiritual needs of this generation? What changes will help or hurt a ministry? Without a clearly articulated vision, it is virtually impossible to know the answers.

A third characteristic of a church without a vision is an affinity for the status quo. The words, "If it isn't broken don't fix it," echo through the halls of visionless churches. The problem is that statistics indicate that many churches *are* "broken." Some leaders tell overworked pastors, "The reason you are struggling is because you are not working hard enough!" They add, "The answer to ministry plateau and decline is to continue what we have always done, but to do it harder." The timeless principles of God's Word never change. However, advance often requires change. Of course, churches hoping to impact society in the twenty-first century must adjust *how* they practice biblical principles.

Multiple Visions

While some churches have no vision, others go to the opposite extreme by having multiple visions held by individual members. One board member may feel the church's *unique* role is to establish a Christian school where his children and others are educated in the context of Christian values. Another person sees a church that finances missionaries all over the world. A third board member envisions evangelizing a nearby community. Though each has its merits, a better approach is for a church to embrace a single, umbrella vision that includes Christian education, missions, evangelism, and so on.

Some might argue that multiple visions are better than no vision. This is not necessarily the case. While churches with no vision tend to go nowhere, churches with multiple visions are moving in different directions at the same time. Most often the results are angry people and church splits.

The Wrong Vision

Some churches have a single, clear vision but it is the wrong vision. This is seen in a number of specialist churches scattered across urban America. Specialist churches focus on a specific area of ministry such as counseling,

9. See Aubrey M. Malphurs, *Pouring New Wine into Old Wineskins: How to Successfully Change a Church Without Destroying It* (Grand Rapids: Baker, 1993), chap. 2.

family life, teaching, or preaching. One church in the community is known primarily for a pastor with a strong counseling ministry. Another church may be known for its in-depth Bible teaching. A third is known for its pulpiteer. The fourth has an excellent reputation for a strong family ministry.

While we do live in an age of specialization, this approach caters to Christian "consumerism." People develop a "shop-around" mentality, moving from church to church depending on their most immediate needs. This presents several problems. One is transfer growth, which involves the repopulation of larger churches at the expense of smaller churches in the area that cannot compete in the area of programming. If someone is disciplined at one church, he or she simply transfers to another church with no questions asked. Another problem is a lack of commitment. If one church ceases to meet people's needs, they feel no commitment to it, and so they go to another that can. Barna predicts that "In the coming decade . . . increasing numbers of people will instead select between two and five local churches and consider these to be their group of home churches. On any give weekend, they will determine which church to attend according to their own most keenly felt needs, and the programs each of their favored churches has to offer."[10]

When Jesus gave the church its marching orders, did he have specialist churches in mind? Did he envision sending his disciples into the world to start counseling churches in some communities and family churches in others? Actually he had something more inclusive in mind.

The Great Commission Vision

It is vital that church leaders periodically ask the basic question, What is the church to accomplish in the world? This forces the ministry to examine its vision regularly. The biblical answer to the question is the Great Commission (Matt. 28:19; Mark 16:15). Yet there will always be a subtle temptation to stray from the basics over a period of time. A pastor may start a church and later discover that he is gifted at counseling or teaching. Then the ministry may begin to focus on that area to the exclusion of other important areas of church ministry. For example, an individual may be so gifted as an evangelist that he focuses on evangelism to the exclusion of nourishing Christians in the Scriptures. Another may focus on teaching to the extent that little evangelism takes place.

While the church's vision is the Great Commission, this raises a second question: What is the Great Commission vision? Jesus' mandate consists of three components that unfold chronologically.

10. George Barna, *The Frog in the Kettle* (Ventura, Calif.: Regal, 1990), p. 142.

The Pursuit of Lost People

The first component of the Great Commission is the intentional pursuit of the unsaved. This component is found in the word "go" in Matthew 28:19: "Therefore go and make disciples of all nations, baptizing them in the name of the Father, and of the Son and of the Holy Spirit." This is repeated in Mark 16:15: "He said to them, 'Go into all the world and preach the good news to all creation.'" In these passages Christ is exhorting his church to pursue or seek lost people. This "invasion" mentality is modeled by the Savior in the first century and is to characterize his church in the twenty-first century.

Pursuing lost people in the first century. The intentional pursuit of lost people is a common theme in the Gospels. Luke developed this theme in several places in his Gospel. In Luke 5:27–32 Levi the tax gatherer had come to faith through the ministry of the Savior. He in turn invited his lost friends to a banquet for the purpose of introducing them to the Messiah. The scribes and Pharisees observed this and strongly criticized Jesus for attending and befriending "sinners." Regardless, Jesus went to the banquet, demonstrating that lost people, even "sinners," matter to God. While he did not accept their sin, he did accept them and pursued them in contrast to the religious people who did neither.

In Luke 15 the Pharisees and teachers of the law again criticized Jesus because he ate with tax collectors and "sinners," something a religious Jew would never do. Liefeld writes, "In OT times it was taken for granted that God's people did not consort with sinners (cf. Ps!), but the Pharisees extended this beyond the biblical intent. To go so far as to 'welcome' them especially to 'eat' with them, implying table fellowship, was unthinkable to the Pharisees."[11]

Jesus responded to these accusations with several parables. The first is the parable of the lost sheep (15:1–7). It concerns a shepherd who was missing only one of one hundred sheep but searched for the animal until he found it. In the analogy the shepherd is Jesus and the lost sheep represents tax collectors and "sinners." The point is that lost people are of such concern to God that the Savior is willing to look for them until he finds them. The same is true of the parable of the lost coin, in which a lady lost only one coin but searched for it until she found it (Luke 15:8–10).

A third reference to pursuing the lost is found in Luke 19:1–10. Jesus summarized this section in verse 10: "For the Son of man came to seek and save what was lost." This verse lays bare the Savior's heart. "Verse 10 could well be considered the 'key verse' of Luke. . . . The verse itself expresses the heart

---

11. Walter L. Liefeld, "Luke," in *The Expositor's Bible Commentary* (Grand Rapids: Zondervan, 1984), 8:981.

of Jesus' ministry as presented by Luke, both his work of salvation and his quest for the lost."[12] To understand verse 10 is to grasp the message of Luke. The two infinitives "to seek" and "to save" reveal the structure of the section and divide it into two parts. The first is the "seeking" section found in verses 1–7 where Zacchaeus is seeking the Savior (v. 3); more important, the Savior is pursuing him in line with the theme of the Gospel of Luke (vv. 5–7). The second is the "saving" section (vv. 8–9): While these verses have several things in common, one relates to the kind of people who are pursued. In each case they are not the religious people of the first century but those who for various reasons were outside the religious establishment. They were described by Luke as tax collectors and "sinners." These are the "nontempled" people of the first century.

Pursuing lost people in the twenty-first century. The Savior pursued lost, nontempled people in the first century, and his church must seek lost, unchurched people in the twenty-first century. Several factors are to be considered in accomplishing this mission.

First, America has become predominantly an unchurched culture. Thirty to forty years ago this nation was a churched culture. Church attendance and membership were expected whether or not one was a Christian. Today that has changed. In 1978 George Gallup conducted a survey of unchurched people in America and discovered that 41 percent of all American adults (18 or older) were unchurched. In 1988 he conducted the same survey and found that the figure had climbed to 44 percent.[13] Peter Wagner estimates that at the beginning of the 1990s the number of nonchurched people was approximately 55 percent.[14] Most recently, the figure has climbed to 60 percent according to *Leadership*.[15] Commenting on this shift, Kennon Callahan writes, "Statistical research, analysis of this culture, and long-range projections all clearly indicate that ours is no longer a churched culture. Study after study and the steady decline of many mainline denominations confirm this fact. We are clearly and decisively entering the mission field of the 1990s."[16]

Second, the church in America must pursue this lost generation. Prior to the shift in the culture, most evangelism was conducted within the four walls of the church facility. Again, it was easier because the custom was for non-Christians as well as Christians to attend church. "Within the broad-based culture after World War II, people held the value that church was important.

12. Ibid., p. 1008.

13. George Gallup, Jr., *The Unchurched American—10 Years Later* (Princeton, N.J.: Princeton Research Center, 1988), p. 2.

14. "Church Growth Fine Tunes Its Formulas," *Christianity Today,* June 24, 1991, pp. 46–47.

15. "To Verify," *Leadership* (Spring 1992): 133. This publication states that only 40 percent of the U.S. population "attend worship services in a given week."

16. Kennon Callahan, *Effective Church Leadership* (San Francisco: Harper and Row, 1990), p. 13.

There was a commonly held belief that participation in church helped one to live a good life. Newcomers, when they moved into a community, were asked, 'What church do you belong to? We want to invite you to visit our church.' People sought the church out and self-initiated their own participation. It was 'the thing to do' to go to church."[17]

Today this is the exception rather than the rule. Thus, the evangelical church must intentionally and aggressively pursue nonchurched people if it is to accomplish the Great Commission vision in its community in this generation. This is not as difficult as some imagine. Many lost people are not unchurched because they are angry with the church or have an antichurch mentality. They simply would rather do other things on Sunday morning. "In an unchurched culture, people do not necessarily view the church as harmful or hurtful. Rather people simply view the church as not particularly relevant or helpful."[18]

In fact, the 1988 Gallup survey revealed that today's unchurched generation is most interested in spiritual matters:

> While the number of "belongers" has declined over the past decade, the number of "believers" has actually increased. The percentage of adults who believe Jesus Christ is God or the Son of God increased from 78 percent in 1978 to 84 percent in 1988; the percentage of those who say they have made a "commitment" to Christ increased from 60 to 66 percent. While these changes are modest, they are significant because Gallup trend surveys have shown that levels of belief and commitment tend to change at a very slow rate.[19]

We must keep in mind that in this report Gallup was citing the responses of people in a telephone survey. When 84 percent of the respondents stated over the phone that they believe that Jesus Christ is God or the Son of God, this does not necessarily mean they are all evangelical or even Christian. However, it does mean that a considerable number of people are interested in spiritual things. Therefore, the 1990s and the early years in the twenty-first century must be viewed as a time of unprecedented opportunity for evangelism in America.

The problem is that many of these unchurched people are not interested in today's typical church. Sims observed that the average baby boomer attends church only 6.2 times a year.[20] Why do these boomers avoid church? Sims explains:

> Most of the baby boomers I have interviewed describe their experience with church and religious media as boring, irrelevant or high-pressured. They say

17. Ibid., p. 8.
18. Ibid., p. 20.
19. Gallup, *Unchurched American—10 Years Later,* p. 3.
20. Jack Sims, "Baby Boomers: Time to Pass the Torch?" *Christian Life,* January 1986, p. 24.

things like: "I don't like the music. It sounds old-fashioned and strange." "It's too one-sided politically." "They are always asking for money." Some young believers I meet as I travel around the country are trying to hang on to a religion programmed to the tastes of the older generation. Others are hoping to find spiritual homes within parachurch organizations. But a growing number are deciding that the cultural pain of living inside traditional organizations is greater than the pain of pulling up their spiritual and emotional roots. Tom Stipe, the 33-year-old pastor of Colorado's second largest church says, "The church is the last standing barrier between our generation and Jesus."[21]

It is true that some of these unchurched boomers will come back for another look at the church. This often occurs after a marriage, and especially when the couple starts a family. Gallup refers to this as the "life cycle effect" and explains that young people often leave the church in their late teens or early twenties but may return in their late twenties.[22] Regarding this effect, Barna writes that "millions of Boomers were driven by a desire to raise their youngsters with some formal religious education. Toward that end, they temporarily suspended their own concerns about churches and came back to the fold, primarily for the sake of their offspring."[23]

Some believe that baby boomers are now returning to the church in large numbers.[24] Gallup does not see a return in record numbers but predicts a slow return. He says that within the next five years more than a third will increase their attendance in church.[25] Barna both agrees and disagrees. He acknowledges that baby boomers have been returning to the church in record numbers, but that now the pendulum has swung again in the opposite direction. He writes:

> Being rational people, though, boomers also constantly analyze their environment and compare the benefits received against the costs incurred. After a few years of gathering the information necessary to draw a conclusion, the verdict is now in. The Church is guilty of irrelevance. Kids or no kids, literally hundreds of thousands of Boomers are exiting.
>
>   The aberrant child-bearing patterns of the generation—and a steady stream of boomers who dropped out of the Church from 1965–1980, and are now flowing back to religious institutions—have protected some churches from this effect. The reason why things are at a crisis point now is that the balance has shifted: there are now more leaving than there are newly returning.[26]

21. Ibid.
22. Gallup, *Unchurched American—10 Years Later,* p. 4.
23. George Barna, *Ministry Currents,* January–March 1992, p. 2.
24. This would include such notables as CNN, *USA Today,* and the *Wall Street Journal.*
25. *Leadership* (Spring 1992): 133.
26. Barna, *Ministry Currents,* p. 2.

Regardless of whether they come back or not, the church's mission is now and always has been to pursue them wherever they are. Just as the Savior spent much time with Levi, Zacchaeus, and the lost, untempled generation of the first century, so churches that significantly impact the twenty-first century will spend time with the lost, unchurched boomers of this generation.

For revival to take place, many churches will have to change. This does not mean that churches must change what they believe as long as those beliefs conform to the eternal, unchangeable principles of the Bible. But it does mean that they will have to change how they practice what they believe (1 Cor. 9:19–23), which will be frightening and threatening to many churched people. But churched people must remember that the principles of Scripture, not its practices, are unchangeable. In fact, churches must regularly evaluate and update their practices if they are to be biblically and culturally relevant. Callahan believes that "The loss and the decline should be teaching us something. The ways in which we have been doing leadership are no longer working on this mission field on which we now find ourselves. In a clear sense, I think this is God's way of teaching us that what we have been doing no longer works. Ultimately, we will continue to lose members until we finally figure that out."[27]

The church of the 1990s must answer this question: What are we willing to give up to obey the Great Commission vision and seek lost people? Scripture clearly teaches that the Father gave up his Son (John 3:16), and the Son gave up his life (Rom. 5:8). Paul was willing to give up his salvation and spend an eternity in hell (Rom. 9:3). Certainly the church must be willing to flex in its cultural customs and practices to become more relevant and pursue a lost, dying generation of baby boomers and baby busters for Christ.

The Evangelism of Lost People

The second component of the Great Commission is evangelism. Christ commanded, "Go into all the world and preach the good news to all creation" (Mark 16:15). A church with a Great Commission vision makes evangelism a high priority. Besides its people actively *seeking* lost people, they are also *reaching* lost people. These churches are growing not because Christians are transferring from other churches, but because they are reaching out to lost unchurched people. There are several characteristics that distinguish Great Commission churches from most typical churches in the area of evangelism.

The first is the style of evangelism. People in typical evangelical churches view evangelism as primarily confrontational and often adversarial. This is not a problem for those who are gifted in evangelism, but they often make up only about 5 to 10 percent of the people in a church. The result is that most fear this style of evangelism and do not share their faith with lost

27. Callahan, *Effective Church Leadership*, p. 26.

people. As Barna observes, "In the past seven years, the proportion of adults who have accepted Christ as their personal Savior (34%) has not increased."[28]

The evangelistic style of Great Commission churches is much broader. First, their people are quick to make friends with lost people. They sincerely believe that lost people matter to God. Lost people are valued. Next, these churches believe that their? people have various styles of evangelism according to each member's divine design. This concept is illustrated by Hybels, who in response to a single, stereotypical style of evangelism, writes,

> How can we counter it? By understanding that there are many styles of effective evangelism. In fact, there are probably as many effective styles as there are evangelists.
>
> Only a tiny fraction of the unbelievers in this world will be reached by the stereotypical evangelist. The unbelieving world is made up of a variety of people: young and old, rich and poor, educated and uneducated, urban and rural, with different races, personalities, values, political systems, and religious backgrounds. Isn't it obvious it would take more than one style of evangelist to reach such a diverse population?[29]

Hybels suggests that six different evangelistic styles are found in the Scriptures. The first is a confrontational style as used by Peter in Acts 2. "Some people will only come to Christ if they are 'knocked over the head with truth' and confronted by someone like Peter."[30] The second is an intellectual style used by Paul in Acts 17, which involved reasoning with Jews and God-fearing Greeks from the Scriptures. "He has given proof of this to all men by raising [Christ] from the dead" (17:31). The third is a testimonial, demonstrated in John's record of Jesus' healing of the blind beggar. When questioned by others, the beggar testified, "One thing I do know. I was blind but now I see" (John 9:25). A fourth is a relational style found in Mark 5. Jesus cast a demon out of a man who then desired to live with the Savior. Instead, Jesus told him, "Go home to your family and tell them how much the Lord has done for you, and how he has had mercy on you" (5:19). The point is that he was to go share the gospel with his family and friends. The fifth is an invitational style illustrated by the conversion of the Samaritan woman. After trusting in the Savior, she went back to her people and invited them to come to hear Jesus (John 4:28–29). The sixth style is service. Dorcas models this style of evangelism in Acts 9:36 through her acts of kindness.

A second characteristic of Great Commission churches is proper motive. The motive for evangelism in many typical churches is guilt. If people share

28. Barna, *Frog in the Kettle*, p. 115.
29. Bill Hybels, *Honest to God?* (Grand Rapids: Zondervan, 1990), p. 126.
30. Ibid., p. 127.

the gospel, it is not because they want to but because they feel they have to out of guilt. This is due to the ministry of a well-meaning pastor who wants people to share their faith but does not understand the implications of motivation by guilt. The result of this approach is that people do not share their faith and suffer emotionally.

The proper motive in Great Commission churches is gratitude. Members of these churches are excited about what Christ has done, and they want to see others come to know him and experience that same joy. They believe that Christianity is not simply a better way to live but the only way to live.

A third characteristic of Great Commission churches is variety in method. Most churches typically employ one or possibly two methods in their evangelism attempts. It is most common to hear an evangelistic sermon followed by an altar call. Others rely on Good News Clubs or Awana programs. Great Commission churches, however, use numerous methods in their efforts to reach the lost. They may use an evangelistic sermon and even an altar call, but they also employ other methods such as various evangelistic children's programs and evangelistic Bible studies for adults.

The Edification of Saved People

The final component of the Great Commission is edification. Great Commission churches are not evangelistic "headhunters." They do not reach lost people only to drop them. Instead they work hard at enfolding and discipling them toward the goal of Christ-likeness (Eph. 4:11–16). In short, they take responsibility for their fruit. This involves several elements.

First, they teach new believers the Scriptures (Acts 2:42). Peter wrote that Christians are to crave pure spiritual milk, so that by it they may grow spiritually (1 Pet. 2:2). This spiritual milk includes good Bible teaching. This teaching involves much more than the communication of biblical content. It includes living the truth as well. The road to spiritual maturity is not Bible knowledge but *applied* Bible knowledge. James admonishes Christians to be doers of the word as well as hearers (1:22). In Matthew 7:24–28 Jesus concluded the Sermon on the Mount with the story of the wise and foolish builders. Wise builders are those who, having heard Christ's word, choose to practice it in their lives.

Second, Great Commission churches encourage new Christians to fellowship with other more seasoned Christians who are following Christ (Acts 2:42). It is critical that new believers see what it is they are to become. They need Christ-like models (1 Cor. 11:1). However, this does not mean they cut themselves off from contact with non-Christians. That is a false view of separation. How will they reach lost people if they do not know any? In his high-priestly prayer (John 17) Jesus did not pray that his people would stay out of the world. Instead he prayed about their being *in* but not *of* the world. The problem for Christianity in the 1990s is that too many professing Christians are *of* but not *in* the world. The result is that Christianity loses on both counts.

Third, Great Commission churches teach new converts to worship God (Acts 2:47). According to Romans 12:2 an important aspect of commitment to the service of Christ is worship. Churches make a big mistake if they ignore the emotional side of people. Worship, and particularly music in worship, involves people in knowing God not only with their minds but also with their hearts. Good worship accomplishes both. It starts with the mind in terms of its content but does not stop there. It proceeds to touch the emotions and move the worshiper's total being toward adoration and commitment to Christ.

This can take place with either a contemporary or traditional worship format. Churches must be sensitive to the people who prefer traditional worship while remaining open to those who prefer contemporary worship. Often new converts prefer the latter. In some contexts, both styles can be blended in the same service. In others, it is preferable to have two separate services. If this is not possible, then established, traditional churches must become involved in planting churches that provide more contemporary worship alternatives.

Other elements, too, are part of the edification process. Acts 2:42 mentions the breaking of bread (probably the Lord's Supper) and prayer. Acts 2:46 indicates that those in the early church were actively involved in small groups. And it is imperative that new believers become involved in a ministry in which they discover and exercise their spiritual gifts.

Presently, 80 to 85 percent of the churches in America are plateaued or in decline. This indicates that the North American church is facing a significant crisis in the area of leadership. Actually the problem exists because of a leadership vacuum. The church of the future will look to an emerging group of younger leaders to replace the retiring senior post-World War II evangelical pioneers. As the church envisions ministry in the twenty-first century, it is critical that its new leaders have a clear concept of the ministry and embrace the Great Commission vision.

Tribute

Dr. Donald K. Campbell is a man of inspiring courage who in difficult times has held passionately to the centrality of the Scriptures and preached them as relevant and vital to the lives of God's people.

The Role of Encouragement in Leadership

Michael Pocock

He crouched in the doorway of the doomed Florida Airways airplane, now resting nosedeep in the icy waters of the Potomac River. This unknown man assisted frantic passengers one after another through the exit to safety. Many later would attribute their survival to his unselfish service. What he was saying to passengers has been lost since he did not survive. But the picture of a self-sacrificing man leading others from the dark cabin to safety remains etched in the minds of those who saw the footage from the 1982 crash of Florida Airways Flight 90. He did not ask to be a leader when he boarded the plane, but circumstances combined with some deep-set inner values to make him a key leadership figure for a brief but significant moment. Some passengers never made it to safety. Those who did were encouraged to keep moving through the dark and rising waters by the direction of that man at the door. More than words, his actions showed the key value of encouragement in the crucial minutes following the crash.[1]

Leadership: Many Models, Same Fuel

People assume leadership in many ways. Some are elected to it, others inherit it, a few seize it by force, but most just work their way up the bureaucratic ladder.[2] By whatever means a leadership role is obtained, the challenge is similar: to motivate and direct others toward joint action that will achieve agreed-on goals. The only major variables are how the leader will motivate and direct.

If a leader is elected, it means that many people recognize his or her qualities of leadership and vision. The degree to which an elected leader can encourage followers is a good indicator of potential success in reaching goals. Franklin D. Roosevelt became president of the United States in March

---

1. R. Rosenblatt, "The Man in the Water: Unknown Hero of Air Florida Jet Crash Near Washington, D.C.," *Time*, January 25, 1982, p. 86.
2. David J. Hesselgrave, *Planting Churches Cross-Culturally* (Grand Rapids: Baker, 1980), p. 356.

1933. Only a few weeks before, there had been a banking panic in which five thousand banks closed. The country was in deep depression. Fast action on the banking crisis and the beginning of his encouraging "fireside chats" helped restore the people's confidence. It was the beginning of a slow but steady recovery.[3]

Others inherit their role as leader, and here, too, encouragement or the lack of it can make the difference. Rehoboam had a sterling opportunity when he inherited the kingdom from Solomon, the wisest of the Hebrew kings. Instead of capitalizing on the good will of the people, however, Rehoboam told them, "Whereas my father loaded you with a heavy yoke, I will add to your yoke; My father disciplined you with whips, but I will discipline you with scorpions" (1 Kings 12:14, NASB). These discouraging words cost Rehoboam the heart of the people. The angry crowd stoned a chief official to death, and Rehoboam fled for his life.

Dictators seize power and maintain their leadership role by terror. Encouragement is not one of the weapons in their arsenal—and a mass of poor, disorganized, and wretched countries from Haiti to Somalia are testimony to the hopelessness brought on by the policies of such dictators.

The situations that demand leadership vary, and to some extent the style appropriate to each will be distinct. The scene of an automobile accident or an emergency in a crowd requires someone to assume a leadership role until appropriate authorities can get to the scene. That was the case with the airplane disaster in Washington. No appointment, no election, no inherited role. A man simply rose to the occasion. His style was simple and direct—nothing complicated. He assumed leadership because of a pressing momentary need.

Though leadership roles are gained in varied ways, and the specific leadership tasks vary in nature and size, encouragement is always a key ingredient. Some leaders, like dictators, motivate by lighting fires *under* people. The more successful leaders, particularly those leading volunteers and highly motivated workers, light fires *inside* them, as someone has said. Encouragement fuels that inner fire.

Vision—and the ability to communicate it—is an essential component of any leadership style or task.[4] For some leaders, their visionary ability is their key contribution to the organization. It may be the main reason a leader was chosen in the first place. When vision assumes this level of importance, and a visionary outlook is the primary characteristic of the leader, those around that leader must be good implementers and managers! Subordinates of a visionary leader must be willing to assume a role complementary to that of

3. *Collier's Encyclopedia* (1988), s.v. "Roosevelt, Franklin D.," 20:205–10.
4. Aubrey Malphurs, *Developing a Vision for Ministry in the 21st Century* (Grand Rapids: Baker, 1992), p. 51.

the leader. Like the caulking between the logs that form the strength and essence of a delightful woodland cabin, these subordinates make the structure functional and comfortable in the rough winter weather. The weight of the logs on the caulk of a visionary's "log cabin," like the responsibilities of working under all the styles of leadership previously mentioned, can only be borne when the leader exercises the one indispensable ingredient of effective leadership: encouragement.

For lack of encouragement, willing workers find that the vigor they otherwise would contribute to the organization is crushed out of them. For lack of encouragement, those who would work overtime, accept, and overcome huge obstacles in the way of progress simply run out of steam. For lack of encouragement, those who would attempt imaginative new enterprises consider it not worth the effort. They did not need others to do their work for them; they simply needed to get the green light of encouragement in order to move ahead. This green light of encouragement is the "go ahead" ingredient indispensable for leading motivated people.

One frustrated worker once wrote of his superiors, "Why don't they recognize that I went to a lot of trouble to get some continuing education so I could do this job better? It seems that I can only move ahead with this project if it costs them nothing and if I take all the responsibility. It's not much motivation, you know!"

Solomon said, "A word aptly spoken is like apples of gold in settings of silver" (Prov. 25:11). That is how encouragement looks to workers intent on accomplishing a leader's vision they accept as their own. Why is it that some leaders defeat themselves and defraud their workers by withholding encouragement? It is probably due to one of several false assumptions. Those assumptions find expression in a number of ways:

"The workers are only in it for the money."

"I expect all my workers to do a good job. I believe encouragement is superfluous."

"As a leader I have assumed burdens greater than any of the workers. Therefore, I am entitled to more praise or encouragement than the workers."

"My role as the leader is to be concerned about reaching the goals of the organization."

"Innovative ideas are the province of the leader, not the implementer."

All these assumptions lead to discouragement among workers regardless of the style the leader may use. Indications are that today's generation feels "discouraged, depressed, tired, lonely, and guilty."[5] The answer to Leith

---

5. Leith Anderson, *A Church for the 21st Century* (Minneapolis: Bethany House, 1992), p. 201.

Anderson's question "Should Sermons Beat Up or Lift Up?"[6] seems obvious: people need encouragement. These discouraged workers are also the workforce that needs to be led through encouragement. If people need encouragement in the pews, they need it even more in the workplace, whether that place is itself a ministry or an opportunity in a secular field.

Bewildering challenges like the economy, the environment, family collapse, drugs, and AIDS have given rise to a sense of uncertainty, distrust of simple solutions, and fear of what the future holds. Even though the leader may have a reliable plan to navigate through troubled waters, workers will require repeated lubrication with the oil of encouragement.

Barnabas: A Biblical Model of Encouragement

The Book of Acts presents Barnabas as a model of how encouragement serves as a key to success in the New Testament. What better personal role model could we have than a man whose very name is synonymous with encouragement? Barnabas was the man who helped launch Paul's ministry.

Barnabas first appears in Acts 4:36–37 where Luke indicated that his encouraging ways had caused the apostles to change his name from Joseph to Barnabas, which means "son of encouragement." The new title was similar to that given by Jesus to the Holy Spirit in John 14:16. There Christ called the Holy Spirit the Paraclete, one who pleads the cause or renders beneficial service on behalf of another, an advocate or helper.[7] The basic idea of Barnabas's name implies not only that he served through encouragement, but also that he was a motivator, one who incited others to action and stood as an advocate for those who needed help. In contemporary terms he was a "persuasive mobilizer." Every time Barnabas is mentioned there is an aspect of encouragement to his role.

The Encouraging Leader Is Generous

Initially Barnabas is seen as a generous man who sold some land so the proceeds could be used to help needy believers (Acts 4:36–37). No doubt this was an encouragement to the whole church.

The Encouraging Leader Is Farsighted

Barnabas was a trusting man with the vision of seeing future greatness in a new convert. Having established himself as a man of sufficient credibility, Barnabas was able to persuade the Jerusalem church to trust the reality of Saul's conversion to Christ (9:27). The church was naturally fearful of the

---

6. Ibid.
7. *Theological Dictionary of the New Testament*, s.v. "παράκαλέω," by Karl Ludwig Schmidt, 5:799, and "παράκλητος," by Johannes Behm, 5:813–14.

man made famous by his murderous opposition to the Lord's people. But as Luke noted, "Barnabas took him and brought him to the Apostles. He told them how Saul on his journey had seen the Lord and that the Lord had spoken to him, and how in Damascus he had preached fearlessly in the name of Jesus. So Saul stayed with them and moved about freely in Jerusalem, speaking boldly in the name of the Lord" (vv. 27–28).

This act of reassurance by Barnabas clearly gave the green light for Paul's ministry to begin in earnest. It also established Barnabas as an influential leader who, though already having a fine reputation in Acts 4, was not named as one of the seven chosen to administer aid to widows (chap. 6). This may be due to his status as a teaching leader (15:35). Barnabas was the one appointed to consolidate the movement of the Holy Spirit when many were converted in Antioch (11:22).

The Encouraging Leader Sets Doubts at Rest

Barnabas's action in the new church at Antioch fit his name exactly. "When he arrived and saw the evidence of the grace of God, he was glad and encouraged them all to remain true to the Lord with all their hearts. He was a good man and full of the Holy Spirit and faith, and a great number of people were brought to the Lord" (11:23–24).

The Jerusalem church was just emerging from its ambivalent feelings about the possibility of God's working among the Gentiles. Apparently the conversion of Cornelius occurred just before the events in Antioch. The conversion of Cornelius proved to both Peter and the Jerusalem church that God was working equally among Gentiles and Jews (11:18). Either because of curiosity, skepticism, or genuine spiritual interest, the Jerusalem church sent Barnabas to Antioch. Their actual motive is not revealed, but this is the first reported case of God working among Gentiles following Cornelius's conversion. Barnabas was again the one to report positively on a new movement and to provide encouragement for its continuation.

The Encouraging Leader Is Selfless

The sheer numbers of men and women coming to faith in Antioch caused Barnabas to secure the services of Paul to help him teach the new believers. There is no attempt to consolidate this movement on his own or to be the sole responsible leader among the church at Antioch. This again reveals the selfless quality of Barnabas's leadership. As a man who had already shown himself to be a facilitator of God's working, he would not limit the growth of the church at Antioch by attempting to control it himself. The action of bringing in alternate leadership had an encouraging effect because it shows that others can rise to leadership and are welcome to do so. No doubt this facilitated the rise of indigenous leadership among this church.

The Encouraging Leader Is Dependable

The believers in Antioch demonstrated that they had caught the spirit of grace and generosity modeled by Barnabas. After hearing of needs in the Jerusalem church that had originally sent Barnabas to Antioch, they sent assistance to that "mother church." They also reiterated their confidence in their new teachers/leaders, Barnabas and Paul, by sending the help in their care (11:29).

The Encouraging Leader Stands Behind Emerging Workers

Barnabas continued to figure in the leadership of the new mission to Gentiles when he and Paul were appointed by the Antioch church for a more extensive ministry (13:1–3). This became what is known as Paul's first missionary journey. Barnabas was a key partner even though Paul emerged as the leading speaker. Their comparative roles are perhaps well noted by the Lycaonians in Derbe and Lystra who mistook them for the gods Zeus and Hermes. Paul was seen as Hermes because he was the chief speaker (14:12). This is understandable because Hermes (Mercury) was the wing-footed messenger of the gods. No textual explanation is given for why Barnabas is seen as Zeus, but Zeus (Jupiter to the Romans) was considered the father of the gods, including Mercury. Zeus, or Jupiter, always appears as an older, bearded man,[8] so Barnabas may have been viewed as a father figure to Paul.

Observers identified Barnabas as a leader even though Paul was the chief speaker. Our picture of Barnabas as the strong, though sometimes silent, facilitator of a younger man's ministry is enhanced or confirmed by this perception of the unconverted. Some young Japanese believers once approached an old missionary to help them with a presentation to the city council. What they needed, the Japanese explained, was his "face" to lend credibility to their request. Could it be that the elder Barnabas filled the same function for the younger, dynamic Paul—to lend credibility to the amazing message he brought to the Mediterranean world? Is not this a function older leaders today can perform in making a way for the ideas of younger leaders?

The Encouraging Leader Liberates Followers for Action

The stamp of encouragement was on the ministry of Barnabas from beginning to end. Barnabas and Paul reported on the response of Gentiles during the first missionary journey—and this very report constitutes an encouragement to believers all along the way back to Antioch and Jerusalem (15:3). Barnabas and Paul took up the cause of Gentile believers who were intimidated by Judaizers seeking to bring them under the Mosaic law. Peter led the way in arguing for liberty for these believers, but Barnabas and Paul were

8. *The New Encyclopedia Britannica*, 15th ed. (1982), s.v. "Zeus," 10:877–78.

appointed to share by letter the encouraging result of the Jerusalem conference of Acts 15. The results were predictable: "The people read it and were glad for its encouraging message" (v. 13).

The spirit of encouragement spread to Judas and Silas, two other individuals in Antioch who themselves became agents of encouragement (v. 32). And in the final scene featuring Barnabas (vv. 36–40), he was arguing for a second chance for John Mark, who for unknown reasons had abandoned the first apostolic mission in Pamphylia.

By the end of Acts 15, Paul's own ministry had been firmly established and he no longer needed Barnabas with him. But those who have leadership responsibilities should never forget Barnabas's role in legitimizing, facilitating, and encouraging the emergence of a great man of God. Oh, that a double portion of Barnabas's spirit or gift would fall on Christian leaders today! Praise God that in many cases it has.

Tribute

I joined the faculty of Dallas Theological Seminary a year after Dr. Donald Campbell became the third president of the school. He has always exhibited the encouraging attitude this chapter advocates, and he has communicated that attitude to all the faculty, which has made it a genuine pleasure to serve together.

Leadership: A Team Effort in a Fragmented World

James O. Rose

People who see their individual rights as life's most important single issue have a hard time submitting to leadership." A former United Nations representative, now living in this country, recently made this observation on the present American culture. The church has not escaped the effects of society's fragmenting condition. Radical individualism, which is dissolving the unity and community of America, has put a noticeable strain on the community of faith. Some cultures and Christian organizations have gone beyond strain to the disastrous state of fragmentation. Someone recently commented that our national motto, *E Pluribus Unum,* has suffered a terrible change. We have the *pluribus,* but we have lost the *unum.* This loss of unity that is seriously affecting our nation is creating chaos in the church. And yet the unity Christ prayed for, and which is presently one of Christianity's greatest needs, seems to be slipping farther and farther from the church's grasp. With the destruction of unity, leadership would seem to be almost an impossibility. The stress cracks appearing in the Christian community are the result of the same observable causes as those tearing at the seams of society. The gender, generational, and ethnic stresses pulling at the community are tugging away at the Christian family circle.

Below the surface of such visible forces we find what the former United Nations representative observed, namely, a fanatical desire for individual or group rights. Fanatical individualism does not reason nor does it compromise. This form of individualism does not care whether the desired rights are unreasonable or even hurtful to others. The authors of *Habits of the Heart,* a survey of individualism in American life, noted that "Utility replaces duty; self-expression unseats authority."[1] This self-expression of individualism rejects the authority of most leadership models presently in operation. Fran-

---

1. Robert N. Bellah, et al., *Habits of the Heart* (Berkeley, Calif.: University of California Press, 1985), p. 77.

cis Fukuyama, consultant with the Rand Corporation, touched the exposed nerve of radical self-expression when he concluded that the individualism of the 1990s is driven by a desire for self-value and recognition. "The propensity to invest the self with a certain value, and to demand recognition for that value, is what in today's language we would call 'self-esteem.'"[2]

In the 1990s the church and other Christian organizations are made up of people who, sometimes quietly, sometimes loudly, are demanding both self-value and recognition. How can effective leadership function in such a fragmenting situation? The answer is a return to the biblical leadership structure, the leadership team model. We need spend only a little time digging into the historical soil in which first-century Christianity was planted and flourished to discover a world splitting at the seams. Yet as James Hind said of Christ, "He recruited and motivated twelve ordinary men to become extraordinary. He molded their diverse personalities, with appetites and ambitions, and internal disagreements, into a 'glorious company.'"[3] And he did it in a world that, according to Tacitus's *Annals,* was tearing apart. Christ brought into being this "glorious company" in an empire to which, in spite of all his power, resources, and effort, Caesar was not able to bring unity. Palestine was a microcosm of that disintegrating world. Yet Jesus of Nazareth brought together revolutionaries and Roman sympathizers, liberals and conservatives, and shaped them into a leadership team that would gather a company that challenged and changed the world.

In their relationship with Christ these diverse individuals found the self-value and recognition they searched for. Finding this self-esteem they, with all their individualism, followed him as leader and became the team that would lead the "glorious company."

The definition of a leadership team emerges from this model. The leadership team is a company of individuals within an organization who are charged with the responsibility of inspiring, training, empowering, and encouraging the members of the organization in the accomplishment of the organization's mission.

A Leader among Leaders

The most acute need of any team is an effective leader. The success of the team depends on a leader who is committed to the concept of team leadership and energetically pursues subsequent responsibilities. Too often a leadership team is little more than a group of people an individual has recruited for support in the pursuit of personal success. In such situations the supporting members have little idea about the ultimate mission.

2. Francis Fukuyama, *The End of History and the Last Man* (New York: Free Press, 1992), p. xvii.
3. James F. Hind, "The Perfect Executive," *Wall Street Journal,* December 18, 1989, p. A15.

The effective team leader is committed to the mission, not to a self-fulfilling personal agenda, and continually communicates vision and the organization's mission to the team members. Communication from the leader must be both informational and motivational. The motivational aspect of communication has two components: the leader's total commitment to the mission, and the essential part each member plays in accomplishing the mission. The leader must therefore be a communicator whose total commitment to the mission is evident to every member of the team.

The church, as well as other Christian organizations, has been suffering from the same sickness paralyzing so much of the American business community. Management has been substituted for leadership. Managers are concerned with maintaining and operating the organization's existing structures.

Leaders, while responsible for existing operations, direct, inspire, and prepare the organization to meet the opportunities and challenges of the future. Harvard University's John Kotter commented recently, "Most firms are overmanaged and underled. . . . Leaders, after all, do fuzzy things like define a firm's mission, express a vision, inspire managers and provoke change."[4] For the team to succeed, the leader must define the mission and be mission-driven.

Motivational communication is to be coupled with the empowerment of the team members. By definition, each member has a crucial position and vital part to play if the mission is to be carried out successfully. A group of people is transformed into a team when every member begins to realize he or she is responsible for an essential piece of the operation. A successful leader empowers each person with the responsibility and authority to carry out the assigned objectives necessary to fulfill this responsibility.

In the leadership process a caring approach is as crucial as communication, motivation, and empowerment. The caring or servant-leadership attitude exhibited by Christ is foundational to a functioning team. When those on the team realize the leader is there to serve them, they begin to develop a sense of self-esteem. They are not tools to be manipulated. Instead they are valuable people, God's people, who are there to serve him. The team's willingness to function as servant-leaders depends on the caring, selfless attitude their leader has toward them. A selfless, caring approach displays the leader's security in Christ.

Critical evaluation does not negate a caring attitude. Team leadership, and leadership in general, is weakened significantly if evaluation is neglected. Evaluation of each team member's accomplishment of the objective agreed on is essential to personal growth. Evaluation is at the heart of true motivation and ongoing training and keeps individuals focused on the objectives of the mission.

---

4. John Kotter, cited in, "A Survey of Management Education," *The Economist*, March 2, 1991, p. 15.

Two aspects of a successful team leader are inherent in his or her relationship to the organization and its mission. The leader who develops an effective team is the embodiment of total dedication to the vision and mission. The leader's passion for the mission is the fire that ignites the team. The second and equally important inherent characteristic of a successful team leader is that of being a risk-taker. Warren Bennis and Burt Nanus call the leader the "main stem-winder." They describe the leader as "one who commits people to action, who converts followers into leaders, and who converts leaders into agents of change."[5]

To be an agent of change within the Christian community one must take risks. If members of the leadership team become risk-takers and thus agents of change, it will be the result of the converting work of a risk-taking leader. The tendency to canonize tradition and to trivialize God's truth makes risk-taking an essential element in Christian leadership.

The team leader is then a risk-taker, committed to the team model with a passion for and total dedication to the mission. The leader's objective is to communicate, motivate, instruct, empower, and engage the team members in the aggressive pursuit of the organization's mission.

The Team

Churches as well as other Christian groups consist of individuals experiencing the same forces of fragmentation as the general public. The pressures to pursue self-value and self-recognition at the expense of others is as real for them as for those living secular lives. The only way to achieve unity of purpose regarding the vision and mission of the church or a Christian agency is for leadership to be a team function.

Peter, when giving instructions to elders, the leadership team of the church, wrote, "Shepherd the flock of God among you" (1 Pet. 5:2). Engraved in the apostle's instruction is the reason team leadership works, no matter how diverse the organization or the church. The people of God are *among* the elders, and the elders as Christ's designated leaders are to be *among* them. *Among*-leaders, not *over*-leaders or *distanced-from*-leaders, become the catalysts that involve the rest of the organization in accomplishing its mission.

The catalytic effect of the leadership team is the result of contact with and observation by those in the organization. Because the leadership team functions *among* the members of the organization, their commitment is evident to all. For these individuals submission to their leader and the mission has not caused them to sacrifice self-esteem.

5. Warren Bennis and Burt Nanus, *Leaders: The Strategies for Taking Charge* (New York: Harper and Row, 1985), p. 3.

Contact with members of the organization is the essential element that completes the catalytic action. The group each team member leads is decided by his or her assignment. Such an assignment may be function-oriented (minister of music) or level-oriented (leader of young adults). In function-based leadership, the team member has the added advantage of leading among a multioriented group. For example, the minister of music gives leadership to people of different ages and interests.

In Christian leadership, unlike leadership in the secular world, the spiritual development of every member of the organization is a special consideration. This aspect is as important as engaging them in the mission of the organization. Because spiritual development is the result of regular, personal contact, it is best accomplished through team leadership. An effective team member will make this one of his or her objectives. Through this process—which the Bible calls discipleship—followers are developed into leaders who, in turn, develop others.

While developing a core group, each team member is to be inspiring the larger group for which he or she is responsible. Inspiration is the combination of two elements: communication and motivation. The vision and mission, if communicated clearly, is the foundation for motivation. Through the team the vision and mission are communicated personally and continually. Against the background of a clear understanding of the mission and vision those in contact with the leader can be motivated to have a part in reaching the assigned objectives.

Motivation creates an openness for the training necessary to accomplish objectives. Personal involvement in the training enables each team member to empower those being trained with a sense of ownership. Through the leader's personal input the individuals begin to realize the mission belongs to them. In the team model each leader is anxious to give ownership of the mission to those led. As Eugene Kennedy wrote, ambition is the most mature "not when we know what we want and how to get it, but when we understand what we possess and how to give it."[6]

This becomes a reality when each leader is committed to the team model in both directions. He or she is not only teamed with other leaders, but is also a team member of the larger organization. For such servant leaders Ephesians 4:12 provides a foundational principle. They are to use their gifts "to prepare God's people for works of service, so that the body of Christ may be built up."

For the entire organization to emerge as a functioning team two other leadership characteristics are necessary. First, the team members, like the team leader, must be risk-takers. Risk-taking can be observed when the team

---

6. Eugene Kennedy, cited in Hind, "The Perfect Executive," *Wall Street Journal,* December 18, 1989, p. A15.

model is operating. Those serving with the leader will see his or her willingness to risk flack and failure to accomplish the mission. They become part of the risk when the leader places the mission and objectives in their hands, knowing failure is a possibility. In risk-taking, failure becomes part of the training and empowerment process. Because the leader is personally involved with the one who failed, he or she can immediately begin the process of recovery, evaluation, and retraining. On the other hand when leadership is long-distanced, failure usually means the loss of the one failing.

The second characteristic necessary for completing the team leadership process was described by Admiral Hyman Rickover. As he put it, "Good ideas and innovation must be driven into existence by courageous patience."[7] A leader's courageous patience is essential in producing innovative individuals who will have an effective part in reaching a defined objective. A courageously patient leader enables others to become effective members of the team and competent servants of Christ. The patient investment of inspiration, instruction, and empowerment also energizes an individual's willingness to follow the leadership of another. In this process self-esteem is not sacrificed; it is enhanced in that each member of the organization realizes he or she is accomplishing a key part in the mission of Christ.

The drift of time has a way of dulling excitement and diluting involvement in the mission, unless contact with leadership is continuous. The team model limits the scope of leadership responsibility so personal contact is maintained. Thus, those pursuing the mission have encouragement that is far more personal than a memo from the president or a verbal "pat" from the pulpit. With encouragement there is opportunity for periodic evaluation and advanced training.

A Final Observation

Those who would be part of a team leadership structure must operate under the conviction that their primary mission is the people they lead. They are to exercise spiritual authority not for their own benefit, but for those whom they serve. Wanting a sense of self-worth and wanting to be recognized are not illegitimate desires. The Savior assures those who are his sheep that he knows them by name, and that out of this recognition he will lead them (John 10:3). Recognition by the Son of God guarantees infinite self-worth.

A leadership team is to be a company of Christ's undershepherds who recognize his sheep and who assure them of their infinite worth, while leading them into the green pasture of his mission.

7. Hyman Rickover, cited in Tom Peters and Nancy Austin, *A Passion for Excellence: The Leadership Difference* (New York: Random House, 1985), p. 51.

Tribute

Dr. Campbell's career at Dallas Theological Seminary has been character-ized by strength and graciousness. He is genuinely a man of steel and velvet. His wise leadership has taken the seminary forward to the next millennium. His sensitivity to both faculty and students has brought the seminary through a time of transition to a new era of excellence in theological education. The privilege of knowing him as a professor, president, and friend continues to shape my life in the service of Christ.

The Effective Leader

Joseph M. Stowell III

Leadership is tougher today then ever before, particularly for those sovereignly called to lead in the arena of ministry. The prevailing antiauthoritarian mood, in which final authority is vested in each person individually, makes it difficult for people to look to someone outside themselves for leadership and direction. It also creates a debilitating sense of skepticism and cynicism. This attitude has been complicated by the fact that in the past three decades high-profile ministry leaders have given the sheep cause to be cynical about their shepherds. Added to these realities is the mobility of the masses, who can move on to another pasture when things under their present leader seem unsatisfying. The scenario is further complicated by the availability of tapes, books, seminars, and television productions with voices presenting agendas for individuals to follow. Given the manipulative way these messengers are presented, it is no surprise some are led to follow another.

Of course, the nemesis of ministry leadership is that most leaders are called to lead volunteers. None of the workers can be fired (except the leader); pay cannot be withheld; there are few if any performance evaluations; and many volunteers in churches and Christian organizations feel that they can bypass the directions of their leader and do what they want, especially if they feel, "This is what God has told me to do."

Yet the issue is not how tough the challenge of leadership is. Those who are gifted, called, and placed will struggle with the challenge of the assignment most of their lives. The issue is what *kind* of leaders we will be. The temptation will be to want to be a great, nationally acclaimed leader, while quite frankly, that dream will escape nearly all of us. What is obtainable, however, is the capacity to be an effective leader. And after all, since as authentic leaders we are not in it for ourselves, the most compelling aspect of leadership is the ability to lead people to embrace a non-negotiable commitment to God and his Word. Effective leadership leads people from their ways to God's ways, from their thoughts to God's thoughts, from hurting to healing, from despair to hope, from serving fleeting passions and worldly pleasures to becoming passionate about eternity. It is about leading others to know the joy of living to bring pleasure to God. The good news is that while all of us may not be world-class leaders, all of us can be *effective* in our tasks.

If our goal in leadership is to be effective, a fundamental issue needs to be resolved. Without it, there is little hope of effectiveness. With this ingredient in place, leaders possess the potential to be used by God in the advancement of his church.

Saint Simeon, a monk in an ancient village, was having difficulty capturing the attention of the townspeople. Simply mounting his pulpit within the four walls of the church seemed to have little effect. Wanting to be a more effective leader, he felt he needed to do something dramatic to capture their attention. He built a sixty-foot tower in the village square, with a platform near the top of the tower; he lived there for twenty years, preaching all his sermons from that precarious perch. Obviously this captured the attention of the people.[1]

Fisher relates this incident to leadership asking from what kind of platform have we chosen to lead?

False Platforms of Leadership

Some are prone to lead from the platform of *personal charm*. Those with a wonderful personality can draw people to follow them simply because they are so charming. Leading from this platform can be successful until the first crisis hits, and then charm carries little clout. In addition, some people with little charm may take it on themselves not to like anyone who has charm and to be as negative as possible about charming people.

Other leaders may be seduced to take *popularity* as their platform. They feel they can please all the people all the time. However, no one stays on this platform for long, especially if he or she is realistic about ministry. How does one please both the charter members and the recent baby boomers? How does one please those who love Bach and those who love rock, or those who love George Beverly Shea and those who cannot worship well unless it is to the strum of a guitar and the pulsating sounds of drums? The platform of popularity leads to big trouble in leadership. Ministry leadership is not a popularity contest, and those who seek to please everyone may soon find themselves looking for another flock to shepherd.

Some seek to lead from the platform of the latest *programs* and ministry fads. While programs and new techniques have their place, a leadership style that is built on programming and reprogramming will soon have people out of breath. They may sense that they are there to serve the leader's whims. A pastor once told me the only way to keep his people excited about church was to keep them in a building program. It struck me at that time that there was something flawed about that perspective on leadership.

1. James L. Fisher, *Power of the Presidency* (New York: Macmillan, 1984), p. 1.

Some like to lead from the platform of rallying people to *causes*. Some leaders keep their people stirred up about causes against which they can protest. Leading people to vent their frustrations about abortion, homosexuality, infidelity in doctrine or society, or the demise of education in America cultivates a climate in which people are concerned about various evils but in which they may feel unfortunately exempt from the challenge of growing in Christ.

Other leaders seek to lead from the platform of *self-promotion*, subtly turning the focus of the ministry on their own qualities and capabilities. This perhaps is the most costly platform because it plays directly into the myth that effectiveness is based on the leader's ability to control the admiration of those who follow. Those who lead from this basis tend to criticize others to keep themselves on top of the pile, to take credit for things for which other people should rightly get the credit, to compete with staff and lay leaders for the limelight, and to initiate efforts to remove or sideline those who are threatening and reward those who affirm him and happily follow his control. The critical, self-promoting spirit of this kind of leader soon is reflected in the attitudes of those who follow, which in turn creates an environment of competition, division, and dissension. And sometimes leaders themselves are the ultimate victims.

What then is the platform from which leaders can effectively lead?

The Platform of Respect

Interestingly Paul admonished Timothy along this very line, when he wrote, "don't let anyone look down on you because you are young" (1 Tim. 4:12). Paul was exhorting Timothy to do what was necessary to engender a sense of respect among those he was called to lead.[2] The difficulty youthfulness presents to the achievement of effective leadership can be overridden by living the kind of life people readily respect. While respect is not glamorous or even trendy, it is the element that can keep a leader leading over the long haul. Even when people disagree, they can still respect the leader. Leaders who engender respect draw people's attention to their character and stimulate a hunger in those who follow to replicate that character in their lives. Though he may call them from their comfort zones and challenge them to deeper levels of commitment requiring personal sacrifice, their respect for him will keep their hearts open to the challenge. People feel safe with leaders they respect. They feel certain about their future with a leader they respect. Respect is the proper platform from which Christian workers can lead effectively in ministry.

---

2. William Hendriksen, *Exposition of the Pastoral Epistles*, New Testament Commentary (Grand Rapids: Baker, 1957), p. 157.

Unfortunately people rarely give respect as a gift to a new leader who comes into a ministry context. True, a few will say, "We believe God has called you here and we are ready and willing to follow you." But many will wait to see what kind of leader he or she will be. In a past series of television commercials for Smith-Barney Securities, a studied older gentleman, casting an image worthy of respect, stated, "We make money the old-fashioned way; we earn it!" Similarly, respect comes the old-fashioned way; it must be earned. Paul made this clear to Timothy when he challenged Timothy to focus his life and ministry in three areas. These three realities define the kind of respect that enables individuals to be effective leaders.

Personhood

Paul did not begin with technique, style, or task performance. He began with *personhood*. "Don't let anyone look down on you because you are young, but set an example for the believers in speech, in life, in love, in faith, and in purity" (1 Tim. 4:12).

In my third pastorate I felt that for the most part, things were going well. Most of the parishioners seemed responsive and supportive, but to my surprise I found myself pondering the fact that at a particular board meeting things seemed different. The difference I sensed was that the board members were interacting with me on a deeper level. They were listening carefully to what I had to say, interacting with my thoughts and ideas as though they had weight and significance, and while I had always sensed that they had listened, this night was different. As I was driving home, I sensed that I had moved into a new phase of ministry. I felt I had been received and perceived as a colleague by those to whom God had called me to minister. What I realized was that when one first leads a group of people, their verbal agenda will probably be something like, "We're so glad you're here. What are your ideas for this ministry? What can we do that will be significant?" While that is their verbal agenda, their heart agenda may be different. They may be saying in their hearts, "Who are you? What will you do with us? Can we trust you?" Not until those questions are adequately answered will people be willing to follow their leader.

Personhood is ultimately the make-or-break issue in effective leadership.

So Paul gave Timothy a short list of issues to be concerned about in his life. First was his *speech*—what he said about people, what he said to people, what he was not willing to say, and what he was willing to proclaim courageously.

Second, Paul referred to Timothy's *conduct* as a critical element in personhood. Today this includes conduct toward our children and spouses, toward individuals of the opposite sex, and toward those who oppose us and those who support us. Conduct is how we carry out the business of life and how we relate to others around us. Conduct is what those who follow a leader constantly scrutinize.

Third on the list is the standard of *love*. Leaders should ask themselves, Are people able to see that I genuinely care about them and others or am I in the business of basically caring about me? Am I protecting, enhancing, enlarging, defending, and advancing myself, or do I have a genuine heart of concern for the needs of those entrusted to my care? As the old adage states, "People will not care how much we know until they know how much we care." Effective leaders love others as Christ loved them (John 13:34). This raises to the surface issues like loving our enemies, loving unconditionally, loving with our time and our talents, loving regardless of the temperaments or idiosyncrasies of those we are called to love, and loving not just those who are like us.

A fourth personhood issue Paul mentioned in 1 Timothy 4:12 is *faith*. Faith is that capacity to trust in God to accomplish his will through our lives, regardless of the pain or pleasure. It is the capacity to realize that he will deal with our enemies, to realize he will supply our needs, and his Word will not return void. Basically it is confidence in God's Word, will, and character.

The fifth quality in Paul's list is *purity*. Besides sexual propriety, godly purity involves purity of motives, purity of heart, purity of conscience, purity in regard to money, and purity in managing time and relationships. Purity simply means that in all matters of life we are not perfect but we keep ourselves clean.

If you were around a person who exemplified these five qualities not perfectly but on a consistent basis, you would be compelled to respect him or her. In fact this would be the kind of person to whom you could listen and the kind of person you would feel ready to follow. Personhood is the beginning point for leading a life that can be respected.

Leaders who have failed as leaders usually do not fail in management principles or leadership capacity. Instead they have had a fatal flaw in their personhood, a flaw that has given the adversary opportunity to accomplish subterfuge and to either discount or debilitate their capacity to lead.

Paul summed up this first aspect of the three non-negotiable elements of respect by calling Timothy to be an exemplary believer. As believers in Christ, we are to be followers of him. Only in that believing relationship, in which we humbly submit to his leadership, can we develop the kind of character from which we can then lead. Interestingly leaders must first be followers—followers of Christ. When we cease being good followers, we sacrifice respect and diminish our capacity to be good leaders.

Proclamation

The second issue undergirding respect is proclamation. Paul told Timothy, "until I come, devote yourself to the public reading of Scripture, to preaching and to teaching" (1 Tim. 4:13). The fundamental need of every believer is to understand and know the Bible and to live in light of its truths. People come to our ministries expecting that their innate spiritual hunger will in some measure be satisfied. When that spiritual hunger is satisfied by the one who leads them, their respect for him or her is enhanced. Again, we need to define what it means to be one who effectively proclaims the Word of God. Only a few will be recognized nationally as leading spokespersons for God. While many in their early years of leadership dream of being known as outstanding leaders, few if any will be sovereignly placed there by God. The goal should not be to become the greatest preacher or teacher, but rather to be an *effective* preacher or teacher, one who effectively communicates the truth of God to meet the spiritual needs and hunger of his people.

When people's basic spiritual needs are being met, respect is a natural byproduct.

Effective proclamation relates directly to several issues, including accuracy in dealing with Scripture. Spending our words on our own ideas, philosophies, and perspectives makes us just another voice among many in people's lives. Communicating clearly and concisely what God has said in a Bible passage puts our communication in a different realm, gives it the authority of God's truth, and becomes a compelling point of accountability for attitude and behavior.

Effective proclamation also relates directly to the needs of the flock. While the shepherd may find pleasure in scholarly pursuits and minute nuances of language and context, most of the sheep have been struggling against the wolves in their lives and are perplexed about how to survive in the marketplace and at home, and how to face issues that doggedly pursue and confuse them. The public ministry of Christ was focused on practical matters. The proclaimer of God's Word should not ignore the intricacies of the Scriptures in study, but needs to get beyond that and bring the food to the sheep where they are and in terms of what they need.

In my first pastorate, one of the deacons was a successful businessman from the hills of Kentucky. He was full of great backwoods sayings, one of which was, "Pastor, don't hang the hay too high for the goats."

Effective proclamation must also be contemporary. It needs to be anchored in the ancient, changeless truth of God's Word and then adapted to the contemporary context, which may vary according to where we are and who our people are. Also, effective proclamation must be based on sound doctrine. Yet it must recognize that every doctrine has valuable implications for living. Doctrine guards our thinking, and can transform the value systems of our lives. Great application without doctrine is foundationless. Great doctrine without application is cognitive and tiresome. Effective preaching is not manipulative, controlling, self-serving, or bullying. It is simply the clear, concise, contemporary communication of the changeless truth of God to people's needs.

If our people sense that we have concocted Saturday night and early Sunday morning specials for their dining pleasure, they will remain hungry and disappointed. That disappointment has a way of settling into a dissatisfaction that often breeds less than a respectful appreciation of the leader.

Proficiency

Paul wrote of a third non-negotiable element in the matter of respect. He urged Timothy not to neglect "your gift, which was given you through a prophetic message when the body of elders laid their hands on you" (1 Tim. 4:14). While personhood and proclamation are essential, the matter of *proficiency* must be added to the list of elements that engender respect. God has given spiritual gifts to those who are called to lead, and he expects us to exercise those gifts in ministering to others. Some are gifted to be teachers, others are mercy people, servants, or exhorters. Others are gifted in prophetically pointing out evil and calling people to the good, while some leaders have been gifted to lead from administrative strengths. One thing is sure, however. None of us has all the gifts and each of us has a lead gift by which we can carry on the work of our ministry.

Unfortunately many leaders spend time needlessly coveting the gifts of others instead of recognizing God's sovereign decisions in making us the way we are and bestowing on us his wisely chosen gifts. Exhorters may covet the ministry of those who are gifted as scholars and teachers. Those with the gift of mercy, those who minister to people who are hurting, may wish they had stronger administrative skills. Others may admire those who are gifted in exercising a servant's heart. In reality, we are all responsible to fulfill the qualities reflected in each gift, but we have a lead strength through which these qualities are to be exercised. Our challenge is to maximize that spiritual gift and to avoid the distractions of people's expectations who may think we are gifted otherwise. We must avoid the distractions of demands people may make on us that we are not gifted to fulfill.

Proficiency also demands that we not spend all our time focusing on our weaknesses. A friend of mine said that he had spent many years trying to shore up the weak sides of his spiritual gift and had neglected to maximize the gift itself. Of course we should be attentive to the potential casualties that could be mounted if we let our weaknesses flourish. But we must commensurately give ourselves to the strengthening of the equipment God has wonderfully bestowed on us.

When our sheep see that we are proficient in what we do, it will engender a sense of admiration. Not that we are the best they have ever seen, but that we do what we do well because we are seeking to exercise our spiritual gifts with proficiency.

Admittedly seeking to build respect through personhood, proclamation, and proficiency may seem an impossible task. Some leaders may feel they will never attain perfection in these areas so they give up trying to lead. However, they need to note that Paul concluded this section of Scripture by writing, "Be diligent in these matters; give yourself wholly to them, so that everyone may see your progress" (1 Tim. 4:15).

In other words, Paul was calling not for perfection but for progress. Effective leaders are out in front; that is the nature of leadership. But if their lives grow stagnant and static, if they are distracted by the lesser things of life that stymie growth, then in time some of their sheep will pass them by.

Progress, however, is a compelling trait in a leader's life. I try to be around people who are out in front of me, people who stimulate my heart to say, "I need to be like that." I try to associate with people who have strength in a quality I need to develop. So if a shepherd is to be an effective leader, he or she must be making progress. People need to be saying, "You know, he (she) is a better person, a better proclaimer, and more proficient today than he (she) was two years ago." While some may be tempted to see such a comment as a negative reflection on their past, they really ought to see it as an affirmation of the fact that people are noticing they are making progress.

Leaders who desire to see their people grow must themselves be growing. Effective leadership demands progress, not perfection.

Conclusion

Effective leadership demands that we examine the platforms from which we have chosen to lead. If we find that we have left the platform of respect for more comfortable and convenient platforms, then our leadership will be discounted. Others of us may have a series of platforms on which we rely, conveniently skipping from one to the other as circumstances dictate.

Leadership should be built on God's platform, which is the platform of respect. This is respect that is earned the biblical way through making progress in our personhood, our proclamation, and our proficiency. As Paul wrote to Timothy, "Persevere in [these things], because if you do, you will save both yourself and your hearers" (1 Tim. 4:16).

Tribute

It is a joy for me to submit this chapter on godly leadership in a book dedicated to the ministry of Dr. Donald K. Campbell. He exemplifies the principles of this chapter in both his public and private life. As a student at Dallas Seminary, I watched his leadership and now as a friend over many years, I have observed these qualities exemplified outside the classroom and in the president's office. His consistency in these areas has provided a model for us who have had the privilege of being associated with him. This is indeed honor to whom honor is due.

Leading with Sustained Excellence

Jack A. Turpin

The subject of this essay is sustained excellence in leadership. Charles Swindoll has defined a leader as one who influences others. Few people do not qualify as leaders. Certainly every parent is a leader. Those in business, government, the military, and education exert influence on others. All Christians are called to have an influence on others. Anyone who chooses to do so can influence other individuals. The word "sustained" denotes longevity. This suggests maintaining leadership in the face of frequent changes in circumstances. "Excellence" is doing and being the best one can with the abilities, gifts, and capabilities he or she possesses.

For every person we could name on a list of leaders characterized by sustained excellence, many more leaders could be named who have not met the "sustained" dimension—leaders who have dropped by the wayside either in total failure or in some form of partial demise. Other leaders have dramatic shifts in effectiveness, with peaks and valleys characterized by inconsistency. The present generation is marked by failed leadership in nearly every walk of life. Sadly, the failure of family leadership is jeopardizing the fabric of our nation. Why do a few individuals demonstrate sustained excellence in leadership while many more fail to do so? This essay focuses on the reasons why some succeed.

My search of the Scriptures has led me to what I consider to be three processes that must be deliberately energized if we are to achieve sustained excellence in leadership. These processes and the principles from which they are derived have been confirmed in my own personal experience, and applied by many leaders in business, education, church, family, and individual pursuits.

Knowing

The first process that must be energized if one is to achieve sustained excellence in leadership is *knowing*. But knowing whom or what? In the order of priority we must come to know God, ourselves, our families, our culture, and those whom we endeavor to lead. The process of "knowing" a person must include a growing "knowledge of" the person and a developing "relationship with" the person. We come to know those we endeavor to lead only as we sustain a proper relationship with them. Both dimensions are essential.

Knowing God

Sustaining excellence in leadership without knowing God is impossible. However, knowing God involves more than a mere knowledge *about* God. The leader must have a relationship *with* God. And this relationship can only be established through his Son, Jesus Christ. Those in leadership roles must provide leadership to others who may not have such a relationship with God. In the past generation America has managed to remove God from major segments of its culture, including public schools, government functions, courts, sports activities, business activities, and even religious holidays. For most individuals in our society God no longer has a place of significance. The greatest need in our nation is for individuals to come to know God better. The primary cause of the crisis in leadership today is the failure to know God.

How can a person know God better? Four elements are necessary: God's Word, the Bible; prayer; worship of God at a local church; and relationships with others through whom one can experience the realities of God's sovereignty and grace. Local churches must provide environments in which individuals can come to understand and gain confidence in God's Word, develop their prayer life, worship God, and develop relationships. Packer, author of the modern-day masterpiece *Knowing God,* says, "What is the best thing in life, bringing more joy, delight and contentment than anything else? The answer: the knowledge of God, to know God."[1]

Do we know God as a God of wrath and judgment as well as a God of grace and love? Do we view God as the infinite and awesome One as well as the God who is personal and intimate? Do we comprehend the uniqueness of God in his omnipotence, omniscience, omnipresence, eternality, immutability, sovereignty, and holiness? A person's ability to lead with sustained excellence is directly related to his personal knowledge of God.

Years ago someone asked me, "How much do you know about God?" I answered, "Not much, but everything I do know has changed my life." The ultimate test in a person's life is whether he or she personally, unshakably, directly, and immediately knows God. Without knowing God we will not lead with sustained excellence. In fact, we will be far removed from sustained excellence.

Knowing Ourselves

Leaders cannot come to know themselves until they have come to know God. As our Creator, God has a plan and a purpose for our lives. Until we

---

1. J. I. Packer, *Knowing God* (Downers Grove, Ill.: InterVarsity, 1973), p. 29.

know God, we can know little about ourselves. And if we are to lead with sustained excellence, we must know ourselves.

Galatians 5 points out two forces within us that are constantly endeavoring to steer our lives: our own natural desires and the Holy Spirit. The Holy Spirit is God's Helper who indwells us when we accept Jesus Christ as our Savior. In verses 19–21 Paul enumerates fifteen traits and actions that may exist in our lives when we are following our own natural desires. Then in verses 22–23 he lists nine traits that may exist when the Holy Spirit controls our lives. A thoughtful, objective study of Galatians 5 can be a meaningful step in coming to know oneself.

When I first became a parent, I came to realize how totally inadequate I am to meet life's challenges. As the years progressed, this feeling of inadequacy spread to every area of my life. My search of the Scriptures led me to 2 Corinthians 3:3–6. There God states that though we are inadequate of ourselves our adequacy is from God. In the process of knowing ourselves, we must attain the position of dependence on God if we are to lead with sustained excellence.

To know ourselves we must know what motivates us. What causes us to act? What causes us to do things we know are not right? What causes us to react on the spur of the moment—either positively or negatively—to certain stimuli? Worldly motivations may be grouped into three progressive categories: (1) the physiological needs of food, rest, shelter, and sex; (2) the need to protect the above physiological needs once they are acquired; and (3) self-respect, acceptance, and recognition.

When we entrust our lives to Jesus Christ, God provides an overriding plan of motivation. My search of the Scriptures, aided by Ray Stedman's insightful book *Authentic Christianity*,[2] led me to realize that our motivation is to come initially from a fear of God and is to mature into love for Jesus Christ.

If we are to know ourselves, we must think through the question, What is the goal of my life? Once that question is answered, the strategies and plans to achieve that goal or goals can be formulated. The maxim, "If we have no goal, we will certainly achieve it," highlights the importance of purpose and direction in sustaining excellence. If we are to know ourselves, we must determine the goals and vision for our lives.

Knowing Our Families

Knowing our families is a high priority if we are to lead effectively. If we do not provide leadership within our families, all else pales in significance. According to 1 Timothy 5:8 failure to take care of our families is a sin worse than unbelief. To provide for one's family then is not an option. I have seen

2. Ray C. Stedman, *Authentic Christianity* (Portland, Oreg.: Multnomah, 1975).

many men and women whose intentions were appropriate, whose commitment levels were high, and whose sacrifices were great—but they failed to lead their families with sustained excellence because they did not know their own families. James C. Dobson wrote, "If America is going to survive the incredible stresses and dangers it now faces, it will be because husbands and fathers again place their families at the highest level on their system of priorities, reserving a portion of their time and energy for leadership within their homes."[3]

Knowing Our Culture

If we are to lead with sustained excellence, we must know our culture. If we are to lead those whose lives are enmeshed in the present worldly culture, we must know that culture. Obviously we can know only limited dimensions of our total culture, but we must strive to comprehend its influences on our lives and on the lives of those we lead.

A related cause of the crisis in leadership in our nation, mentioned earlier, may be the reality that there exists also a crisis in cultural authority. Colossians 2:8 addresses the problem of our deteriorating culture: "We are to see to it that no one takes us captive through philosophy and empty deception according to the tradition of men, according to the elementary principles of the world, rather than Jesus Christ." Could there be a better description of what has happened to our nation?

Most of America's educational process, if not the world's educational system, has been captured exactly as Paul warned the Colossians. We can trace the decline back to the philosophies and empty deceptions of Jean-Jacques Rousseau in the seventeenth century, views that were expanded, refined, and promulgated in the nineteenth century by John Stuart Mill, Charles Darwin, Sigmund Freud, Karl Marx, Julius Wellhausen, John Dewey, and others. In the twentieth century, America has seen the adoption and implementation of these philosophies through our courts, our education system, our government, and every dimension of culture, including our individual lives. Our culture has been taken captive through these philosophies, all of which deny the existence of God and his sovereignty. God is no longer our Authority; secularism is the spirit of our age. We have become a neopaganistic society. Our culture is governed by relativism, humanism, and materialism.

If we are to lead with sustained excellence, we must strive to know our culture better. If we earnestly and diligently pursue knowing God and knowing ourselves, the Holy Spirit will lead us to intelligent, biblically based, personal answers to the complex questions posed by such a culture. First John 2:15–16 identifies three influences on our lives in today's culture: the lust of the

3. James C. Dobson, *Straight Talk to Men and Their Wives,* rev. ed. (Dallas, Tex.: Word, 1991), p. 49.

flesh, the lust of the eyes, and the boastful pride of life. In today's language, these influences are pleasure, possessions, position, and power. God could not have been more straightforward or plain in arming us with the knowledge of our culture. Most of us have little difficulty acknowledging the condition and description of our culture. But we have not applied God's course of action to attack the causes of such conditions. To lead with sustained excellence, it is imperative that we comprehend our culture better.

Knowing Those Whom We Endeavor to Lead

While this is the most obvious identity we need to know, it is also the most illusive, complex, challenging, and often overlooked identity. Every comment made earlier about knowing ourselves applies to this group.

In vast segments of American industry, including the electronics industry in which I have spent my entire business career, we have failed to recognize the need to know our "customer," the ultimate recipient of our influence whom we want to encourage to do business with us. In the case of the corporation for which I have worked for over thirty-two years—having started the business in 1962 and having served as its chief executive officer for most of its history—I am firmly convinced that an emphasis on "knowing the customer" that was initiated in its second year of existence was one of the primary reasons for its survival, growth, and continuing existence.

Today we have seen the astounding growth of megachurches and the numerical decline of major denominational churches. The megachurches came to know those they were endeavoring to lead and responded with a capacity to address their needs. Many denominational churches, on the other hand, did not seek to know those they were endeavoring to lead and so they remained unresponsive to significant segments of needs.

Caring

The second process that must be deliberately energized if we are to achieve sustained excellence in leadership is *caring*. But caring about whom? We must come to care about God, ourselves, our families, our culture, and those whom we endeavor to lead—the very same elements we must come to know.

God's second greatest commandment is "love your neighbor as you love yourself" (Matt. 22:39). When I gradually caught the full meaning of Christian love, which involves active relationships with others, this command became the foundation on which my concepts of leadership were built. In our secular culture and in our fast-paced electronics industry, in order to avoid confusion or misunderstanding, I adopted the term "care" in lieu of "love." Caring for others is the key to sustaining excellence in leadership. The degree to which a person truly cares for another, however, is not readily discernible. Neither our desire nor our capacity to care for others is a measure of our actual caring. Only God knows the degree of excellence we achieve in our actual caring for others.

Second Peter 1:5–7 outlines the process by which we can develop the capacity to care for and love others. The seven steps in the process are sequential, each step building on the preceding one. As in the case of the knowing process, the caring process encompasses repetitive, ongoing cycles. This process that leads us to an ability to love others is one of the most applicable principles of leadership. It provides clearly understandable and achievable steps of growth along with daily action goals that lead to recognizable progress toward sustained excellence in leadership. Seven characteristics are mentioned in this passage: goodness (i.e., moral excellence), spiritual knowledge, self-control, perseverance, godliness, brotherly kindness, and Christian love. Two of these are readily recognized as vital to effective leadership—moral excellence and perseverance. The remaining five are seldom considered at all in lists of leadership characteristics. All seven are absolutely essential if we are to achieve sustained excellence in leadership.

Without moral excellence, all other elements are impossible. Spiritual knowledge provides the direction for moral excellence. Self-control or self-discipline enables the process to be maintained. Perseverance provides integration into our lives. Through the power of the Holy Spirit our lives begin to reflect Christ-like traits. Concern for others results. The love of Jesus Christ flows through our lives to others. We learn how to care for others.

I have seen this process work in my own life and in the lives of others. I have also seen the process break down in my life and in others. The most frequent cause of breakdown is the loss of self-discipline, the third step in the process. Self-discipline is foreign to much of our society, but it is essential. We need to maintain the self-discipline of daily prayer, the study of God's Word, proper care of our bodies, daily planning, regular church attendance, pursuit of certain fundamental skills of leadership, and the "practice" itself of self-discipline. Self-discipline relates not only to the mastery of our passions, time, thoughts, and energies but also to the ability to wait on God. Self-discipline is a mark of sustained excellence in leadership.

Serving

The third process that must be deliberately utilized if we are to achieve sustained excellence in leadership is *serving*. But serving whom? We must serve those whom we endeavor to lead. This concept of serving those whom we lead is radical in the business world, and the practice of the concept is not as prevalent in our churches as we might think.

Mark 10:42–45 records some startling things Jesus said about leadership and serving: "You know that those who are regarded as rulers of the Gentiles lorded over them and their high officials exercised authority over them. Not so with you. Instead, whoever wants to become great among you must be your servant and whoever wants to be the first must be slave of all. For even the Son of Man did not come to be served but to serve and give His life as a ransom for many." How many times have we heard these words but failed to reflect on what they really mean, to reflect on how they should affect our leadership roles?

When Jesus washed the feet of his disciples at the Last Supper, he vividly demonstrated that he practiced what he preached. He followed that act with the appropriate exercise of authority that he held as the apostles' leader as he directed them to subsequent action. What Jesus preached and lived was radically different from that of the religious leaders of his day. Like him, we are to be servants, not bosses. Our emphasis should not be on our authority as positioned leaders but on the humility of servant leaders.

For anyone accustomed to functioning in a normal leadership mode, servant leadership requires a dramatic change in attitude. This attitude change stands little chance of being sustained without continuing development of the functions of knowing and caring. Ten years after the founding of our electronics company, I asked God for wisdom on the direction the company should take. As I searched the Scriptures, the Lord led me to Galatians 5:13, "Serve one another in love." God had provided the opportunity for me to pursue a career in the electronics industry, and he was now providing the vision to guide it. The name of our firm is Hall-Mark Electronics Corporation. Over twenty years ago the ongoing operational vision, the governing management theme, and the daily employee-wide creed became "Hall-Mark Cares / Hall-Mark Serves." This radical but simple concept works. We have concentrated on five identities denoted by the acronym CARES: customers, assets, resources, employees, and suppliers. By knowing, caring, and serving, the Lord has enabled us to maintain a level of sustained excellence in leadership.

J. Dwight Pentecost has said, "What a man truly knows, he will love, and what he truly loves, he will serve."[4] "Servant leadership" is often discussed, described, and desired, but it is seldom effectively applied on a sustained basis. Why? Because the vital prerequisites of caring and knowing do not exist. We may achieve knowing without caring, and may be caring without knowing. But we cannot achieve serving on a sustained basis without knowing *and* caring. The essential link between caring and serving is awareness of needs. The result of caring must be the discernment of others' needs. The purpose of serving is to help meet those discerned needs. When we provide leadership to meet needs, we then are serving and can achieve "servant leadership."

---

4. J. Dwight Pentecost, cited in Peter V. Deison, *The Priority of Knowing God* (Grand Rapids: Discovery House, 1990), p. 7.

Leaders Are Made, Not Born

"The people who know their God will display strength and take action" (Dan. 11:32). We can take action today if we strive to lead with sustained excellence. The three processes of knowing, caring, and serving require action. Pogo, one of the most quoted cartoon "philosophers" of our generation, stated, "We is confronted by insurmountable opportunity." Opportunity challenges us to action. Edmund Burke is credited as having said, "All that is necessary for evil to triumph is for good men to do nothing." We need to act. Though potential leaders are born, effective leaders are made. In the "making" or development of effective leaders, certain skills add greatly to the ability to maintain sustained excellence with the appropriate expenditure of effort, time, resources, and thought. Two such skills are the ability to anticipate and the ability to persuade.

Anticipation is one of the least recognized leadership skills, but this skill separates excellence from mediocrity. An excellent business anticipates the customers' needs; an excellent education anticipates the graduates' needs; an excellent ministry anticipates the people's needs; an excellent athlete anticipates his or her competitors' moves. In every endeavor the value of anticipation is immense. In a television interview Wayne Gretsky, the great hockey player, was asked the secret of his success. He answered, "I skate to where the puck is going to be, not where it is."

God's Word provides much wisdom to help us anticipate our own thoughts and actions. The process of "knowing" gives us the knowledge base on which to have the best chance for accurate anticipation. It is far easier to "react" rather than "act" in response to the challenges and opportunities of leadership. Anticipating how people will respond to our words, how they will react to our actions, and how they will perceive our thoughts should be an integral part of leadership.

Persuasion too is essential if we are to influence others. Three means of persuasion are emotion, authority, and comprehension. To a large degree, advertising is a form of emotional persuasion. Much political persuasion draws on emotions. Parents exercise authority as a primary means of persuasion; the military also utilizes authority as its primary means of persuasion. Persuasion based on comprehension provides the best opportunity for sustained excellence in leadership. When we lead others to understand the task, idea, or challenge, then there is a greater possibility of sustained excellence.

In many parts of the world Christians boldly face challenges to their faith, even to the point of having to stand against opposition and persecution. But in America some Christians fear an eyebrow will be raised if they live in obedience to God's standards. Our nation desperately needs men and women who will develop the skills to lead others in the footsteps of Jesus Christ, the ultimate Leader. As Charles Colson has written, "Culture is most profoundly changed not by the efforts of huge institutions but by individual people being changed."[5] Leaders of sustained excellence can be made.

Tribute

Most people could acknowledge that a small number of individuals have had a profound influence on the course, direction, and nature of their lives. It is my distinct privilege to pay tribute to the man who has influenced my spiritual walk more than any other, Dr. Donald K. Campbell, by sharing thoughts and experiences about leadership principles, all of which are clearly exemplified in his life.

5. Charles Colson, with Ellen S. Vaughn, *Kingdoms of Conflict* (Grand Rapids: Zondervan, 1987), p. 255.

Vision-Casting Through Preaching

Timothy S. Warren

A student once asked me, "If you were planting a church, what would be your first series of messages?" The question bothered me not so much because I could not give an answer, but because it assumed that I could answer without some knowledge of the people I would address. For too long too many preachers have plodded along week after week, year after year, preaching whatever series seemed appropriate to them. Sometimes a series might consider the listeners, but often it would spring from a recently recovered set of antique class notes or a new commentary making its way onto the market. All too seldom preachers have chosen sermon topics and series strategically—that is, with the audience in mind.

The failure to preach strategically may exist for at least two reasons. First, the preacher may have no goal, dream, or vision for the church. Second, the preacher may not know how to move from a God-given vision to communicating that vision to God's people through preaching. Schaller argues that leaders who transform listeners "(1) can conceptualize a vision of a new tomorrow, (2) can articulate that vision so persuasively that people rally in support of it, and (3) know how to turn that vision into reality."[1] The purpose of this chapter is to propose a paradigm for vision-casting that enables the preacher to share, specifically through preaching, his or her God-given vision in the experience of the believing community, motivating them to spiritual participation.[2]

The approach is essentially rhetorical,[3] for it is through rhetoric that spiritual vision is secured, shaped, and shared. God activates vision in spiritual

---

1. Lyle E. Schaller, *The Seven-Day-a-Week Church* (Nashville: Abingdon, 1992), p. 58.
2. This is not to imply that a preacher may pull off a humanly devised and humanly orchestrated vision for Christ's church without the will of God or the enablement of the Spirit. Spiritual leadership cannot function outside God's will or without God's Spirit. At the same time God has chosen to work with human means, including planning and communicating, to accomplish his purposes.
3. "Rhetoric" refers to legitimate and necessary means of persuasion rather than coercion. According to Aristotle, "Rhetoric is the faculty of discovering in the particular case what are the avail-

leaders through the rhetoric of Scripture. The leader then accommodates the vision to the believing community through the rhetoric of dialogue with other spiritual leaders. He or she then articulates the vision through the rhetoric of preaching. Aristotle warned, however, that persuasive strategies may be misused by unscrupulous speakers or go unused by speakers who mean to represent the right:

> The art of Rhetoric has its value. It is valuable, first, because truth and justice are by nature more powerful than their opposites; so that when decisions are not made as they should be, the speakers with the right on their side have only themselves to thank for the outcome. Their neglect of the art needs correction.[4]

Clevenger summarized the communication task of the preacher when he distinguished between the speaker who exploits the audience through coercive tactics and the speaker who persuades an audience through rhetorical strategies.

"Much of the presumed audience control of skillful public speakers resides not so much in their ability to manipulate audiences as in their adroitness at fitting their speeches to ongoing behavioral patterns and tendencies in the audience."[5]

Because of the power of rhetoric in the work of vision-casting, attention must be given to it. I often demonstrate this power for students in my preaching classes. Early in the semester, before they have preached a sermon, I invite two student volunteers to role play with me as I critique the imaginary sermons they have just preached. To the first student I present a positive and encouraging picture of past and future preaching. To the second I offer a negative and discouraging picture. Even though the evaluation is merely "play," the effect is dramatic. I ask the first student how he feels about his preaching, "even though you realize we were play acting." The student replies that he feels optimistic. I ask the second student how he feels about his preaching, "even though you know I was pretending with you just now." Invariably the student replies that he feels rather pessimistic and discouraged. If the entire class picks up on the fantasy, adding their own constructive or destructive comments, the effect can be overwhelming.[6] Words clearly have the ability to "create reality."

---

able means of persuasion" (*The Rhetoric of Aristotle,* trans. Lane Cooper [New York: Appleton-Century-Crofts, 1932], p. 7).

4. Ibid., p. 5.

5. Theodore Clevenger, Jr., *Audience Analysis* (Indianapolis: Bobbs-Merrill, 1966), p. 7.

6. I am always careful in my choice of students so as to not devastate a sensitive personality. We also take classtime after this exercise both to make light of what happened and to discuss exactly how the effect was created.

The Paradigm

Bormann argued that the oral dramatizations of life that occur in small groups as members express and test their visions of reality continue on into public discourse.[7] If a personal vision, dramatized by a member of a group, is not accepted by the group, the vision dies. But if the vision, expressed as a dream or "fantasy" by the group member, is accepted by the group, it is then adjusted and enhanced by the group. That "rhetorical vision" is ultimately delivered to the public as a "reality."

> The dramatizations which catch on and chain out in small groups are worked into public speeches and into the mass media and, in turn, spread out across larger publics, serve to sustain the members' sense of community, to impel them strongly to action (which raises the question of motivation), and to provide them with a social reality filled with heroes, villains, emotions, and attitudes.[8]

There are three stages to spiritual vision-casting through preaching. In the first stage the vision is secured within the preacher. Seeing the drama[9] of life as it is played out between God and a particular community of people, preachers secure a vision that excites, motivates, and changes them. They now see how things should, could, and will be. In the second stage the vision is shaped within a small group of community leaders. The drama of life as secured by the preacher is specifically developed to fit the larger corporate vision of the group. This newly shaped vision excites, motivates, and changes this leader/influencer group. In the third stage the vision is shared by preachers in their preaching with the community at large. This public expression of how things should be, could be, and will be invites the community of believers to participate in the shared drama of life as they become excited, motivated, and changed by the vision.

Progressing through the first two stages are necessary prerequisites to the third stage, preaching the vision. Unfortunately many pastors have a vision for God's people, but do not cast that vision through their preaching. Others desire to cast a vision, but do not move through the essential preliminary stages.

A Vision Secured

The securing of the vision must originate in the preacher's understanding of God's will through his Word. "Since our vision must be God's vision, we

---

7. Ernest G. Bormann, "Fantasy and Rhetorical Vision: The Rhetorical Criticism of Social Reality," *Quarterly Journal of Speech* 58 (December 1972): 396–407.

8. Ibid., p. 398.

9. Bormann described vision in terms of "a dramatizing message or part of a message and includes characters (personae) in action within a given scene" (Ernest G. Bormann, "Fetching Good out of Evil: A Rhetorical Use of Calamity," *Quarterly Journal of Speech* 63 [April 1977]: 130).

must gain it from the Scriptures."[10] This cannot be taken for granted. With an increasing interest in consumerism and professionalism, the vision-caster must critically evaluate the true sources of a vision. Recognizing the influence of counseling as a pastoral skill and television as a cultural influence, Shelley warns that experience and entertainment must not take the place of Scripture in the Christian's drama of life:

> If this preaching . . . like television, tends more and more to evoke feelings from listeners rather than thoughts, then churches will have to supplement such preaching with serious adult education programs in order to communicate the Christian tradition to believers and to nurture the community of faith. Christian community is simply impossible apart from Christian truth.[11]

Wells provides an even more outspoken critique of the influence of professionalism and management in contrast to the influence of the Scriptures in the work of the ministry. Lamenting Christian journals and books that "freely dip their buckets into pop-psychology and pop-management theory in place of a serious reckoning with Scripture," Wells illustrates his concern from the pages of *Leadership Journal*:

> This publication . . . is geared specifically to pastors and addresses every conceivable problem the church could encounter in the modern world. But a review of all the essays appearing between 1980 and 1988 shows that less than 1 percent made any obvious attempt to root the answers in anything biblical or doctrinal—despite the fact that many of the problems addressed are addressed directly in the Scripture. Instead, the answers were taken heavily from the insights of the managerial and therapeutic revolutions. Furthermore, despite that this magazine attempts to offer wisdom on how to handle the problems of modernity . . . less than 1 percent of the essays attempt to understand the modern world in which the problems arose.[12]

Contemporary preaching fares only a little better in Wells' estimation. He cites a study of two hundred sermons preached by evangelicals between 1985 and 1990 in which less than half were biblical either in content or organization. Wells then wonders "whether the reality, character, and acts of God were the explicit foundation for what was said about the life of faith, and whether in fact that life of faith made an internal sense without reference to the character, will, and acts of God."[13]

10. Haddon Robinson, cited in Aubrey Malphurs, *Developing a Vision for Ministry in the Twenty-first Century* (Grand Rapids: Baker, 1992), p. 2.

11. Bruce Shelley and Marshall Shelley, *The Consumer Church: Can Evangelicals Win the World Without Losing Their Souls?* (Downers Grove, Ill.: InterVarsity, 1992), p. 198.

12. David F. Wells, "The D-Min-Ization of the Ministry," in *No God but God,* ed. Os Guinness and John Seel (Chicago: Moody, 1992), p. 181.

13. Ibid., p. 185.

If preachers expect to lead the church into a God-given vision, they must lead from a firm biblical underpinning. Malphurs outlines several steps in the development of a spiritual vision: Envisioning Prayer, Thinking Big, Written Brainstorming, Questioning the Dream, and Demonstrating Patience.[14] Although Malphurs does not state explicitly the importance of the biblical grounding of a vision, he implies as much when he notes the importance of "a daily quiet time for prayer and the study of God's Word."[15] At the least, the preacher will secure a vision through interaction with the Spirit of God through the Scriptures and an understanding of the existing rhetorical situation.[16]

From its biblical underpinnings, the vision will emerge out of "a recollection of something that happened to the group in the *past* and a dream of what the group might do in the *future*."[17] The nostalgic look backward and the futuristic look forward combine to give a vision its motivating power.

In the world of sports, for example, Jerry Jones' purchase of the Dallas Cowboys football team in the winter of 1989 illustrated a vision secured on the part of an individual, a vision-caster. Jones was motivated by the dream of a future National Football League dynasty. That dream was dominated by a recollection of something that happened in the past as well as an unrealized dream of what might become a future reality.

Jerry Jones and Jimmy Johnson, both on the 1964 University of Arkansas National Championship football team, "used to lie in bed at night talking about how much they wanted football always to be a part of their lives."[18] When the Dallas Cowboys went up for sale in 1988, Jones went after them aggressively, recollecting the past glories of "America's Team." "The Dallas Cowboys are the only team I would want to own. I will sell my house in Little Rock and move to Dallas. My entire office and my entire business will be at [the Cowboys] complex."[19] Jones dreamed of reliving the five Super Bowl appearances and two Super Bowl wins by the Cowboys of the past.

"We'll win the Super Bowl within five years," Jones predicted at the time of the sale. His vision included a five-point strategy for success.[20] Not many

---

14. Malphurs, *Developing a Vision for Ministry in the Twenty-first Century*, pp. 62–83.
15. Ibid., p. 239.
16. The vision-casting preacher will have to understand not only the vision, but also the context into which the vision will be cast. Bitzer identified three constituents of a rhetorical situation: an exigence, an audience, and a set of constraints that limit the discourse (Lloyd Bitzer, "The Rhetorical Situation," *Philosophy and Rhetoric* 1 [Winter 1968]: 1–15).
17. Bormann, "Fantasy and Rhetorical Vision," p. 397.
18. W. O. Johnson, "A Chapter Closed: New Dallas Cowboys Owner Jerry Jones Replaces Tom Landry with Jimmy Johnson," *Sports Illustrated,* March 6, 1989, p. 24.
19. Ibid.
20. K. Kelly, "Jerry Jones: The Man Who Fired Tom Landry," *Business Week,* April 24, 1989, p. 148. The vision included the hiring of Jimmy Johnson as head coach, the signing of a star quarterback, dropping the price of end-zone tickets from $25 to $19, trimming costs, and seeking lucrative cable and pay-per-view television contracts.

observers believed that the new owner could pull off his dream. For Jerry Jones, however, the vision was secured deep within his being. That year the Cowboys went from a 3–13 win/loss record to a 1–15 record. But three years later, and with a Super Bowl win to his credit, Jones commented, "It feels great to be the best in the world."[21] *Sports Illustrated* proclaimed the beginning of the dream come true. "Get used to the Dallas Cowboys, folks, because they're going to be with us for a long time. Here comes that dread word—*dynasty*."[22]

Nehemiah serves as a biblical example of vision-casting. He remembered how things had been in the past. "Why should my face not look sad when the city where my fathers are buried lies in ruins, and its gates have been destroyed by fire?" (Neh. 2:3). He had a vision of how things should be, could be, and would be in the future. "Come, let us rebuild the wall of Jerusalem and we will no longer be in disgrace" (2:17). His personal vision, based on his knowledge of God's promises in the Scriptures,[23] became the vision of a nation that experienced not only the physical rebuilding of their city, but also a spiritual revival as seen in Nehemiah 8 and 9.

The vision-casting preacher must secure a God-given vision from the Word of God for the particular people of God among whom he seeks to minister. That authoritative yet relevant vision will look back to the past, remembering God's former work among them, and look forward to the future, envisioning God's blessing on them.

A Vision Shaped

The second stage takes place when the vision is shaped among the spiritual leadership of a believing community. The preacher's vision of the life's drama is "chained out,"[24] adopted and expanded, by the spiritual leadership. As they adjust the vision through the dynamic of discussion and debate, they too become excited, motivated, and changed. The vision, as it is pictured in the dreams of the preacher, must be taken to the spiritual leadership of the church for evaluation and adjustment. "Birthing the vision begins with the visionary leader. Again, it takes a visionary to develop a vision. However, he cannot and must not do it alone. It is imperative that he involve others, 'significant others,' in the process."[25]

21. *The Dallas Morning News,* February, 1, 1993, p. A1.

22. Paul Zimmerman, "Big D, As in Dynasty," *Sports Illustrated,* February 8, 1993, p. 54.

23. Nehemiah's prayer in 1:5–11 was based squarely on the covenant promises of Deuteronomy 28–30 and Leviticus 26.

24. When a personal vision that mirrors a small group's life situation is expressed in the group setting, the vision is extended and develops in a chaining fashion. Bormann speaks of a "drama played out somewhere else or in some other time . . . just as an individual's repressed problems might surface in dream fantasies so those of a group might surface in a fantasy chain" ("Fantasy and Rhetorical Vision," p. 397).

25. Malphurs, *Developing a Vision for Ministry in the Twenty-first Century,* p. 51.

Whereas some would limit the role of the vision-shapers to articulating rather than adjusting the vision,[26] Bormann argues that the role of the leadership group may include significant additions, deletions, and changes as deemed necessary. "A rhetorical vision is constructed from fantasy themes that chain out in face-to-face interacting groups."[27] Often the vision will not "play" well until it has been shaped by influencers who are in touch with the diverse segments of the ultimate audience.

The role of the vision-caster within the leadership group is that of "explaining past events" and "expressing future expectations." In the civil rights movement Martin Luther King, Jr. illustrated the vision-caster whose dream was shaped by a host of leader/influencers who met in smaller group settings. King's characteristic nostalgic glimpses back to the promises of the founding fathers and futuristic visualizations, like those composing his "I Have a Dream" homily, were nurtured by years of leader/influencer dialogue. This strategy accounts, at least in part, for the success King enjoyed as a civil rights advocate.

> King's unmatched words galvanized blacks and changed the minds of moderate and uncommitted whites. Others could embrace nonviolence, get arrested, and accept martyrdom. But only King could convince middle-of-the-road whites about the meaning of the revolutionary events they were witnessing on their television screens. His persuasiveness did more than surpass that of his colleagues. It enabled him to accomplish what Frederick Douglass, Sojourner Truth, W. E. B. DuBois, and his own models and mentors had failed to achieve.[28]

King's small group of leader/influencers had many segments. He

> succeeded largely because he . . . drew on two powerful and popular rhetorical traditions. The first is the veritable torrent of sermons delivered and published by Harry Emerson Fosdick, [J. Wallace] Hamilton, [Harold] Bosley, and other prominent (and mainly white) preachers. The second, underlying, and more significant influence was the black folk pulpit of King's grandfather, father, Rev. [J. H.] Edwards, and several generations of anonymous, often illiterate folk preachers.[29]

Whether lifting extended passages from the sermons of the influential preachers in white pulpits or immersing himself in the folk preaching of his own African-American tradition, King allowed his vision to be shaped in

26. Ibid., p. 83.

27. Bormann, "Fantasy and Rhetorical Vision," p. 398.

28. Keith D. Miller, *Voice of Deliverance: The Language of Martin Luther King, Jr. and Its Sources* (New York: Free Press, 1992), pp. 10–11.

29. Ibid., p. 7.

both formal and informal settings. King "expertly blended others' voices with his own; in his public discourse, no matter how much he borrowed, he invariably sounded exactly like himself."[30]

As a renowned minister, King followed the same pulpit circuit the noted preachers of the north traveled. As a civil rights activist, he met and traveled with the spectrum of leaders representing that movement. There was a constant exchange, not only of ideas, but also of images and styles. "For Martin Luther King to be the Martin Luther King he was, there had to be a whole lot of little folk, a whole lot of unsung heroes. . . . And they made their contributions. They were just not heard loudly."[31] King gathered his materials from the input of these many sources, revising his vision along the way. He adapted, sometimes word for word, the language of scores of writers, speakers, civil rights leaders. He especially "borrowed from himself, moving material freely from speeches to sermons and sermons to speeches."[32]

Perhaps the influence of the leadership groups in which King moved was seen on August 28, 1963, the day King delivered his "I Have a Dream" homily. There was little question that King would stay within the limits of propriety at such a precarious moment for the civil rights movement. In contrast to King's placing himself under the influence of the civil rights leaders he understood so well, John Lewis, a more militant young speaker, created a real crisis when the text of his speech was circulated among the leadership of "The March on Washington for Jobs and Freedom." "March leaders were shocked when they read Lewis' words. His remarks, they thought, would mar the unity of the occasion. In a huddle hastily convened just before the meeting opened the SNCC leader was pressured to moderate his attack; reluctantly he gave in."[33]

Like King before him, Lewis had learned a lesson in vision-shaping through the influence of the group. King's vision, shaped over the years by scores of leader/influencers, will be remembered as one of the great speeches of all time.

A biblical illustration of vision-shaping is that of Paul and Barnabas bringing to the apostles their vision for Gentile entrance into the church without the rite of circumcision (Acts 15:1–2). Within the small group of leaders in Jerusalem, Paul and Barnabas told of God's work among the Gentiles. Peter affirmed their vision that Gentiles are saved by grace without the necessity of circumcision. James agreed, but added that it would be well for the Gentiles to abstain from certain practices that would be offensive to the Jewish broth-

---

30. Ibid., p. 9.

31. Ibid., p. 11, quoting from an interview with Juanita Abernathy, August 21, 1990, in Atlanta.

32. Ibid., p. 150. Miller's thesis is that King blended his voice with the voices of the African-American folk church and the printed sermons of liberal, white Protestant preachers.

33. Lillie Patterson, *Martin Luther King, Jr. and the Freedom Movement* (New York: Facts on File, 1989), p. 117.

ers. Then the apostles and elders sent both representatives and an accurately constructed letter along with Paul and Barnabas to articulate the original vision statement as shaped by the Jerusalem leadership.

Preachers' explanations of past events must also be run through the grid of a leadership that carefully shapes the message for future public and general consumption. For example, they may not be aware of events that occurred before their coming to a church, or may not remember certain events, decisions, or programs as vividly as others. Therefore it is helpful for the group to reconstruct the vision to suit a broader consensus.

Preachers, then, will lay out their vision for the future and invite the leadership to shape and chain out that vision anew. At times, as legitimate barriers are surfaced, this may mean going back to the beginning. Sometimes the changes, though significant, will not change the essence of the original vision. In still other situations the dream will be left intact with little or no change at all. Whatever the case, the visionary preacher must be willing to cast a dream before a group of recognized and respected spiritual leaders with an attitude of humility. Communities grow and change only

> by taking an imaginative leap from an accumulated and consolidated body of information on a subject and then by undergoing the risk of confronting self and others with the claim that results, a risk that may lead to the disconfirmation or modification of the claim.
>
> A person confronting self has no public risk . . . but the private risk is that an important claim or an important part of a self may have to be discarded. When two persons engage in mutual confrontation so they can share a rational choice, they share the risks of what that confrontation may do to change their ideas, their selves, and their relationship with one another.[34]

More than one pastor has gone to church leaders with a dream of a facility or a ministry program only to have it changed or dismantled by a group of wise and godly believers. Certainly it is obvious that wisdom and godliness are requirements of a leadership team. Without the cooperation, contribution, support, and honest communication[35] of qualified leaders, a vision generally fails to be realized.

A Vision Shared

Step three takes place when the vision is shared before the congregation, the believing community. The reshaped vision of the "drama of life" is "chained out" before the congregation, stirring their emotions, stimulating

34. Wayne Brockriede, "Where Is Argument?" *Journal of the American Forensic Association* 11 (Spring 1975): 179–82.
35. Malphurs, *Developing a Vision for Ministry in the Twenty-first Century*, pp. 52–53.

their motives, and inviting their involvement in the ongoing "fantasy." Vision-casting in a public setting incorporates a nostalgic "explanation of the past" and a futuristic "expression of the future."

What is true of vision-casting from a positive, spiritual perspective has also been recognized as true from a negative, evil perspective as well. In 1944 Konrad Heiden explained Adolf Hitler's political success:

> One scarcely need ask with what arts Hitler conquered the masses; he did not conquer them, he portrayed and represented them. His speeches are daydreams of this mass soul; they are chaotic, full of contradictions, if their words are taken literally, often senseless, as dreams are, and yet charted with deeper meaning. . . . The speeches begin always with deep pessimism and end in over-joyed redemption, a triumphant happy ending; often they can be refuted by reason, but they follow the far mightier logic of the subconscious, which no ref-utation can touch. Hitler has given speech to the speechless terror of the mod-ern mass, and to the nameless fear he has given a name. That makes him the greatest mass orator of the mass age.[36]

Hitler's "deep pessimism" explained the past injustice committed against the German people at the end of and following World War I. Hitler was "driven by so many hatreds—hatred of the Treaty of Versailles, which branded Germany with 'war guilt,' hatred of the French, of the Russians, and especially of the Jews (who were identified in his mind with the Commu-nists)."[37] As a result his speeches told how Germany had been stripped of its former and requisite glory.

> If anyone reproaches me and asks why I did not resort to the regular courts of justice for conviction of the offenders, then all that I can say to him is this: in this hour I was responsible for the fate of the German people, and thereby I became the supreme justiciar of the German people!
>
> Mutinous divisions have in all periods been recalled to order by decimation. Only one state has failed to make any use of its articles of war, and this state paid for that failure by collapse—Germany. I did not wish to deliver up the young Reich to the fate of the old Reich.[38]

Hitler then would speak of moving ahead to a future glory:

> To millions of my former opponents, on behalf of the new state and in the name of the National Socialist party, I offered a general amnesty; millions of

---

36. Konrad Heiden, *Der Fuehrer: Hitler's Rise to Power*, trans. Ralph Manheim (Boston: Hough-ton Mifflin, 1944), p. 106.

37. Houston Peterson, *A Treasury of the World's Great Speeches* (New York: Grolier, 1965), p. 756.

38. Ibid., p. 758 (Adolf Hitler, July 13, 1934).

them have since joined us and are loyally co-operating in the rebuilding of the Reich. . . .

May we all feel responsible for the most precious treasure that there can be for the German people: internal order, internal and external peace, just as I am ready to undertake responsibility at the bar of history for the twenty-four hours in which the bitterest decisions of my life were made, in which fate once again taught me in the midst of anxious care with every thought to hold fast to the dearest thing that has been given us in this world—the German people and the German Reich![39]

The message of Isaiah followed the same look back/look forward perspective. As the prophet shared his God-given vision with the people of God, he articulated not only the rebellion of the past, but also the glories of the future. The entire message of Isaiah may be understood as a warning concerning past sins (chaps. 1–39) and a promise of future blessing (chaps. 40–66). Smaller units, as well, look both backward and forward. For example, "'Come now, and let us reason together,' says the Lord. 'Though your sins are as scarlet, they will be as white as snow; though they are red like crimson, they will be like wool. If you consent and obey, you will eat the best of the land; but if you refuse and rebel, you will be devoured by the sword.' Truly, the mouth of the Lord has spoken" (Isa. 1:18–20, NASB).

Fred Craddock articulated the dynamic that takes place when the preacher shares a spiritual vision of the reflections and aspirations of the congregation:

> When the pastor stands among them to preach, the parishioners who have said, "Pray for us; we do not know how to pray as we ought," just as eagerly say, "Preach for us; we do not know how to speak as we ought." And when the pastor does so, the people say in their hearts, "Yes, that is it; that is our message; that is our faith." In many black churches, this response would not be in the heart but from the heart and on the lips. The dynamic of the preacher giving voice to the congregation's message is a major contributing factor in the high level of participation in preaching in the worship of black churches. Such congregations are able to recognize the sermon as their own much more than in those churches in which the sermon is the minister's own possession, before which the congregation sits silently waiting to see what the preacher has brought to them today.[40]

The Gospel of Mark provides an example of vision-casting on at least two levels. Mark, the author, secured a vision along the way of his experience. He later shaped that vision in the presence of Peter and the other apostles. Ultimately he shared the vision with the world through the Gospel of Mark as

39. Ibid., p. 760.
40. Fred B. Craddock, *Preaching* (Nashville: Abingdon, 1985), p. 44.

we have it today. Mark participated in the vision and continues to invite us to participate.

Through his Gospel, Mark portrayed a "Drama of Life" in which we are, at first, merely observers, but ultimately participants. We follow the lead of Mark who is following the lead of Jesus, in word as well as deed. We gradually accept the invitation to think, feel, and act out the new reality of going God's way.

In the Gospel of Mark we observe the disciples going through a similar experience. Jesus' calling them to follow him that they might become fishers of men (1:17) secured for them a new way of viewing life. However, they struggled with shaping a clear vision of what this new way of living looks like. In order for us to see how Jesus shaped the vision for them, and in order for that vision to be chained out in our dreams, Mark presented three passion narratives in which Jesus stimulated clear sight in the disciples. These three narratives are enclosed by two healings. In 8:22–26 Jesus healed the blind man in Bethsaida. His vision became clear only after a two-step healing, suggesting that clear vision results from a shaping process through exposure to the truth. In 10:46–52 Jesus healed blind Bartimaeus. Seeing clearly, Bartimaeus began to follow Jesus. The three passion narratives (8:27–38; 9:1–50; 10:1–45) clearly present what it means to go God's way. Finally, Jesus' followers understood that the discipleship vision includes both immediate sacrifice and death, and the promise of future glory. Not until after the resurrection did the disciples, fully seeing the vision as it was presented by Jesus,[41] share the vision with the world.

A Case Study

On Father's Day, 1979, Steve Stroope preached his first sermon as the pastor of the newly formed Dalrock Baptist Church eventually located in Rowlett, Texas. Steve was a student at Southwestern Baptist Theological Seminary, Fort Worth, Texas, and had served as a Young Life leader, a fulltime youth pastor for over three years, and was presently serving as an associate pastor. He had taken the pastoral position because he believed the vision of the new church, reaching the lost people of the Lake Ray Hubbard community by whatever means necessary, was compatible with his own.

---

41. Whether one takes the shorter ending or the longer ending of Mark's Gospel, the failure of the disciples to grasp the vision is unmistakable. Taking the shorter ending, 16:8, the disciples deserted (14:50) and denied (14:66–72) Jesus. Only the loyal women followers, having witnessed Jesus' death (15:40–41), burial (15:47), and resurrection (16:6) are left. But even these failed to tell the good news. Taking the longer ending, 16:9–20, the disciples did not believe Jesus' resurrection (16:11, 13–14) until they actually saw him resurrected. Only then did they fully grasp the vision. Only then did they share the vision with the world.

That personal vision grew out of a biblical conviction and Stroope's own spiritual experience.

The vision began to take shape when Stroope was a fourteen-year-old camper. Asked to present a devotional for his cabin mates, young Steve turned through the pages of his Good News Bible for inspiration. The stick figure of Jesus hanging on the cross struck a familiar and heartfelt theme. He spoke that night on the crucifixion of Christ. "This is what Jesus has done for you; what have you done for him?" A positive response by all his fellow campers encouraged Steve. But that night as he lay on his bunk he could not get his own question out of his mind. The desire to serve Jesus Christ later grew into a vision to reach out to other young people, particularly those who were unchurched. That vision was confirmed through an active devotional life and ongoing retreat and camping experiences.

Later in his teen years, Stroope and several friends organized their own one-night youth crusade. The evening before school began in the fall Steve spoke to nearly eight hundred teenagers under a tent in Dallas, Texas. Thirty to forty classmates' profession of faith in Christ overwhelmed him. The vision that had begun with the biblical truth of Christ's death for sinners had taken a firm grasp on Steve Stroope's life. His vision was to reach young people with the gospel message.

During and after college, Steve reached out to young people who were not responding to the traditional ministries of local churches. Even in a full-time youth pastorate he enjoyed the freedom granted his youth ministry status. But while in seminary he could not find a youth pastor position and so he took an associate position in a traditional Southern Baptist church. His commitment to pastoring teens was solidified there as he saw how unwilling churches were to do whatever was necessary to reach all ages of lost people. Only youth pastors were allotted the freedom to be culturally relevant. Then, at their invitation, Stroope met with seven families committed to the same vision of reaching the unchurched. Out of that joining of visions, Dalrock Baptist Church was born.

The original vision statement of Dalrock had been "Let's Get Together." The slogan caused Stroope to be wary of the group, but when he learned that they had merely adopted it from the Baptist General Convention and that they too were interested in reaching the unchurched of any age by whatever means possible, the dream became a reality. The new vision statement became "Sharing His Miracle." The goal was to disciple those outside the church with a "Reach and Teach" strategy. A key theme in Stroope's early preaching was balance between the reach and the teach parts of the vision. The teaching aspect had been added to Stroope's vision through a study of the Great Commission. He knew that keeping the balance of this new vision would be difficult for him since his gift and inclination were toward the reaching aspect. Over the months, the church council, composed of a representative from each member family, became the leadership core that helped shape the ongoing vision.

As the church grew it became apparent that the church council could no longer fulfill the burden of vision-shaping. That responsibility eventually fell to the staff. New ways of stating and effecting the vision were evaluated by the staff at weekly staff meetings and at staff retreats held three times a year. Then, because the church was being confused on a regular basis with a charismatic church nearby, both the name of the church and the vision statement were changed. The new name became Lake Pointe Baptist Church and the new vision statement became "Sharing His Love." Keeping the balance between reaching and teaching constantly challenged both pastor and staff.

A growing church attracts churched as well as unchurched people. Stroope faced a new crisis, for both groups had certain expectations. Many of those expectations were not being met. Trying to maintain what was already in place by appeasing all reasonable demands, the pastor and staff of Lake Pointe lost immediate touch with the vision over a period of months. No longer was the main question, "What has God called us to do?" The main question was, "How can we keep all these people who are coming happy?" Then one day at a staff meeting when Stroope referred to the church's vision, a staff member asked, "Well, Steve, what is our vision?" Once again the story was told of the securing of the vision, of past shapings of that vision, and of the present status of the vision. The original vision was reaffirmed in essence, but refined and replaced with a more developed statement, "Sharing God's Love with the People of the Lake Ray Hubbard Community." The concept of discipleship became more pronounced so that the vision included the making of disciples who "walk with God, live by God's Word, contribute to God's work, and impact God's world." A greater effort was made to keep the vision before both the staff and the congregation.

About that time Stroope became aware of the Willow Creek Community Church in suburban Chicago. He began attending yearly conferences on church growth. The encouragement he received there did not change the vision, but confirmed the vision that was already in place. The emphasis was on "doing what God has called you to do wherever you are." Knowing the mind of God, knowing the needs of the people, and knowing the resources of the local congregation were affirmed as the prerequisites of a particular church's vision.

As Stroope worked with the staff as his core leader/influence group, he soon came to realize that he had unwittingly placed the staff in a compromising position. How could they make unbiased decisions regarding the vision and its implementation if their own budgets and/or jobs might be threatened by adjustments in the vision? He began to pull away and make more of the vision decisions on his own. That was not satisfactory either. Even if church members and staff trusted his integrity and wisdom, Stroope decided he could not take that burden on himself. As a result, a board of elders was formed with the approval of the congregation. Now this board, formally, along with other leader/influencers informally, helps shape the vision of Lake Pointe Baptist Church. The major contribution of the board comes not so much in securing a new vision for the church, but in clearly identifying the present vision's theological underpinnings and shaping its reality and timing. For example, the elders often slow down the implementation of certain plans in order to prepare better for their success.

Over the years, another aspect of the Lake Pointe vision had been forming in Stroope's mind and heart. Influenced particularly by the ministry of Jesus in the Gospels, Stroope eventually articulated a missing piece of the vision. Jesus reached people who otherwise would not have been reached by ministering to their physical, emotional, and psychological needs. What Lake Pointe needed to do was reach out, not only to those who attend church already, not only to those who would attend if invited by a friend, but also to those who would never think of attending a church. There was a third field out there to harvest that would be reached only if the church met them on their own turf. At least two results have followed the securing of that new aspect of the original Lake Pointe vision. First, a new vision statement more fully reflects the target people and the ultimate goal of Lake Pointe. "God has called us to share his love with the unchurched people of the Lake Ray Hubbard Community in such a way that they have the greatest opportunity to become fully developing followers of Christ." Second, a new $2.2 million Lake Pointe Community Center building is being built on five and one-half acres of land adjacent to the church. The building, which will be physically unconnected to the present facility, will be used specifically for community outreach.

Over the years the vision of Lake Pointe, at whatever stage of development, has been shared in a number of ways. Church literature, mailings, and billboards have carried the slogan. Outreach ministries have emphasized the message of "Sharing God's Love." New members classes and receptions have provided opportunities to state and explain the vision to those who have not previously been exposed to it. Congregational meetings and town hall meetings provide the same opportunity for long-standing members and other interested attendees. Leadership summits, as well as staff and elder retreats, keep the vision before the leader/influencers for ongoing discussion.

For the congregation as a whole, however, no means is more effective than when Pastor Steve makes reference to the Lake Pointe vision in a sermon. It usually comes in the form of an allusion to his original vision as a teenager, a reference to the bait house where the original group met and articulated that first vision statement, or a reference to plans that are underway to fulfill the vision in the future. The recollections of the past are nostalgic, but realistic. The dreams of the future are presented as possible and necessary. At least twice a year Stroope preaches on the church's vision, usually in January and in June, on the anniversary of the church. The emphasis is on how the Lake Pointe vision is intentionally grounded in the Bible. Throughout the year, when a sermon's theme in any way alludes to the church's vision, Stroope demonstrates how the Bible and the vision are connected. This pastor maintains an enduring commitment to articulating the vision to the church and inviting God's people to participate. He has learned that the preacher cannot make the assumption that his listeners understand and live the vision. Even as it is constantly being renewed and revised, the vision must be shared again and again.

Tribute

The ministry is more than teaching the Scriptures and leading God's people. While I was a student at Dallas Seminary Dr. Campbell's telling about his son's football accomplishments caused me to realize that he, my teacher, was a genuine person. Years later when I was recovering from a long and serious illness, Don's showing care and patience caused me, one of his faculty members, to see his heart for those whom he served. I have known Don Campbell as not only my teacher and my leader, but also my friend. Thank you, Don, for your ministry and the difference you have made in my life.

Insights into Pastoral Counseling from John Owen

John D. Hannah

The annals of Christian history witness to a rich heritage of concern and compassion for the troubled. The phrase used in previous centuries to express pastoral care was "the cure of souls"; its more contemporary designation is "counseling."[1] The rise of the Enlightenment in the eighteenth century, with its emphasis on the role of the individual and the importance of the mind or reason as the final arbiter of truth (i.e., a focus on the internal, subjective self rather than imposed external authority such as the church or the Bible), brought profound changes in the methodology and content of advice-giving. Because it established insight into malevolent motives and their remedy in pre-Christian sources, the emerging movement became a powerful rival to the traditional views pastors offered.

In a counseling ministry two crucial and underlying questions must be faced. First, an accounting for the person's plight is important. Here the issue is the discovery of the fountainhead of the client's or parishioner's dilemma. What causes a person to manifest certain negative behavioral traits? Second, a perception of the methodology of behavior modification is vital. Here the question is about change and how it is brought to fruition. What is a person capable of doing? How can a person be directed to change?

A wide variety of solutions to these questions have been suggested. Secular psychologists, including behaviorists, psychoanalysts, personalists, and transpersonalists, have identified the root of behavioral dysfunction in a variety of external and internal factors. John Watson and B. F. Skinner rejected the role of the unconscious as the determinant of behavior to suggest that actions are a function of social influences. Sigmund Freud (1856–1939), followed by Alfred Adler (1870–1937) and Carl Jung (1875–1961), argued that

---

1. The history of pastoral care has been summarized in two particularly useful volumes: John T. McNeill, *A History of the Cure of Souls* (New York: Harper and Brothers, 1951); and William A. Clebsch and Charles R. Jaekle, *Pastoral Care in Historical Perspective* (Englewood Cliffs, N.J.: Prentice-Hall, 1964).

348

the key to behavior patterns is in the realm of the unconscious (i.e., the world of memory). For Carl Rogers, a personalist, the catalyst is the quest for the true, deeper self. In Maslow's transpersonal terminology it is the human quest for self-realization or self-actualization, a labyrinthine journey into the self. In each case the roots of dysfunction are to be found in external forces that have come on the client as an involuntary victim; the solutions, other than the environmental or statist behaviorism, is in the discovery of the self and one's potential (i.e., self-worth, the realization that *I'm OK, You're OK*,[2] to quote a well-known book on transactional analysis).[3]

Realizing that the fundamental weakness of secular psychology is its unbiblical, humanistic anthropology, Christian counselors have responded in one of two ways. Segregationalists (to coin a term) like Jay Adams have argued that the insights of secular psychology are not only misleading but are also completely useless and destructive. To quote Tertullian's much-used question, "What has Jerusalem to do with Athens, the church with the academy, the Christian with the heretic?" Accepting Cornelius Van Til's sharp dualism between Christ and the world, as well as correctly faulting secularists for errant views of God, creation, and man, Adams stridently rejects psychological insights for an aggressively perceived, Bible-only approach to counseling.[4]

Integrationists like Larry Crabb, on the other hand, have argued that insights drawn from the social sciences should not be rejected out of hand (though extreme caution is warranted) because there is much to be gained from this form of natural revelation.[5] While the use of information derived from the observation of behavior has been criticized by some Christian counselors,[6] others have embraced some of its interpretive insights and remedies,

---

2. Thomas Harris, *I'm OK—You're OK* (New York: Harper and Row, 1969).

3. I am dependent on Roger F. Hurding's excellent volume, *The Tree of Healing: Psychological and Biblical Foundations for Counseling and Pastoral Care* (Grand Rapids: Zondervan, 1985), for an analysis of the various approaches to counseling.

4. Jay E. Adams' approach, known as nouthetic counseling, is set forth in his *Competent to Counsel* (Grand Rapids: Baker, 1973). Adams, however, tends to be one-sided in his biblical approach; that is, he has reduced to a formula what the biblical revelation has left less rigid and simple. Simply stated, the Bible is more complex in its remedy for the struggling saints' dilemmas than Adams' perspective implies. For him, the key to unlocking a person's problems is confrontational and verbal. He overemphasizes the necessity of the counselor to the point (seemingly) of deemphasizing the necessity of the Spirit of God to work change in the heart. No doubt he embraces the biblical truth of the work of the Holy Spirit, but it is not evident in his biblical description of nouthetic counseling (ibid., 41–64).

5. Hurdling, *Tree of Healing*, pp. 243–74.

6. The most strident criticism of integrationalism by segregationalist counselors has been in the writings of Marton Bobgan and Deidre Bobgan. Bobgan is an educational psychologist who expressed his antipathy for much of general Christian counseling in the book, *The Psychological Way/The Spiritual Way* (Minneapolis: Bethany House, 1979). A summary of their counseling approach is presented in Hurdling, *Tree of Healing*, pp. 291–92. Their most bombastic criticism of their peers is found in *Psychoheresy: The Psychological Seduction of Christianity* (Santa Barbara, Calif.: East Gate, 1987) and *Prophets of Psychoheresy I* (Santa Barbara, Calif.: East Gate, 1989).

written various self-insight books, and emerged as well-known biblical counselors.

In addition to professional Christian counselors, theologians have set forth a dizzying array of procedures for dealing with behavioral dysfunction (most are agreed as to the root of man's problem). Unlike secularists, Christian theologians generally have perceived the human dilemma through the lens of Scripture. However, they often speak of the issue in theological jargon (e.g., sanctification) rather than using psychological terms. Whether it is a Holiness, Keswick, or Pentecostal model for the Christian life, the emphasis on faith (i.e., "you believe it, so simply trust") is often little more than psychological gymnastics. These theologians often err in being simplistic and reductionistic. As sometimes presented, victory over sin is a matter of following correct procedures with wholehearted trust; inability to obtain the promised results often leads to delusion and despondency. Some such schemes, at least as popularly presented, promise too much, thus bringing confusion to tenderhearted realists. This approach does not take into account the struggle with sin as an ever-enduring process, and results in discouragement for those anticipating a quick fix. All this can easily lead to an even greater sense of guilt; they simply do not deliver according to their own promises.[7]

In the preface to an edition of John Owen's works, J. I. Packer recounted his own struggle with the Holiness theory of the victorious life and his sense of haunting failure. As a result, he turned to the saving insight of the biblically oriented wisdom of that master counselor, the chancellor of Oxford University in the seventeenth century, the puritan divine, John Owen.[8] Packer wrote, "I still think after thirty-five years that Owen did more than anyone else to make me as much of a moral, spiritual, and theological realist as I have so far become. . . . It is not too much at all to say that God used him to save my sanity."[9]

This brief essay is offered with the prayer that those who struggle to maintain their sanity in the battle with sin will find in Owen's description and pre-

7. For a review of the various views on sanctification, see J. I. Packer, *Keep in Step with the Spirit* (Old Tappan, N.J.: Revell, 1984). A recent poignant criticism of the Holiness-oriented notion of sanctification is found in Douglas W. Frank, *Less Than Conquerors: How Evangelicals Entered the Twentieth Century* (Grand Rapids: Eerdmans, 1986), pp. 167–231. Two insightful articles compare Owen's view to Holiness and Keswick interpretations: Peter Golding, "Owen on the Mortification of Sin: 1," *Banner of Truth* (June 1990), pp. 13–16; and idem, "Owen on the Mortification of Sin: 2," *Banner of Truth* (July 1990), pp. 20–24.

8. For a biography of John Owen, see Peter Toon, *God's Swordsman: The Life and Work of John Owen* (Grand Rapids: Zondervan, 1973). Owen has been called "the John Calvin of England" and the "Atlas and Patriarch of Puritanism" (Allen C. Guelzo, "John Owen, Puritan Pacesetter," *Christianity Today,* May 21, 1976, pp. 14–16).

9. J. I. Packer, in John Owen, *Sin and Temptation: The Challenge to Personal Godliness,* abridged and edited by James M. Houston (Portland, Oreg.: Multnomah, 1983), p. xxix. In another place the same author noted that Owen "lived in an age of giants, and I think he over-tops them all" (quoted in Guelzo, "John Owen, Puritan Pacesetter," p. 14).

scription of the human dilemma a realistic, practical, and workable approach to the task and joy of becoming more Christ-like.

John Owen and the Human Dilemma

Owen's major works on the doctrine of the spiritual life—namely, mankind's fault and rescue, or man's sin and redemption in Christ—are in the sixth and seventh volumes of his collected works. They include *A Treatise of the Dominion of Sin and Grace; Of Temptation: The Nature and Power of It; The Nature, Power, Deceit, and Prevalency of the Remainders of Indwelling Sin in Believers;* and *On the Mortification of Sin in Believers.*[10] Three other works provide further insight: *The Grace and Duty of Believing Spiritually Minded; A Discourse of the Work of the Holy Spirit in Prayer;* and *A Discourse of the Holy Spirit as a Comforter* (the latter two are in the fourth volume of his collected works). These will be analyzed in an effort to offer Owen's timeless insights into the two major questions faced by secular psychologists, Christian counselors, and theologians: What is the fundamental cause of behavioral dysfunction? How is it corrected?

The Dominion of Sin: The Reality of Brokenness

Owen's treatise, *The Dominion of Sin and Grace,* is a detailed explanation of Romans 6:14: "For sin shall not be master over you, for you are not under law, but under grace." Owen's point is that believers, by their identity with Christ, have been set free from the deceitful, universal grip of sin. This, he argues, can be seen by reflecting on the characteristics of sin's dominion, which has an unrelenting vicelike hold on the unbeliever. Dominion is evident when, for example, there is a state or condition of perpetual continuance of evil practices, when there is a consistent rejecting of warnings, when there is a malicious contempt for the ways of God, and when there is a resolute rejection of any means of grace.[11] In brief, "The dominion of sin is present when sin exercises control over the will of a man with no opposition from another principle."[12]

Though sin, says Owen, remains in the believer, never to be eradicated in this life, and its general design is total domination through deceit or force, the believer has experienced the wonderful reality of degrees of victory over sin. This is evident for several reasons. First, sin is now occasional; though its roots lie deep in the heart, wickedness is now easily discerned. Second, sin is now afflictive; it is a burden to the soul whereas previously it was a delight. Third,

10. William H. Goold, ed., *The Works of John Owen,* 16 vols. (reprint, Carlisle, Pa.: Banner of Truth Trust, 1965).
11. Ibid., 7:517–22, 534–42.
12. Ibid., p. 518.

the lust or desire that causes sin is detested by the heart and mind. Sin is an offense to the child of God that gravely disappoints and profoundly wounds.[13]

To illustrate the point Owen invokes the image of a forest. Before the Lord's mercy in redemption a person's life can be characterized as a dense tangle of trees, vines, and underbrush. The ground is completely covered; there are no clearings and the light never penetrates to the soil. Sin, like a dense jungle, completely dominates the entire landscape of man's being: intellect, emotions, and will.

The Indwelling of Sin: An Ever-Present Reality

While the Bible suggests that the dominion of sin has been utterly crushed, the Bible also attests to the believer's continual struggle with sin. In his treatise *The Nature, Power, Deceit, and Prevalency of the Remainders of Indwelling Sin in Believers,* Owen grapples with Paul's statement in Romans 7:21; "I find then the principle of sin in me." Owen attempts to deal with the apparent contradiction between sin's defeat and its ongoing activity. In essence, the universal hold of sin endures. Ferguson has stated, "The nature of sin does not change in regeneration or sanctification, but its status in us is radically attired."[14] Owen is quite explicit: "Grace changeth the nature of man, but nothing can change the nature of sin."[15] Indeed, "the man that understands the evil of his own heart, how vile it is, is the only useful, fruitful, and solid believing and obedient person."[16]

To return to the illustration of the dense forest, Owen argues that the dominion of sin no longer exists for the believer, not because the forest has been completely cleared, but because many of the trees and some of the underbrush have been destroyed. The totality of sin's hold has been broken because the grip of its power over all the trees has been decidedly reduced. Some areas (i.e., trees) where sin reigned without any influence to the contrary no longer exists. The forest is still present, but there are now clearings, areas where trees have been uprooted and the tangle of vines removed. To express it another way, in God's mighty act of redemption his renovating, revivifying grace removed some of the towering trees in the believer's life. Among some of the trees the growth has been retarded by pruning; others remain untouched by grace. In it all, however, sin no longer controls one's totality.

Owen describes the reality of indwelling sin graphically: "Men harbor spirit-devouring lusts in their bosoms, that lie as worms, at the root of their obedience, and corrode and weaken it day by day."[17] The mind, the arena of

13. Ibid., pp. 522–24.
14. Sinclair B. Ferguson, *John Owen on the Christian Life* (Carlisle, Pa.: Banner of Truth Trust, 1987), pp. 125–26.
15. *Works of John Owen,* 6:177.
16. Ibid., p. 201.

spiritual battle, deals with sin in several ways. First, the mind reflects on sin in generalities, not on sin in terms of specifics; it is the idea of wickedness, not one's own act of wickedness. Therefore a believer dismisses the gravity of sin through deceit. Second, the mind enjoys secret sins while simultaneously attempting to glorify God in other ways. Third, the mind can become so engaged in activities that it is often unaware of sin's danger; that is, sin literally catches us by surprise. Fourth, sin causes the mind to become slothful, unwilling, weak, ineffective, and unable to fight off discouragement.[18] In the same treatise Owen comments that "where it [sin] is least felt, it is most powerful."[19]

The Temptation to Sin:
The Constancy of Outward Solicitation

The potency of evil in the believer can be seen in Owen's analysis of the way an individual falls into sin. To Owen, sin is such a common fact of life that temptation, its instrumental cause, became the focus of a treatise. *Of Temptation: The Nature and Power of It* is an exposition of Matthew 26:41, "Keep watching and praying, that you may not enter into temptation." A person may be displeased with sin, but is often disposed to temptation. Until the believer fears temptation he or she will never have victory over it. Owen offers the perceptive inquiry, "How [can] a man . . . know when he is entered into temptation?"[20] It occurs when lust and solicitation meet with occasions and opportunities for its provocation. "Also a person may know he or she has entered into temptation when there is the discovery that the duties of the Christian life are performed with no satisfaction or joy."[21]

In addition to the fact of outward or external solicitations that frequently find fertile soil for sin's growth, there are times when temptations arise within the believer; these seasons require careful scrutiny. "There are sundry seasons wherein an hour of temptation is commonly at hand, and will unavoidably seize upon the soul, unless it be delivered by mercy in the use of watchfulness."[22] Owen enumerated four such seasons: times of unusual outward prosperity ("prosperity and temptation go together"[23]), times of spiritual coldness and periods of formality in duties, times of great spiritual success ("men cheat their souls with their own fancies"), and times of self-confidence as in Peter's affirmation, "I will not deny thee."[24]

17. Ibid., p. 162.
18. Ibid., pp. 189–90.
19. Ibid., p. 159.
20. Ibid., p. 119.
21. Ibid., pp. 117–22.
22. Ibid., p. 127.
23. Ibid.
24. Ibid., p. 130.

That the Scriptures warn believers of the need for constant watchfulness is an incontrovertible evidence of the reality of indwelling sin. To Owen, if sin is not an ever-present possibility the Bible's warnings to be watchful are ludicrous.

John Owen and the Human Solution

Secular psychologists, who suggest that the locus of the human dilemma is some form of victimization (i.e., environmental and involuntary), have sought to establish the remedy in personal insight and self-determination. Integrationist psychologists have generally sought to use the insights of their secular counterparts and go beyond natural theology in the description of both the human condition and its amelioration; they have attempted to combine the insights and benefits of both spheres. Christian theologians have intended, at least as evidenced in the major schemes of sanctification, to exclude emotional, environmental factors for rational, "objective" explanations and solutions.

For Owen, like his English contemporaries, the remedy for sin's *dominion* has a single cause: it is the regenerating work of God the Spirit. The solution to *indwelling* sin in the believer involves both a divine work and a human response. Ferguson has succinctly summarized the point as follows: "As in the inauguration of the new life, there is the *act* of regeneration, producing the *exercise* of God-given faith, so in sanctification, there is the *work* of grace, producing the exercise of duty, and the response of obedience."[25] Owen states the point this way:

> Sanctification is an immediate work of the Spirit of God on the souls of believers, purifying and cleansing their natures from the pollution and uncleanness of sin, renewing in them the image of God, and thereby enabling them, from a spiritual and habitual principle of grace, to yield obedience unto God, according unto the tenor and terms of the new covenant, by virtue of the life and death of Jesus Christ. Or more briefly: It is the universal renovation of our natures by the Holy Spirit unto the image of God through Jesus Christ.[26]

While the objective cure for sin's destruction is the redemptive work of Jesus Christ applied through the grace of God and bestowed by the Holy Spirit, the subjective cure is the Spirit's work in the redeemed by which he calls them to daily obedience. The latter ministry of God's Spirit focuses on the progressive diminution of the power of indwelling sin. This work is described by the Puritans as twofold, according to Packer: "Sanctification has a double aspect. Its positive side is *vivification*, the growing and maturing

25. Ferguson, *John Owen on the Christian Life*, p. 55.
26. *Works of John Owen*, 3:386.

of the new man; its negative side is *mortification,* the weakening and killing of the old man."[27] Though the focus of this essay is on the latter aspect of sanctification, a brief notice of facets of the former will be delineated.

Vivification: The Renewal of the Believer

According to Owen a variety of acts help foster spiritual progress. His work *The Grace and Duty of Being Spiritually Minded* capsulizes numerous important points. The treatise pivots around Romans 8:6, "For the mind set on the flesh is death, but the mind set on the spirit is life and peace." For Owen the sphere of sanctification is the mind, while the end of sanctification is renewed affections. Central to the duty of being spiritual-minded is a constancy of reflection for God himself.[28] When the mind is filled with such delight or relish for God, the affections are spiritual;[29] opposite preoccupations of the mind are either earthly worries or vain imaginations. One of the means for the promotion of spiritual-mindedness and heavenly affections is prayer. "One principal end of it [prayer] is to excite, stir up, and draw forth the principle of grace, of faith and of love in the heart, unto a due exercise in holy thoughts of God and spiritual things, with affections suitable unto them."[30]

The corporate aspects of positive steps to diminish the grip of indwelling sin (i.e., the fruit of the flesh) are also crucial. In fact, the duties of saints to the church and its ordinances are vital. For example, on the importance of hearing the Word of God proclaimed, Owen writes the following:

> Such a means is the *preaching of the Word itself.* It is observed concerning many in the gospel, that they heard it willingly, received it with joy, and did many things gladly, upon the preaching of it; and we see the same thing exemplified in multitudes every day. But none of these things can be without many thoughts in the minds of such persons about the spiritual things of the word; for they are the affects of such thoughts, and, being wrought in the mind of men, will produce more of the same nature.[31]

Also essential for spiritual progress is the often-neglected art of meditation and memorization. "Whosoever shall sincerely engage in this duty," says Owen, "and shall abide constant therein, he will make such a refreshing progress in his apprehension of heavenly things as he will be greatly satisfied withal."[32] In a moving passage Owen writes, "Think much of *him who unto*

---

27. J. I. Packer, *A Quest for Godliness: The Puritan Vision of the Christian Life* (Wheaton, Ill.: Crossway, 1990), p. 199.
28. *Works of John Owen,* 7:351–52.
29. Ibid., p. 298.
30. Ibid., p. 284.
31. Ibid., p. 282.
32. Ibid., p. 319.

us is the life and centre of all the glory of heaven; this is, Christ himself. . . . Our hope is that ere long we shall be with him; and if so, it is certainly our wisdom and duty to be here with him as much as we can."[33]

Mortification: The Death of Sin in the Believer

Returning to the forest image, the dense impenetrable forest of huge trees and entangling underbrush has been broken forever; the dominion of sin, its universal power without any ameliorating influences, has been ended. There are now clearings in the jungle; some of the trees (i.e., sins) have been entirely uprooted; other trees have been pruned to varying degrees. This new condition is the state of the believer in indwelling sin (i.e., sin remains, but it is no longer all-pervasive). The goal of the spiritual life is that of continuing the work of clearing the forest, opening ever-enlarged clearings, and discovering new trees to uproot (if uprooting is not possible, the goal should be to remove as many branches and cut away as much undergrowth as possible). The negative activity of putting sin to death is what Owen calls mortification. It is as much a duty as the work of vivification. In this sphere the compatibility of integrationist psychology with Owen's biblical view of the solution to the human dilemma can be evaluated.

Owen's treatise *On the Mortification of Sin in Believers* is an exposition of Romans 8:13, "If by the Spirit you are putting to death the deeds of the flesh you will live." Of crucial importance to Owen is that believers grasp the significance of the phrase "by the Spirit" because mortification is God's work, in which he breaks up the stony heart through the gift of Christ granted by the Spirit.[34] Though a work of God, it is also a duty of each believer. "He doth not so work our mortification in us as not to keep it still an act of our obedience," says Owen.[35]

The believer's responsibility toward indwelling sin. Owen argues that the lifegoal of the Christian is to weaken and root out the remnants of sin's dominion. Three reasons make this endeavor important. First, sin is always present in believers and toward them (i.e., the external ravages of the evil one are an ever-present fact). "When sin lets us alone we may let sin alone; but as sin is never less quiet than when it seems most quiet, and its waters are for the most part deep when they are still, so ought our contrivances against it to be vigorous at all times."[36] Second, if left alone, sin becomes progressively active, thereby causing the inner man to atrophy.[37] Third, the Spirit has been granted to the believer for the purpose of putting to death the deeds of the flesh. "Not to be daily employing the Spirit and new nature for the mortify-

---

33. Ibid., p. 344.
34. Ibid., 6:18–19.
35. Ibid., p. 20.
36. Ibid., p. 11.
37. Ibid., p. 12.

ing of sin, is to neglect that excellent succor which God hath given us against our greatest enemy. . . . Not to daily mortify sin, is to sin against the goodness, kindness, wisdom, grace and love of God, who hath furnished us with a principle of doing it."[38]

The qualifications for the mortification of sin. Owen was a realist in his teaching concerning indwelling sin; he refused to offer promises about the outcome of duties that are contrary to experience and Scripture. He strenuously argues, for example, that while sin can be weakened and some forms of wickedness uprooted, it cannot be utterly killed or destroyed ("it is not in this life to be expected"[39]). Further, mortification is not simply the presence of a quiet, sedate demeanor. In the context of a stern warning, he states:

> Some men have an advantage by their natural constitution so far as that they are not exposed to such violence of unruly passions and tumultuous affections as many others are. Let now these men cultivate and improve their natural frame and temper by discipline, consideration, and prudence, and they may seem to themselves and others very mortified men, when, perhaps, their lusts are a standing sink of all abominations.[40]

Mortifying sin is, also, not simply the creation of a diversion or cover-up; it is not the hiding of evil with other positive qualities. Owen observes that "men in old age do not usually persist in pursuit of youthful lusts, although they have never been mortified of any of them."[41] Also he suggests that uprooting sin is not simply an occasional conquest; the fact of sin's reoccurrence provides ample evidence that it has not been mortified.

The method for the mortification of sin. As often stated in Puritan writings, the praxis of mortification is "the heart of the matter," the essence of sanctification. The dysfunction of man, according to Owen, differs vastly from the dilemma proposed by secular psychologists. Man's dilemma stems from a voluntary choice that has resulted in the corruption of the very core of man's being (i.e., the heart) and all his subsequent actions (since acts spring from man's inner being). The remedy, as one would expect, is also radically different from that of the secularists; it is not to be found in a pity-party of the helpless victim seeking restoration and adjudication. Instead the remedy comes only when man as a responsible, culpable agent recognizes his own guilt and seeks forgiveness.

Owen points out that the believer must recognize sin for all its terrible potential, meditate on its destructive power, and load the conscience with the

---

38. Ibid., p. 13.
39. Ibid., p. 25.
40. Ibid.
41. Ibid., p. 26.

heavy weight of its guilt as the first step in mortifying sin. He writes, "Get a clear and abiding sense upon thy mind and conscience of the guilt, danger, and evil of that sin wherewith thou art perplexed."[42] This advice stands in stark contrast to Harris's *I'm OK—You're OK*, but it is not distant from Crabb's integrationist approach in *Inside Out*.[43] In the latter work the author, though he uses psychological terminology to express his views, roots man's dilemma in his relationship with Adam and man's unsuccessful attempt to devise self-protective behavioral patterns that, being wicked, merely worsen his plight.[44] Owen and Crabb, it seems, view man as a culpable agent of his own destruction, not simply a victim of others' crimes. To both writers, external factors can contribute to behavioral dysfunction, but voluntary choices have resulted in unbiblical, isolationistic, corrective methodologies that only contribute to man's alienation and trauma.[45]

Owen also suggests that a careful analysis should be made to determine whether sin has a deeper cause than its external manifestation. "Consider whether the distemper with which thou art perplexed be not rooted in thy *nature,* and cherished, fomented, and heightened from thy constitution."[46] Describing the carelessness of people, he suggests, "this is the folly of some men; they set themselves with all earnestness and diligence against the appearing eruption of lust, but, leaving *the principle and root untouched,* perhaps *unsearched out,* they make but little or no progress in this work of mortification."[47] Or, again, "The root must be dealt with, the nature of the tree changed, or no good fruit will be brought forth."[48] That is, a particular manifestation of sin may have a deeper root. If that root is not dealt with through painstaking analysis, its manifestation will never be defeated. "That thou art peculiarly inclined unto any sinful distemper is but a peculiar breaking out of original lust in thy nature, which should peculiarly abase and humble thee."[49]

This sentiment is capsulized in one of Jonathan Edwards' famous personal resolutions. The Puritan pastor, philosopher, and evangelist wrote, "Resolved, whenever I do any conspicuously evil action, to trace it back, till

---

42. Ibid., p. 51.
43. Larry Crabb, *Inside Out* (Colorado Springs, Colo.: NavPress, 1988). I have chosen to derive my interpretation from this text rather than his previous books (*Basic Principles of Biblical Counseling* [Grand Rapids: Zondervan, 1975]; *The Marriage Builder* [Grand Rapids: Zondervan, 1982]; and *Understanding People* [Grand Rapids: Zondervan, 1987]) because it is his most recent work. A forceful criticism of Crabb's approach, not shared by this writer, is given in Bobgan, *Prophets of Psychoheresy I*, pp. 107–220.
44. Crabb, *Inside Out*, pp. 14, 16, 19, 30–32, 39, 69, 72, 115–16, 131–32, 155–56, 182–85, 194–200.
45. Ibid., pp. 201–18.
46. *Works of John Owen*, 6:60.
47. Ibid., p. 30.
48. Ibid., p. 36.
49. Ibid., p. 60.

I come to the original cause; and then both carefully endeavor to do so no more and to fight and pray with all my might against the original of it."[50] In Crabb's psychological terminology, dealing with sin involves a stripping away of the self-protective barriers people erect to hide their fallenness from exposure. However, this only further exposes their fallenness by adding layers of insulative defense mechanisms that obscure the deeper underlying problem.[51]

Owen encourages Christians to react quickly and decisively against sin, not minimizing its wickedness or neglecting to recognize its potential for destruction: "Rise mightily against the *first actings* of thy distemper, its first conceptions; suffer it not to get the least ground."[52] The believer must become an astute observer of the occasions when he or she is vulnerable to sinning, and carefully endeavor to avoid them. As Owen suggests, "Consider what ways, what companies, what opportunities, what studies, what businesses, what conditions, have at any time given, or do usually give, advantages to thy distempers, and set thyself heedfully against them all."[53] Though Owen states several more points (this is only the briefest summary), he concludes the discussion by arguing that the saint must carefully keep before him or her the wonderfulness, majesty, and kindness of God, being ever-mindful of his or her own vileness.[54]

Three emphases in Owen's writings are less apparent in Crabb's writings. First, Owen's richly stated explanation of the ever-present sinfulness of man is lacking in Crabb's popular presentation. Second, Crabb does not have the same emphasis as Owen on the elevation of the beauty, majesty, and compassion of the awesome God in Christ as revealed by the Holy Spirit. Though this may be assumed in Crabb's writings, it is not explicitly stated. Third, in contrast to Owen's minute attention to explaining various texts of Scripture with depth of insight and clarity of explanation, Crabb's use of the Scriptures is sometimes forced, if not inaccurate.[55] While he does seem to grasp the essence of man's dysfunctionalism and offers accurate procedures for its

---

50. Jonathan Edwards, "Resolutions," in *The Works of Jonathan Edwards* (1834; reprint, Carlisle, Pa.: Banner of Truth Trust, 1974), 1:xxi.

51. Crabb, *Inside Out,* pp. 23–37, 51–57, 116–29.

52. *Works of John Owen,* 6:62.

53. Ibid.

54. Ibid., pp. 63–70.

55. For example, at a recent conference Crabb suggested that Adam and Eve's sin was to question, doubt, and reject God as being good because he withheld something beneficial from them (Crabb, Devotional, Center for Christian Leadership Seminar, Dallas Theological Seminary, Dallas, Texas, October 22–23, 1992). Crabb is reading a psychological motive into the couple's decision, a motive that is simply not stated in Scripture. The Bible indicates that Satan's appeal to Eve was to greed and pride ("you shall be as God"); the biblical account gives no clue that they doubted God's essential goodness. Adam and Eve's error was their desire to be as God; they did not doubt God's goodness. They did not see a defect in God; they wanted to be as good as God.

amelioration, his writings lack the richness of the Puritan's insight into the character of God and the Scriptures.

What would be Owen's evaluation of contemporary explanations of the human dilemma and its resolution? To the secular psychologists from Freud to Rogers and Maslow there is no important ground of continuity; secularist remedies emerge from a bankrupt system, superficial in its estimate of man's nature and lacking meaningful solutions. While Crabb's vocabulary differs from that of Owen, Crabb does evidence some compatibility with Owen's position. The human dilemma, its remedy, and the methodology of change bear similarities; there is a qualitative correspondence. Yet the majestic richness of Owen's theology is lacking. Owen's devastating critique of human inability and ineptitude is difficult for secular culture (and even enculturated Christianity) to accept, but the beauty of Owen's God is wonderfully attractive. To gain even a passing glimpse of that beauty, like the momentary passing of clouds that enshroud a majestic peak of a mountain range, is to see reality and embrace joy. Mankind's only hope and encouragement is paradoxically to see the depths of human vileness and the majesty of God's grace in Christ. Owen would have Christians resolve with Jonathan Edwards, "Never to give over, nor in the least to slacken my fight with my corruptions, however unsuccessful I may be."[56]

Tribute

The purpose of our seminary is to educate godly servant-leaders for the Lord's earthly work. At the helm of our school has been a man who has sought to exemplify the character traits that qualify anyone to undershepherd the flocks of God. His model of kindness, care, and moral integrity has been in the forefront of his leadership. In these matters, I am grateful to God for Dr. Donald K. Campbell.

56. *Works of Jonathan Edwards*, 1:xxii.

A Christian View of Politics, Government, and Social Action

J. Kerby Anderson

In the past two decades evangelical Christians have become more involved in government and social action. In the nineteenth century, Christians were involved in a vast array of social concerns, but the rise of the social gospel among ecumenical denominations turned evangelicals away from social involvement. With renewed evangelical activity in the 1980s and 1990s, Christians need to think biblically about politics, government, and social action.

A Christian View of Government

Government affects our lives daily. It tells us how fast to drive. It regulates our commerce. It protects us from foreign and domestic strife. Yet we rarely take time to consider its basic function. What is a biblical view of government? Why do we have government? What kind of government does the Bible allow? Are Christians to be involved in the political process? These are just a few questions we will address in this essay.

Developing a Christian view of government is difficult since the Bible does not provide an exhaustive treatment of government. This itself is perhaps instructive and provides us with some latitude for these institutions to reflect the needs and demands of particular cultural situations. Because of this ambiguity, Christians often hold different views on particular political issues because the Bible does not speak directly to every area of political discussion. However, Christians are not free to believe whatever they want. Christians should not abandon the Bible when they begin to think about these issues because there is a great deal of biblical material that can be used to judge particular political options.

The Old Testament includes clear guidelines for the development of a theocracy in which God is the head of government. But these guidelines were written for particular circumstances involving a covenant people who were established by God. These guidelines do not completely apply today because modern-day governments are not the direct inheritors of the promises God made to the nation Israel.

Apart from that unique situation, the Bible does not propose or endorse any specific political system. The Bible, however, does provide a basis for evaluating various political philosophies because it clearly delineates a view of human nature. Every political theory rests on a particular view of human nature. British historian Hugh Trevor-Roper once remarked that a "political theory which does not start from a theory of man is in my view quite worthless."[1] It is impossible to think about government without thinking about human nature. Christians therefore have a basis for rejecting those political philosophies that start with and embrace an incorrect view of human nature. Christians have a mandate to construct a workable government system with a realistic view of human nature.

Government and Human Nature

The Bible describes two different elements of human nature. This viewpoint is helpful in judging government systems. Because we are created in the image of God (Gen. 1), we are able to exercise such noble human traits as courage, judgment, compassion, and reason. However, we are also fallen creatures (Gen. 3). This human sinfulness (Rom. 3:23) has created a need to control evil and sinful human behavior through civil government.

Many theologians have suggested that the only reason we have government today is to control sinful behavior due to the fall. But there is every indication that government would have existed even if we lived in a sinless world. For example, there seems to be some structuring of authority in the garden (Gen. 1–2). The Bible also speaks of the angelic host as being organized into levels of authority and function.

In the creation God ordained government as the means by which human beings and angelic hosts are ruled. The rest of the created order is governed by instinct (Prov. 30:24–28) and God's providence. Insect colonies, for example, may show a level of order, but this is due merely to genetically controlled instinct.

Human beings, on the other hand, are created in the image of God (Gen. 1:27) and thus are responsible to obey God's volitional commands. We are created by a God of order (1 Cor. 14:33); therefore we also seek order through governmental structures.

This Christian view of government is quite different from that proposed by many political theorists. The basis for civil government is rooted in our created nature. We are rational and volitional beings. We are not determined by fate as the ancient Greeks would claim, nor are we determined by our

1. Hugh Trevor-Roper, "Human Nature and Politics," *Listener,* December 10, 1953.

environment as modern behaviorists would say. We have the power of choice. Because we have this power of choice, we can exercise delegated power over the created order. Thus, a biblical view of human nature requires a governmental system that acknowledges human responsibility.

While the source of civil government is rooted in human responsibility, the need for government derives from the need to control human sinfulness. God ordained civil government to restrain evil (cf. Gen. 9). We cannot consider anarchy as a viable option because all have sinned (Rom. 3:23) and are in need of external control.

A Christian view of human nature gives a basis on which to judge political philosophies. For example, Christians must reject political philosophies that ignore human sinfulness. Many utopian political theories are guilty of this. Plato postulated in *The Republic* that the ideal government would be one in which enlightened philosopher-kings led the country. The Bible, however, teaches that all are sinful (Rom. 3:23). Therefore Plato's proposed leaders would also be affected by the sinful effects of the fall. They would lack the benevolent and enlightened disposition necessary for Plato's republic to work.

Another example is the Marxist scheme of government. Karl Marx (1818–1883) had a naive view of human nature.[2] He felt that society, in particular the capitalistic economy, was the reason for human failing. His solution was to overthrow the capitalistic economy and replace it with a communistic society in which human potential would be liberated. He located the problem in an economic system and believed that the solution would emerge by the destruction of capitalism. Marx felt that people are only the innocent victims of this menace.

Christians should reject the utopian vision of Marxism. Although the Bible does talk of believers becoming new creations (2 Cor. 5:17) through spiritual conversion, even then the effects of sin are not completely overcome in this life. The new birth is just the beginning of the growth process that continues throughout our earthly existence. Furthermore the Bible teaches that we will always live in a world tainted by sin. Marx's view of the New Man in a New Society therefore contradicts biblical teaching because it teaches human perfectibility on earth by humanity's own efforts.

A Christian view of government is based on a balanced view of human nature. It recognizes both human dignity (we are created in God's image) and human depravity (we are sinful individuals). Because both grace and sin operate in government, we should be neither too optimistic nor too pessimistic. We should view governmental affairs with a deep sense of biblical realism.

2. Claus Bockmuehl, *The Challenge of Marxism* (Downers Grove, Ill.: InterVarsity, 1980).

Most early political theorists in Britain and the United States accepted this balanced view of human nature. Edmund Burke (1729–1797), an English Christian, developed his description of what government should be in his *Reflections on the French Revolution,* based on a balanced view of human nature. So did the founders of the American form of government. Even though many were not Christians, they were frequently influenced by the Christian milieu.

James Madison (1751–1836), fourth president of the United States, believed in this balanced view of human nature. He asked the following question in the *Federalist Papers:* "But what is government itself, but the greatest of all reflections on human nature? If men were angels, no government would be necessary. If angels were to govern men, neither external nor internal controls on government would be necessary. In framing a government which is to be administered by men over men, the great difficulty lies in this: you must first enable the government to control the governed; and in the next place oblige it to control itself."[3] Framing a republic requires a balance of power that liberates human dignity and rationality and controls human sin and depravity. "As there is a degree of depravity in mankind which requires a certain degree of circumspection and distrust, so there are other qualities in human nature, which justify a certain portion of esteem and confidence. Republican government presupposes the existence of these qualities in a higher degree than any other form."[4]

This does not mean that Christians must support every aspect of the American governmental system. The Constitution represents a compromise of Christian principles and humanistic principles from the Enlightenment. And evangelicals have often been guilty of substituting a civil religion for biblical principles. The American political experiment has nevertheless been successful because it is based on a balanced view of human nature that avoids the dangers of utopian experiments in human government.

Civil Government

Civil government is necessary and divinely ordained by God (Rom. 13:1–7). Government is ultimately under God's control. It has been given three political responsibilities: the sword of justice (to punish criminals), the sword of order (to thwart rebellion), and the sword of war (to defend the state).

Citizens, too, have been given a number of responsibilities. They are to render service and obedience to the government (Matt. 22:21). Because it is a God-ordained institution, they are to submit to civil authority (1 Pet. 2:13–17) as they would to other institutions of God. But Christians are not to give total and final allegiance to the secular state. Other God-ordained

3. James Madison, *Federalist Papers,* no. 51 (New York: New American Library, 1961), p. 322.
4. James Madison, *Federalist Papers,* no. 55 (New York: New American Library, 1961), p. 346.

institutions exist in society alongside the state. Our final allegiance must be to God. We are to obey civil authorities (Rom. 13:5) in order to avoid anarchy and chaos, but there may be times when we are called to exercise civil disobedience.

A number of instances of civil disobedience are recorded in the Bible. Moses' mother defied the order of Pharaoh to kill all male babies (Exod. 1–2). God ordered Samuel to deceive King Saul (1 Sam. 16). Shadrach, Meshach, and Abednego defied the order of Nebuchadnezzar (Dan. 3). The apostles continued preaching even when they were commanded to be silent (Acts 4:13–20; 5:22–28). In situations in which a major conflict arises between biblical absolutes and governmental policy, we are to obey God rather than men (Acts 5:29). However, in many cases, we may be able to find a creative alternative that avoids a conflict and allows us to be obedient to both the Lord and the government (Dan. 1).

Many Christians have mistakenly felt that since government is made up of fallen individuals, we are to limit our involvement in it. Yet we must recognize that government is part of the creation order. Like other institutions, government has fallen into sin, but that should not limit our involvement with it. We are to be salt and light (Matt. 5:13–16) in the midst of the political context.

Though governments may be guilty of injustice, we should not stop working for justice or cease being concerned about human rights. We do not give up on marriage as an institution simply because there are so many divorces; we do not give up on the church because of its many internal problems. Each God-ordained institution manifests human sinfulness and disobedience. Our responsibility as Christians is to call political leaders back to this God-ordained task. Government is a legitimate sphere of Christian service, and so we should not look to government only when our rights are being abused. We are to be concerned with social justice and should see governmental action as a legitimate instrument to achieve just ends.

One of the greatest flaws with the American form of government is the tendency to assume that the public good is the sum total of all special interests. In this regard, we have been excessively influenced by utilitarianism. We have focused too much on pragmatic policies and questions of majority rule and not enough on public justice.

Interest-group politics dominates the political landscape. Each special group of individuals in society has a desire to see its competitive interests represented in public policy. As a result, interest-group politics often predominate over the just and moral action that should be taken. Rather than consider the normative (what should be done), we frequently focus on the strategic (what can be done with the political forces involved). We focus too much on the form of government rather than on the moral content of policy. We should be more concerned with justice than with satisfying public interests.

A Christian view of government should also be concerned with human rights. Human rights in a Christian system are based on a biblical view of human dignity. A bill of rights, therefore, does not grant rights to individuals, but instead acknowledges these rights as already existing. The Declaration of Independence captures this idea by stating that government is based on the inalienable rights of individuals. Government based on a humanistic view of government, however, does not see rights as inalienable and thus opens the possibility for the state to redefine what rights its citizens may enjoy. The rights of citizens in a republic are articulated in terms of what the government is forbidden to do. But in totalitarian governments, the rights of citizens are spelled out. In essence, a republic limits government, while a totalitarian government limits citizens.

A Christian view of government also recognizes the need to limit the influence of sin in society. This is best achieved by placing certain checks on governmental authority. By doing this we can protect citizens from the abuse or misuse of governmental power that results when sinful individuals are allowed to exercise too much governmental control.

The greatest threat to liberty comes from the exercise of power. Our experience in history has shown that power is a corrupting force when placed in human hands. In the Old Testament theocracy there was less danger of abuse because the head of state was God. But when power was transferred to a single king, dangers ensued. Even David, a man after God's own heart, abused his power and brought great calamity on Israel (2 Sam. 11–20).

Abuse and misuse of power characterize human governments. The contribution of modern democratic theory was to recognize human sinfulness and to devise an ingenious method to tame its effects. Madison and others recognized that since government could not rid human nature of sinful behavior (which Madison called passions), the only solution was to use human nature to control itself.

Again, we can see the genius of the American system. Madison and others realized the futility of trying to remove passions (human sinfulness) from the population. Therefore they proposed that human nature be set against human nature. This was done by separating various institutional power structures. First, the church was separated from the state so that ecclesiastical functions and governmental functions would not interfere with religious and political liberty. Second, the federal government was delegated certain powers while the rest of the powers resided in the state governments. Third, the federal government was divided into three equal branches: executive, legislative, and judicial. Each branch was given separate but rival powers, thus preventing the possibility of concentrating power into the hands of a few. Each branch had certain checks over the other branches so that there was a distribution and balance of power.

In addition to this, the people were given certain means of redress. Elections and an amendment process kept power from being concentrated in the hands of governmental officials. Each of these checks was motivated by a healthy fear of human nature. The founders believed in human responsibility and human dignity, but they did not trust human nature too much. Their solution was to separate powers and invest each branch with rival powers.

The effect of this system was to allow ambition and power to control itself. Each branch is given power, and as ambitious men and women seek to extend their sphere of influence, they are checked by the other branches. This is what has often been referred to as the concept of "countervailing ambitions."

For example, the executive branch cannot take over the government and rule at its whim because the legislative branch has been given the power of the purse. Congress can approve or disapprove budgets for governmental programs. A president cannot wage war if Congress does not appropriate money for its execution.

The legislative branch is also controlled by this structure of government. It can pass legislation, but it always faces the threat of presidential veto and judicial oversight. Since the executive branch is responsible for the execution of legislation, the legislature cannot exercise complete control over the government. Undergirding all of this is the authority of the ballot box.

Modern democratic systems (whether the American form of government or the British form of parliamentary rule) function well because they protect liberty and allow the greatest amount of political participation. A benevolent dictator might be more efficient, but he or she would probably be less objective and less keen at adjudicating rival interests. Each of us has biases, and the potential for being corrupted by power is very great in a dictatorship. But the greatest fear would be that a benevolent dictator might be replaced by a malevolent one. A modern democratic government prevents the unleashing of human sinfulness that might occur through concentrations of power. Democracy is a system in which "bad men can do least harm, and good men have the freedom to do good works."[5] Unlike other political systems, it takes human sinfulness seriously and thus protects its citizens from major abuses of power.

Governmental Authority

One of the most perplexing problems in government today is determining the limits of governmental authority. With the remarkable growth in the size and scope of government in this century, it is necessary to define clearly the lines of governmental authority.

---

5. This is a portion of a statement I use when speaking on college campuses on American political theory.

At the outset, one must acknowledge that it is often difficult to set limits or draw lines. The Old Testament theocracy was different from modern democratic government. Though human nature is the same, drawing biblical principles from an agrarian, monolithic culture and applying them to a technological, pluralistic culture require discernment.

Part of this difficulty can be eased by separating two issues. First, should government legislate morality? This will be discussed later. Second, what are the limits of governmental sovereignty? The following are a few general principles that can be helpful in determining the limits of governmental authority.

As Christians, we recognize that God has ordained other institutions besides government that exercise authority in their particular sphere of influence. This is in contrast to various political systems that see the state as the sovereign agent over human affairs, exercising sovereignty over every other human institution. A Christian view is different.

The first institution ordained by God is the family (Eph. 5:22–32; 1 Pet. 3:1–7). The family is an institution under God and under his authority (Gen. 1:26–28; 2:20–25). When the family breaks down, the government often has to step in to protect the rights of the wife or children because of abuse. The biblical emphasis, however, is not so much on rights as it is on responsibilities and mutual submission (Eph. 5).

The second institution is the church (Heb. 12:18–24; 1 Pet. 2:9–10). In the New Testament Jesus taught that the government should work in harmony with the church and should recognize the church's sovereignty in spiritual matters (Matt. 22:21).

A third institution is education. Children are not the wards of the state, but belong to God (Ps. 127:3) and are given to parents as a gift from God. Parents are to teach their children (Deut. 4:9) and may entrust them to tutors (Gal. 4:2).

In a humanistic system of government, the institutions of church and family are usually subordinated to the state. In this atheistic system, the state ultimately becomes a substitute god and is given additional power to adjudicate disputes and to seek to bring order to society. Since institutions exist by permission of the state, there is always the possibility that a new social contract will allow governmental intervention into the areas of church and family.

A Christian view of government recognizes the sovereignty of these spheres. Governmental intervention into the spheres of church and family is necessary in cases in which there is threat to life, liberty, or property. Otherwise, civil government should recognize the sovereignty of the other spheres of God-ordained institutions.

The Moral Basis of Law

Law should be the foundation of any government. Whether law is based on moral absolutes, changing consensus, or totalitarian whim is of crucial importance. Until fairly recently Western culture held to a notion that common law was founded on God's revealed moral absolutes. As one legal scholar put it, "There never has been a period in which common law did not recognize Christianity as laying at its foundation."[6]

In a Christian view of government, law is based on God's revealed commandments, not on human opinion or sociological convention. Rooted in God's unchangeable character, law is derived from biblical principles of morality.

On the other hand, in humanism humanity is the source of law. Law is merely the expression of human will or mind. Since ethics and morality are man-made, so also is law. Humanists' law is rooted in human opinion, and thus is relative and arbitrary.

Two important figures in the history of law are Samuel Rutherford (1600–1661) and Sir William Blackstone (1723–1780). Rutherford's *Lex Rex,* written in 1644, had a profound effect on British and American law. His treatise challenged the foundations of seventeenth-century politics by proclaiming that law must be based on the Bible rather than on the word of any man.

Up until that time, the king had been the law. Rutherford's work created a great controversy because it attacked the idea of the divine right of kings. This doctrine had held that the king or the state ruled as God's appointed regent. Thus the king's word *was* law. Rutherford properly argued from passages such as Romans 13 that the king, as well as anyone else, was under God's law and not above it.[7]

William Blackstone (1723–1780), an English jurist, is famous for his *Commentaries on the Law of England,* which embodied the tenets of Judeo-Christian theism. According to Blackstone, the two foundations for law are nature and scriptural revelation. Believing that the fear of the Lord was the beginning of wisdom, Blackstone taught that God was the source of all laws. Interestingly even the Swiss humanist Jean-Jacques Rousseau (1717–1778) noted in his *Social Contract* that someone outside the world system is needed to provide a moral basis for law. He said, "It would take gods to give men laws."

Unfortunately modern legal structure has been influenced by relativism and utilitarianism, instead of by moral absolutes revealed in Scripture. Relativism provides no secure basis for moral judgments. There are no firm moral absolutes on which to build a secure legal foundation.

Utilitarianism looks merely at consequences and ignores moral principles. This legal foundation has been further eroded by the relatively recent phenomenon of sociological law. In this view, law should be based on relative

6. Joseph Story, in his 1829 inaugural address as Dane Professor at Harvard University, quoted by Perry Miller, ed., *The Legal Mind in America* (Garden City, N.Y.: Doubleday, 1962), p. 178.

7. Full discussion of this idea can be found in Francis Schaeffer, *How Should We Then Live?* (Old Tappan, N.J.: Revell, 1976); idem, *A Christian Manifesto* (Westchester, Ill.: Crossway, 1981); and John Whitehead, *The Second American Revolution* (Westchester, Ill.: Crossway, 1982).

sociological standards. No discipline is more helpless without a moral foundation than law. Law is a tool, and it needs a jurisprudential foundation. Just as contractors and builders need the architect's blueprint in order to build, so lawyers need theologians and moral philosophers to make good law. The problem is that most lawyers today are extensively trained in technique, but have little training in moral and legal philosophy.

Legal justice in the Western world has been based on a proper, biblical understanding of human nature and human choice. We hold criminals accountable for their crimes, rather than excuse their behavior as part of environmental conditioning. We also acknowledge differences between willful, premeditated acts (e.g., murder) and crimes without malice (e.g., manslaughter).

One of the problems in society today is that we do not operate from assumptions of human choice. The influence of the behaviorist, the evolutionist, and the sociobiologist is quite profound. The evolutionist and sociobiologist say that human behavior is genetically determined, and the behaviorist says that human behavior is environmentally determined. Where do we find free choice in a system that argues that actions are a result of heredity and environment? Because of the influences of these secular perspectives free choice and personal responsibility have been diminished in the criminal justice system.

It is therefore not by accident that we have seen a dramatic change in our view of criminal justice. The emphasis has moved from a view of punishment and restitution to one of rehabilitation. If our actions are governed by something external and human choice is denied, then we cannot punish someone for something he or she cannot control. If the influences are merely heredity and environment, then we must rehabilitate the criminal. Such a view of human actions diminishes human dignity. If a person cannot choose, then he or she is merely a victim of circumstances and must become a ward of the state.

As Christians, we must take the criminal act seriously and punish wrong human choices. While we recognize the value of rehabilitation (especially through spiritual conversion [John 3:3]), we also recognize the need for punishing wrongdoing. The Old Testament provisions for punishment and restitution make more sense in light of the biblical view of human nature. Yet today we have a justice system that promotes no-fault divorce and no-fault insurance, and continues to erode the notion of human responsibility.

A Christian View of Social Action

In the nineteenth century, Christians were significantly involved in social action. Many of the social movements of the time were led by Christians. Unfortunately conservative Christians lost this vision for social action in the twentieth century. Fundamentalists emphasized evangelism and personal piety often to the exclusion of social action. Evangelical leaders after World War II began to speak to the issue of social action, but only recently have evangelicals become strategically involved in social and political activities.

Evangelical Disinterest in Social Action

For decades evangelical Christians have assumed that their theology excludes any significant emphasis on social ethics. They rightly believe that preaching the gospel is their primary task. But that does not mean that Christians should therefore neglect the social arena altogether. Evangelism and social action are intimately related. Christians are called not only to save souls (James 5:20) but also to be the salt of the earth (Matt. 5:13).

Missionaries have long understood the importance of developing a comprehensive approach to reaching a culture. Feeding hungry stomachs will allow missionaries to feed hungry hearts also. Social reformation follows spiritual revival. Evangelism and social action are both important to the missionary task. Evangelical Christians who desire to reach a society must also give due attention to the social circumstances of that society.

Evangelical Christians sometimes resist focusing on the social and political circumstances of a society because they believe that social and political involvement is a worldly activity. Building roads, schools, and hospitals could also be considered a worldly activity, yet mission agencies see the importance of these activities in advancing their goal of reaching a culture for Christ.

Christians often retreat from social and political involvement because it involves conflict and compromise. Evangelicals feel they will be forced to compromise biblical principles if they enter into the social and political arena. While it is true that there is conflict and compromise in these arenas, compromise need not take place at the level of fundamental principles. Every area of human endeavor (including church government) involves some form of compromise. Evangelical Christians must not compromise biblical principles, but they can cooperate with others to achieve a positive solution in the social, economic, or political realm. Government is under God's authority (Rom. 13:1–7), and Christians must exercise their responsibility to affect change within this God-ordained institution.

Some Christians have withdrawn from social and political involvement because they feel that political systems are evil and that current events are a fulfillment of prophecy. Evangelical Christians, especially premillennial evangelicals, have developed a "psychology of eschatology." They see politics as worldly and ultimately a culmination of the work of the Antichrist (Dan. 7:23–28; Rev. 17:9–18). Believing that the current social, economic, and political systems are headed for destruction, some evangelicals avoid any active involvement in social and political activities.

This fatalistic view of the world does not square with the Bible. Jesus taught that believers are to occupy the world until he returns (Luke 19:13). While it is true that the Lord may soon return, we should not presume that he will. Though we should expectantly await his return, we must also plan for the future (Isa. 32:8). Jesus did not set a time limit on being salt and light (Matt. 5:13–16). Christ's return in the future does not negate the need for us to be strategically involved now. Jesus Christ may soon return; but if he does not, then Christians have a responsibility to be socially and politically involved.

Biblical Guidelines for Social Action

How then should Christians be involved in the social and political arena? They should be distinctively Christian in their approach, and they should learn from the mistakes of other Christians in the past so that they might be effective without falling into compromise or sin.

First, Christians must remember that they have a dual citizenship. On the one hand their citizenship is in heaven and not on earth (Phil. 3:17–21). Christians must remind themselves that God is sovereign over human affairs even when circumstances look dark and discouraging.

On the other hand the Bible also teaches that Christians are citizens of this earth (Matt. 22:15–22). We are to obey government (Rom. 13:1–7) and work within the social and political circumstances to affect change. We are to pray for those in authority (1 Tim. 2:1–4) and obey them (Rom. 13:5).

Jesus compared the kingdom of heaven to leaven hidden in three pecks of meal (Matt. 13:33). The meal represents the world and the leaven represents the Christian presence in it. We bring about change by exercising our influence within society. Though the Christian presence may seem as insignificant as leaven in meal, nevertheless in a similar way we are to seek to bring about change.

Second, Christians must remember the sovereignty of God. The Bible teaches that God is sovereign over nations. He bestows power on whom he wishes (Dan. 4:17), and he can turn the heart of a king wherever he so desires (Prov. 21:1).

Christians have often been guilty of believing that they alone can make a difference in the political process. Christian leaders frequently claim that the future of this country depends on the election of a particular candidate, the passage of a certain bill, or the confirmation of a specific Supreme Court justice. While it is important for Christians to be involved in social and political affairs, they must not forget that God is ultimately in control.

Third, Christians must use their specific gifts within the social and political arenas. There are different gifts and different ministries (1 Cor. 12:4–6) to which each Christian has been called. Some may be called to a higher level of political participation than others (e.g., a candidate for a school board or a congressional representative). All have a responsibility to be involved in society, but some are called to a higher level of social service (e.g., a social worker or crisis pregnancy center worker). Christians must recognize the diversity of gifts and encourage believers to use their individual gifts for the greatest impact.

Fourth, Christians must channel social and political activities through the church. Christians need to be accountable to one another, especially as they are seeking to make an impact on society. Wise leadership can prevent zealous evangelical Christians from repeating mistakes made in previous decades by other Christians.

The local church also provides a context for compassionate social service. In the New Testament, the local church became a training ground for social action (Acts 2:45; 4:34). Meeting the needs of the poor, the infirm, the elderly, and the widows is a responsibility of the church. Ministries to these groups can provide a foundation and a catalyst for further outreach and ministry to the community at large.

In our needy society we have abundant opportunities to preach the gospel of Jesus Christ while also meeting significant social needs. By combining preaching and ministry, Christians can make a strategic difference in today's society.

Tribute

In his many years of leadership at Dallas Theological Seminary, Dr. Campbell has been a model of grace, compassion, and godliness. To students, faculty, and staff he exhibits a leadership style and a ministry heart that is evident to all who come in contact with him. May God bless him in his future opportunities for ministry and service in the body of Jesus Christ.